RIDE TO HELL
PRISONER OF A DUBIOUS PEACE

PAUL RIDE

RIDE TO HELL
Prisoner Of A Dubious Peace
Copyright Paul Ride 2022
ISBN: 9798354602445
THE MORAL RIGHT OF THE AUTHOR HAS BEEN ASSERTED
Apart from any fair dealing for the purposes of research or private study, or criticism or review, as permitted under the Copyright, Designs and Patents Act 1988, this publication may only be reproduced, stored or transmitted, in any means, with the prior permission in writing of Gate 17, or in the case of reprographic reproduction in accordance with the terms of licenses issued by the Copyright Licensing Agency. Enquiries concerning reproduction outside those terms should be sent to the publishers. enquiries@gate17.co.uk

Editing, typesetting and design: Mark Worrall
Proofreader: Tim Rolls
www.gate17books.co.uk

CONTENTS

FOREWORD by MARK WORRALL 1
TELL US WHO YOU'RE SPYING FOR? 5
I DIDN'T EXPECT THIS 9
COME BACK TOMORROW 15
THE WORST JAIL IN BASRA 18
ROAD TRIP WITH THREE MAD MEN 25
MUKHABARAT INTERROGATION 35
FAISALIYAH: THE NIGHTMARE MUTATES! 58
AL ALWIYAH 63
"SEVEN YEARS!" "DON'T WORRY, IT'S NOT TOO LONG!" 72
MADE IN ENGLAND! 76
ABU GHRAIB 79
MUSTER MADNESS 84
YOU'RE GOING ON TV: "IF YOU WANT TO?" 91
A VISIT FROM MADAM JULIE AND WILLIAM 100
THE TROUBLE WITH JERJES! 105
GOODWILL TO ALL MEN, AND A TIN OF LUNCHEON MEAT! 110
HAPPY NEW YEAR! WELCOME TO 1993! 117
YOU WILL PAY FOR EVERYTHING! 125
YOU SELFISH BASTARD! 130
OI! BIRTHDAY BOY 136
AMNESTY, WHAT AMNESTY? 145
WE'VE GOT A NEW SEPTIC! 156
ONE TRIP AROUND THE SUN 169
RESEARCH STUDENTS, RUMOUR AND RHETORIC 186
PSYCHO 198
FAMILY COME AND THE SWEDES GO! 218
HURRY UP AND GET US OUT! 230
SOUR GRAPES! 237
SIR EDWARD TO THE RESCUE! 248
THREE MONKEYS! 254
MAGIC CARPET RIDE! 263
FLIGHT TO FREEDOM! 268
AFTERMATH 273
EPILOGUE 295

FOREWORD

Football isn't just a sport it's a way of life. The experience of going to matches concentrates the defining characteristics of supporters; loyalty, camaraderie, passion, intensity, and hope – there is always hope and there are always dreams. I've always preferred going to games as opposed to watching them on TV partly because during my formative teenage years there wasn't much football screened but more so because I quickly became fascinated with terrace culture and the personalities associated with it. On the pitch, mavericks like Peter Osgood and Alan Hudson who played for my team Chelsea, and George Best, Rodney Marsh, Stan Bowles and Frank Worthington who I wished played for Chelsea interested me the most. Off the pitch and sometimes on the pitch, it was the faces who marshalled hundreds of urchins just like me gathered on The Shed terrace that caught my eye. At Stamford Bridge we had Eccles and Greenaway and I studied them with an unbridled curiosity only ever matched when I occasionally wandered into Soho to the Marquee club to watch live music and gaze at the latest wannabe rock stars and the people gazing at the wannabe rock stars.

As time passed, I made friends with people I encountered at football matches and gigs and some of these friendships have endured to this very day which is truly wonderful and fulfilling. I never lost the curiosity I had about people and what granular details of their lives might explain the sometimes happy, sometimes sad, sometimes angry, sometimes taciturn, expressions on their faces and it's a strange fact of life that even though I've seen some of these individuals countless times down the years, communication has never got beyond an anonymous, "hello mate", wink, or nod. That faint flicker of recognition can be fleeting as you pass someone by and then the moment is gone and your mind moves on. This might seem extraordinary, but the chances are, even if you don't go to watch football, you'll know exactly what I mean as the same thing applies anywhere people gather repeatedly; pub, church, gym, supermarket, place of work, public transport – the list goes on.

For many years Paul Ride was a familiar face I'd occasionally see at Chelsea games that I was sure I recognised from somewhere else and it was only in August 2017 when by chance we had our first conversation the penny finally dropped. For a brief moment in time Paul had been front-page news. He was the Blues supporter taken hostage by the Iraqis in 1992 during the aftermath of the first Gulf War. A decent, honest fella who worked abroad to generate a better level of income to support his family and unwittingly found himself an imprisoned pawn in a political game of chess.

At that time, the internet and mobile phone technology were still in their infancy and social media was the stuff of fantasy. News was read in newspapers and viewed on TV, and you only got to read and see what the moguls who controlled the media wanted you to. I knew Paul was a Chelsea fan because the story of his abduction had been reported not only in the press but also in 'Onside' the Chelsea FC 'official newspaper' of that time and the 'Chelsea Independent' fanzine. As time passed I remember thinking the Government of the United Kingdom should be doing more to secure his release and wondered what was going on behind the scenes but there was nothing to keep his story at the forefront of my mind.

In the modern day and age there would have been a massive and relentless campaign visible 24/7 on social media lobbying politicians and humanitarian pressure groups to bring Paul home and a fundraising exercise would have been coordinated to help him get back on his feet when he returned. Mental health care would have been provided immediately meaning the consequences of this traumatic event might have been significantly less destructive and Paul would also have had a huge support network to protect him from media misdemeanours. The old saying, 'Today's news is tomorrow's fish and chip paper' wouldn't have applied to his story and the suffering and injustices he endured would not have been swept away and lost in the mists of time.

The calendar on my wall tells me it's exactly 30 years to the day that Paul was taken hostage and I'm pleased that I have been able to help him finally get his version of events out there. It's a heady cocktail of misfortune, fear, sensory deprivation, violence, injustice and loss twirled by an unscrupulous media and served in a jagged glass to largely uncaring government officials whose impotence at times beggars belief.

Turn the pages and you will journey to inhuman places where touch and taste often eclipse sight and the rule of law is handed down by desperate psychopaths with no sense of morality who crush Paul's spirit and leave him mentally scarred and feeling suicidal. A steely survivor, he has persevered through a pantheon of problems and thankfully lived to tell the tale. By the time you have finished reading 'Ride To Hell' you may well conclude that the truth can sometimes be stranger and infinitely darker than fiction and I guarantee you will never go to the toilet at night without first switching a light on! Joking aside, one things for certain, you will definitely want to give Paul a big hug and wish him well as he continues to rebuild his life which was so maliciously interrupted.

Mark Worrall
London
28th June, 2022

RIDE TO HELL

Dedicated to Julie, William, Rhian,
and my other 'family' at Stamford Bridge.

TELL US WHO YOU'RE SPYING FOR

I had only been in the cell a short while when a guard opened the gate and said something to me in Arabic. I looked at him but didn't reply. He repeated the words and when I didn't reply again he slammed the gate shut. I heard the guard's footsteps recede across the concrete floor outside my cell and then a conversation took place and then the footsteps approached once more.

The guard opened the heavy metallic gate to my cell and spoke slowly. I understood what he said. "Elf Miah wo Khamseen?" He was asking my name. 1150, the 'name' given to me by the Mukhabarat (Iraqi Secret Police)! I answered, "Aywa!" (Yes!), and he threw a blindfold at me. I stood up quickly and put my sandals on while he mimed that I was to button my top. With this done, I put the blindfold on and followed him across the landing. This was accomplished by hand signals, not a word was spoken. To 'follow him' I tilted my head back and tried to obey his directions. Suddenly he moved from being in front, to walking behind me and 'directing me' with shoves in my back.

The guard pushed and prodded me as we descended the slope I'd come up on my arrival. He shoved me towards the central stairwell, and we descended two floors. I realised that he was leading me back to my vehicle, a Land Cruiser. I quivered with anticipation. Spoken Arabic echoed up the stairwell as I was manhandled onto a small kerb and shoved into a room. The guard pushed me into a seat and left the room. I was still wearing the blindfold, but for a moment I was out of my cell and alone.

Seconds later someone entered the room. He passed in front of me and went behind a desk and sat. I could make out nothing but shadows. The blindfold obscured my vision, but with the aid of a window behind him, I could 'see' that the man was dressed in traditional Arabic attire.

The first question he asked was, "Who are you spying for?"

As he spoke, he rose and came towards me. I flinched as he passed my shoulder. I felt certain he was about to strike me. Instead, he said something to someone at the door.

My emotions fluttered; fear, foreboding, disbelief. *Christ almighty! They think I'm a fucking spy!* I thought. *These pricks think they've got James Bond in a T-shirt!* This latter notion made me smile but I was scared; the smile was a rictus grin of trepidation and terror.

He then said, "Tell us who you are spying for, then you will be released. We will put you on the next flight for London!"

I struggled. The offer was freedom, but the caveat was the requirement to lie and say I was a spy to win the reward. I had the good sense not to go for the easy answer. I didn't go for the flight to London. I told him that I was not a spy and added I was sorry if that was what they believed as nothing could be further from the truth.

This was not what he wanted to hear. He got up and rushed towards me again. I was sure he was about to hit me and so I held myself rigid. Again he passed me, went to the door, spoke to the guard, and then slapped me on the shoulder saying, "Come now, we know you are a spy. Tell us who you work for, and all this will be over."

I was flabbergasted. *What makes these idiots think I'm a spy?* I denied the accusation again, and said pitifully, "I'm a chef!" It was the only moment in my life when I remember thinking I wanted to be in a hot, sweaty kitchen right now!

He asked the same ubiquitous questions. "How did you get into Iraq?"

I replied, with as much conviction as I could. "I didn't. I couldn't, my passport is in Kuwait. An Iraqi soldier took me across the border. I was still in northern Kuwait!"

"No!" Spat the interrogator. "You were inside Iraq on a spying mission! Who do you work for?"

Time stood still. Fear made me shiver. My brain, used to learning song lyrics and churning out quick-fire comedic one liners, began to seize. All I could hear was the repeated accusation getting louder and louder!

"Who are you spying for?"

"Who are YOU spying for?"

"WHO ARE YOU SPYING FOR?"

My pathetic retort. "I work for a British catering company. I'm a Chef!

"What were you doing in Iraq?" Was his next question.

"I was in northern Kuwait looking for a friend of mine," I blustered. I've worked with him in both Algeria and Saudi Arabia."

My interrogator raised his voice and asked, "Is he a spy too? Is he your contact?"

"No! He's not a spy. NEITHER AM I. He works for UNIKOM (United Nations Iraq Kuwait Observation Mission) in Kuwait." I realised that I'd shouted at him as he demanded, "What is his job? How do you know he works for UNIKOM?"

"He is feeding people. He's in charge of feeding the UNIKOM mission. I've met him many times in Kuwait."

"Where did you meet him? What is his name?"

"His name's Mike Walsh. He has been to my accommodation at Fintas on many occasions."

"Why did you want to see him?" asked the irritatingly persistent Iraqi interrogator.

"I was arranging a barbecue for the company that I work for. I thought he might be able to help us with some things needed for the job."

What I didn't inform the obsequious little shit were the 'things' that I hoped Mike could help with – principally alcohol for a 4th of July

(American Independence Day) party. UNIKOM personnel could source alcohol but I didn't tell him because I felt stupid. Secondly, I didn't want the horrible little bastard to get all pious on me.

"How did you get to Umm Qasr? (Where the Iraqis had taken me into custody.)

The questioning had gone from accusatory to stupid. I couldn't allow my distress to blind me to the danger I was in, nor could I make a slip. I had seen these bastards execute people, I didn't want to become another victim so I replied, "I had passes that allowed me access to certain areas in Kuwait. I was allowed to enter the sector by the Kuwaiti guards."

"Why did you go to Umm Qasr?"

A redundant question. I had to stifle my contempt. "To see Mike – he is working with the UNIKOM mission!"

As I said the words my mind was deciding that the interrogator was either enjoying a sick game with me, as a cat would with a mouse, or he was a complete idiot.

"Did you know this (Umm Qasr) is an important military site?"

I replied, "No! Until I was told the name of the place, once I was in Iraq, I'd never heard of it before!"

I don't think that this was what he wanted to hear and he quickly launched a salvo of other questions.

"What is your company's name, and what do you do?"

As fast as he threw the questions at me, I delivered an answer, and we continued to verbally parry and thrust. "I work for Taylors International, we are contract caterers. We provide support and catering services to various clients in Kuwait."

"In your car were three pairs of glasses. Who do they belong to?"

This question itself didn't worry me. All three pairs were mine. It was the way in which the question was slipped into the interrogation that worried me. "They are mine."

"All three pairs belong to you?" This was asked with some incredulity as if owning three pairs of glasses was a crime in itself!

"Yes," I replied. "One pair are prescription and the other two are sunglasses. I use them on different occasions!"

His next question threw me completely.

"And this machine we found, what is it?'

"What machine?" I then realised he was speaking about a solar-powered calculator I had with me. "That is a solar-powered calculator."

"Why did you have it with you?"

"I had been closing a business deal and needed the calculator to price the function that I was costing."

His next statement sent shivers through me and made me realise I was in a very vulnerable situation.

"Really! We know that this is not true. You are lying to us, and we will ask you these questions again. When you tell us the truth we will decide what to do with you, but we know you are a spy!"

My interrogator then called out some instructions and the door opened and I was grabbed from behind, physically hauled from the chair and dragged, pushed, and shoved back to the cell. With every accusation I felt more confused and unsure of what I knew and running through my head were his taunts and allegations.

"Who do you spy for?"
"Is your friend your contact?"
"We know you are lying."
"We know you are a spy!"

As he shoved me into my cell the guard ripped the blindfold from my head. I stood alone not able to understand what had just happened to me. My head swam, I felt sick. *What the bloody hell was that all about, and what did it all mean? Was I a spy?*

I DIDN'T EXPECT THIS

Sunday, 28th June, 1992.

I joined Taylors International in June 1991 providing a catering support contract for Bechtel, an American construction company, who were putting out oil well fires started by the Iraqis earlier in the year as the first Gulf War ended.

I lived at the Ahmadi 'Guest House' along with firefighters and other support workers. Everything was organised to ensure that the firefighters were as happy as possible, not easy when the most 'high-tech' war in history had just been fought in the surrounding desert. Kuwait's infrastructure had been destroyed. The firefighters, mostly American or Canadian, demanded a functioning environment. When I arrived, Kuwait was not 'fully-functioning' by any stretch of the imagination. The country was full of war debris and covered in unexploded ordnance. The air was unbreathable due to the smoke and soot from over 750 oil well fires. All the water to fight the fires and for domestic use was brought in by tanker.

As the firefighting contract finished, in May 1992 Taylors opened a contract in Jahra, a small town about 40 klicks (kilometres) north-west of Kuwait City. The contract was with an American EOD (Explosive Ordnance Disposal) company called EHRT (Environmental Health Research and Testing). There were two camps either side of Jahra which were about four klicks apart. In the north-west was the senior (American expatriate) mess and accommodation which comprised three small blocks of flats that also housed Taylors staff who were looking after the clients, most of whom were Vietnam veterans.

While inspecting the senior camp I'd gone into the toilet and seen a huge land mine in the bidet! When I mentioned it to one of the Americans he had a good laugh and told me that it was a harmless casing used as an ashtray.

The camp on the south-east side of town was a different kettle of fish. At the junior camp, as the EHRT management called it, I had five staff who were having issues. The camp housed 130 residents including a large number of Gurkhas. There was also an eclectic mix of ethnicities many of whom appeared to detest each other. Iranians, Turks, Egyptians, Syrians, Palestinians, Pakistanis, Indians (Christian, Sikh, and Hindus), Sri Lankans, Filipinos, plus some Kuwaiti overseers stirring the pot! All-in-all, it was challenging environment for our Sri Lankan staff to control.

I got up daily at 2.00am to collect the packed lunches (prepared at Latifa by the night shift) and take them to Jahra, where the working day began at 3.00am in the junior mess and the American Mess was not far behind at 4.00am.

It had been emphasised that the packed lunches had to be available as and when required by the client personnel to prevent any delay to their working day. I set out on the Fahaheel expressway taking ring roads Five, Six and Seven and then made for Jahra via the by-pass. I had been making this trip three, four, five, and more times a day, becoming a familiar sight at the Kuwaiti military check-point where I was waved straight through.

I drove to the junior mess. On more than one occasion our staff had overslept and breakfast had been served late, which was unforgivable, so I got there as early as I could to prevent any issues.

Later that morning at the EHRT offices I negotiated the price and menu for a 4th of July, American Independence Day, barbeque.

I made a daily trip to the Kuwait Flour Millers, but the sliced bread, (we used 25 loaves a day), was unavailable. The machinery was broken! I asked when it would be available and was told, "About four or five hours, Inshallah!" This phrase, which means, 'By the grace of God', or, 'If God allows it' can also mean, 'If you're lucky'.

No bread until after 2.00pm. I tried to think of things I could do in order not to have to drive back to Latifa. I was already tired from the 50-minute drive along the windswept, empty road between Latifa Towers and Jahra. I thought I'd go and see Mike Walsh who I'd worked with in Algeria a few years before. I knew he was working in northern Kuwait with UNIKOM so heading north for a few hours seemed like the solution!

I was expecting to be transferred back to Algeria soon and so this would be a good opportunity to find out when I could return Mike's film videos and music cassettes he'd loaned me before I left Kuwait. I also wanted to find out how things were with him as he was a nice bloke.

I'd never been to the UNIKOM camp but all the signs north out of Jahra were pointing towards it. During the first Gulf War all road signs north of the Jahra by-pass had been removed. Now, nothing but the UNIKOM camp was signposted. I'd gone about a klick north of the by-pass when I was stopped at a Kuwaiti check-point. I handed my pass to the soldier. He asked where I was heading and I told him I was going to see a friend who was working with the United Nations. He handed back my pass and waved me on.

The aim of my trip was to kill four or five hours so I drove, slowly and carefully, along the single-track road. Either side of me was chaos, the detritus of war. Swathes of the desert were covered by burned-out tanks, lorries and various vehicles, shattered cases of grenades and a multitude of other weapons. I gazed at the sight spread out around me. Boxes of missiles and mines, anti-aircraft guns, bandoliers and assorted weapons poked through the sand. Caution and curiosity encouraged me to drive vigilantly.

Many years later, I watched a film called 'The Hurt Locker' which follows an Iraq War explosive ordnance disposal team and contains a scene that brought my 'trip north' flooding back to me. The main character is stood on the peak of a sand dune and as he gazes down he sees the scene of utter devastation which I drove through in 1992.

About 25 klicks later I arrived at a second army roadblock. A repeat of the first stop and I was allowed to proceed. A light 'shamal', the local name for a wind carrying sand, was blowing and its pulsing heavy gusts obscured my view and caused the road ahead to drift in and out of focus.

20 more klicks up the road, I encountered a third check-point. I went through the usual patter and was told to proceed but not to turn left or right – the only directive I'd had on the road from Jahra. I followed the signs for the UNIKOM camp and two klicks later the road disappeared turning into rubble and sand.

'Information films' on Kuwaiti TV advised that thousands of mines, bombs, explosives and weapons covered Kuwait and not to drive across open ground. With this in mind, I decided to follow a tarmacadam road. When the soldier said not to turn left or right, he obviously meant that I shouldn't deviate from the United Nations signs, remaining on the 'blacktop' as Americans termed a road. I turned left, travelled about half a klick and saw a sign indicated < UNIKOM – Doha>. After another 200 to 300 metres the road split again and I followed signs to the UNIKOM camp and passed chainlink fencing which protected cranes and assorted equipment including the remains of hundreds of marine pumps, motors, maritime engines and the hulls of naval patrol boats, MTBs (motor torpedo boats), and other vessels. This was different and something new for me, as all I'd seen for weeks was sand and desert.

As I reached the end of the chainlink fencing the road split again. Ahead, signposts for the UNIKOM airfield or the HQ and camp. I followed the sign for the camp and arrived at a mini-roundabout which the route from Jahra would have led me to had it not broken up. I didn't want to be 'caught' sneaking about in the United Nations camp so I decided to get directions from the HQ. That way I couldn't go wrong could I?

I turned the Land Cruiser left and saw soldiers up ahead grouped around a small 'Arabic-style' arch. I pulled in to one side of the road and stopped well before the arch. I could see the soldiers looking at me as I climbed out of the vehicle. As I did so I caught sight of flags flapping on poles high above the archway. I couldn't decide what it was that was 'wrong' with the flags but I knew something was 'wrong' and suddenly the penny dropped and my mind screamed at me, *THAT'S THE IRAQI FLAG!*

I reached back through the Land Cruiser's door which was still open, lunged at a Union Flag pennant stuck in the middle of the dashboard and shoved it under the driver's seat. The only way to proceed was to 'front' it out. The last thing I needed to do here was antagonise the soldiers. Suddenly I felt 'blasé' and thought, *What's the problem? I am in Kuwait. That is the border. At the very worst this is the UN zone, so what can they do?*

A tubby and poorly dressed Iraqi soldier, initially I was thinking the local equivalent of a character from TV sitcom 'Dad's Army', approached the Land Cruiser. As he did so, his colleagues unslung their machine guns and spread out across the width of the road. *Whoah!* I thought, as a 'Mexican stand-off' shaped up with five or six of them armed to the teeth against me with a Union Flag on a stick!

Captain Mainwaring's doppelganger, or maybe he can better be imagined if you think of Private Schultz, the bumbling German guard from the American TV comedy 'Stalag 17', approached me and asked me in Arabic where I was going. I told him I wanted to get to the UNIKOM mess hall and then without invitation he got into the passenger seat of the Land Cruiser, pointed straight ahead towards the arch and the armed soldiers and shouted, "YALLA!" (Let's go!)

Taken aback, I replied, "La, hadda Aleiraq!" (No, that's Iraq!)

Again he shouted, "YALLA!"

I replied in Arabic, "No, I work in Kuwait, and that," I said, pointing ahead, "is Iraq. That's a problem!"

We played out this cameo four or five times as Schultz ordered me to cross the border and I point-blank refused. He tired of 'our game' and pulled open the flap on his holster and began to withdraw his pistol, saying in Arabic, "You and the car are the problem, now GO…!"

I'd heard stories about shootings at the border and not wishing to become a statistic I complied! His gun was in his hand and with a sick feeling in my stomach I drove the Land Cruiser into Iraq. I concentrated on driving. I didn't want to have an accident as I thought this would give the Iraqis a reason to detain me.

I had no doubt that I should have attempted to leave when I'd first seen the soldiers. Having never been in the military, all soldiers looked alike to me. The soldiers all became Arabs with no 'throbe' or 'guttra', the traditional headgear of the Arab – if you've seen the film 'Lawrence of Arabia' you'll know what I mean!

I was directed to drive over a central area between the two lanes of traffic. This frightened me. For the previous year everyone in Kuwait had been told how dangerous this was. Not all the 'Gulf War ordnance' had gone BANG!

I was directed into a car park and ordered to drive up to an Iraqi border control office. Schultz indicated that I was to get out of the car and I followed him into the building. As I was over the border, and in Iraq, he had calmed down and re-holstered his gun. He knocked on the office door, entered, saluted, and then proceeded to explain to a uniformed man sat behind a desk that I had driven up to the border in a Saudi registered vehicle.

At this point I didn't understand the importance of my vehicle being 'Saudi registered' and why it was problematic. I now believe that the Saudi registration was the cause of my spending too long in various squalid Iraqi jail cells and prisons.

Having explained his version of events, Schultz summoned me into the control room and my stomach churned as I looked first at the Iraqi officer sat behind the desk, then at a photo of a smiling Saddam Hussein that was hanging on the wall, and finally at seven other Iraqi men who were seated and staring at me as if I was an exhibit in a zoo.

The officer behind the desk asked why I was in the area? I replied that I was looking for a friend. He asked why my vehicle was from Saudi Arabia, I replied it wasn't and that to my knowledge it had been in Kuwait for over 13 months.

He asked how I'd got to Iraq, I explained that my pass was valid in certain areas of Kuwait and that I'd passed three check-points and been allowed to proceed. He shook his head in disbelief explaining that the "evil Kuwaitis" were always allowing people to get into the UN zone which he said was Iraq. This was a part of the Kuwaitis provocative tactics. He said that this sort of thing happened all the time and was not a major problem and that as soon as his commanding officer returned he would arrange for me to return to Kuwait.

My passes were handed around the office. I assumed that all the men were Iraqi military, or at least there in some 'official' capacity, meaning they all had a bearing on my situation. Only two of them spoke to me, the others never did.

I was offered a cup of tea, Arabic chai, sweet and black. As I was drinking it the Iraqi officer told me that I could, if I wished, go next door to the UNIKOM HQ.

I knew that Arabs liked to be regarded as honourable and so I decided, rather stupidly, to demonstrate I 'trusted' the Iraqis and didn't feel troubled saying I was fine with them and it wasn't necessary to go to the UNIKOM HQ. Actually I was petrified as I considered where I was and who the people holding me were. I tried to understand why I acted as I did and questioned if going to the UNIKOM offices might have prevented the entire episode taking place. Who knows?

At about 12.15pm I was told we were going to go into an adjoining room, a dining area, to eat lunch, a meal of rice and some vegetables in an Arabic sauce. The Iraqis said they were embarrassed by the meal and pointed out this was Iraq's meagre diet since the imposition of sanctions by the West. Lunch was a short affair and I was soon back in the room I'd first been questioned in and sat down facing Saddam Hussein's smirking image. It all felt a little like a visit to the headmaster's office – which in my experience had always resulted in a caning!

As I waited, a very imposing UN commander entered. He was a huge Nigerian officer by the name of Colonel Abdulkader and he shook hands with everyone in the room, me included. As I was the only English speaker in the room, I later wondered why Colonel Abdulkader hadn't taken more notice of me. *How was I allowed to get through the UN zone, 'unseen', to the Iraqi lines? Why, when my abduction was noticed, didn't the UN or Colonel Abdulkader report the fact that I'd been seen at the border? What exactly were the UN troops observing?*

Apart from my own feelings about the UN, and Colonel Abdulkader, it was just a small piece in a much larger picture. The whole Kuwait/Iraq situation was a problem of British Imperialism and failed diplomacy. Abdulkader's concern was that the Iraqis were technicians, there to carry out work on an Iraqi communications station. He asked them, in brusque terms if their alterations were designed to interfere with the UN transmissions? They assured him they were not and then they all left leaving me alone with one guard.

I spent time later in the afternoon with various soldiers being told that I would be going to Basra to answer a few questions and then I would then be returned to Kuwait. I was told this was a mere formality on numerous occasions. I remember thinking to myself that I was now playing this game by Iraqi rules and I wasn't fond of formality.

COME BACK TOMORROW

Escorted by two armed Iraqi guards, I walked out of the border office and got into the Land Cruiser. The relief of the familiar was a comfort for me, when separated from the vehicle I'd felt lost and stranded. The guards also climbed in. One sat in the passenger seat next to me, the other in rear and he instructed me to drive out of the compound. Off we went, heading in what, as far as my immediate welfare was concerned, I perceived to be the wrong direction! Kuwait was now behind me and receding in the rear-view mirror! I glanced at the guards and their guns and wondered if all Iraqis were armed, and concluded that they were.

As we left Umm Qasr I noticed that all the buildings we passed showed signs of war damage. Rippling in the scorching late afternoon heat, the road to Basra stretched ahead of me; empty and windswept, disappearing into a desert void.

The journey was uneventful until we reached the outskirts of Basra and the road became increasingly congested. I became aware of the 'interest' the Land Cruiser was attracting from passing vehicles. Suddenly, a pick-up truck crammed with Iraqi youths squeezed past me – then it dropped back only to blast past me again. They raced through traffic blocking other vehicles from trying to overtake and agitating their drivers whose overtaking manoeuvres became increasingly more desperate. Unexpectedly, the pick-up took a position directly in front of me and the youths began to gesticulate and verbally abuse me and the Land Cruiser. I tried to overtake their vehicle but after my third attempt, all abject failures, the guard sat next to me indicated that I should hold my place and suffer their taunts.

As we entered Basra the pick-up went in one direction and I another as directed by the front seat guard. Basra's road system was in chaos; every carriageway, roundabout and junction was being rebuilt. Vast tracts of the road had disappeared entirely and traffic was required to cross sections of desert. It would be ironic, I thought, to be killed here by bombs dropped by the Royal Air Force!

Driving through the outskirts of Basra, I could see no war damage. Shops were open, roads were jammed and the streets teemed with vast crowds. Abruptly, I was ordered to pull over and stop. As I did so, the guard in the rear got out and said goodbye. My Land Cruiser had just been used as a taxi by a guy who was travelling home from his shift at the border! I know this might seem odd in the context of my situation, but I felt a bit 'used'.

I was tersely ordered to drive on by the remaining guard and rejoined the traffic which brought with it chaos at every turn. Clouds of toxic black fumes spewed from the exhausts of ancient buses struggling with the weight of the Iraqis hanging all over them like ripe fruit on a tree. We drove beside a stinking and filthy river, past three bridges and left over a fourth. Crossing the river, I drove through the centre of town and along a dual carriageway heading out of Basra. At a roundabout the guard gestured that I should drive back in the direction we'd come from. I was motioned to slow down as we approached a pair of gates on our left and as I braked to a halt the soldier on guard unslung a machine gun from his shoulder and pointed it at me. My guard climbed out and spoke with the sentry. When he returned, he told me to reverse to some bollards, park up and get out. He then led me through the gates. Weeks later I found out that I'd just entered the Basra compound of the Mukhabarat (Iraqi secret police)!

The compound was surrounded by an two-and-a-half-metre-high wall, and on either side of a road which bisected it were a series of n-shaped buildings interconnected with paths and walkways. In the centre was a large but fairly empty car park which had corrugated iron shades over its parking spaces to protect vehicles from the fierce Iraqi sun. It reminded me of the bicycle sheds at my secondary school!

I was led into a small office appointed with household-style furniture and a picture of Saddam Hussein hanging on the wall. I was sat down and for the next two hours spoken to by six different Mukhabarat officers, several of whom were dressed in Hawaiian shirts open to the waist! Some were guarding me, and asked questions out of curiosity (or so I presumed), others were interrogating me and asked structured but repetitive questions. I heard later that this was normal and that they were checking for discrepancies in a prisoner's story.

As the afternoon turned into evening, I was told that I would be going to the visa office in Basra in two hours time. At 8.30pm Iraq time (it was 7.30pm in Kuwait according to my watch), just as the light was fading, a young, uniformed guard came in and in good English introduced himself as my escort to the visa office. He politely instructed me to get into the Land Cruiser which had been brought into the compound while I was waiting in the office. I climbed into the passenger seat as I didn't fancy driving through southern Iraq or northern Kuwait at this time of night. Tensions were high and I had no wish to be mistaken, by either side, as the enemy!

With the guard driving, we moved off towards the bridge I'd crossed that afternoon. The streets were brightly lit and teeming with people and I noticed that women were dressed in Western clothes rather than traditional Arabic attire. There were no signs of the poverty associated with war which was being peddled by Iraqi propaganda merchants.

The guard drove like a madman with the horn used as much as the accelerator and every other vehicle around us being shouted at and gestured towards. He explained to me that he was in a hurry. This was his last task of the day and then he was going to a party so he wanted this sorted out as quickly as possible. He mentioned the war and that it was the Iraqi nature to stand up to a challenge. He then said that the people of Iraq were peace-loving, but that if struck they would not turn the other cheek, but instead, "Strike back hard!" His words, not mine!

Eventually, we stopped outside a huge anonymous office block several storeys high and the length of a football field. We parked up, got out of the Land Cruiser, and walked into the dimly lit building, crossing its entrance lobby and turning left onto a long corridor. In the gloom we approached an enquiry counter.

Behind the desk, an official spoke with the guard. The tone and volume of their conversation soon changed becoming increasingly tense and heated. They looked at me throughout their exchange and became animated with arms being thrown about. There was a pause when the official made a phone call and when he got off the phone more dialogue ensued which developed into an argument and concluded with the guard instructing me to follow him.

Outside, we got back into the Land Cruiser and drove away from the visa office and the guard explained that the official had said that it was too late to grant me the documentation now and I would have to return in the morning. I'd never 'factored-in' a night in Iraq. It was a huge blow, and I shuddered. As we sped through the crowded streets my head struggled with the growing fear lurking at the back of my mind about what an overnight stay in Iraq might include; assault, torture and pain!

After we'd arrived back at the Mukhabarat compound I was placed in a lecture hall behind the room I'd been questioned in during the afternoon. It was dimly lit and musky, but I found a sofa which I laid down on and attempted to sleep. I found this impossible however. I tossed and turned continually and was still tossing and turning when a different guard came in and told me to sleep in the room I'd initially been sat in so that the sentry at the gate would only have to walk 30 metres or so to check on me. As I lay on an even more uncomfortable bench than the lecture hall sofa, I spent my first night in Iraq trying not to give free rein to my worst fear that this could take days, rather than hours, to sort out!

THE WORST JAIL IN BASRA

Monday, 29th June.

At 6.30am the sentry from the gate indicated that I should get myself up and ready for the day. A pair of men I'd not seen before came in and asked the same questions I'd been asked previously and received the same answers. They soon bored of me and turned their attention to members of the public arriving and making enquiries about members of their families who had gone missing, or that's how it appeared.

I gathered that Saddam Hussein's regime didn't have respect for most human life but the elderly were shown deference and I witnessed a stream of older Iraqis arriving at the compound to make requests and enquiries; younger Iraqis, I learned, feared being thrown in a cell, as a witness or co-defendant.

I was given 'breakfast', a piece of Arabic bread, a blob of disgusting fruit jam, and a scoop of cheap catering margarine. It was foul but I ate it all and washed it down with a glass of tea. I'd had nothing since the 'meal' at the border the previous day. I needed the lavatory, but the disgusting state of the facility made me feel like throwing up so I decided to 'hold on' until I was back in Kuwait which I hoped wouldn't be too long now.

The young guard who'd taken me to the visa office the night before entered the room and told me that very soon we would be going back there now to get the papers I required to return to Kuwait. *Brilliant news!* I thought confidently as he departed to receive further orders.

As the only Westerner, I was conscious I was attracting the attention of other occupants who clearly viewed me as an 'enemy'. Sitting in a roomful of people looking at you with barely concealed hatred and contempt is very disturbing. *I never ordered the missile attacks, I promise*, were typical of the thoughts in my head as I sat and waited.

Eventually the guard returned and we made our way to my Land Cruiser. I felt propelled by an invisible force and could feel my heart pumping furiously as we set out once again for the visa office with the soldier driving. I asked about the party. The guard said it had gone well, but he was tired. *Christ!* I thought. *I hope he doesn't wreck the vehicle!* I wasn't worried for my own safety but thought an accident would delay me and be difficult to explain back in Kuwait!

Basra was scorching. The streets were busy but nothing compared to the crowds of yesterday. In the Middle East the heat of the day is widely avoided. When we arrived at the visa office I was led in through the front door and told to sit in what was now a very busy waiting area. The guard left – I thought to arrange my travel documents. When he reappeared, he shook my hand and told me I was no longer his responsibility. I stood open-mouthed not really understanding what was happening. With thoughts of a fairly immediate release and return to Kuwait evaporating, things fogged as I tried to recalculate and accommodate a new schedule – whatever that was going to be.

I started to feel 'Stockholm Syndrome' gnawing at me. This condition takes its name from a six-day hostage drama inside a Swedish bank in which the detainees developed a psychological bond with their captor. My English-speaking guard had been decent enough, but my mind was whirring. *Who will control me next? Will it be a sadist? Will I be worse off, and how? Will this delay my return to Kuwait?* The permutations seemed endless and his goodbye stripped my confidence. Now my worry grew as I waited for the next turn of events to unfold.

An officer in green military fatigues led me to a top floor office. He pointed at a chair – I sat. A tirade of questions followed. "How did I get to the border? Why was I there? Who did I work for? What was my job? How long had I been in Kuwait? What was the company I worked for doing in Kuwait? What were the company I was sub-contracted to doing? How long had they been there?"

The officer wrote down my answers and then without warning sprang to his feet and indicated I should follow him. We descended two floors and went through an exact repeat of the interrogation, however this time another person was present. He was dressed in civilian clothes. He, and his room were in a disheveled state. His clothes were crumpled and dirty and the office was full of debris. Cabinets, the desk and the floor were covered in rubbish. Windows were unwashed, dustbins full, and a mess of cups, filled ashtrays and assorted filth filled the room.

This session was more humane, with the scruffy man adding asides to the flow of the first interrogation. He mocked my predicament, not unkindly, more in a 'good-cop-bad-cop' manner and then suddenly this interrogation was also terminated.

I asked for the toilet and was shown into a filthy urinal, but amazingly enough, it was just that, a proper stand-up male urinal as opposed to the holes in the ground I'd already had to become accustomed to! I left the toilet and was instructed to wait in the corridor. I looked out of a window and down at my Land Cruiser trying not to overthink the situation as I had already been doing and trusting to common sense for a quick end to all this nonsense.

The most difficult captive moments are during a change of environment, location, or situation. Fear of the unknown is horrible and 'suggestion' caused me more 'fear' than it probably deserved. During these moments I was aware of my own vulnerability and my isolation increased during these events. My alarm was intense but quickly subsided when the changes were over.

The officer then led me into another room. *Jesus Christ! This is an Arsenal.* Guns, pistols, automatic weapons, magazines covered every surface. It was a war waiting to happen and I twitched nervously as I was asked the same questions for a third time. When the questions stopped I was ushered out of the room in a daze. The changes and three sets of near identical questions had left me feeling tired and exhausted with a desire to get as far away from the visa office as possible!

The officer then led me through a door and out into a rear car park. After three hours inside, the sunlight blinded me and the heat was stifling. When my eyes grew accustomed to the light I spotted my Land Cruiser. I stifled a cry of joy and walked across and mentally prepared to get in my vehicle and go.

The officer handed me a notebook, and said, "Check the contents of your car. Write everything in the book, sign it, and lock the vehicle."

I did as ordered and then he snatched the notebook saying, "Your car will be staying here, safe, until your problem is over!"

The bastards! The rug had been pulled from under my feet again and a surge of fear shot through me. Chilled to the bone in 40 degrees of of Iraqi heat, I shuddered. This situation was starting to get away from me. I was losing control and things were about to change again.

The officer pointed me to another car and I got in. I was petrified at the thought of being separated from my Land Cruiser. I tried hard to stay calm and relaxed and failed miserably. Everything on my part was now bravado with very little to back it up!

The back streets of Basra were quiet as we drove along roads covered in rubbish. We passed a shop with a window full of alcohol and for a second it felt vaguely reassuring knowing that I was among drinkers! A smile passed my lips as I thought about a party I'd attended in Kuwait. My driver, an Iraqi guard in military uniform, glanced at me and asked me in Arabic why I was smiling? I replied, It was nothing, just the drink!

The rest of the trip was silent and we travelled about six blocks on a circuitous route eventually arriving at what looked like a military base. Soldiers were lazing about at the gate with automatic weapons over their shoulders. They looked ready to sleep rather than take aim. My guard barked at me to get out and led me through a small archway and into a room on our left. I followed him through a second door and he pushed me back and entered alone. I stood in the room with the armed soldiers gaping at me opened mouthed.

I heard a conversation, understood none of it, and then my guard emerged snarling that I should sit down and then he left. This was a positive change as he struck me as a man capable of violence and so his departure was a bonus and I already understood that bonuses needed to be savoured. I was in a small, smelly room furnished with an easy chair and a sofa. The room was also occupied by a huge swarm of flies and I spent the first hour swatting them.

One-by-one, soldiers came in. I was offered a cigarette and asked, "You Inglisi? What your name? What your Job? Where you come from?

You soldier?"

I took this as natural curiosity, still believing it to be so. Occasionally, a 'barked' order from the office would cause one of the guards to dash into the inner office, take instructions from the unit commander, and dash out through 'my' room to carry out their orders.

I heard my name being called from the 'inner sanctum', my full name is Paul Stephen Ride, but the 'Iraqi translation' as I heard it, "Mr Bol Stebhen", rang out and I leapt to my feet resolved not to keep these mad sods waiting a second more than necessary.

I stood and cried out, "Aywa!"

The same voice from the 'inner sanctum' called out, "Ta'al!" (Come here !)

I knocked and entered. In the room two men were sat in what looked like a bedsit. I stood there being stared at with contempt, or disgust, I really couldn't tell which.

The commander of the unit was a well-built man with a bored expression on his face which told me he didn't give a toss. He asked the usual questions and when he'd heard enough he gave me a dismissive wave of his hand wafting me back to the outer office and the flies.

I asked to use a toilet and the commander allowed me to use the lavatory in his room. Oh God! It was awful. I could hear 'things' moving! I tried to find a light switch and touched the walls which were wet, slimy, and mouldy. The smell was overpowering and it was so dark I couldn't see a bloody thing. I could barely manage to urinate and got out of the disgusting cesspit as fast as I could.

Shortly after the commander left. Back in the room with the flies, as I sat contemplating my situation, a dragging, scraping, sound interrupted my musing. I got up and looked out of the window and saw a man, his ankles in bandages, sitting on what looked like a large waiters tray or platter using his hands to propel himself backwards across the space from the main gates to the office block steps. As he dragged his legs behind him, the soldiers mocked and teased him. I couldn't understand what was happening. As the invalid 'Platter Man' approached the stone steps a mechanic in dirty overalls appeared in the doorway and said to me, "I speak English, a little. I help with your problem, come!"

I thought this was a wind-up so more in hope than expectation I followed him out of the room. We passed a cell filled with the saddest humans I'd ever seen. They resembled whipped animals cowering in the corner of a dungeon. Some were holding the bars of their filthy, cramped cage and their eyes appeared to be begging for freedom. The space was so full of suffering it shocked me. I'd been just across the hall and not understood the evil in this place. I shuddered and walked on.

The mechanic led me to an office. Another question and answer session followed with an older officer, so overweight his uniform looked ridiculous. My replies passed through the mechanic who was acting as interpreter. The accuracy of his translation I cannot comment on, but I decided that he'd blown it when the officer said, "There will be charges!"

"What charges?" I blurted.

"Illegal entry," came the officer's reply in perfect English!

Illegal-bloody-entry, to this shithole was crazy. No one, and I mean no one, would enter this mad house voluntarily or deliberately!

The mechanic returned me to 'my room', said sorry and left. I had about £200 in my possession, made up of Kuwaiti Dinars and Sterling, which I hoped would be enough to pay my fine for illegally entering this open-plan, mental asylum.

When would I go to court? How would I explain this back in Kuwait? My employers had started to send people off to Bahrain for a long weekend so I thought my story upon my return should be, *I didn't fancy a weekend in Bahrain, I've been there before, so I decided to go somewhere that I hadn't seen before – Basra!*

I forced a smile but I was on edge. I clasped at a keyring I had in my pocket which had my son William's photo embedded in it. I couldn't relax. The flies were tormenting me and the heat was so oppressive that sweat was dribbling out of every pore of my body and then there was the smell! I asked one of the guards for a broom. His look suggested he thought I'd lost my mind. He gave me a small hand brush. I swept all the corners of 'my room' and moved the furniture around so I was able to clean out the muck accumulated beneath and behind it. There were three benefits to this. The smell wasn't as bad, the flies declined and I'd filled half-an-hour.

It became very quiet during the afternoon and then towards 6.00pm I heard the dragging sound of Platter Man. I watched as slowly, painfully, one-by-one, he descended the stone steps. Two passing soldiers ruffled his hair, pulled his cheek and leaned down to whisper something into his upturned ear. The man grinned sardonically and joked with the soldiers. As he bumped onto the bottom stair he spotted me and said something I didn't understand. In Arabic I replied, "Ana Inglisi" (I'm English). His expression was incredible. He stopped shaking his head, regained his composure, furtively checked around to make sure nobody was listening, and then spoke to me in fractured English telling me I was being held in a police station.

Christ! I thought. *This is a police station! Why does everyone look like an Iraqi soldier? Why are they all carrying guns? Why do I think this is a military camp?*

He then said, "This worst police station in all Basra, very bad, very dangerous, you be careful." He told me he was a Chef who'd been mugged. His assailant had dropped a wheelbarrow on him during the robbery and his ankles had been broken. With this guy's warning ringing in my ears, the commander, or police chief, returned and I went back to 'my room'.

I'd asked all day for water from the soldiers at the gate. Initially they'd been happy to oblige, but as the day wore on they'd become less enthusiastic about carrying water into me and permitted me to walk to a water tap mounted on the outside wall of the compound where I helped myself. This allowed me to walk a few metres and also meant the guards didn't fetch my water keeping possible hostility to a minimum. I drank the water from a metallic beaker which gave it a shocking chemical flavour.

The police station was an ebb and flow of victims, offenders, and armed policemen. At 11.00pm a soldier brought me two of the worst samosas I'd ever tasted. I had not eaten since 'breakfast' at the Mukhabarat compound but I couldn't manage to finish these foul items. In retrospect though, I applaud the humanity of the gesture!

I used the toilet again and had to run the gauntlet of the 'other occupants'. I couldn't see in the dark but I could hear 'them' and their sound made my skin crawl. The night was punctuated with frenzied activity. Drunks and revellers were given the benefit of the police officers training in crowd control – hit them and hit them again. I dozed off and was woken repeatedly by the blood-curdling screams of both sexes. I heard a man being interrogated as he was physically abused. His wife or girlfriend screamed and begged his assailants to stop. Similar sounds continued throughout the night and haunted my spasmodic sleep. I was now praying that I would have enough to pay my fine and wouldn't need anyone to plead for mercy for my wracked body.

Tuesday, 30th June.

I staggered outside to put some water on my grimy face and rinsed my foul-tasting mouth. Brushing my teeth already felt like a long-lost luxury! I hoped I'd go to court and this 'mistake' would be dealt with swiftly and I'd be taken to the border at Safwan and allowed back to Kuwait. This was so far out of my experience that I didn't know what to expect next and alternatives swung between credible and wildly incredible possibilities.

At 7.00am, a woman with a child and an elderly man arrived. They went to the deputy's office where the beatings of the previous night had been administered. I recognised her. She was one of the women I'd seen during the night who'd come to plead for her husband. She was well dressed and wearing make-up. The child was the usual childlike mixture of playfulness and curiosity, exploring everything. She scolded him gently while the older man just sat and looked worried. The woman was very beautiful and I was about to try to speak to them when my guard from the previous day arrived, spoke to the deputy, and marched out instructing me to follow.

I walked outside and there was 'my' Land Cruiser. I was so happy to see it, I nearly kissed it. I leapt into the passenger seat, and we drove off circling the backstreets until I recognised the Mukhabarat compound. The guard said, "Put your head down." I must have been wearing my stupid-head; I just stared at him and then he screamed, "GET DOWN!"

I ducked my head below the dashboard, not far down enough as he grasped my neck and using terrific force, rammed my head virtually onto the floor. I didn't understand I'd arrived at this compound three or four times, what did I care where the damned place was? I could hardly breathe and was on the verge of blacking-out as we entered the gates. Once inside and parked up I was allowed to get up and out of the vehicle. 24 hours after my departure, I was back. The officers I'd been interrogated by previously appeared with polite handshakes all round. I began thinking, *This is it son, saying goodbye, you're on your way!*

The younger officer who'd taken me to the visa office approached and said hello but when I extended my hand he shook it reluctantly not looking at me. It was strange. He'd been so friendly during our previous meetings, but again, I thought, *I'm off, so who gives a toss?*

The group went into the office, and I stood by the Land Cruiser with a guard. Three uniformed men I'd not met previously came out of the office and approached me with smiles and handshakes. The tallest, obviously in charge, spoke the best English and told me to get into the vehicle. I settled in the front passenger seat and he opened the driver's door and said, "No, you must be in the back."

I climbed out and got in the rear, sitting behind the driver's seat. The eldest of the trio sat next to me and with the other two in the front off we went. I was full of hope. Even though I'd seen people locked up at the police station and I'd been told that there would be charges, I'd not been put in a cell which I took as evidence that what had happened to me was a mistake!

The man I perceived to be in command drove. There was a lot of traffic and no conversation. I just sat there happy to be out of the dirty, smelly, dangerous, police station. Inquisitive, I asked a question. "Where are we going then? Which part of the border, Safwan?"

"Where would you like to go?" replied the driver.

"I don't mind. Anywhere I can get across the border!" I said.

"Have you seen Baghdad?" came the reply.

I laughed a hollow, frightened laugh. "No never."

Slowly, the driver sank the knife in. "Would you like to see it?"

I felt sick, my confidence evaporating and I regretted asking the initial question. Looking for an easy way out, I fired back, "No thanks. Let's just go to the border?"

His next line, was, in the history of one liners, unequivocally, the worst I'd ever heard. He tore the heart out of me!

"No! We must take you to Baghdad. These are our orders. Okay?"

My mind raced. Millions of connections a second – and all I could come up with was, "How far is Baghdad then?" Thinking, *If it's not far this may only add a day or two to my time in Iraq!* His reply scared me.

"Oh 800 kilometres!"

All my years on the earth, my whole life focused on this one moment, and all I could say by way of a reply was, "How fucking far?"

ROAD TRIP WITH THREE MAD MEN

I sat for an age in silence, I felt numb. Incomprehension and fear are the memories. Why would the Iraqis want me in Baghdad? I couldn't understand what was happening. I felt sick and started to panic. I think I wanted to scream. I know I wanted to be heading in the opposite direction. Fear was quickly converted to anger and aggression. I wanted to hit out at the person who had decided that I should be taken to Baghdad. Seething, I felt myself slowly drowning in a sticky mixture of panic, hate and apprehension.

I began to watch the road and passing signs. In most desert countries there isn't much to look at once you get out of the urban areas. A band of road running ahead of the vehicle usually meant hope and good times. There was nothing on this road for me but anxiety. The thought of how long this journey might take bounced around my head as the Land Cruiser found every bump in the road.

What was that? Whoah! Stop! Shit! We passed a sign which said turn right for the motorway to Baghdad. *Where are these jokers taking me?* This 'development' helped me find my voice and I said, "I thought you said we were going to Baghdad, the road sign said that Baghdad was a right turn at the junction we just passed?"

The reply didn't fill me with much optimism.

"Don't worry Mr Paul. "We are going on another road through the quiet area!"

My three 'companions' were armed. What their weapons were, as a lifelong civilian, I couldn't say. Why would I warrant such security? The fact that we were heading off into the 'Iraqi bondu' – me alone with these armed soldiers filled me with dread. Visions of a shallow grave and my body, with a questioning expression on my now dead face, passed through my mind. A desolate end. *What would happen to my family? Would I be missed? What would be said? What story, if any, would be told?* Fear is a wonderful memory jogger. I'd not said a prayer in years but I recalled the 'Lord's Prayer' and the 'Hail Mary' quickly and gave them a good airing!

The road was punctuated with roadblocks, armed soldiers, and armoured vehicles. As we approached every roadblock, we'd pull out of the flow of traffic to one side of the road and our driver, who I'd nicknamed 'Tall Smiling Boy', would give a couple of toots on the horn, receive a wave of recognition from the guards, and we'd speed on our way. I found this weird, I wondered if the entire Iraqi 'system' knew about me, the Land Cruiser, our journey? If not, why were we being waved through?

At one point, the flow of traffic was brought to a halt by some Iraqi soldiers steering colossal amphibious craft into the marshlands. I thought at the time they were hunting for insurgents who were employing metaphoric bows and arrows against Saddam Hussein's lightning!

While the other vehicles were behaving in a deferential way to Tall Smiling Boy he seemed happy enough. If another vehicle dared to encroach on any piece of the road that he was planning on using, a torrent of Arabic would explode from him and his driving would become 'erratic', if not plain bloody dangerous. At this juncture, I changed his nickname to 'Tall Road Rage Boy'.

I had a few music cassettes in the vehicle with me, each was put in the player by Tall Road Rage Boy and quickly rejected and so most of the journey was made listening to an Iraqi radio station, complete with prayer times! I recalled I'd crossed the border to the sound of Def Leppard's 'Armageddon It!'. Strange but true.

Approaching a town with, once again, a road sign pointing in a different direction for Baghdad, Tall Road Rage Boy pre-empted my next question and said, "We are getting some food here."

His comment made me realise that they knew I was aware of my surroundings and our general direction of travel. We parked outside an Iraqi 'transport café' complete with ovens built into the wall. Once inside we sat around a small table and I excused myself and went to the toilet. After checking it out, my bottle went. I couldn't bring myself to do it. *Christ, I'm not going to wipe my backside with my hand!* The thought made me squirm. I re-took my place at the table and was asked what I would like to eat. I requested the same as they were eating although I didn't really want any food.

We were drawing the looks of everyone in the restaurant. Once again, I found the hostile gaze of so many Iraqis very unsettling and was glad when our food arrived. Two small kebabs which were a little greasy but actually tasted nice. These were served with a small salad and Arabic bread, not over filling but pleasant.

After eating, I definitely needed the toilet. The horror of performing the act of defecating caused me to grimace but fortunately the onerous task was soon over. I exited the cubical and washed my hands repeatedly as I'd never done in my entire life! Eventually I did manage to forget the thoughts which kept bombarding me and with as much composure as I could gather I reentered the restaurant and it wasn't long before we were on our way again with a change of driver, the youngest of the three guards taking the wheel.

Along the road there were many large brown earthen constructions. It never occurred to me that they could be of any strategic significance as they looked more ancient than modern. I asked what they were? Puzzled glances were exchanged by the trio who eventually shrugged and said they didn't know. I suppose they weren't tourist guides but guards. I mention this to demonstrate my naiveté to the entire situation. Also, I think it demonstrates how the Iraqis regarded me.

We drove on through the barren landscape and the driver realised that the Land Cruiser was using more fuel than he expected. The tension in the car rose and communication ceased. For better economy, the radio was switched off and then the air conditioning which made the journey increasingly unbearable given the windows were shut and the midday sun was beating down. It didn't take long in the stifling heat for the odour of four men, one of whom might be about to die, to stink out the vehicle.

For what felt like an eternity we didn't pass any buildings, let alone a bloody petrol-station and my emotions were now as tight as a drum. I felt close to an idiotic gesture such as trying to get out of the now slow-moving Land Cruiser thinking that if it ran out of petrol I would be done for. I would sooner not see the bullet coming and considered I'd prefer to be shot trying to escape which was an irrational idea given there was nowhere to run and certainly nothing to hide behind. *Would I become excess baggage on this trip to God knows where?* Not for the first time, I had visions of a desert grave – this could be the end of my world!

The horizon shimmered, sweat trickled into my eyes. *What is that I can see in the distance? A building? Please don't let it be a mirage.* No, it was real – my guards had also seen it. We drove towards this tiny, wavering dot on the horizon which deep inside Iraq felt like salvation. The atmosphere in the vehicle lifted and the easing of tension was like a draught of cool air in the furnace of the vehicle. I checked the fuel gauge. We were running on vapour. The driver pointed and spoke to the other two. I didn't think we'd make it. I'd never run the Land Cruiser that low on fuel and, knowing how 'thirsty' it was, I felt sure and terrified that we'd run out of juice.

The dot grew and solidified and miraculously we made it and parked up. Literally dripping with sweat I climbed out of the vehicle and stood on the tarmac with a huge grin of relief on my face as I surveyed the oasis – a petrol station! The scorching desert wind felt cold on my body which was so sweaty that I appeared to have had a shower with my clothes on!

The youngest guard filled the Land Cruiser with fuel which cost six Iraqi Dinars (about £1.50) and we each had a soft drink. I drank mine thanking every deity that I'd ever heard of for the fact that we had made it to the petrol station and that I was still alive. Reluctantly, I climbed back into the vehicle with my sweat still dripping from me and we set off again travelling on for a couple of hours with little or nothing happening and then suddenly, without warning, the youngest guard who had returned to the passenger seat drew his pistol, spoke a few urgent words to Tall Road Rage Boy who was now driving and then stuck the gun into his side and cocked it!

Fuck me! What the bejesus is going on now? I know nothing about guns, but I do know that you don't play around with them. The idea that 'Gun Boy', as I instantly nicknamed the youngest guard, had turned on his team leader terrified me. I held my breath and couldn't bear to think what might happen next. For what seemed like an age, but surely was only seconds, Gun Boy maintained his position and I held my breath and then the guards started laughing! Almost immediately after this Gun Boy re-holstered his pistol and the laughter grew in intensity.

I couldn't laugh as I didn't know what the joke was and I had visions of a horrible end to my life flashing through my head. I had no idea where I was, I'd seen no road signs for many klicks and now the three armed lunatics I was with were playing with their guns. I was sure I was going to die at the hands of these armed juvenile delinquents. It was just a matter of when and this thought preyed on my mind. I started to measure, in terms of minutes, my own mortality and at the same time I became aware, with the road becoming increasingly busy, that we were approaching the outskirts of a city.

A sign confirmed we had reached Baghdad, a welcome sight after so much sand and scrub. My visions of a shallow grave subsided as we came to a halt in the early evening traffic. The guard sat beside me leant forward, said something and then got out. I sat in the rear alone and as we drove off again I wondered what was going to happen next? During the long hot drive, I had lost the will to keep track of what was happening and I was happy to arrive anywhere by the time we got to Baghdad. I asked what was happening next and was told I was being taken to, "answer a few questions that needed clarification."

The Land Cruiser had become a talisman and I felt that no serious problems would happen if I was able to stay close to it. I asked if it would be staying with me? I thought I'd been brought into the bloody country in the first place because of the vehicle and hoped that soon I would be using it to get the hell out of the place as well.

Tall Road Rage Boy said, "Yes, your vehicle will be staying with you, but maybe we will take the vehicle to Jordan tomorrow!"

An electric jolt passed through me. *Jordan! Why take my vehicle to bloody Jordan?*

All at once a nonsensical mix of Arabic and English words poured into my head. *Min fadlik – please – excuse me – ya rab – wait – hold on – ta'al – come here – ya rayal – one minute – bi sharafak – Christ!* Finally I spat out, "Where my vehicle goes, I will go too?"

Tall Road Rage Boy assured me this would be the case. "Of course, we will come for you tomorrow and take you there with us," he said with a grin on his face!

I'd been brought over the border at gunpoint and into Iraq with no passport – it was still safely locked in my room in Kuwait! "How the bloody hell could I go to Jordan?" I asked the guards and Tall Road Rage Boy replied, "Don't worry, we can fix all things."

Don't think me stupid, but I believed all of this. What reasons did I have not to? Rather than believing everything I should have doubted it, but at this stage I was totally naive.

Baghdad, in heavy traffic, trickled past the windows as I sat struggling with the permutations of a trip to Jordan. *How the hell would I get the vehicle back to Kuwait?*

Tall Road Rage Boy pulled into the side of the road and said that I was worrying too much and should relax! He'd obviously never spent ten hours in a car with three armed lunatics! "We must now put a blindfold on you, this is nothing to worry about," he said. "It is for security reasons so get out of the car – Okay Mr Paul?"

I was hardly able to refuse, or even complain, so with as much swagger as I could manage I was accompanied by Gun Boy to the back of the Land Cruiser. He rummaged around in his bag for something. *Oh Christ!* I thought. *What's he searching for?* Then he pulled out a shirt and wrapped it around my head over my eyes and then shoved me back into the vehicle and off we went again. Petrified at the prospect of being blindfolded and shot by the side of an Iraqi road, I then smelled something which took a few seconds to identify – body odour! These half-wits had tied a worn and very smelly shirt around my head as a blindfold. You never read about or saw situations like this in spy novels or films – I just couldn't catch a break!

A Land Cruiser is nearly all windows and here I was sitting blindfolded in the back of one with Union Flags on it, paintwork used to identify 'friendly vehicles' in Kuwait after the first Gulf War. Any locals looking on would have been suspicious had they seen me which prompted Tall Road Rage Boy to say, "Mr Paul, we think it would be best if you laid down. Yes?"

I complied and as I laid across the back seat I wondered what was going to happen next on a trip that was getting more bizarre by the minute. The Land Cruiser slithered around roundabouts and swerved past other cars and each time it did so I slid up and down the rear seat with varying degrees of force. I hit my head so hard on the door a couple of times it's a wonder I didn't break my neck!

We arrived at a check-point and words were exchanged. The Land Cruiser was crashed into reverse, spun round and my 'ordeal by blindfold' resumed. A short drive followed to another check-point and the same shouted greetings and requests were repeated, only this time we were allowed into wherever this place was and immediately started to ascend a ramp as if we were driving into a multi-storey car park. The nauseating smell, the heat and the sensation of driving round and round disorientated me. I wondered what the hell was going on and if I was going to throw up?

We eventually juddered to a halt and my guards got out. In the distance I could hear voices and footsteps but for a long while I was left on my own. I was bathed in sweat from the heat but in truth feeling cold and frightened about what these mad men might have in store for me next? My guards had promised me that my situation was easily resolved, but I didn't think blindfolding a man then driving him to a secret location was 'taking the heat' out of the situation.

In truth I was so naive that I still believed that my situation hadn't come to the attention of anyone senior enough to treat 'an Englishman with the respect he deserved'. At this point I wasn't aware of just how despised the British were in the Middle East and thought that as soon as my plight was known by someone with enough rank the situation would be corrected. What an idiot I was!

Footsteps approached the Land Cruiser, the door flew open and in English a new voice said harshly, "Close your eyes and put this on when I take the cloth off."

I waited with my eyes shut as swiftly the smelly shirt was replaced with a purpose-made, elasticated blindfold that was adjusted with such force it made my ears burn. Next, my arm was grabbed and I was pulled from the vehicle. With my eyes totally covered, I was pushed across a concrete floor. We stopped and the blindfold was pulled up a centimetre or two so I was able to see some steps and I was then dragged up three or four flights whereupon the blindfold was pulled down again so I couldn't see anything at all. We moved on again until I could hear voices and someone asked me if I spoke Arabic, I told them I spoke very little. Something was said in Arabic which I didn't understand and I was spun around and propelled along not able to see where I was going before being abruptly brought to a halt by restraining hands on my shoulders.

Then the shit hit the fan! I was pushed down onto my knees and heard the sound of footsteps retreating. I knelt, helpless, vulnerable and scared with snapshots of the day flashing through my mind. I tried to understand why I would be driven 800 klicks from Kuwait to be shot in the back of the head in a multi-storey car park in the suburbs of Baghdad. Flashbacks of atrocities I had regulary seen on Kuwaiti TV showing the Iraqi military murdering Shias in the southern marshes blitzed my mind and stirred my confusion. For seconds that felt like minutes and minutes that felt like hours, I knelt and strained my hearing to catch the sound of a gun being cocked that would mean my life was about to end.

This was just how I'd seen the Iraqis execute prisoners. Blindfolded, defenceless, on their knees. I shook and waited but I didn't hear a gun being cocked. Finally, someone marched up behind me. I felt sure I was about to experience pain beyond belief. Would my life pass before me as I'd read and heard so often was the case? I tensed, waiting. What a stupid way to die. Something touched me, this was it. *Oh fuck!*

The guard shouted something and I flinched. I felt both of his hands resting on me and then I was spun round and sat on my backside. It was a huge relief because I'd never seen the Iraqis execute anyone sat on their arse!

I was left to sit and worry for maybe 20 minutes. I heard footsteps coming towards me and braced myself once again for what I thought was the inevitable but this time I was simply dragged to my feet and pushed in the direction of voices I could hear in the distance. I felt a change in the air temperature as I was pushed into a room where immediately a voice said, "You may take off the mask now."

I did as instructed and initially I was blinded by fluorescent strips that lit the room. Slowly my eyes adjusted and I took in my surroundings. I was in a small room with a partition wall that looked out onto a car park. Everything was constructed in concrete while the office was finished in a beige plaster.

At first the huge man whose voice I'd heard was kind enough to me, but the longer things went on, the more obvious it became that he was really a grade 'A' shit! I was reminded of an old saying I'd heard that goes, 'You can pick your friends but not your jailers!' And then the litany of standard questions started with, "Why did you come to Iraq?"

I got the impression that it didn't matter a damn what I said, my fate was sealed. As I was later to discover, Iraqi agencies and courts are only there to 'rubber stamp' decisions made by 'higher authorities'.

When my interrogator had all the necessary paperwork in front of him completed, I was ordered to take everything out of my pockets. I removed my keys, wallet, loose change and my passes, including my KOC (Kuwait Oil Company) passes; one with Al-Awada Project, another with Al-Tameer, along with my Taylors ID which attracted particular interest.

My personal items were brought up from the Land Cruiser and I was made to explain the purpose of each item at some length.

"Why have you got five cassettes in the vehicle with you?"

"Er, well I like music, and er, well the desert is really boring and it's just for entertainment!"

"But why five, isn't that too much?"

"No. I've got around 70 tapes in my accommodation in Kuwait, I like a good variety you see."

At this, I received a knowing gaze, a deeply suspicious "hmmm" and the cassettes were given another examination.

This went on and on with all my belongings. My cash was counted, keys were identified. "Which doors did they open? Why was I carrying so many?" I was instructed to remove gold chains from my neck, a puzzle ring I had on a finger on my right hand and finally my wedding ring. I hadn't removed this is over five years and it really pissed me off.

My possessions were placed into a large manila envelope and I signed for them. I asked if I could retain the keyring which had William's picture in it and a fat, pig-like guard behind the desk sneered at my weakness and said in a voice that sounded both insincere and content when denying me, "No Mr Bol (Paul), you must keep nothing."

I tossed the keyring back onto the desk with all the bravado I could summon and shrugged, boiling with rage, ready to lash out at this prick who was obviously very happy in his work. I was terrified at this stage. Pulling my wedding ring off had not proved easy and I hated these men for reducing me to nothing. They had taken away everything I possessed, I had nothing familiar to cling to for support. I was 800 klicks from Kuwait and bullshit and bluster were simply not enough here. I had been isolated and now stood alone and frightened.

After a few more questions about why I'd made the trip to northern Kuwait, the officer I nicknamed 'Pig Man' told me that when I was asked my name I was to reply, "Elf Miah wo Khamseen. Your name is not Mr Bol, it is now the number Elf Miah wo Khamseen."

Puzzled, and given my limited knowledge of Arabic, I politely asked for confirmation. "Is that 1005?"

Pig Man yelled, "NO! NO! NO! ELF MIAH WO KHAMSEEN is ONE, ONE, FIVE, ZERO, 1150!"

After this little bit of confusion he calmed down and in a matter of seconds I'd forgotten what I'd just been told! Then came the ultimate insult. A subordinate entered the room and threw a muddy-grey laundry bag at my feet and Pig Man told me to remove my clothes and put them into the bag.

As I undressed, I felt self-conscious and vulnerable. I've undressed in sporting environments where nudity is universal, but this was hostile – alone with four guards watching me. It's a strange feeling, being naked in front of four sneering men, all wearing Village-People-style moustaches watching and leering. Pride cannot be salvaged as your wedding tackle does it's best to totally disappear.

Pig Man raised his head and instructed me to put my underpants back on and also the 'pyjamas', which had been thrown on the floor during my getting-naked performance. I felt stupid dressed in pyjamas and then there was also a pair of plastic sandals in the bag that were too small for me that I also told to wear. Couldn't the Iraqis tell that I was not the 'Cinderella' they were looking for! The Iraqi footwear and clothing made me feel like a poorly-presented clown.

I asked if I would be going to prison? Pig Man scoffed and said no. I was then made to sign for my clothes and taken outside back to the area where I had been knelt. Without a blindfold on I saw that I had been knelt close to a concrete wall. Adjacent to the wall were three or four plastic bowls and some small plastic cups. I was told to collect one of each and then I was led back towards the office. A thin blanket was thrown at me and I was grabbed by the arm, spun through 180 degrees, and shoved in the back across the car park. As I approached a ramp leading up to the next level I heard footsteps coming down the incline towards us, the guard grabbed my head and rammed it against the wall to prevent me seeing the other person. As the footsteps receded behind me, I was grabbed and shoved up the ramp. My head swam with a sickening mixture of fear, hate, anger, and bewilderment.

Why are these bastards doing this to me?
Where am I being taken now?
What have I done to deserve this treatment?

The guard grunted and shoved me in the base of the spine and we went up the ramp. Hands held my arms and twisted aggressively to control my speed of movement and direction of travel. We went up the ramp and onto a wide landing where I was directed toward a steel gate. I recognised a cell when I saw one, and this was a cell. If this was not a prison then the Iraqis certainly had a strange idea of what the word meant! I was shoved towards cell 49. As my escort held my arms, another guard stepped in front of me and unlocked the cell with a vast black bunch of keys that were medieval in appearance. As the door was drawn open, I struggled as Pig Man's statement reverberated through my head. *NO WE ARE NOT GOING TO PUT YOU IN PRISON!* Memories of a workmate of mine in Saudi flashed through my mind, he would say when dealing with an obvious lie, "You fucker, you lie like a flat fish!"

I was shoved and stumbled into the cell as a shiver of fear ran through me. Each day of this piss-take I had been told that it would "be over soon" – "a mistake easily rectified" – "you will be going back to Kuwait very soon" – but every developement further distanced me from the relative safety of Kuwait. Every bloody word that I'd been told was a lie. *Bastards, all of them!* I thought.

Words cannot describe the feelings, fears, and disgust of being shoved into a dark, dirty, foul-smelling, concrete bunker. Disbelief was the first thing to hit me, then logic kicked-in and I struggled to come to terms with the realisation that this may not be 'right and just' but unfortunately, it was my lot – at least for the night.

The fetid air in the cell was heavy with the stench of urine. The smell came from every millimetre of the chamber. I know this as I made a circuit of the floor on my hands and knees, like a human bloodhound, trying to find the least fouled area to sleep on. I marked out 'my patch' by laying the blanket on the floor. Trying to get comfortable was impossible as the whole cell was concrete and I couldn't find a way of lying that didn't hurt!

After a while I heard the bolt on my cell being opened again and I sat up and waited for the next act in this farce to unfold. Images of the dozens of Iraqis that had informed me in the previous 60 or so hours that this was a "mistake" and that "you will be free soon" filled my head. I expected to see a friendly smiling face explaining that the "mistake" was over and I'd be going back to Kuwait!

A pair of thin blankets thrown in my direction smothered my hopes. Luxury, two more layers of 'toilet-tissue' that I could fashion into a bed! I slept for most of the night because the previous two had been disturbed and as my third day of captivity came to an end, I realised that this "mistake" would have to be sorted out tomorrow. If I could have managed tears of self-pity they may have been justified as my situation had become more complicated, but the sad truth was I just felt angry and totally exhausted.

Lying there in the dark, I was shrouded in trepidation. This wasn't related to the probable conseqences of trying to escape or fighting back, as far as I was concerned that was 'Hollywood' bravado. For myself it was a stark realisation. *You're fucked now son! Better make the most of it!*

MUKHABARAT INTERROGATION

Wednesday, 1st July.

When I woke up I couldn't feel certain parts of my body, the concrete floor had been a wonderful anaesthetic. I had a sensation akin to being drugged, or of having a hangover.

My fourth day of captivity began and I had not been able to brush my teeth or clean myself in any way at all. I remember sitting on the floor breathing in a mixture of body odour and other people's urine. I felt dreadful; physically and mentally, and no doubt I looked and smelled the same as I felt.

Light filtered in from a high grill in the rear wall and I examined the boundaries of my world. Nearly rectangular in shape, my cell was about five metres in length from the gate to the rear wall and approximately three metres across at its widest point. In the corners there were small piles of cardboard which on closer inspection turned out to be stale bread! One of the walls had a small dogleg out of view of the guards, in it was a small yoghurt pot! This had the remnants of a bar of soap in it. I had no idea how long the Iraqis were going to keep me here so I decided to use the soap to record the days that I spent in solitary confinement.

I am no longer surprised at the conditions people can exist in. A human being can adjust and cope with far more than I would have ever have believed possible. I could hear very little noise, occasional footsteps, whispered conversations, nothing more. I wondered how long it would take the Iraqis to establish that I wasn't who they thought I was?

Later, I heard a strange and anguished wailing. It grew louder and I heard cell doors opening. Tortured squealing sounds of gates opening were sometimes followed by a few words of abrupt spoken Arabic then the metallic clang of a cell door being slammed rang out. More wailing followed and I realised the sound was being made by the wheels on a trolley. Each cell was opened and closed, then the next and the next. The squeaking of the trolley wheels filled the space between apparent moments of freedom.

I tried not to get excited and attempted to ignore what was going on however questions pervaded my thoughts. *Supposing my cell isn't opened? What if the person opening the cells isn't aware I'm in here. Will he shoot me?*

I realise that the last question seems extreme, but I had no idea of where I was, or what these armed, mad sods were capable of. I didn't know how to play this, I thought of standing by the gate to be ready for whatever happened next and worried that I might spook whoever opened the cell and what might happen. I decided to play it cool and remained seated in the middle of my cell on my filthy blankets. I tried to appear as relaxed as I could, hoping and praying that my cell door would open.

A metallic clang at my door heralded disappointment. My cell remained firmly shut instead a small 'Judas gate' which was about 15 centimetres in diameter and high up on the door opened. A hand appeared in the gap accompanied by Arabic words I didn't understand. I panicked, what the hell was going on? I looked closer. The hand was holding a disc of bread. It was feeding time! The bread was thrown into the cell and the hand reappeared holding a bowl with something hot in it. I took the bowl and immediately the hand withdrew and reappeared holding a cup with hot liquid in it. The Judas gate slammed shut almost before I'd managed to lower the cup and bowl from above head height to gaze at their contents. The entire process, even allowing for the words that were snarled at me, had taken seconds. My 'breakfast' consisted of half a cup of Arabic tea and a concoction that filled the bowl which my 20 years in the catering trade couldn't help me identify.

Christ! I thought, *I'm in worse trouble than I'd imagined!* I felt nauseous looking at the slop in the bowl which appeared luminous. As my mind was revolting at the thought of eating the slop, an internal voice, the one that had seen the film 'Papillion' was saying, *Eat everything. You never know when you will next be fed!*

Both the bowl and cup were child-size. Eating was another problem. I gazed at the slop and realised I had no cutlery to eat it with. I felt debased as I used the putrefying piece of bread like a shovel to scoop up the contents of the bowl. After a few mouthfuls I deduced I was eating 'rice soup' which I would come to learn was a staple part of the Iraqi penal system diet. When compared with some other culinary delights which my body would attempt to digest, the 'soup' was one of 'Saddam's boys' better offerings!

Silence followed which was eventually broken by a metallic clang and seconds later the scurry of feet on the floor. One-by-one the occupants of each cell were being released and then re-caged before the next cell was opened. The patter of fast feet was mingled with tired legs being dragged slowly across the concrete. I laid on the floor on my chest, peered under my cell door and watched as the feet, some individual and some in groups, went in the same direction past the right-hand side of my cell and out of my field of vision.

I heard running water and guessed that people were being allowed to visit the toilet which I had been desperate to use for some time. I sat on the floor of my cell waiting for my turn. I didn't want to give the guards any reason to give me a hard time. When my door opened I didn't hang about when the guard indicated that I should do as everyone else had. He waved me out, stepping away from the door, and pointed me in the direction the others had gone.

I put my plastic sandals on and minced out of my cell at which point fear ambushed me. It wasn't cold, yet I shivered. I had my bowl and cup with me and entered a white tiled area containing toilets, a shower, hand basins and rubbish bins. It was brightly lit and appeared surprisingly clean.

Two wall-mounted hand basins and two large wheelie dustbins, where I discarded the remains of my bread and emptied the last of the still luminous rice soup, were in the lower section of the space. I washed my bowl and cup and climbed the stairs that ran between the bins and basins. To the left were two shower stalls and to the right two toilets, both surrounded by a chest high wall covered in peeling white paint.

A guard began shouting at me. I didn't understand what he said but his tone told me all I needed to know. I am not sure if I feared these guards, but when they yelled I reacted. I'd figured I wouldn't get released quickly by behaving like an idiot. I gesticulated that I was about to use the toilet and the guard yelled and used sign language to indicate that I should hurry up!

The toilets were not only foul, but full! By toilet, I mean a hole in the floor that brimmed over and provided a meal for the thousands of flies hovering and buzzing nearby. I used the unpleasant facilities and got the hell out as fast as I could. I then used sign language to request a shower but the guard indicated very firmly, no, and that I should return to my cell immediately. This was a serious blow to my morale as I still had the grime of four of five days worth of travel and captivity clinging to my body. I felt like hell. A clean up denied, I grabbed my cup and bowl and returned sullenly to my cell. The door slammed shut behind me, and a long wait began.

Time meant nothing. As my watch had been confiscated by Pig Man the hours stood still as I waited for something, anything, to happen. I'd done nothing wrong and did not understand what my captors wanted of me.

As the day wore on my squalid cell became hotter and the now familiar prison stench increasingly nauseating. I was incredibly thirsty and realised I'd need to bring water back to my cell at the next opportunity. No one teaches you how to survive in solitary, you have to figure it out yourself. Stripped of my humanity and liberty and fearing what could happen next I sat and brooded over my situation. I was alone, guilty apparently until I could prove otherwise. Trial and painful error were teaching me the rules. I would need to learn quickly or I might become another grim statistic.

I paced my cage. Hours passed, I don't know how many. I had resigned myself to a day without anything happening when my cell door squealed open. I was led out by a guard and shoved towards a small glass-fronted office opposite my cell where I was pushed onto a chair. Moments later, another guard entered holding a small camera and took a photograph of me. All of this was accomplished without a single word being spoken. As the 'photographer' left, the first guard reappeared and dragged me out of the chair, shoving me across the landing and into my cell that I'd left seconds before. The metallic ring of the key turning in the lock after the door closed mocked me.

More time passed. The squeaking and wailing of the food trolley indicated the prospect of a lunchtime meal which I took as a positive. Wrong! If I thought breakfast had been dire, then lunch was the end of the world!

The Judas gate opened and I thrust my bowl and cup into the small gap. The cup was pushed back, with an oath being uttered by the 'hand' serving the slop. The prison chef's 'pièce de résistance' was passed into the cell and the Judas gate rang out as it was slammed shut. I gazed expectantly at my bowl which contained rice so badly burnt that it was virtually inedible but I forced down all I could.

More time passed. I sat in my cell alone with my thoughts. The sound of the trolley told me we had moved from lunchtime to dinnertime. The Judas gate opened and I thrust my cup and bowl out. As before, the cup was pushed back and the bowl snatched away and filled. I put it on the floor and tried my luck with the cup again. This time it was ripped from my grasp and hurled across the cell. I realised that tea was a breakfast luxury!

Evening 'meals' were water, a tin of tomato puree, then either a 'vegetable of the day', okra, aubergine, courgette, potato, or if we were very lucky butter beans, or pasta (whatever shape the kitchen had) and the whole concoction was boiled – furiously by the look of it. On two occasions, I received a small piece of very tough fatty meat. I'd sooner have had the butter beans! I should say here that these were the only pieces of meat that the Iraqi 'system' gave me in the entire duration of my detention.

Although shocking, the food at this Mukhabarat complex in Baghdad was the best, with the largest portions, of all the prisons I was to be held in. Just thinking about it now reminds me of the depths to which I would have to descend in the next three or four months simply to stay alive.

Following 'dinner' I was allowed out of my cell to use the toilets. I found the visits quicker after lunch and dinner as no one was permitted to shower. Post-food was the only times we were allowed out of solitary. I say 'we' – I never saw another prisoner in all my time in the complex except for one glimpsed fleetingly when I was first taken to my cell.

After being locked up once again I lay on the floor of my cell, frightened, confused, and with a headful of questions no one was answering. This time I'd remembered to take water to my cell which was constructed of concrete breeze blocks that absorbed heat during the day and kept it searingly hot at night.

Nothing happened for the next couple of days as I followed my dreadful routine apart from a stark realisation that I was now depressed rather than scared. This period of my detention is confused. Trips to the toilets and the squealing of the trolley were the only respite from the isolation of solitary confinement.

Solitude gave my brain the time and opportunity to recall episodes from my life that I had not considered in many years. In all honesty, for a very 'earthy' person, I found it disturbing. I know what I think, and I like to understand what is happening to me. In all honesty, I felt as if I'd lost control over my mind and some of the places it took me.

Friday, 3rd July.

I was allowed to shower for the first time! I ran to the toilet area, enthusiastically thinking about hot water and being clean! Washing powder that was piled on the top of the wall was to be used as soap! I stood under the shower, delighting in the refreshing sensations that my filthy, sticky body was now revelling in. Finally, when I was sufficiently wet, I picked up some of the soap powder, and put it onto my hair. *DEAR GOD!* My mind screamed as I felt my scalp burn! The 'washing powder' was some kind of concentrated biological detergent. I could feel the heat burning my scalp as a chemical reaction of sorts took place on my fucking head!

By the time I'd finished the guard who'd escorted me to the shower was having a fit, shouting at me to hurry up. I had no means of drying myself so I simply put my 'pyjamas' on over my still wet body and then collected my bowl and beaker of water and returned to my cell.

Later, as I was prodded and pushed to my first interrogation I understood why I'd been allowed to shower. It was Friday, The Muslim holy day, things got cleaned on a Friday. Obviously, it was the same in solitary!

After my first blindfolded interrogation, I paced around my cell trying to make sense of it. My head cleared, I realised that this was the day of the barbecue I'd been organising in Jahra. Today had been my first 'goal' date I'd hoped to be released by. I felt damaged, used, and abused, I resented the accusation I was a spy, this was turning into something I didn't understand, want to think about, or believe possible. It was a nightmare, only conceivable in works of fiction – or was it?

In the afternoon, my cell was unlocked and a floor squeegee was propped up against the wall. The guard indicated that I should wash my cell! I couldn't remove with the cold water the smell of urine that filled the cell. If anything, the liquid acted as a catalyst making the odour overpowering. Fortunately, this only lasted while the floor stayed wet, which in July wasn't long.

Following my release, it took a couple of years to be able to write about my experience of solitary confinement. As time passed, I could recall small, sanitised snippets but alone, sat in front of a blank page the horror of the Mukhabarat complex in Baghdad came back. I was not exposed to physical torture but that didn't stop my mind from anticipating it, expecting it and preparing for it every waking moment of my incarceration.

I woke the day after my first blindfolded interrogation feeling positive and I fluctuated between boredom and fear that yesterday's activity would not change things. Today I was ready. As soon as the guard opened my cell door and said my 'name', "Elf Miah wo Khamseen," I replied, "Aywa!" The blindfold was thrown at me and as I was pushed and poked down to the interrogation room I felt positive as I believed the way to resolve this was to provide the Iraqis with any information they wanted. I thought that this would demonstrate my innocence!

The session was with at least two men, possibly more. The questions started with a statement. "We know that you were lying to us yesterday, and today we want you to tell us the truth. Do you understand this?"

This was ridiculous. I'd been telling the mad bastards the truth since I'd been brought across the border. I understood fear, but now the pangs of terror started. Nothing I said was being heard. Their version of the 'truth' was 'the' answer. These guys were serious; they believed I was a spy! I was told to stop lying and tell them who I was working for.

"Who are your contacts in Kuwait?"

"I don't have contacts."

"Do you work for British Intelligence?"

"No!"

"Do you work for the Americans?"

"No!"

"Do you work for the Kuwaiti Mukhabarat?"

"No!"

"Are you Jewish? Do you work for Mossad?"

"No!"

"Who is your contact at the American Embassy?"

"I don't have a contact at the American Embassy. I don't really know where it is. I've been past it, but I don't know Kuwait City very well at all!"

"You are lying to us. Who do you pass your information to?"

"Nobody! I am a catering worker, I am not a spy. I have never been in the military, nor am I interested in politics. I mind my own business!

"Do you expect us to believe this? What were you doing in a restricted area?"

"I didn't realise I was in a restricted area. Believe me, it's the truth!"

"Tell us who you are working for and you can go home."

"I am not a bloody spy. I am a catering manager and have been in catering all my life. Okay?"

They didn't believe me and said they had plenty of time and eventually I would tell them the truth. They repeated the questions I'd answered the previous day and I was asked what I'd seen in Kuwait. Where exactly I had worked, and what exactly I had been doing?

I told them about the firefighters, the Thai and Filipino labourers, the sites that I'd worked at, and my role at each camp. I gave them everything that I had, but the Iraqis always wanted more detail, more information, more of something, more of everything! That's how it felt. They asked me what each group of people did.

"The firemen, what do they do?"

"They are putting out fires!"

"What fires?"

"The fires you started during the Gulf War!"

"Oh, those fires!"

I couldn't believe it. The biggest act of ecological vandalism ever carried out and these pricks had forgotten doing it!

"What about the Thais and Filipinos?"

"They are mostly involved in labouring, and are being fed up in the Ahmadi area."

"What sort of labouring?"

"Putting back together the oil-producing infrastructure that was damaged during the war."

"What about the Americans?"

"They all live and are fed down at Latifa Towers."

"No! What sort of work are they doing?"

"Supervising only now."

"What sort of supervising?"

"Technical, civils, logistics, engineering."

At the mention of engineers there was a perceptible rise in the level of interest in the room.

"What are the engineers doing?"

"Putting the damaged equipment and structures back together. Mostly in the oil industry."

The disappointment was palpable. I seriously think the Iraqis were expecting some major revelations and their next questions were odd.

"Did you see any Saudis? Were Aramco (Arabian American Oil Company) there giving technical advice?"

"No. I didn't see any Aramco personnel."

"The Kuwaitis claim to be exporting crude oil again. This is a lie isn't it?"

"As far as I know the exports have been going on for some time now. We feed the pilots at the jetty."

"We hear that they are exporting water, is this true?"

"I couldn't tell you."

"Come, you must know? Things were so badly damaged that they could not be operational so quickly!"

"The damage was not so bad apart from the fires. Yes the repairs are nearly finished. We were promised five years work, but are already being made redundant after only one year!"

This didn't seem to be what they wanted to hear, but as I have already said I believed that telling the truth was to be the best way of getting out of Iraq.

The questions continued and became personal.

"Are you married?"
"Yes!"
"Is your wife with you?"
"No!"
"Where is she?"
"At home."
"In Kuwait?"
"No, my home is in London. I work in Kuwait!"
"Do you have children?"
"Yes two. A boy, William, and a girl, Rhian."
"They do not go with you to Kuwait?"
"No. I am on a bachelor contract, no wife or family allowed."
"Where do you live, tell us your address?

Without a second thought I told him my address. I know that this sounds a totally stupid thing to do, but I had nothing to hide.

"So your wife never goes to Kuwait?"
"I wouldn't take her even if I could!"
"Why not?"
"It's too bloody dangerous, that's why."

The next set of questions concerned my friend Mike Walsh.

"Did he know you were coming to see him?"
"No. I suddenly found myself with four or five hours to kill. I didn't fancy driving back to Latifa Towers just in time to return to Jahra!"
"Did you phone him to find out the way?"
"No. I simply followed the signs to the UNIKOM area."
"You came all the way with no knowledge of the area?"
"Yes."
"Why? It is too far just to see a friend."
"I had heard that Mike was about to be transferred to Cambodia, working with the UN. I had some of his personal possessions which I wanted to give back to him before he left. Also I was due to be going back to Algeria soon in any case so I wanted to see him to say goodbye. It was business, and personal!"
"The Kuwaiti check-points simply allowed you to drive into the restricted area?"
"Yes. I showed them my pass, said I was going to see a friend in the UNIKOM area and was waved on three times. My pass was not valid for all areas. So if an area was restricted or I was not allowed to go any further, for any reason at all, I was expecting to be stopped and turned around. I was travelling as far as my pass would take me! This all sounds incredibly stupid and lame now, but I swear it is the truth."
"Did you not know that the UN area was in Iraq?"
"No, I believed it to be between Kuwait and Iraq."

The questions then took a new direction.

"What does your company do – exactly?"

I gave them a general overview of what Taylors did starting with the provision of food and labour to ensure that the sites we ran were clean and tidy. I told them we carried out janitorial services as well as arranging the logistics and catering for functions. I am not sure of the detail I gave them, but they kept asking more questions. I remember saying, "For example, we did the catering for the ceremonial extinction of the last oil well fire. It was at BG 118, in the Burgan Oil field. It was a huge affair, with the last real fire being put out in the northern oil fields in the morning. Then the Emir could legitimately perform the symbolic extinction of a 'last' oil well fire."

I also boasted of a number of other important jobs that Taylors had taken care of all including Kuwaiti Royalty, or top Kuwaiti, American or British dignitaries.

"So, your company is taking care of the Al Sabah family?"

This is the Family name of the Royal household in Kuwait so I told them the truth.

"Yes, sometimes, depending on the situation."

This seemed to satisfy their curiosity on matters about my employment. My vehicle was the next topic the Iraqis started questioning me about.

"How did you get from Saudi Arabia to Umm Qasr?"

"I didn't come from Saudi. I will have been working in Kuwait for a year next week."

"No! Your vehicle had Saudi registration plates on it, it is from Saudi!"

I reacted angrily and started raising my voice. "To my knowledge that vehicle has been in Kuwait for at least 13 months."

"This is impossible. All Gulf states require vehicles staying more than six months to re-register. One year is too long. You are lying!"

"The vehicle was involved in an accident on the 6th of November, 1991, on the way to a ceremony at BG118 and five men were hospitalised. It's true, you've got to believe me. I am telling you the truth."

I was panicking. It didn't matter what I said as I was continually accused of lying. Accusations that made me furious. There was no room to manoeuvre, no back tracking, nowhere to run. I was stuck – with the truth I was telling denounced as a lie.

The obstacle was the dammed Land Cruiser! Questions rang around the room. I answered, but each answer was condemned a lie. I denied these accusations but the rapidity of the questions, the blindfold and the lack of food all conspired to confuse me. Eventually, I wondered if they were correct about the lies. I was muddled. *Which part of what I'm saying has a lie in it?* I wanted this to stop.

The interrogators kept coming back to the theme that I had some link with one of the security agencies. This was incorrect on every level but I was powerless to convince them otherwise.

The interrogation was terminated. Was it only a day? I felt like Doctor Who – a 'Time Lord' who could cram several lifetimes into a weekend! The Mukhabarat didn't believe that I was a chef and were convinced I was a spy. I would stay in their custody, they said, until I changed my story and my lies and told them the truth!

As a parting shot, something for me to brood over in the 'comfort' of my cell, they said, "You know, we can bring your wife here. She will make you tell us the truth. We can do this, have no doubt!"

Everything moved; the chair I sat upon rocked, I felt physically sick. Immediately, anger surged in me and I shouted, "YOU LEAVE MY FUCKING FAMILY ALONE! THEY HAVE NOTHING TO DO WITH YOU OR KUWAIT!"

This outburst angered the interrogators, one of whom immediately said in one of the most chilling tones I've ever heard, "Do not shout at us, you will answer questions and do as you are told!"

I shook with both fear and rage. I couldn't even help myself, let alone my family. I believed them. These lunatics were capable of anything, I knew it!

Next they said, "You can go now. You will be held here until you tell us the truth!

"It is the truth!"

"No, you are lying!"

With this I was dragged out of the chair by a guard and manhandled back to my cell. The thought of an Iraqi turning up on my wife Julie's doorstep nauseated me. *Would I stay here till I changed my story? Would they involve Julie?*

During Saddam Hussein's dictatorship a national paranoia was created perpetuating a myth that the rest of the world was against Iraq. Eventually, I suspect, the regime believed their own propaganda and the psychosis developed into a national xenophobia.

Iraq existed in an air of splendid isolation, the populace was fed with lies, half-truths, and distortions. The regime maintained total control with fear as its primary tool. A system of national informants reporting on everything and everyone. Nobody in Iraq trusted anyone, not even their neighbours. I have been in their prisons and seen what the Ba'ath Party cancer did to the Iraqi people.

In my cell, memories of past events came to me. One was a recollection of a family holiday I spent in Tenerife two months before I had returned to Kuwait on this trip. My wife Julie went on a day trip to Teidi, the volcanic mountain on the island, and my son William and I spent the day around the hotel having a lovely time. I had a tender memory of the occasion. As we'd shopped for lunch, William, then a 13-months-old baby, had stretched out from his buggy and pointed at what he wanted for to eat. A lot of the items he chose I presumed he wouldn't like and I would have to eat. We went down by the sea and I proceeded to feed him the yoghurt, biscuits and snacks that he'd selected. To my delight, and surprise, he ate some of every item he'd chosen. This doesn't sound like much of an event, but I'd been a distant father and suddenly it appeared he had grown up and was now a little boy. Feeding him was the closest I'd ever felt to him, and I hoped that in years to come he would understand how much I loved him.

Thinking about William was a trigger for me to recall my own formative years. I came into the world at a time in history that existed in the shadow of the second major conflict of the 20th Century. My memories of my childhood home in Chelsea and the tumble of local streets and terraces that surrounded it are in monochrome. A dark sky, bleak buildings, grey cranes mounted along the banks of the River Thames that clawed the sky like macabre skeletal fingers. It was a dirty, dusty world of black and white. White; the clouds of powder from the flour mill opposite our front door, billowing along the gutter, racing toward an iron grating to be washed away periodically by an outbreak of rain. Black; the grime associated with the rubbish-handling yards that punctuated the length of our street and were responsible for transferring refuse from the local boroughs onto river barges to be floated away. Our mean little houses, further sub-divided into flats, were kept back from the edge of the Thames by these monoliths of dirt, dust and detritus.

When I was a small boy, we lived on the ground floor of a house in Lots Road. I would regularly get out of bed having been woken by one of the seemingly never-ending arguments between Mum and Dad. The subject matter? Bills, money, horses, gambling, alcohol, family, work – the list became a familiar one to me at a very early age. I recall once, the screaming reached fever pitch and as I shuffled from my bedroom into the passageway my grandmother came in through the front door which she had a key for. As she stepped into the hall her face contorted when she heard my mum's screaming which was suddenly punctuated by the sound of smashing crockery. My Nan pushed her way into the front room where the commotion was coming from, and I crept in behind her. What we saw has stayed with me for life. Across the room stood my Dad with an umbrella and beside my Nan and myself stood my Mum. Turning halfway around she pulled another dinner plate from the cabinet behind her and then spinning through 180 degrees she launched the next salvo in her 'tea-service bombardment' of Dad's position which he manfully defended with his brolly in a defensive-hook-style similar to legendary England international cricketer Ian 'Beefy' Botham!

On the corner of our street was a pub, destroyed at the behest of Adolf Hitler. Similarly, the house directly behind ours on Stadium Street was a Second World War bombsite and the houses on either side of the gap were propped up by wooden cross-members! The Cremorne Arms as the pub had been known was a shell, rather than a gap, but that made it a place of fascination for a small boy from a poor background. In my youth, it was a jumble of scarred brickwork, shattered wood, and smashed fittings. Twisted piles of bar stools, tables, chairs, and every accessory that had once made the Cremorne a place to gather and drown sorrows, share stories, laugh, cry, sing, swear and love over a pint of Mild, Stout, or Bitter and bitter is how I remember the early pre-Swinging Sixties Chelsea.

This was my Chelsea, the Chelsea of my youth; London SW10 not SW3. Cheap, bleak and broken. I went to a school in the Fulham Road and slowly slipped further and further behind as the teaching progressed proficiently. This is the start of my life story, a story I have heard from so many other men, repeated in so many ways, and in so many minute variations, with a kaleidoscopic array of mothers, fathers, guardians, and carers. A story of confusion, of fear, of hate, of violence, or retribution, or revenge; pitiful and cold, perpetrated upon the young, and defenceless. Forgive them, they know not what they do!

Estate Agents of the 21st Century refer to the area I lived in as the 'Desirable Lots Road Triangle' but as a child I remember it being a lot more like the 'Bermuda Triangle' as the terraced housing in Dartrey Road, Luna Street, Seaton Street and the surrounding area were demolished to be replaced by the World's End Estate. As a small child, I would call for a classmate who lived on Dartrey Road and we would walk to and from our school together. Then came the 'slum clearance' and the streets were emptied of the working-class kids and smashed into a billion pieces. Along with the streets and people went the local community I'd known as a kid.

I was 11-years-old when we moved out of Lots Road to a new development not too far away on Finborough Road. I hated the place, but it was a stones throw from Stamford Bridge, the home of my favourite football team Chelsea, which was a short-lived consolation because my Mum and Dad soon relocated the Ride family to North Devon!

The culture shock of living near the Kings Road, during the 60's and suddenly finding yourself in a small town called Bideford in 1971 was overwhelming. I got a place at the local grammar school but realised straight away I was going to struggle. I told stories, trying to ingratiate myself with my new peers, of the weird and wonderful things I'd seen around the Swinging Sixties scene in London. Not only did this not win me any friends, my tales were the catalyst for a torrent of recriminations and abuse from my new classmates. "We don't like you. You lying cockney bastard!" Imagine that being repeatedly said in a strong Devonian accent and you'll understand that the 'mates' element of classmates didn't apply to me.

I spent four years in Bideford, most of it on 'Headmasters Report' having to report to every teacher at the end of every lesson to get this stupid report card signed to state whether, or not, I had been disruptive in class, usually I had, and they all said so. No one liked the stupid cockney kid! I fucking hated Bideford Grammar School! I failed miserably at anything academic and my only success there was sports-related. I set a long jump record that stood for about 20 years! Ironic given my experience at the school; it really should have been the high jump!

To earn a bit of money as I got into my teenage years, I spent my summers working at the 'Malibu' fish and chip shop in Westward Ho! My winters were split between working for 'Supreme Magic', suppliers of magic paraphernalia, and cooking burgers at the Wimpy restaurant in Bideford. I purchased lots of great music with the cash I made; vinyl by T. Rex, Slade, Roxy Music, Alice Cooper, Led Zeppelin, David Bowie, and many others, which I still have and treasure today.

At the age of 15 as I sat in front of a 'Careers Advisor' who toured the schools of the county and imparted pearls of wisdom upon the likes of me and the rest of the kids it became clear that my options were limited.

"So what do you think you're going to do when you leave school?" asked the advisor.

"I want to be a journalist," I replied.

"How's your English?"

"I'm gonna fail the exam." I said with a shrug of my shoulders.

"Maths?"

"I'm gonna fail that too."

"The Sciences?"

"I'm going to fail all of those as well."

The advisor, safe in the knowledge that the answer wasn't going to be study-related, looked at me quizzically and asked me, "What do you do in your spare time?"

"I work in a fish and chip shop in the summer and Wimpy's in the winter," I replied, not expecting any kind of reply that would steer me in any kind of direction as far as a future career was concerned.

The advisor rubbed his chin in a thoughtful manner for a few seconds and then looked me squarely in the eyes to make sure he had my attention. "You are going to be a chef!" He said authoritatively.

And that was that! I had nothing to argue with and no fall-back qualifications. All I knew was that in a few months I'd be getting out of this awful school and shortly after doing just that I was sent back to London to live with my Aunt and her family in Damer Terrace, Chelsea. I'd only been there for a few weeks when it was decided I'd be 'better off' with my Nan in Lots Road.

Based on the careers advice I'd been given, I went for an interview with Trusthouse Forte for a position as an Apprentice Chef at the Royal Festival Hall on London's South Bank and was offered a job. This was my route into the catering trade. In late August 1975, I commenced full-time employment on a basic wage of £16 per week.

If I hadn't taken those holiday jobs in Devon I wouldn't have had the same conversation with that smart-arsed careers advisor and almost certainly woundn't have ended up working in catering overseas – and been taken hostage. Oh well, nevermind! There was no going back on the past, I had to deal with the present and so I dissected the interrogations I'd endured and came to the understanding that I 'represented' Iraq's nemesis; the West. Despised, reviled and ultimately disbelieved. Being the target for so much hatred and animosity was distressing and something I was very clearly ill-eqipped to deal with. I tried praying again but felt hypocritical.

Saturday, 4th July.

Morning began like any other in solitary; warm, dirty, distant, lonely, the reality of another day. I was expecting to be interrogated daily until the Mukhabarat discovered that I was not a spy. I'm not sure they ever decided this throughout my detention!

My next interrogation began with what seemed like five or six people present. Not everyone spoke, but even though I was blindfolded I could discern movement all around the room. I was dizzy and confused, whether from exhaustion or poor diet I had no idea. Now I began openly laughing when they asked me questions connecting me with spying. This infuriated the Iraqis.

"What are you laughing at? We do not find spying amusing."

"If only you knew how silly the question sounds then you would understand why I'm laughing. The idea that I could be a spy! If my mates heard you they would all be laughing too!"

"You should understand that you are in a lot of trouble, and only by cooperating with us will you help yourself. Do you understand?"

"Yes I understand, but the idea that I should be a spy is so fantastic, it really is funny!"

I answered all the same questions as in my previous interrogations. What? Why? When? With whom? I found this distressing, knowing I'd made no progress at all in persuading these idiots of my honesty. The session stumbled along with a constant change of interrogator and tempo, then suddenly came the key questions.

"You stated that your company does many functions for the Emir?"

"We do a lot of functions, and yes, the Emir or members of the Royal Family have been present at a lot of them."

"We want you to do a mission for us?"

"What do you mean a mission?"

"We will grant you your freedom and send you back to Kuwait. In return you must do a mission for us?"

"What sort of mission?"

"Ah, we want you to use one of the functions that your company is organizing to kill the Emir or members of his family!"

What my expression suggested in response to this I had no idea. I shuddered as the enormity of the statement hit me. I was silent. I couldn't hazard a guess at the length of the silence in the room. When I later mentioned it to the UK Foreign Office, the idea was laughed off.

In time, I would come to form an opinion that the Foreign Office is fond of hiding facts and will tell any amount of lies to keep 'truths' as deeply buried as possible. The only thing it cares about is preserving the status quo. It should be remembered that in April 1993, an attempt was made to kill George Bush (by then the former President of the United States), in Kuwait. This was organised by the Iraqi Mukhabarat, the very people who asked me to return to Kuwait and kill the Emir, or members of his family!

When I had regained the power of speech I said, "I have no military training!"

"Don't worry, we will train you," was the swift reply. "You will be sent back well trained!"

"I don't have any weapons I couldn't do the job."

"We will supply the arms you will be sent back well equipped!"

"Why?"

"The reasons are ours."

My head swam. *Is this a serious offer? Will I gain my freedom? What's it like to kill someone? Will I get caught? Can I kill someone? What is happening to me?* This was total madness! *Say something,* I thought. "I am not a soldier, I have no wish to kill people, and I am not about to become a terrorist!"

"We will let you go. This is all we want from you!"

These Bastards were trying to coerce an innocent man into committing a killing that they had not been able to carry out themselves. The rage at my unwarranted detention and treatment in the most appalling conditions spewed out as I said, "Wait a minute. I want to be put in touch with the British Embassy!"

"Why? For what purpose?"

"The questions you are asking me are not the sort of thing you ask of an innocent man. I don't like the direction your questions are taking. I'm not a fucking terrorist. I want to speak with the British Embassy!"

Why it had taken me the best part of a week to remember the British Embassy, or at least mention them, I can't imagine, but the effect it had on the Iraqis was interesting to say the least.

"Don't talk to us like this. We are not frightened of you. There is no British Embassy here in Iraq. Even if there was, we would not let you contact them. Not until you tell us the truth. Do you understand? Just be quiet and answer our questions, all right?"

The voice had a threatening tone and I realised that this was not a situation for audacity and bravado so I sat and waited. I did feel the Iraqi was very brave in pointing out that, "We are not frightened of you," as part of his admonition. After all there were five or six of them in the room, all fully-clothed and armed. I was sat blindfolded and defenceless in pyjamas and plastic sandals. The 'odds' were definitely in their favour. *Bastards!*

Again, I was invited to tell the truth and state who I was spying for.

"I am not a spy. I have nothing to do with the CIA, MI5, Kuwaiti Mukhabarat or Mossad. For God's sake! I'm telling you the truth!"

Questions were repeated continually. Was this abject boredom or were they amusing themselves – 'playing' with me?

Once more I was told I'd be held until I changed my story, stopped lying and admitted that I was a spy. My body shuddered with fear and apprehension as I said that if that was the case I would be there for the rest of my life, as I had been telling them the truth. They told me to think carefully about my situation and be ready to change my story when they next saw me. I was then yanked to my feet and shoved back to my cell.

Sunday, 5th July.

A day of sheer hell. I was not interrogated and absolutely nothing happened. The piece of soap I'd used to mark the days on the wall ran out. I hadn't helped by writing 'I AM INNOCENT' in large letters on my cell wall. Detention is damaging and solitary confinement an extra burden. I started having jumbled thoughts and realised it was vital to keep a track of the date. Carefully, I pulled one of my blankets apart. I had seven pieces of white cotton for the month, and 31 pieces of green cotton, for the day/date. It probably didn't help, but at least I felt aware of my situation as opposed to just drifting.

Tuesday, 7th July.

40 hours of worst-case scenarios later, a guard delivered me to the usual location for my next interrogation. I came close to thanking them for giving me the chance to answer their questions! Bloody idiot that I am!

By the time I reached the interrogation room I was already high on adrenaline. As soon as I entered I could detect an atmosphere. I could sense seven or eight people in the room today and the air was heavy with anticipation, or was that anger, and tarty Arabic aftershave!

As the week had gone on the duration of the interrogations and the number of Mukhabarat present had increased. Today, I'd drawn a crowd, and I felt like a freak show. *Roll Up! Roll Up! Come and see the blindfolded English buffoon!*

I sat and the questions began. They were initially easy-going and then the tempo picked up a little, and again the accusation came that I was a spy!

"Today is your last chance. Tell us who you are working for. Now!"

I didn't really understand the implications of what "last chance" meant and wasn't sure if I was meant to read anything into it, so I replied, "I've told you this day after day. I am not a spy, please believe me."

"We know very well that you are a spy. It will be better if you tell us who you are working for. It will go in your favour."

Again my temper and big mouth got the better of me. "What do you mean, you know? I have been here a bloody week! Haven't you checked out a single word of what I've been saying to you? Christ! How long will I be here waiting for you to find out the truth?"

This really upset my interrogator. "Shut your mouth," he retorted. "Don't speak to us in this fashion. Just keep your mouth shut and answer our questions!"

There were some exchanges of spoken Arabic around the room and then I was told, "We have someone here who will record your statement now. You will simply answer the questions truthfully, understood?"

I replied that I understood but the "last chance" phrase was now playing on my mind. It's finality made me feel very uncomfortable. What followed next was the longest interrogation I was to undergo in Iraq. Every question was first asked in Arabic so that the scribe could record it. Each of my answers, were also translated into Arabic. All this took a very long time and broke up the flow of the questioning. My mind started to wander and I lost track of the questions. The Interrogators were annoyed by my lack of concentration and voices barked when they had to repeat a question – some of which were new.

"Why did you choose to work in Kuwait?"

"The war ended, and the job came up!"

"No special reason? You don't love Kuwait?"

"I don't love Kuwait any more or less than I do Algeria. It is a job."

"There is no other reason? Belief? Politics?"

"None whatsoever."

"Why didn't you come to work in Iraq?"

"Because of the sanctions, there is no work in Iraq now!"

"You would work in Iraq?"

"Sure, why not? Expatriates are international prostitutes. We go where there are jobs and money!"

"Maybe you can return when the sanctions are lifted to enjoy Iraq as a free man?" This question was asked with an inflection of laughter.

"Yes," I replied, laughing. "That would be nice!"

This may sound as if I'd developed a rapport with the Mukhabarat, nothing could be further from the truth! I was petrified, and many of the comments, humour and bravado occurred in a state of absolute terror. I went into autopilot mode and my actions and dialogue became virtually involuntary.

The questions then went back over old ground until finally I was asked about catering. It had taken over a week, but here I was on home ground!

"What sort of food do you prepare?"

"I'll try my hand at anything although I trained in classical French Cuisine."

"Do you know any Arabic dishes?"

"I have worked with Arabic chefs, but don't have a lot of experience in Arabic food preparation."

"How do you make an Escalope?"

Now this really stumped me. Nothing was further from my mind at that moment than preparing food. Eventually I blurted out, "You take a piece of beef. Remove a thin slice, bat it out with a meat hammer, coat it with, flour, egg and breadcrumbs and then shallow fry it."

With a note of total incredulity the head Interrogator asked, "What sort of a chef are you?"

"What do you mean?" I enquired, my professional pride severely dented.

"You say an escalope is beef!"

"You can make an escalope out of any sort of meat," I replied, defending my position and integrity. "It is not the meat but the style of preparation that is different. You can have chicken, turkey, veal escalopes, usually prepared thinly sliced and bread crumbed, okay?"

Now we know you are not what you say you are! I thought to myself as I smarted from this accusation. I never liked bloody catering anyway!

Today's interrogation was also different because my entire family were discussed.

"Your Father, what is his job?"

"Machine operator in a factory."

"Your Mother?"

"She also works in a factory."

"You have one brother, what job does he do?"

"He is a bakery manager in a supermarket."

"Does he own this supermarket?"

This brought a smile to my face, as he was working for one of the 'majors'. I replied, "No!" They spoke as if all British people were living in the lap of luxury. Why I was asked, were we, expats, out furthering Imperialistic British attitudes? I did try to explain that most British people were barely scraping a living while the rich were exploiting everyone, not only non-British people.

When I got off my soap box one of my interrogators said, "We have a story in Iraq. Do you want to hear it?"

I was hardly in a position to say no I didn't! "Yes," I replied. "What is it?"

"There are two fish in a pond, they are friends. One day the two fish start fighting. What does this mean?"

I thought for a couple of seconds and then said, "Sorry, I don't have a clue."

The punchline was emphasised with a thump on the table, great relish and obvious satisfaction. "When two fish who have been friends for many years start fighting. This means that the British are close by!"

This was followed by an unnecessary explanation. "You see, you British make trouble and cause arguments wherever you go!"

I don't know if it was expected that I would 'offer' to be held responsible, and forgiven, for the British Government's crimes over centuries. If it was, then my captors were disappointed. I feel that the British Government has treated the indigenous population of the UK in a shameful way for centuries. I feel no responsibility for its abuse of others worldwide. In the same way as most of the populace of the UK, my family never earned vast wealth from the exploitation of foreign nationals or their countries. I feel sorrow for people who have suffered, but only a similar sorrow as I have for many people used, abused, and cast aside by an uncaring ex-Empire.

What did they expect me to say? I couldn't think of a retort that was quick, clever or witty enough so I sat in silence – a straw man being burned. I was sick. Sick to the back teeth of being the target of all this hate. Sick of being held for no reason, and now sick of being the butt of Iraqi humour.

The interrogator then asked about my political interests and affiliations. To this, I answered that I didn't have any. I believed that all politicians were out to further their own ends and if people were helped or hindered along the way then that was a mere by-product of the political games played at Westminster.

Then they asked me for my home telephone number! I jolted as if I'd been slapped and said, "What do you want my fucking telephone number for? I'm here!"

Again, my outburst angered the Mukhabarat who retorted, "Your job is to sit still and answer all of our questions in full. This is for your benefit!"

Then I heard a voice that I recognised. It was Pig Man, the huge oaf who had inducted me into the building. He was speaking Arabic so I didn't have a clue what he was saying and then a voice addressed me, "You have a message written on your underpants, what does it say?"

I told them that it was my name written on my underwear by the laundry in Kuwait. This was the truth.

"Are you sure it is not a message about your spying activities?"

This was too ridiculous. It was obvious that the writing in my 'skiddies' was my name, what did I have to do to convince these mad sods that what I was saying was the truth, and their accusations were totally unfounded?

The next order really caught me by surprise and I sat back in the hard chair as if I had been punched.

"Show us the message!"

There was nothing to do but comply; outnumbered, and alone I realised that I was theirs to do with as they pleased, the realisation disgusted me. I sat in my chair, unbuttoned my pyjama bottoms and displayed the front of my underpants.

"We cannot see the message. Show us the message!"

The only thing I could do was to turn my underpants inside out. During the time spent in solitary, I'd obviously put them on the wrong way around. This happened because I rinsed them out as often as I could in the shower block to remove the sweat from them.

I pulled my underpants out exposing my genitalia. As I sat there, the Mukhabarat in the room surrounded me, I could feel their breath upon me as they gathered around. I felt totally humiliated. There I sat exposed as seven or eight Iraqis gazed at my rapidly dwindling manhood. I was told later that this was a ploy to check my penis and to confirm that I was not circumcised. I had been very, very close to a Jewish demise.

When they were satisfied that 'the message' was a laundry mark, and that my penis was intact, they all sat down. The questions, once again took on a cooking orientation. I was asked if I enjoyed Arabic food and what dishes I liked. It was all very light-hearted or so it seemed and then the game changed.

"Now you will sign this statement!" I was told, then dragged up and pushed to a desk where my blindfold was pulled up a a couple of centimetres. A document was placed in front of me and I was given a biro to sign it. My first thought was, *I'm not fucking signing that!* What I actually said was, "Sorry. I cannot sign this!"

"What do you mean? Why can you not sign?"

"This is written in Arabic. I don't read Arabic. So I don't know what it says, therefore I'm not signing it!"

"You must sign it!"

"All right, can I sign it and write 'unread' by the side of my signature?"

"No! You just sign it, understand?"

"No! I can't sign this!"

"This will help you to be released. If you do not sign you will be here longer."

I had a little think, for just a second. In that moment I decided that anything that would get me out of here had to be done. I felt that I was already up shit creek without a paddle. What further trouble could my signature on these papers cause? When you become reliant on your captors the Stockholm Syndrome I mentioned previously develops. It exists – trust me!

Suddenly, the atmosphere got very jovial and chatty. I was offered a cigarette, which I accepted. I was asked why I accepted the cigarette as after a week in solitary this would be a good time to give up. I replied I'd felt like giving up on some things but right now I wanted a cigarette!

Then suddenly the mood swung again as a voice said, "We will be releasing you in two or three days after we have verified your story. This will be no problem. Then you will go!"

"Excellent! Thank you," I replied.

Then the voice added, "When you are released, do not think of going to the media, or newspapers. All that has been done to you here is totally legal in Iraq. If you go to the newspapers, it will be on your own conscience, understood?"

"Yes!"

"Your family will not be happy if you do go to the media. Do you understand?"

The inference here was impossible to miss. It was an open threat to the security of my family. I told them that I understood, then I did something totally out of character, I recited the 'Lord's Prayer', trying to emphasise the line 'Forgive us our trespasses, as we forgive those who trespass against us'. Judging by what would follow, my attempts at religion fell on deaf ears!

I was dragged out of the chair still smoking the cigarette. When we were clear of the interrogation room, the guard smacked the cigarette from my hand and gave me an extra firm dig in the back. I didn't care, they were going to let me out in two or three days! Shoved into my cell, I spent the rest of the day thinking about what I was going to do when I got back to Kuwait.

Wednesday, 8th July.

The day passed with thoughts of explaining being AWOL more than a week. I believed the Mukhabarat saying I'd be released. What reason would they have to lie? I had to bide my time, and I would be back among friends. Routines were no problem, I could cope with anything they threw at me for two or three more days it was a simple matter of sitting and waiting.

I became a little concerned when nothing happened on Thursday. I was hoping to get back to Kuwait by the weekend, the European weekend, Sunday.

Friday was slow, I cleaned the cell with little enthusiasm. The food trolley arrived, and I realised it was lunchtime. *Christ! They are hanging about a bit. If they don't get a move on, I will either spend another night in Baghdad or spend the whole night driving back to Basra.*

All afternoon I waited for something to happen. It never did, the bitter taste of the burnt rice and watery soup was even more difficult to stomach that evening.

Saturday, 11th July.

I became hyper-vigilant, every noise outside the cells became a portent of a guard coming to collect me. Every key in another lock was a mistake, *This is the cell you want, come and get me.* The food was inedible, the air hotter, trips to the toilets more rushed. Every action heightened my distress.

I could scarcely believe it when lunch finished and I was still caged. *Why have they not come for me? Why is my release delayed? What question needs clarification? Which facts can't they confirm? I should be half way to Basra by now!*

Sleep was fitful. I struggled with the idea of being moved out at night. Days passed and I was not interrogated again. I'd had four interrogations in a two-week stay in the Mukhabarat complex in Baghdad and I thought that this was an affront but I discovered some had it far worse than me.

Suffering is a very personal thing. Two people have the same experience, but react in totally different ways; one person showing little distress, while another has a breakdown. Was it heat exhaustion, lack of fluids or a mental aberration? I can't say, but I spoke to and saw my grandfather who died in 1973 and relived huge episodes from my youth while in post-interrogation solitary confinement.

The dank cell drained my ability to be positive. When I was allowed to go to the toilet, I shuffled out of there in a manner which belied my 33 years. I had no defiant glare for the guard, instead I preferred not to look in his direction in case I saw a smile on his face. Composure fled, I became mortal remains running around a wheel in a Mukhabarat cage. I ran myself to exhaustion. Jumping about until rivulets of sweat coursed down my body, I never became fit, but day-after-day I increased the amount of time I spent exercising with no reason but to fill up the hours.

My days were fused into a memory that seemed weeks long. There was little to differentiate day and night and I became so angry that logical thought was impossible. Nightmares about dying in this hole, alone, half-naked, with no mourners, no marker, simply gone, filled my mind. Time passed with nothing but the wailing trolley and trips to the toilets to fill my mind, and self-loathing and bitterness about my own situation filled every moment. Hatred for everything was my initial thought every morning and my final reflection as I tried to sleep in the heat and half-light of my bunker at night.

Tuesday, 14th July.

I walked around and around my cell, with each step asking God to send down one of his curses on the bastards who were doing this to me. I was so distressed I remember beating the floor with my fist as my head screamed, *WHY ME? WHAT HAVE I DONE THAT'S SO BAD? DO SOMETHING, ANYTHING. JUST DON'T LEAVE ME SAT IN HERE!*

There were no mirrors and so I was unable to see how I looked. Very rough, I'm sure. The guards did start to give me strange looks, so I think my deteriorating state of mind was apparent or was that paranoia?

Wednesday, 15th July.

By now I think I would have admitted any number of crimes to secure release from my solitary cell. Fortunately, I didn't have to. My 'luck' changed in the shape of an Iraqi guard with a razor blade! He entered my cell and said, in English, "Follow me."

At long bloody last, the stupid bastards remembered they had me in a cell! He led me to the toilets and said, "I'll shave you. Do you keep your moustache?"

I kept the moustache. He told me to lather my face, but the bar of carbolic soap would not make any lather. He was eventually satisfied that my face was suitably slimy and shaved me. I was disappointed when he led me back to my bunker and left. Alone in my cell I panicked. A voice in my head yelled, *DON'T LEAVE ME HERE! DON'T LET A SHAVE BE TODAY'S ACTIVITY!*

An hour-ish later another guard took me, without a blindfold, down to the room where Pig Man had inducted me. The layout had changed and an Iraqi sat behind a desk on the left-hand side of the room. I entered and he asked my name while brandishing a sack I'd filled with my clothes a fortnight earlier.

By now I had the drill off to a tee. "Elf Miah wo Khamseen!" was my immediate and knowledgeable reply.

"No what is your name!"

This was repeated until at his fourth attempt, he asked, "Are you Bol Stepan Ridd?"

I knew he meant Paul Stephen Ride. I confimed my name and the Iraqi threw the sack at me in a manner suggesting he wanted it to have been a grenade! When I had carried out his instructions and dressed in my own clothes, which resembled the sort of rags you keep in the boot of a car, he got out a manila envelope. This contained my personal effects; rings, wallet, jewellery etc. which were returned to me.

I was then blindfolded and led I thought to the interrogation room, but then I made out we were going down to another floor. When the blindfold was removed I could see my Land Cruiser. Never in my entire life have I been so emotional about a car, but the sight of this vehicle brought a lump to my throat as I thought, *Finally I'm getting out of here!*

The Iraqi showed me the contents of the vehicle and then without warning he grabbed me and dragged me away and shoved me towards a white Sherpa van. The van had its widows white-washed so that passengers couldn't see out and the public couldn't see in. The side door was opened revealing a bare storage area. I was pushed inside and told to sit on the bare metal floor and the door was slid shut. After about ten minutes the engine started and we were off.

I remember thinking, *This is the beginning of the end. Please let this be as fast as possible, no more hold ups. Just get me back to my vehicle and then get me back to Kuwait!*

As we pulled out into the late morning heat and joined the traffic madness of Baghdad I said the first thing that came into my head, "Home James!"

FAISALIYAH: THE NIGHTMARE MUTATES

The van drove around Baghdad for what seemed an age, and due to the heat in July the metal floor became so hot that it began to scald my hands and backside. Unable to remain seated, I lifted myself and put my weight on my shoulders and jammed them into the back of the van's wall so that only my shoes were touching the scorching floor, and then we stopped.

The heat was suffocating, after about 15 minutes the door slid open. The light blinded me. I had not been outside in daylight for some time and it took an age for my eyes to adjust to the glare. I felt extremely dizzy and realised that I was very dehydrated. In the Mukhabarat complex my access to water had been limited. Sweating profusely now in the back of the van, I was dripping wet, and with nothing to drink I felt as if the last drops of fluid were leaving my body.

The driver dragged me to my Land Cruiser which must have followed us. I didn't know it then, but this was the last time I saw my talisman. The contents of the vehicle; tapes, sunglasses, etc. were thrust into my arms and I was shoved towards an office block. I remember there were many corridors and stairs and in a dream-like state with faces looming towards me, as everything gyrated, I 'floated' through the establishment. There seemed to be thousands of people watching me and we walked for what seemed like miles before I was propelled into an office.

An Iraqi asked me if I was okay. I gasped, "Water, I need water." I was given a jam jar full of water. I drank it in one draught. Immediately the Iraqis started to interrogate me but I was unable to speak or put any sentences together coherently. Asked if I wanted to continue the 'interview' later I was petrified that I would return, in the heat of the van, to the Mukhabarat complex and be left there – forever!

I was asked if I wanted a cup of tea and I nodded. I drank a jam jar of the sweet black stuff and began to feel better. My vision cleared and I could breathe with increasing ease. Following a litany of 'standard' questions I was given an official document written in Arabic to sign. There was an element of déjà vu now as I refused to sign the document because I couldn't read it. I was told by the man sat behind the desk in the office that if I did not sign I could not be processed or released. I noted that on the desk was a sign which read 'Director' so I signed the damned paperwork straight away.

'The Director' sent one of his men, who curiously placed his gun in a drawer before he left, down to the courthouse in the Karrada district of Baghdad to see a judge to get my release papers signed. About 90 minutes later he returned and spoke to The Director, who with a theatrical show of anguish declared, "This is terrible, the judge wants to see you. I was hoping to get you out today but the judge wants to see you!"

Once again, all my personal possessions were taken away from me, "for safe keeping" they said. This was the last I would see of them – ever!

I was taken outside with around eight other men and we were ordered into a battered old Land Cruiser. I sat in the front with the driver and the others were bundled in the back. Baghdad was an enormous construction site; sewers were being laid and buildings were being repaired and reconstructed. The journey lasted for about 45 minutes and eventually we stopped outside what looked like a military prison which I discovered later was in fact a police holding jail called Faisaliyah.

As soon as we were inside the gates were locked behind us. We were ordered out of the vehicle and into a building. The passages were small, cramped and claustrophobic. 50 metres of shuffling later and we were outside a shabby office. We entered and an officer asked each of us, "What is your name? Problem? Nationality?"

I was approached by a guard asking if I was British? I replied, "Yes!"

He looked at me murderously and said, "I hate the British, you killed my friends in the war."

The guard and his comrades had machine guns. I feared a pack mentality and felt physically sick. Things were getting very personal. Our details were entered in a huge book and then we were led through a maze of rooms and corridors which became darker and darker. We came to a halt at a black metal door and as it opened I was blinded by sunlight.

Eventually, a scene reminiscent of the prison drama 'Midnight Express' came into focus. Rubbish was piled in the doorway; an assortment of food debris, old scrubbing brushes and other detritus. The smell of these things blended with body and cooking odours was phenomenally pungent.

I walked out from under the door's porch and into the main courtyard which was about 20 metres square and surrounded by a five metre high, barbed-wire-topped whitewashed wall, which given the way the paint was flaking had clearly been roasting for years under the hot Iraqi sun.

Looking around the courtyard, I saw some men sat with their backs against the wall. The place was a hive of industry and had a bazaar-like quality to it. I saw a man with three kettles brewing various drinks, another selling food and another dealing cigarettes. Some people were repairing shoes, others clothing and I saw some men doing laundry. I watched as dozens of prisoners walked around a centrally-placed water trough, there was no water in it; it was just a sun-baked trough. As they began to notice my presence, I realised they were all staring at me. I was different – a Westerner!

Suddenly terrified, I felt myself rooted to the spot. I looked around again and remembered that in the Mukhabarat complex I'd had a cell to myself, what was I going to get here? I'd been convinced I was going to die in the prison I'd just come from, but Faisaliyah was frightening in a very different way. I felt weak and sick. I was still very dehydrated. I'd worn the same clothes for four days. They were creased and filthy after spending a couple of weeks in a sack.

I'm not sure how much time had passed when a black guy spoke to me in English with an American accent and broke my silent spell of contemplation by introducing himself as David. He was from the Bahamas, lived in Miami, and asked where I'd come from – solitary confinement at the Mukhabarat complex – and what the charges against me were? – I didn't know!

His next question put my situation into perspective. He asked where my things were and stared at me open-mouthed when I told him that everything I had I was wearing. I explained how I came to be in Iraq and that I'd been told that there might be a charge of illegal entry. I added that the Mukhabarat had told me I was about to released.

"Don't believe the lying bastards, they tell everyone this bullshit," he replied, and then he asked, "Have you seen Mr Michael?"

I shook my head and reminded him I'd been in solitary until this morning. He said Michael was English and continued, "Don't worry, you'll meet Mr Michael. He was transferred to Al Alwiyah after being here for five days."

I said I wouldn't see him as I was going in front of a judge tomorrow and my problem would be resolved. David, roared with laughter and said, "At the courts they tell everyone they will be back in one day. You will have to stay here ten days. Nothing is ever sorted out tomorrow. They say tomorrow, and then it's days or weeks."

I looked around, shuddered and thought, *Eight to ten days here, no thanks!*

"When you are transferred from here," continued David, "it will be to another prison and then you will see Mr Michael, but Mr Michael is strange. His mind is not right."

He then asked me again, "Where are your bags?"

"I have nothing," I replied. "What you see is what I have!" I was wearing jeans, desert boots, socks, underpants, and a filthy, crumpled, once-white, T-Shirt.

David gazed at me with pity in his eyes and said, "Come with me and we'll find you a place to sleep."

Dotted around the courtyard were rooms of varying sizes. None appeared to lock, some were missing their doors. We entered a room about ten metres long and six metres wide. Everywhere I looked, sleeping rolls, blankets and personal possessions were piled. The walls were covered with assorted bags; string, linen, plastic, and suitcases. It looked like a waiting room. About 15 people were in the room. Some asleep, some smoking, some in small groups chatting.

Introducing me as an Englishman, David asked an Egyptian called Nordeen to find me somewhere to sleep adding he didn't want me in the rooms with, as he put it, "those other thieving bastards!" "Paul has no clothes or passport," he continued. "He was abducted from Kuwait, he has nothing."

David and Nordeen offered me a glass of tea. I was instructed not to walk on the mats with boots on – Arabic etiquette. David then took me to his room and advised me that 'spies' informed on everyone and to be careful about whom I spoke and what I said. We ate a tin of corned beef with salad and bread that was shared with four other people. After eating David said, "We will sort you out a change of clothes, now go and have a shower."

Another total stranger gave me a tiny slither of soap. I went into the 'shower' which was a concrete box with a blanket for a door. A 45-litre oil drum filled from a small tap provided the water. A hand-held tin can was then used to pour the water over your body. I tried to undress and keep my clothes dry and free from the greasy slime that covered the walls.

Entering a room full of Arabs I felt very exposed and vulnerable. Two Egyptians, who lent me a towel for the shower, also gave me some clothes. It was a generous gesture. My filthy clothes were washed by the 'Laundry Man'. I learned that every Iraqi prison had one! This was a service that had to be paid for and so I advised David that I had no Iraqi money and he told me that he could get my Kuwaiti Dinars exchanged – problem solved.

David and the Egyptians spoke about Michael. He had been brought from the Mukhabarat complex in Baghdad about ten days previously. They said he had cigarette burns all over his body and he'd been covered in blood and confused. They said that they had cleaned him up and given him clothes.

Each man told me why they were being held along with a personal tale of abuse and wrongful imprisonment. An International Committee of the Red Cross visit was discussed. I was told how everything had been cleaned as the Red Cross had to give notice, where, and when, they wanted to visit. This gave the Iraqis the opportunity to ship half of the prisoners out to other jails and the prison was cleaned with disinfectant. The prisoners were then told to re-space their bed rolls so that they each had three metres of space on either side of them. They said that no one dared tell the Red Cross what conditions were really like and that once they had left the prisoners were brought back and within days conditions were back as before the visit.

Later that night after David had left to go sleep, the room burst into life. Around 20 men formed two lines facing each other and began a loud and animated game of spoof. They had coins and the opponents had to guess how many were held in their counterpart's hands. There was jubilation at a victory and howls of anguish at a loss – the noise was incredible!

Nordeen tired of the entertainment, unfolded his blanket, offered me half of it, and went to sleep. I felt humble and grateful. When the game of spoof finished, the men who'd been playing started dancing and singing. Some played the female roles with scarves tied about their waists; belly dancing, pouting, leering, and sticking out their tongues at the others. This continued until what I deduced were the early hours of the following morning when everyone eventually fell asleep.

I was nervous. Some prisoners looked evil, other dangerous, others let me know they were homosexual! Many evidently required mental health care. Most of my fellow inmates slept outside until the first prayer call at about 4.00am when many came inside and the room, with over 200 prisoners, became incredibly crowded. Bodies were lying everywhere and some without their own bedding lay across the bottom of other inmates mats. I started to realise how lucky I had been meeting David, and how tough this might get.

Thursday, 16th July.

I woke early and walked around the water trough in the courtyard. I circled it several times gasping in the morning air. I had not been able to draw 'fresh' morning air into my lungs for over two weeks, something I'd always taken for granted, and it felt so bloody good.

Breakfast arrived while most of the prisoners were still asleep. The food was in two plastic dustbins each filled two-thirds; one with black tea and the other with rice soup. Prisoners could have one or the other. I had the tea as I was already sick of the rice soup. Someone lent me a jam jar and we went back to our 'spaces' to drink and smoke. Prior to being incarcerated I hadn't smoked for eight months but mainly out of boredom that changed in jail.

David said I'd be able to buy the toiletries I needed once he'd arranged to convert my Kuwaiti money and as we chatted he said, "There's no chance of you getting to court today."

The currency exchange was a rip off. I only got 10% of the value of my Kuwaiti money but I offered to pay for the things I wanted before they were purchased once I had Iraqi currency. Inflation was rampant and the offer was refused as the price today could be more than yesterday and no one wanted to lose money on a deal!

At about 10.00am, some guards came in and began calling out names including mine. David went berserk and kept swearing and repeating that I shouldn't be going to court. He shook his head in disbelief as I bundled together my clothes, some still wet, and enthusiastically joined the line for court. Not for the first time, I truly believed my ordeal was almost over.

AL ALWIYAH

At the courthouse I was taken in front of a female judge and explained my 'situation' through an interpreter. I have no idea if what I said was lost in translation but I got little out of the judge, the court, or the experience. Shortly after, I was brought in front of two male judges. My 'appearance' this time was brief and after an exchange of words I was waved away. Almost immediately, I was taken out of the court buildings and put in a car. *This is more like it*, I thought to myself. *Now I can get back to Kuwait.*

The journey was short but as we parked up outside an anonymous-looking building my heart soared. Parked across the road was a white United Nations vehicle. I was about to be released! I got out of the car and was escorted by the driver who doubled as my guard and interpreter into the building and then along numerous corridors and up several flights of stairs. We climbed higher and higher eventually entering a room where an Iraqi appeared from behind a huge filing cabinet. He approached me and directed me to another office. He put his hand out and I extended mine to thinking it was a friendly greeting. Without warning he clasped my hand and dragged me to a desk and thrust my fingers into black ink. My heart sank as I realised I wasn't being released, I was being fingerprinted!

I stood with my hand being plunged into ink and my fingers stabbed onto a card. The room was full of filing cabinets each with thousands of print cards. My prints were taken twice and then I was taken to another office and my prints were stamped.

We left the 'Fingerprint Bureau' and got back into the car. I asked my 'driver/guard/interpreter' if it would be possible to stop along the way to wherever we were headed next to get a cup, spoon, toothbrush and some sandals as the penny had now dropped that it might take more than my desire and honesty to get out of Iraq and I needed some basic essentials to help me get by.

We stopped at a couple of shops but reached our destination, another dusty, nondescript building, empty-handed. A sign said Al Alwiyah, the place David had told me fellow Englishman 'Mr Michael' had been transferred to. I was swiftly escorted from the car into the building and to a small holding cell. After a few minutes I was frogmarched to another block and left to stand outside a large, barred cell. I looked through the bars and immediately saw it was overcrowded. There had to be at least 80 men in there. Among them, a Western-looking man with a short military-style haircut. I made an assumption that this was 'Mr Michael' and with a sense of relief called through the bars, "Is your name Michael?"

"Aye," replied Michael. "It is that." His accent had an unmistakable Yorkshire twang to it. Definitely English. A uniformed guard arrived, opened the cell and waved me in. With the rest of the cell occupants looking on curiously, Michael and I shook hands and made perfunctory introductions.

As we spoke, I glanced around. To my left as I'd entered were the toilets. The cell, around 12 or 13 metres square, had a tiled floor and was flanked by walls which were about four metres high. Three metres up two of the walls, too high to look out of, were a row of small windows. People were sitting in every available space and blankets, carpets, food, luggage, and clothing were strewn everywhere.

Michael and I made a space for ourselves, sat down on a piece of rug and told each other our stories. I was right about him being a Yorkshireman. His surname was Wainwright and he was from a place called Hebden Bridge and had been on a travelling holiday when misfortune first struck.

In Holland he'd had his rucksack and possessions stolen. He'd done some manual labour to raise money and eventually got a van which he drove across Europe to Greece where he'd made some cash by collecting items to recycle. He then drove to Turkey where he was prevented from driving further as his insurance card was no longer valid. He'd parked the vehicle and purchased a mountain bike which he rode through Turkey! He had taken packets of vegetable seeds with him and told me that whenever he stopped in a town or village he would plant seeds with local children and be given food in exchange!

"So then I goes t'border wi' Syria," he continued, "and they say to me, 'No visa you can't come in'. Then I went to Iran and they says, 'No visa so you can't come in'."

Michael explained that he was advised to go to a town with a regional office for the issue of visas to get into Iran, Iraq or Syria but he was unable to get the correct paperwork. After repeated failed attempts, he travelled to Habur, a Turkish border crossing with Iraq, and presented his British Passport and the Iraqis let him in. At the border he'd sold his bike for a pittance and travelled to Mosul. Heading south, he'd been approached by an official, taken into custody and held in Mosul before being transferred to the Mukhabarat complex in Baghdad and then Faisaliyah where he'd met David. Subsequently, he'd been to a preliminary court hearing and then sent to Al Alwiyah where he'd already been held for five or six days before my arrival.

I told Michael about my route to Al Alwiyah. It had taken me two and a half weeks to get to here – it had taken him two-and-a-half months, he'd crossed the border on the 24th of April 1992.

Michael explained that he was trying to get to Australia to see an uncle. I asked why he was travelling down the Saudi Peninsula and he said it was no problem, he would just get on a boat. I couldn't make him understand that Saudi Arabia and Kuwait were as sensitive as the Iraqis about foreigners and that he could go no further without a visa.

With my very limited Arabic, I also had a few stilted conversations with other prisoners. The first thing I heard from each person I spoke with was a warning about everyone else!

Lunch arrived. A familiar sight. Soup delivered in a dustbin! I met George, a watch smith, in prison for handling stolen goods who was the Maraheb (aka a Red Band in the UK prison system – a trusted prisoner given responsibilities and allowed to work unsupervised) tasked with serving food. George used a saucepan belonging to Michael to get the soup out of the dustbin. God only knows what he'd used prior to Michael's arrival!

I would come to learn that George was also the head 'grass' in our section. He would leave the cell daily, under the guise of cleaning the floors throughout the police station, to file his reports. Because of his position, George was treated with an odd mixture of fear, hatred, and respect by fellow inmates.

I noticed that many prisoners didn't eat the 'dustbin food' and I wondered how they survived. Unlike Faisaliyah, this place had no area for food preparation. That evening my question was answered. Iraqi prisoners received food brought in by family and friends while foreign prisoners who had the means to do so gave money to the guards in exchange for better quality sustenance.

In the evening, Michael was involved in vaudevillian acts with the majority of the other prisoners making fun of him. He didn't care, he used it to his advantage and he told me he was given extra food from some inmates as 'payment' for his clowning around.

I tried to get to sleep at 10.00pm but it was hopeless. Arabs have an afternoon siesta and then are awake until about 2.00am. The cacophony of the day made it impossible to relax and the nervous exhaustion I was already suffering from steadily worsened. The fabric of the jail, combined with the shocking physical and mental condition of a large percentage of the inmates, myself included, was both distressing and frightening.

During my time in Al Alwiyah, I was conscious of always feeling hungry. By now I was working my way through a couple of packets of cigarettes a day and drinking vast quantities of water because it was so hot. I sat for hours, trying to stay as still as possible. I watched the prisoners who had food coming in and eating what they wanted. When they had eaten they moved away from the food. Their hands were greasy after eating with their fingers and they would go to the toilet to wash their hands. As soon as they got up, those prisoners who did not have access to food would scurry across and snatch at the remains devouring them as quickly as they could.

I enquired about the price of food and realised that even by changing all the money I had left I would still only have enough to buy a couple of meals. I had no idea how much I was going to be fined, so I decided to hold on to my money and continue to eat out of the communal dustbin. A couple of Iraqi prisoners invited me to eat their leftover food and out of a false pride I initially refused as politely as possible, however after a few days I became so hungry that I capitulated.

On one particularly bad day, with no food available anywhere, I was absolutely starving and, almost in tears, I prayed for someone, anyone, to buy some food. There were times when I was so desperately hungry that I can remember falling on whatever food was leftover, with not a shred of self-respect. I feel ashamed to recall these episodes. During this period of my detention, I learned that it really didn't matter who you were – an English expat, or a Sudanese building labourer – hunger was the same in any language.

I noted that the Iraqi inmates, while sometimes feeding Michael, myself, and the very poorest of the prisoners, wouldn't offer food to the Egyptians. It was almost as if they were 'untouchables'. Each ethnic group however would be fed by their national kinsman who had contacts on the outside.

The chaos only subsided when the Maraheb decided, or was instructed by the guards, that it was time for everyone to sleep. There was not enough room for everyone to lie down so we were forced to 'tuck in' very close behind the person next to you. We were all cramped together lying side-by-side packed together on the floor, a position I have heard referred to as 'spooning' – humiliated and vulnerable is how I felt. Trying to sleep in these crowded conditions was virtually impossible. I took my shirt off and draped it loosely over my chest and was told off for removing it. This was considered 'haram', forbidden. I have no idea why.

When I did sleep, I was usually awake before 7.00am. This suited me as it meant I could use the toilet and showers before most of the other prisoners. I started this routine by accident, but soon realised it was essential to my cleanliness and mental wellbeing. After other prisoners had used the 'facilities' they invariably became unusable until they were cleaned by George – the same George who often used his fingers to serve food from the dustbin!

Normally, prisoners would wake up without encouragement. Occasionally, the Maraheb, or in extreme cases, one of the guards, would throw water, kick, or scream at those 'lying in' forcing them to get up. I never understood why, because for most of us there was no change in our situation for weeks on end. Maybe sleeping through the misery of a day was seen as 'escaping' the full custodial experience!

As we got up, the noise in the cage (I use the word cage deliberately because in the West animals could not have been legally kept in these awful conditions) rose to a fever pitch as inmates vied, fought, and demanded their share of the totally inadequate facilities.

I spent the first few days in Al Alwiyah trying to stay aware of 'comings and goings' such as court appearances. The level of concentration required to keep up with developments was another source of stress and exhaustion.

I was a 'target' for all the petty criminals and informants in the cage, there was nothing 'reticent' about either group. I decided the set-up in Iraq appeared similar to the system operated by the Nazis in Germany. Everyone watched everyone else and transgressions, no matter how minor, were reported, examined and regularly punished with brutal severity. Some spies were blatant in their attempts to glean information from or about me. Others were so clever that years after my release I was still becoming aware of the very subtle ruses used.

While I was in Al Alwiyah I wrote the first of many letters to my wife Julie telling her of my plight. These were smuggled out by various people and I also wrote letters of no importance sent through the censor to keep the authorities happy. Initially the lack of any kind of response from Julie or the various authorities back home, including the British Government, that I'd requested help from, made me think my letters hadn't reached their intended destinations.

From Saturday to Wednesday, the names of prisoners going to court were called through the bars of the cage. This was a signal for the attendees to wash and maybe change clothes and sometimes to collect vast piles of documents before lining up at the cage door. This wasn't an orderly process. Getting ready to go to court happened in a frenzy and provoked much shouting, dashing about, and panic which was caused by the guards wanting everyone ready almost as soon as their names were yelled!

Michael was more realistic and honest in his appraisal of the situation than I was and frequently derided the Iraqis, their legal system, and their parentage! I soon became aware that he appeared to be going out of his way to wind the Arabs up and was doing nothing that would ease their distress at his habits which included breaking wind very audibly (treated as a terrible breach of etiquette) and then sitting back roaring with laughter as the other inmates went completely bonkers. Like me he considered his detention to be a complete travesty of justice and as a form of retaliation he wanted to, in his words, "Fuck these bog-Arabs off!"

After 10.00am, fortunate prisoners would get family visits which saw them blessed with 'gifts' of foodstuffs, household items, and toiletries. Some received daily visits, others three or four visits a week. A few received irregular visits and the unfortunate, me included, received no visits at all. There were peer groups among the prisoners with the top Iraqi prisoners providing food for their whole group. I would look on with pangs of hunger and wait for the chance to wolf down any leftovers.

On the second day of my stay at Al Alwiyah two Iraqi prisoners had arrived and been introduced as big-time fraudsters. They received huge respect from everyone in the cage and soon arranged that Michael and I should move to the 'privileged' side of the jail to sleep next to them! I quickly realised they were Mukhabarat spies sent to collect information about us. They spoke excellent English and were well placed to hear anything we said. They had quilts to sleep on, insulated containers for their food, flasks for hot drinks, mirrors, toiletries and even scissors which were banned in the prison in case fights broke out!

An Egyptian prisoner called Mohammed tried to build a relationship with me. He was homosexual and interested in me for sex, and I think he thought I could give him access to food left by the Iraqis. Spying meant that many prisoners left the cage daily to report what was going on. Mohammed was among this group. The fraudsters had 'bribed' the guards to use the telephone and disappeared regularly. I'm sure they were reporting on our conversations and contact with other prisoners.

Five young soldiers were imprisoned towards the end of my first week in Al Alwiyah. They playfully arm wrestled with Michael but as soon as they discovered that he didn't understand any Arabic he became an object of derision. One would call out in Arabic, "Ghayr shakl" (Different look) and the others would roar out in English, "On a bicycle" – a reference to Michael's mode of travel when he'd entered Iraq which was common knowledge in the cage.

The number of prisoners in the cage changed daily with a constant flow of people in and out. The overcrowding was unremitting and meant that there was no privacy – ever. I nicknamed the Iraqi legal and judicial system the 'Magic Roundabout' as the perpetual movement of prisoners between prisons saw many return following an absence of many weeks without having been near a court!

If having the dire physical conditions of the jail and some unstable fellow inmates to deal with wasn't enough, the guards, most of whom were nothing more than animals, were also a constant threat. Some of the incidents that happened were as shocking as they were deeply disturbing.

Mohammed was badly beaten when I lost my temper with him. When he lit a cigarette he offered me half and in return he expected to receive half of every cigarette I lit. He tried to apply this to tea and food. He regularly asked me to buy him cigarettes. It had to stop as I knew he was working towards a homosexual encounter. I wasn't comfortable, but not sure how to 'remove' him. I couldn't exactly 'avoid him' as he slept a yard away from me!

A Palestinian prisoner called Jamel had food delivered, a roast chicken with bread and salad. I was offered the best parts of the chicken but declined as others needed food as much as I did. Mohammed was hovering, plucking at my shirt, saying in Arabic, "Give me some bread!" I told him that it was not my bread and tried to ignore him. He took some bread himself then started poking and prodding me, asking for a bit of chicken. I told him again it was not my food to give him but he kept on at me.

My revulsion and fear at the entire situation that had enveloped me was vented at Mohammed. I screamed at him to leave me alone, stay away from me, stop asking for things and stop hanging around. I was abusive, very loud, and my delivery was punctuated with a tirade of foul language. I couldn't continue to let him pester me. I was frightened of him, not physically, but his sexual motives worried me. He had moved his sleeping space next to mine a few days ago but following this altercation the Maraheb moved him into the middle of the room and I tried to stay away from him as much as was possible in the cramped cage. I forgot the incident. I was happy that Mohammed's increasing demands were at an end and felt more relaxed with him five or so metres away.

The following afternoon I was called to speak to one of the guards who was known to be a sadist. A Palestinian professor who spoke good English was called up to translate for me. The guard said, "You had a problem yesterday."

I didn't know what he was on about as nothing 'official' had happened to me and I had forgotten the incident with Mohammed.

"No," I replied.

The guard persisted. "With another prisoner."

Light dawned as he demanded to know who the problem had been with. "It doesn't matter," I replied.

"WHO WAS IT?" he shouted.

"Mohammed." was my timid reply.

"MOHAMMED! COME HERE!" he screamed.

The guard asked me what had happened and so I told him. Mohammed protested that he only wanted some bread. He was told to shut up and then verbally abused, slapped in the mouth, and told to stay away from me.

I thought that was the end of the matter but the guard had other ideas. In his hand he had a thick electrical cable and he struck Mohammed around the head with it repeatedly. Mohammed shrieked in pain and fell to the floor. The beating continued as he cowered and attempted to avoid the blows by scrambling across the tiles. It was futile. Nearby prisoners moved away to avoid getting involved and sickening thuds filled the room as the guard repeatedly hit Mohammed all over his body. His anguished screams appeared to encourage the guard and the violence intensified. When the beating stopped, the guard made a statement to the cage that no one was to interfere with Michael or me and anyone who did could expect the same treatment as Mohammed. I felt sick. I wanted to be left alone, I didn't want this treatment for anyone. This was pure evil having prisoners turn on each other for a 'favour' from the system. I knew from that moment on that I would take no action that might cause another prisoner to be punished as a consequence.

Friday, 7th August.

I don't know if it was a Muslim holiday or an Iraqi public holiday or national day but it was a holiday. There were a number of these holidays while I was detained at Al Alwiyah awaiting 'trial' and holidays which fell on a Friday meant that Saturday became the day off which delayed court appearances. In the days leading up to this particular holiday there was a terrific buzz around the cage because Saddam Hussein sometimes announced an amnesty for prisoners on these occasions.

Late in the afternoon, a young Iraqi got out a radio, a forbidden gem, which he'd kept hidden from the guards. He tuned into a speech Saddam Hussein was delivering to hear if there was an amnesty. The guard who'd beaten Mohammed got wind of what was going on and crashed into the cage demanding the radio. It was handed over and he hurled it onto the floor, smashing it to pieces. He picked up the shattered remains and threw them to the floor again, jumping on them and reducing them to fragments. Something was not right with this madman – he was drunk! The drunk guard struck 'Radio Boy' repeatedly in the face only stopping when he broke down in tears.

Young soldiers and policemen outside the cage, armed with automatic weapons, were drinking from bottles of spirit and images of what a psychopath with a temper fuelled by drink could do terrified me on this and several other occasions.

Another time, a young man was thrown into the cage late one evening. He was was mentally ill and sat and crooned songs which I was told were about his mother. When he stopped a couple of younger guards struck him with a large palm branch shouting at him to sing some more, which he did. When they had been sufficiently entertained they told him to shut up but the man kept on singing. He was beaten until virtually unconscious and whimpering and then thrown onto a piece of potato sacking outside the toilets. The sacking was to soak up all the urine and filth seeping out of the toilet area and this poor incapable soul was made to lie on it and sleep.

Two Egyptian prisoners infested with lice and fleas were brought in from Faisaliyah. Their heads and bodies were shaved and they were washed from head to toe and isolated from the rest of the cage. They were forced to sleep in the area by the toilets and warned not to approach anyone. Their positioning meant that everyone in the cage had to pass them every time they went to the toilets!

People were resourceful in this desperate place. A bright spark had cut into the electrical cable in the shower and with the assistance of a little extra flex and two spoons created a current and element with which to boil water and make tea which was then sold to the other prisoners!

Some inmates were as dangerous as the guards. One day, a new arrival, an Iraqi not of great stature but with a very muscular physique, was being washed by George. The man made a grab for the two electrically wired spoons in a bid to electrocute himself. George grabbed him and dragged him out of the shower room. The man then crouched down as if to whisper something to another prisoner and George 'the informer' bent down to listen. As he did so, the man whipped his head up and butted him in the face. George keeled over screaming and because he was feared and despised the rest of the prisoners roared with delight. When the guards arrived, the man was beaten to a pulp and chained hand and foot to the railings outside the cage.

A couple of days later, he was allowed back inside. He was still handcuffed when a Palestinian prisoner attempted to speak to him and was viciously kicked in the face by way of a response! This act of violence was met with another cheer from the rest of the prisoners. The man was taken out of the cage and beaten again, reappearing in the evening muttering loudly and hobbling around the floor with both his wrists and ankles handcuffed. An Egyptian prisoner lowered his head to listen and with enormous force the man smashed his handcuffed hands into his face. The result was horrific. He had ripped open one of the Egyptian's eyes.

The guards piled into the cage and the man was given another beating. The Egyptian was taken to hospital and we later learned that he had already been unsighted in one eye and had now lost the use of his second eye – he was totally blind! His assailant was a danger to everyone at Al Alwiyah and was shipped out to a mental asylum. The asylum refused to admit him and he returned to the jail but disappeared overnight and was never seen again!

A collection was made to help the poor sod get back to Egypt. He left, but almost immediately was returned to Al Alwiyah as the collection had been appropriated by some guards! More money had to be raised to get him home.

"SEVEN YEARS!"
"IT'S NOT TOO LONG, DON'T WORRY!"

Later in August, a representative of the International Committee of the Red Cross (ICRC) arrived to ask me questions. They were like those I'd been asked repeatedly since my detention but it was nice to have my account listened to and recorded without snorts of derision and clucks of disbelief. When he was finished the representative shook my hand saying he'd be in touch with the authorities and would return to see me in a few days. Hearing a friendly European voice, he was French or Swiss-French, gave my morale a boost although I thought it strange he hadn't asked about Michael as I'd mentioned his name while speaking to him.

Thursday, 20th August.

I'd been told for weeks that I'd be going to court and when the day finally arrived, it was anti-climactic. I was tired of being told "tomorrow, you go" and when I was finally called I'd gone off the idea. My reasoning? With nothing going the way I'd been told it would, why should my court appearance be any different?

I was advised I should prepare myself accordingly, whatever that meant in this mad house. I showered and dressed in my finest clothes, the shirt and trousers the Egyptian prisoner in Faisaliyah had given me, and waited.

I was called to the gate and escorted to the main office, a bizarre mixture of work space, household, and bordello furnishings! A Rococo-style settee sat alongside a filing cabinet. An electric kettle stood on a reproduction Louis XVI table, and in the corner of the room was a bed!

In the office stood the man who'd sent me to Faisaliyah the day I was released from the Mukhabarat complex. He appeared fatter and sweatier than I remembered but I'd been experiencing heat exhaustion and dehydration at our first meeting and my sense of perception might have been out of kilter. 'Fat Man' enquired about my health and how I'd been, as if he gave a damn, and then he led me out to a car and we drove to the courthouse in Karrada where he led me into the building to a 'safe room' where I was to wait until my case was called.

At first I was alone but then more men arrived. One of them was a mouthy old Palestinian who said he'd been part of the revolt against the British in his country. He wanted to know all about me and I assumed he was a 'spy' there to get information about me. I engaged in small talk with him but nothing of consequence as he drove me mad with his incessant questions and I was glad when Fat Man returned to escort me to the court.

We made our way to a natural intersection where two main corridors of the building crossed and I waited to be called into the courtroom. Fat Man appeared as nervous as I felt. He started pacing up and down wringing his hands, mopping his sweaty brow and constantly muttering, "Don't worry Mr Pol. There will be no jail for you."

This annoyed me because, for the past two months I'd already been held in three jails. Maybe he meant that I would not be convicted and that I'd be returned to Kuwait. If that is what he meant, I thought it was not before bloody time!

Eventually, I was called and gestured into the courtroom. We entered together and Fat Man sat at the rear while I was shoved into a dock directly in front of the bench. The courtroom layout was exactly the opposite of what I'd seen in Britain. Here, the lawyers were sat in booths off to the left and right of the court, away from the judges, while the dock area was in the centre of the room.

I stood facing three dark-haired, swarthy-looking Arabs with moustaches. They sat, dressed in robes, and regarded me with disdain. A clerk-of-the-court-type character made a statement in Arabic and then the Iraqi on my left delivered a tirade also in Arabic while gesticulating at me. Finally the Iraqi on my right said a few words. The senior judge then said to me in English, "You are accused of illegal entry. Are you guilty or not?"

I started to speak, explaining that I'd passed no signs telling me that I was leaving Kuwait and that an Iraqi soldier had actually brought me past the 'frontier' when the judge screamed, "ARE YOU GUILTY? THAT IS ALL. YES OR NO?"

I pleaded not guilty!

The judge spoke to the man who'd delivered the long speech which drew another tirade of words and gesticulations. Then the guy on my right delivered another short response. The judge asked me why I had brought a vehicle into Iraq containing 'specialist equipment'. I tried to decide what could be defined as 'specialist equipment'. Finally, it was made clear that the 'specialist equipment' was the solar-powered calculator!

I tried to engage the bench by asking how a calculator could be considered 'specialist equipment'. The senior judge interrupted my question by screaming, "DID YOU BRING THIS INTO IRAQ?"

Technically I thought I hadn't brought it into Iraq since me, the calculator and the vehicle had been ushered over the border by a man with a gun, but by now I'd learned that this chap didn't really give a toss about semantics so calmly I replied, "Yes."

There was a quick-fire question and answer session between the verbose chap on my left and the bench and then the judges got up and left the room and I was left standing in the dock, with conversation, in Arabic, going on behind me. Fat Man spoke to me explaining that the judges had gone to consider their verdict after listening to the prosecution, the verbal chap on my left, and my defence, the quiet person on my right! I'd never seen or met the lawyer who was meant to be my defence, and as the entire proceedings, apart from the questions spat at me by the judge, were in Arabic, I had no idea what he had said. I started to feel nervous because of the aggressive tone of the judge who had shouted at me, but Fat Man told me not to worry, it was normal, and there would be no jail for me.

A few minutes later the judge reentered the room and silence descended in the 'public gallery' behind me. He addressed the court in Arabic and then spoke directly to me in English. "Do you know the sentence for illegal entry?"

I considered lying and telling him that I didn't but I thought that honesty would be the best policy so I said, "Yes. I've been told that it's five years and one month."

The judge glared at me as he spat out his reponse. "This is a military court and we could sentence you to life imprisonment for this crime."

My world stopped, like a record sticking, the phrase "sentence you to life imprisonment" kept repeating itself in a grainy fashion in my head. I gulped and felt sick as he continued, "But as this is Iraq, and we are nice people we are going to give you seven years."

My mind went into free-fall. I clutched at the wooden rail that separated me from the judges. I blinked, I gasped, my body shook with fear at what I'd just heard. *SEVEN YEARS*! My head screamed, I swayed gently and everything appeared to swirl around me in the still cool air of the court room. Seven years for driving up the wrong street with a calculator!

Fat Man pulled me out of the dock and out of the court. We walked into the corridor and he expressed his shock at the sentence. I looked at him and thought, *Do you understand? Do you care? Do you know I'll be nearly 40-years-old when I get out? I'm going to jail. What have I done wrong?*

I was escorted back to the 'safe custody' room where the inquisitive Palestinian asked how long my sentence was. "Seven years," I mumbled. To my horror he replied, "It's not too long, don't worry!"

I was mortified, this fatalistic prick was telling me not to worry. I struggled with the way Muslims put everything down to God. It's almost as if there was no secular authority involved in my detention. They were doing God's work – the freaking lunatics.

I prowled up and down beside one wall in the room. I wanted out of this place. I wanted to start my sentence. The sooner I started the quicker it would be over. *Will I ever see my home again? Will I ever meet anyone who gives a damn about me?* I feared disappearing. I hated my luck. I despised the Iraqis. I wanted to run. I needed to fly. I wanted wings, but all I got was Fat Man with a car!

He took me back to Al Alwiyah, and I was thrown back into the cage. Questions tumbled from the lips of many of the prisoners as they saw me through the bars. My mutterings of a seven year sentence stunned them. Michael said he was sorry to hear this new and surprising development – he was a master of understatement!

A Bangladeshi driver called Musharrif, whose abduction was similar to mine, started crying when he heard my news. Tears laced with self-concern lest he received a similar sentence. I told him not to get so worked up because as a Muslim he would be treated very differently.

The days following my sentence were a nightmare, time turned to ice and moved at a glacial pace. My bleak mood was lifted by an extraordinarily generous deed. A collection organised by the inmates, many of whom were in desperate situations, gathered over 400 Dinars for me, more than a month's wages for most Iraqis at the time! This was an incredibly humbling experience. When I was given the money I gave a short speech expressing my thanks for this act of kindness, and I said that I hoped that they would be excused a trip to the courthouse.

MADE IN ENGLAND!

It soon became apparent after my sentencing that the regime at Al Alwiyah wanted to get rid of me as quickly as possible. Perhaps I'd been cramping their style! It was swiftly arranged I would be moved to a 'transportation depot' called Tasfirat.

When a person is arrested in Iraq they are detained at 'police stations' such as Al Alwiyah and Faisaliyah with holding capability. Those convicted at court are then transferred to Tasfirat prior to being sent to Abu Ghraib, Iraq's central prison.

Monday, 24th August.

On the morning of my transfer I was handcuffed by a young policeman who escorted me out of the Al Alwiyah compound to a waiting taxi which I had to pay for! I was bundled into the back and driven to Tasfirat. As I sat there with the policeman next to me, I lifted my hands to look at the cuffs that were shackling my wrists and I started to laugh out loud. The policemen asked me what was so funny and I told him that the handcuffs, stamped with the manufacturer's name, were made in England – the irony was not lost on him!

At Tasfirat I was pulled out of the cab by my handcuffs and shoved past a row of armed guards into a building which was teeming with men in military garb. I felt like I was being treated as a dangerous criminal, but looking back the young policeman was simply following Iraqi protocol. I was pushed into a room, uncuffed and instructed to wait. In a matter of minutes I was called into an office and asked for my passport. I shook my head and said I had no documentation. Looks of incredulity were etched on every face in the room. I was ushered out and the young policeman handcuffed me again and and shoved me back to and into the taxi and, as we drove off, he explained in a mix of broken English and pigeon Arabic that Tasfirat would not accept me without paperwork and we were going back to Al Alwiyah!

A couple of days later another attempt at my transfer failed again, and my return disappointed most of the prisoners who decided that whatever constituted normality could not be resumed while "The Inglisi", as they'd nicknamed me, drifted between Al Alwiyah and Tasfirat.

Thursday, 27th August.

With an older policeman for 'company', I set off for Tasfirat again. He spoke a bit of basic English and the journey soon passed. We got to Tasfirat and things went as they had previously – a request for paperwork, a shake of my head, grimaces from the Iraqis. This time however there was an unexplained breakthrough. I didn't understand why but I knew things were different because as we left the office the policeman went in one direction and I was sent in another.

I walked across a rubbish and machinery-strewn yard into a tall, dimly-lit, farm-like building that was full of people. When my eyes had grown accustomed to the gloom I saw dozens of confused faces. I looked past them and into the interior of the building and saw a huge room with high walls and nothing between the floor and the roof. Maybe it had been used as a barn in a previous life. It certainly had an agriculture feel to it though perhaps that had something to do with the smell.

I was swiftly surrounded by a collection of curious Arabs in various states of dress and appearance. Most of them were quickly chased away by a Maraheb. The 'barn' was packed with people, some lying down, some sitting, some walking about. This place was vast after the confines of Al Alwiyah however it was more densely populated and I was already beginning to imagine the hellish problems this might present.

I asked to use a toilet and was shown a facility separated from the main room by a corridor. As at Al Alwiyah there were bodies all over the floor leading up to and even inside the toilets which were predictably nauseous.

On returning to the barn I was presented to the 'top detainees' where food and drink was offered to me. It's rude to refuse this kind of hospitality and so I sat down and drank and ate with the resident dignitaries. I'd barely started answering their questions when I was called to the gate and told to get my things, I was on the move again!

Outside, the brilliant sunshine was harsh after the gloom of the barn. I was in a group of 12 prisoners and one-by-one we were counted off against a list by a guard. I was then cuffed by my left wrist to the right wrist of another prisoner and we looked on as some Iraqi soldiers approached and surrounded us talking animatedly. One of them walked over to an old, dilapidated bus which was parked nearby. It reminded me of those vintage Green Line buses that I used to see on the roads during childhood visits to the English countryside, except this bus had no windows in it apart from one adjacent to the driver's seat!

The soldier clambered into the seat and cranked the engine several times attempting to fire it into life. After a short pause he tried again and failed at which point he leaned out of the window and shouted some instructions to his colleagues who ordered us to move towards the front of the bus. I had no idea what was going on but I was pulled along by my left wrist which was firmly secured to an Arab who did. The pathos of the situation then dawned on me. We, the prisoners on our way to prison, were having to push-start our transport. Oh, the ignominy!

We pushed the clapped-out bus backwards until the engine fired up. Fortunately, given the searing heat, this was a quick job. We were then counted on board and herded down the aisle to a sealed compartment at the rear that had no windows and smelled foul.

We set off and a guard entertained himself with a question that each prisoner answered in turn. I understood the question was about the length of our sentences. Most of the others had been given between one and five years, I had been given seven years. I wallowed in self-pity.

A short while into the journey, the guard went to every prisoner and requested a payment of 50 Dinars. I asked what this was for and could not believe the answer. *FOR GOD'S SAKE!* I was having money extorted from me to pay for the diesel to get me to bloody prison! I sat there seething, this entire country was a mad house where convicted prisoners had to pay for taxis and fuel to get to jail!

We stopped at a petrol station where the bus was filled with diesel and we were each given a sweet, carbonated drink. This was refreshing, but never 50 Dinars worth and, given the price of fuel in Iraq, the 600 Dinars collected would have filled the inside of the entire vehicle, let alone its tank!

As we recommenced the journey I felt anger coursing through my body at the injustice of everything that had happened to me since that fateful day in June when I'd decided to visit Mike Walsh. I began contemplating what horrors would be lying in wait for me next and as I did so the driver announced that Abu Ghraib was in sight.

ABU GHRAIB

Upon arrival at Abu Ghraib we were ordered off the bus and shuffled towards the main gate of the prison.

Ibrahim, a Palestinian prisoner who had 'crashed' the border to fight the world by Saddam Hussein's side, said that it was "good and holy" to intone the Islamic phrase, "Bismillah Hir Rahman Nir Rahim", which he translated as we entered the prison gates as, "In the name of God, the most gracious, the most merciful." He added that saying the phrase might keep me safe from harm. I repeated the words exactly as he'd said them and with a shudder I walked on, not knowing what to expect next.

We made our way along well-lit corridors, through locked gates, deeper and deeper into the prison. People stared at us in a detached way. New prisoners meant nothing. The corridors seemed endless and were lined by scores of men performing tasks. It was another custodial marketplace with all the noise, confusion and argument that entailed. Some of the 'market traders' wore traditional Arabic attire, some younger 'businessmen' were dressed in T-shirts and jeans. The heat was staggering and the smell of over-ripe bodies overwhelming.

Eventually we arrived at an administrative area where we were lined up against a wall and left to wait to be 'processed'. As we waited a passing guard questioned me and someone explained my situation. He gestured that he considered me a good candidate for a homosexual liason. He stood there with a suggestive gaze on his face and made another hand gesture and said something I didn't understand. A crowd had gathered and they roared with approval. I didn't know if this was to frighten me or impress the guard. I neither knew nor cared. It shook me for a second but in truth I had other things preying on my mind.

The prison 'traders' approached selling food, drink, and cigarettes. As they passed they were pumping us for information. "Where have you been held? Where have you come from? What are your crimes? What are your sentences? What is the word from the streets?"

I was told that seven years was a light sentence, anything over eight years being heavy. Damn, I'd just missed out! Irony aside, the news that I was serving a light sentence didn't soothe me at all.

We were unshackled from each other and called singularly into a filthy room piled high with what I now recognised all too well as the usual detritus. When my turn came, I was asked a series of shouted questions by an Iraqi prison officer who was flanked by several colleagues. I shrugged and said, "Ana Inglisi, Sayidi." (I'm English, Sir.) Disbelief was writ large on his face. A prisoner who spoke English was called in and translated the questions which I answered.

Eventually I was asked for my passport. I said I didn't have one and hadn't when I went to northern Kuwait which I hadn't intended to leave. The officer asking the questions looked flustered at my reponse while his colleagues simply laughed. He recovered by stating that Kuwait was southern Iraq, an Imperial invention of the British. *Fine*, I thought. *Why then have I got seven bloody years for illegal entry if Kuwait is Iraq?* I was simmering with rage again. Fortunately, my interrogation remained calm but this wasn't the case for other prisoners who received verbal and physical abuse when they failed to comply or respond appropriately.

Our answers were entered into a huge book which I would nickname the 'Kitab al-Hayah' (Book of Life or Bible in Arabic). We were then escorted into another room for more questions and then another to be fingerprinted not once but four times! Fingerprinting done and with our hands blackened with ink we were made to wait in a corridor. I was then called into a room and invited to sit down. I was asked yet another series of questions and told that my situation was political, nothing to do with me, and I should expect to be released in six months! A guard arrived and informed the officers I was being moved, and with polite regrets they told me that I would have to go and wished me good luck! I soon understood why!

After waiting in the corridor with my fellow new arrivals for a short while we were then led up to an area of holding cells with bars from floor to ceiling. Paintings of a grinning Saddam Hussein adorned every wall, mocking me in this rehash of a cheap Western-movie-style sheriff's office!

A cage was opened and six of us entered. It was a filthy space. I'd been told Abu Ghraib was an excellent place with all the facilities imaginable. The reality was a nightmare. My treasures; a plate, cup, some toiletries and a couple of pieces of clothing, secured in two plastic bread bags, were safely placed in a corner of the cell. I felt a little more secure with 'my territory' established. The cell had two, glassless, barred windows and in one corner was a toilet area walled off at chest height. That was it, the cell had nothing else in at all, except for an empty 45-litre oil drum.

I looked over the wall at the toilet area. Reality didn't dawn on me until a Palestinian said, "You must not go to the toilet. Okay?"

I stared at him like an idiot and he pulled me against the wall and gestured over it. "Look! No shitting! Okay?"

This was the same mouthy guy who had been at the courts when I'd been 'tried'. I didn't trust him, I thought, *He's a spy!* I was paranoid about people who 'turned up!' I stared over the wall at the 'toilet'. There wasn't one, just a concrete slab with a tiny waste pipe running horizontally through the external wall!

"You see, only piss. Okay?" said the Palestinian.

I nodded stupidly still gazing at the concrete slab, trying to establish how I was going to survive – and it got worse. An inmate approached the cell with a bucket of water and poured it through the bars to empty it into the oil drum! Not only was this our drinking water, it had to fulfil all our other needs. Now I knew how a caged animal felt. I was distraught and pissed off in equal measures.

We took turns to 'shower'. This involved pouring water over our bodies, applying soap and a community-spirited peer tipping a jam jar of water over our heads to help rinse the lather away. We did this to conserve water and to stop the jam jar from being smashed as a result of a soapy hand dropping it. Nobody wanted to smash someone else's jam jar which sounds pathetic but jam jars were prized possessions!

After I'd had my turn at 'showering' I felt better. However it was late August and with no respite from the heat I was soon as vile and sticky as I had been before my shower. The temporary relief brought with it fleeting comfort though. Someone kindly gave me some 'Arabic underwear' – big white jobs akin to Boxer Shorts. Mine were in tatters. I'd been wearing the same pair for weeks and they were well past their sell-by date!

Iraqi prisoners used new arrivals as a revenue source. Everything cost a fortune. We purchased food made by them. This was very basic but superior to prison fare. The food was passed through the bars of our cell – everything I ate had been handled by at least four people and that was only the people I knew about! There was no point worrying about the consequences of eating this food as the alternative was starving to death. I needed to eat, survive and keep my wits about me. I didn't know what was going to happen next and the Iraqis never let me down in this respect!

Time in this cell was very difficult. I ate the bare minimum as we didn't have the use of a toilet. When I think about this period of my incarceration, I realise it was just one short passage in a litany of mental torture, depravation, and high farce.

Sleeping was a lot easier here than in Al Alwiyah as there were only six of us in the cell. Two Iraqis, two Egyptians, the mouthy Palestinian and myself. The Iraqis were Muslims and the Egyptians were Christians. One of the Egyptians gave me a small picture of a traditional image of the Virgin Mary which I still have today! The mouthy Palestinian also claimed to be Christian but I had my doubts about everything he said!

In the afternoon of the second day in Abu Ghraib, the Palestinian bribed a guard and we moved to another cell with a 'functioning toilet' – well a sort of 'toilet', but it was better than nothing! The luxury of having a 'functioning toilet' meant that we had to tolerate the stench that came from it. The sad thing is that after a few hours you didn't notice the aroma. It was always a struggle for me going behind that little wall to relieve myself with five blokes sat just a few feet away!

Our cell was in the punishment complex and screams and the sound of physical violence became a 24-hour 'soundtrack' to our detention. A stream of bodies flowed through the complex day and night and some of the prisoners never re-emerged. I spent a lot of time lying on the floor variously wondering, *When will I get out of this hole? When will I see my family again? What condition will I be in? Will I have my sanity?*

Saturday, 29th August.

I woke to the sound of weeping. I rose slightly from the concrete floor and one of the Iraqis, his hands raised in supplication, was saying his prayers while tears ran down his tired face. *What the fuck are you crying about?* I thought. He'd only been sentenced to a year. Given my own situation how was I meant to feel sorry for anyone else?

I pretended to sleep and got up when I heard others speaking, another day in paradise was underway! The Biblical gardens of Eden were thought to be in Iraq – be assured, no part of Saddam Hussein's Iraq resembled this bounteous heaven on earth, especially not his bloody prisons!

A couple of hours passed and a guard arrived and took me out of the cage and downstairs through an area where prisoners were allowed out of their cells. I didn't know what was going on and so I panicked. *Christ!* I thought, *I've been separated from all my worldly goods.* I wondered if the Palestinian had anything to do with this. "Where am I going?" I asked, but got no reply.

I attracted considerable interest and a buzz went up as inmates crowded around to 'view The Inglisi'. A scream from the guard dispersed them and I was led into an outside courtyard and stood against a wall.

What the fuck is going on? Is this it? Death by firing squad? My mind whirred. I couldn't see any blood or holes in the wall to indicate I was about to be executed, nevertheless I was absolutely terrified as I stood alone trembling in the scalding sun.

I flinched as a door in the courtyard wall crashed open and an officer strode out. Other uniformed men followed in his wake and I traumatised myself mentally. One of the guards handed me something, I took it and turned it over. It was a photo ID board. *Oh God! They are taking my picture!* I was anxious, terrified and relieved – my panic had been over a photo-shoot! *Jesus Christ! I thought I was going to die!*

I was photographed and then escorted back to my cell and shoved forcefully through the door. I hadn't been away that long, but the smell seemed more overpowering than it had before. There was a blockage in the toilet and excrement had spewed out onto the concrete behind the wall. After my mental ordeal I wanted another shower to help calm me down but I'd have to wait until this latest drama was sorted.

I spoke to the two Egyptians about religion, the Palestinian about how the British Empire had destroyed the Middle East, and the two Iraqis spoke of their families and the injustice of being put in prison by an evil dictator. According to their stories they were all innocent and should not have been in jail. During my detention, I only ever met three men who admitted to a crime!

Sunday, 30th August.

I was taken from the cell to an open area outside the complex and herded together with a couple of dozen other men. An officer screamed something and the other men sank squatting on their haunches. I played the 'I don't speak Arabic and do not understand' card which was ruined by English speakers whispering that I had to sit down which I did begrudgingly. I thought my thighs would seize up, or my knees explode. The pain was awful! We hunched like this for an eternity. It was hot, uncomfortable and after an age we were ordered to stand, which by now I could hardly manage. It was midday and the heat was unbearable. I felt weak. I'd had insufficient food and water since my detention began and been held in appalling, primitive conditions. Looking around I could see that many of my fellow inmates appeared to be in a worse state than I was. I wondered how long it would be before I was consumed by illness, and shuddered.

"March!" barked one of the guards distracting me from my morbid thoughts. I'd never been in the military so marching was something I'd never done and I had an excuse for my immediate lack of coordination. Those with me who had been soldiers appeared to have forgotten their basic training and were as uncertain about how to 'march' as I was.

With no disrespect to the valiant prisoners of war who really built 'The Bridge on the River Kwai' I recalled the movie and thought we must have resembled them. Unshaven, ill-fed, poorly clothed, confused and marching from the main prison to our destination. I felt like a film extra – but no one was shouting, "Cut!"

People began to 'wander' after only a few minutes of this idiotic march and soon we were strung out over 50 metres. The guard at the rear started screaming abuse at the stragglers and I began thinking with every step, *I'm going to die, I am going to die*, because I might be 'marching' through an area that had unexploded ordnance buried in it. It was dreadful.

Across the open ground, I saw other complexes resembling the main prison. We passed a building housing female prisoners and the female guards stood outside received a lot of attention from our 'marching' group of shabby degenerates. Eventually we reached the foreign prisoner complex. My first impression was that it looked more inviting than the main Abu Ghraib block I'd just come from. I smiled and then shook my head. I knew already that I was clutching at straws!

MUSTER MADNESS

We entered the foreigners section of Abu Ghraib and once again I muttered, "Bismillah Hir Rahman Nir Rahim." Religion! The opiate of the people!

Five of us including the Palestinian were led into the administration building which had Saddam Hussain's sycophantic smiling face on every wall. Shoved down a corridor, past display cases full of the 'jewellery' and other items made there; wooden boats, models of the Eiffel Tower made from matches, crocheted footwear, decorative boxes, bracelets, etc. I learned that this 'cottage industry' was how some prisoners stayed alive in Abu Ghraib.

We were corralled in a large empty, apart from the omnipresent Saddam Hussein artwork, room and waited. Instructions were shouted by a guard and my peers retreated into a corner against the wall and I joined them. We stood for an age and then a young guard appeared asking questions. I understood the question was, "What's your sentence?" because I heard the reponses one, two and five years. When he spoke to me, I ignored him so he threw a piece of folded paper at me and with this the Palestinian said in Arabic, "He's English. He doesn't speak Arabic!"

The guard asked the Palestinian what the length of my sentence was and he showed a mixture of surprise and respect when told it was seven years. I wondered what he would have said had he known the sentence was for driving up a road in northern Kuwait?

We were called one-by-one into an adjacent office. "Pol Stevi Rod," I heard. I knew it was me they wanted to see! I entered the room and was immediately rebuffed by a man sat behind a desk. I stopped and stared at the man who was waving at me in a gesture that suggested I was to go out again so I walked back outside. He then called out, "Taal!" (Come here!) I entered slowly this time, but once again he waved me back. I retreated until he indicated I had gone far enough – just inside the door. Apparently he wanted it that way!

I was asked the usual stupid questions and I answered each one in turn and then he screamed, "GIVE ME YOUR PASSPORT!"

"I don't have one!" I replied.

He didn't understand how I'd got from Kuwait to Iraq without documentation – my own recurring question.

The Palestinian was instructed to speak on my behalf. Once again I wondered if he was a spy or an informant. He'd been ever-present since my court appearance and was always eager to involve himself in my situation. Angrily, the officer dismissed me and I re-joined the shabby collective in the main room, relaxing slightly as the chance of a beating for disrespecting the screaming madman receded.

We were told to go outside and wait by a tiny man called Ghassan who I thought was a prison official. He was actually a Syrian prisoner and turned out to be one of the sneakiest men I had to deal with in Abu Ghraib. He called us one-by-one and requested we remove our shirts so he could examine us for any obvious illnesses, wounds or troublesome insect bites – I'd already had problems with Iraqi mosquitos! When Ghassan questioned me and I stated I didn't speak much Arabic he went into rapture screaming, "IT'S WONDERFUL TO HAVE ANOTHER BRITISH MAN AT ABU GHRAIB."

He burbled that he had been a 'friend' to someone called Ian Richter. This was a new name to me but I was to hear Mr Richter's name a great deal in the coming months. Ghassan told me he would become my 'friend' too and said he helped in the prison 'clinic' and would see me in the next few days and that I shouldn't worry about mosquito bites as they would not harm me. I was overjoyed at this news even though I thought it unlikely as I'd seen lots of stagnant water around the prison.

Ghassan then went away and returned with the officer who had inducted us. We were instructed to empty our pockets onto the floor and stand behind them. Some items were confiscated from others but I didn't lose anything because I hadn't taken everything out of my pockets! I was learning! Guards saw prisoners as a way of supplementing their income and I didn't want to give anyone the opportunity of stealing my money.

The officer approached me and enquired if these were all my possessions. I assured him they were at which point he asked, "Do you have money?"

I thought, *Here we go, the Bastard is about to relieve me of it!* I informed him that I did have some money.

"How much?"

"About 400 Dinars," I replied, already knowing how much this represented to him.

Ghassan hovered, sniffing about like a bloody ferret, and the officer came close to me and in an exaggerated aside said, "Be careful, there are many bad men in here. They will steal your money if you let them. Many thieves, many bad men – be very clever!"

This was funny. Here I was entering the notorious Abu Ghraib prison and this idiot was telling me there were lots of thieves and bad men inside its walls!

We were then split up and led to our respective sections. There were five separate sections and I was taken to Section Three which was locked, as it was every afternoon at this time. The Maraheb was summoned. He was a Libyan/Egyptian called Jabber. Referencing the 'Star Wars' film character I immediately nicknamed him 'Jabba the Hutt'. Sleepily, he accepted me and led me through the gloom of the section to his cell where I was instantly surrounded by people shouting questions in Arabic and English.

The questions in English were from four Filipino guys who introduced themselves as Albert, Ronnie, Kid and Obet. The usual subjects were covered and then Albert mentioned I had grown a beard and said that this was not allowed! I was then asked about my personal effects. The cell fell silent when I told them everything I possessed was in the pair of small plastic sacks I had just placed on the floor. New arrivals were expected to bring information and commodities to the meagre prison economy – with no information, and no goods, the inmates were bitterly disappointed with me and most of them left.

The Filipinos went to their cells and returned with things I could use; underwear, sandals, shorts, toiletries etc. They also gave me bedding and a mattress. With little enough for themselves in this dire place, I was, and remain, very grateful for their kindness.

I had a shave and was challenged to a game of chess by Jabba the Hutt. I hadn't played for years but I would have appeared churlish not to accept. I was beaten easily. It turned out that Jabba was one of the top players in the section, I didn't stand a chance.

I then went to Albert's cell to thank him for the shaving kit. He and I were to form a friendship that in time would become mutually beneficial. In my first few weeks in Abu Ghraib I was helpless. I had little money and Albert guided me through the minefield of prison life. He was a veteran of six years and knew every trick going. Albert, along with Ronnie, Kid and Obet, held me together until the cavalry, in the form of diplomatic aid, arrived. Albert told me what to do, what not to do, who to trust and who not to trust. Importantly, he also told me the unwritten rules that made existence possible in the prison.

That evening Albert, who I'd now learned was known to everyone as Abet, provided my evening meal. After we ate a dish of vegetables and rice, Abet, Ronnie and I spent the evening getting to know each other. Abet and Ronnie shared a two-man cell, highly coveted as most cells had up to 18 prisoners in them. I would spend my first few weeks in Abu Ghraib sleeping in the 'ghurfat kabira', a big room that had over 80 people bunking down in its fetid environs!

Abet had been imprisoned for robbery, he and Obet had been accused of breaking into the room of a fellow building site worker. If they were guilty of the crime, something they both hotly denied, then six years in Abu Ghraib was an unbelievable sentence – just like mine was!

After the revelations, I trudged exhausted to the big room which resembled a warehouse and was teeming with the filth that was life for the poor sods confined in there who were now joined by another poor sod – me! Lying down, dog-tired, on a piece of borrowed foam, in borrowed clothes, I wondered how I was going to survive in this shithole for seven years!

The next day I asked Abet if he could find me a scrap of paper I could write on and a biro. He duly obliged and I wrote a letter to my wife Julie asking her to write to Saddam Hussein requesting a Presidential pardon! In previous letters I'd written to her when in Al Alwiyah I'd said that I didn't want her making a trip to Iraq. It was unstable and dangerous. Anyone who has been married will know that was like telling water not to flow downhill! I recall writing, "I would appreciate help from wherever it comes, I have committed no crime, I am a pawn in a game of politics, and seven years is a long game!"

I also asked Julie to record highlights of the Formula 1 season as I'd been following British driver Nigel Mansell's progress closely in Kuwait and had missed the last few races. I realise this was a strange request from a man sentenced to seven years in prison but I was optimistic my situation would change soon and I'd be home in good time to catch up with everything and cheer Mansell on to win the world championship which was due to conclude in November.

In Al Alwiyah I'd been told about the Barcelona 1992 Olympics results and by early September I also realised the English football season had started and so in my letters that followed I asked Julie to keep me abreast of the scores. I was keen to find out how Chelsea were faring the inaugural campaign of the all-new Premier League.

Wednesday, 9th September.

I received my first letter from the United Kingdom! It was from a bloke called Malc Smith who lived in Nottingham. He told me to keep my chin up, not to worry, and that it would all get sorted out. Not only was this a shock but it was a massive morale boost to know that people at home were aware of my situation! I hoped the British Government would become involved and that in a matter of days I would be home again in London with my family, but as the time passed hope soon fell by the wayside.

An improvement in my situation came in form of being able to exercise outside 'properly' for the first time when I got permission to use the prison 'sports field'. The 'field' was actually a muddy patch of earth without a blade of grass in sight. The water table was shallow here and so despite the heat the field was always damp and sticky. Other prisoners could use the field daily, except Fridays – I was allowed on there twice a week! It was my only release and I exhausted myself on the mud by running until I could run no more, burning off the hate and anger that smothered my soul. The longer I was held, the worse my black moods became. I was aggressive and short-tempered and needed to run off my rage.

I was constantly watched and monitored unaware that the Iraqis held the belief that I was a spy and my entry to Iraq had been planned by the British Government and World media – bloody idiots!

Food was a concern. My cash wasn't going far given the spiralling prices that the 'Hanoot' (shop) in the prison charged. Abet and I ate together often, mainly rice and vegetables, although early on I did invest in a reasonably-sized chicken. This, with imaginative portioning, fed the two of us for five meals although it has to be said that Abet did better than me – he would eat the chicken bones as well. I never became brave enough to follow suit.

Life was very repetitive. A day would start around 6.30am with the first prisoners getting out of bed to get into the toilet block which I nicknamed 'hell'. People requiring a visit to hell after waking up was normal – normal until you had 300 men trying to use five toilets! The noise, smell and attitude in that cramped hole was horrific. I have no more unpleasant memory of Abu Ghraib than queuing and using the filthy, evil toilets during the mornings.

"Awal!"
"Thania!"
"Althaalith!"
Meaning –
"First!"
"Second!"
"Third!"

The next in line impatiently called to the occupants of the two toilets and the drain which doubled as a urinal, imploring them to hurry up. The block was always wet and filthy and regularly I got splashed by the piss and shit that formed in puddles on the floor. This frantic activity was because being late for the first of the day's roll-calls (Musters) was to invite a beating from the prison guards and I do not mean a few slaps, I mean an assault with fists, boots, heavy-duty cable, and batons in full view of the rest of everyone in the section. A very visible warning not to be late.

After Muster, an ever-lengthening queue would form at the gate to a yard where Arabic tea was 'served'. The sound of a guard opening the gate always precipitated a scramble and late arrivals whould try to queue-jump as the line moved into the yard where the Maraheb served the tea from a 70-litre container.

I never worked out if the Musters were to count or subjugate us. Forming rows of five, we would crouch onto our haunches which was very difficult to maintain as leg muscles cramped, swiftly causing excruciating pain. We were left crouching for up to 30 minutes before the officer would appear and count us. I detested Muster and looked upon the whole thing as kowtowing to the Iraqis. My hatred was heightened by the insistence of the more obnoxious guards that I stay cowed like a dog along with everyone else.

The area we 'Mustered' on was surrounded by chainlink fencing as were Section Four and Five, directly opposite us, while Section One and Two were hidden from view by administration buildings. Punishments were regularly carried out in full view of the prisoners. I was convinced this was to demonstrate the power the sadistic guards held over us.

After Muster, people ate breakfast. Status in the hierarchy meant that this could range from a jam jar full of ration tea to chickpea fritters and bread with margarine, jam and eggs. A substantial meal could be had by prisoners with the highest status, typically, Marahebs, section spies, informants or the well-connected who had suppliers, family or friends that visited regularly.

Time was then 'wasted' until 9.00am, and a second Muster. I say wasted because with such a short period from the end of the first Muster to the start of the second there wasn't enough time to do anything constructive. The second Muster coincided with a shift change for the guards meaning a refreshed squad of spiteful bastards now had the reins of power.

Musters in bad weather were even more unbearable. The conditions were of no consequence to the guards. We would Muster in sandstorms, rain, and sometimes in the middle of the night! Often, I would stand my ground – literally, after being told to squat by the guards, waiting until the officer came to count us. There were occasions I remember shaking with fear that I was about to be beaten as I'd defied orders – I was lucky, a beating never came.

After the 9.00am Muster the prison 'school' opened. In the school people with a skill would instruct others in their trade. Hairdressing, metalwork, jewellery manufacture, gardening, and handicrafts such as basket weaving and model building were taught. It was was well attended as items made were sold bringing in vital cash to many who would not have survived otherwise.

Exercise on the 'sports field' was an alternative but this was regularly stopped at the whim of the guards as a section punishment. Each section had its day for exercise and certain prisoners had special dispensations to exercise daily, something I was denied for months. 'Spies' were denied many 'privileges'!

At the end of morning activity, exercise people returned to their sections first at around 11.00am. At 12.00pm the 'scholars' returned. After midday, food came from the central kitchen. Usually this was a huge container of boiled vegetable (one vegetable) 'soup' mixed with enough tomato puree to colour it. Dished out by the Maraheb to a squabbling, screeching crowd that was never orderly, the soup was either eaten as it came or incorporated into a meal.

The third Muster of the day was at 1.00pm, which in the full glare of the sun could be a long, hot, uncomfortable event. Once counted we were marched into the section and locked in. Lunch was eaten and there was the opportunity for a siesta, with those who slept doing so until the gate was opened again at 3.30pm. At this juncture, prisoners prepared meals and socialised until the last Muster and lock-up for the night which coincided with sunset. This ranged from 4.00pm in winter to 8.00pm in summer. Cooking was carried out in the Muster area. Gas bottles were not allowed in the sections as they had repeatedly caused fires. I was told that Ian Richter had badly burned his arms putting out such a fire.

Once locked in we were allowed to watch the section TV until the end of transmissions which was a signal for Maraheb Laylee, the night supervisor, to instruct prisoners to sleep.

The routine was simple and repetitive and comprised of days and nights where situations regularly filled me with fear, hate, loathing, and disgust. This picture of emptiness and boredom is existence in many prisons. Time in Abu Ghraib crept like a thief, stealing my life.

YOU'RE GOING ON TV: "IF YOU WANT TO?"

Time passed slowly. I learned new ways to exist and was taught new rules to obey. I developed new targets to aim for and a belief that I would not be in prison for seven years. I had more conversations with the Red Cross who visited Abu Ghraib bi-monthly. They told me about Julie's efforts to get me out of Iraq. This was a result. My letters were getting through! They knew the basics but had no real details which was a major concern, but I thought the British Government would be in the process of resolving matters. I was still being quizzed about the finer points surrounding my circumstances and the situation of others and I answered if I could, and any positive news they had they shared with me. I was delighted to be told that the Bangladeshi driver Musharrif, who'd sobbed when I was sentenced to seven years, had been released by the Iraqis and had returned to Kuwait. I was glad he and his family had been spared further suffering but upset that the Iraqi legal system was blatantly biased towards citizens of nations not involved in the Gulf War, who were given far more lenient sentences.

At the Red Cross meetings I also linked up again with Michael Wainwright, the Yorkshireman that I'd first met at Al Alwiyah who had also been transferred to Abu Ghraib (Section Five) to serve his ten-year sentence – ten years! He outlined his story in great detail and raged about the colossal injustice of his sentence.

Saturday, 12th September.

For the one and only time during my captivity, I saw brief highlights of a Chelsea game on TV. Norwich City were the visitors at Stamford Bridge and even though the Canaries were currently flying high at the top of the Premier League table, when Mick Harford and Andy Townsend put the Blues 2-0 up inside the first half-an-hour I thought we had the job done. "Up the Chels!" I hollered, much to the puzzlement of fellow inmates watching with me. Townsend nearly scored a second against his old club just before the break but a last-ditch tackle by a Norwich defender prevented him making it 3-0. Still, 2-0 wasn't bad. What could possibly go wrong?

My experience of life since the 28th of June should have told me that a reversal of fortune when least expected is always a possibility but even so I couldn't quite believe my eyes at the events that unfolded on the flickering screen in front of me. First, Norwich striker Mark Robbins left Chelsea goalkeeper flat on his back to reduce the arrears. 2-1. Then, Blues defender Mal Donaghy was beaten for pace down the right and from the resultant cross Robins again netted. 2-2. Finally, as I was shaking my fist angrily at the TV, Canaries midfielder David Phillips had a soft shot at goal and what happened next further enraged me. The ball trickled towards Beasant who went down to make what should have been a routine save and somehow allowed it to bobble under his body and over the line! 2-3. I was dumbfounded and hurled obscenities at the hapless goalie who was subsequently dropped and wouldn't feature again for Chelsea until March the following year!

Tuesday, 15th September.

It wouldn't have happened now given Russia's invasion of Ukraine and the sanctions the West has imposed on Moscow, but back then, with the British Embassy in Iraq having been abandoned in 1991, the UK Foreign Office enlisted the help of Russian diplomats to try and secure the release of Michael and myself. Today we had a first visit from the Russian Embassy in Baghdad in the shape of Gleb Desyatnikov, a charming man who was to be our main source of hope, and frustration, for the next 15 months.

I stated in a letter how 'happy' I was at having 'diplomatic contact', unfortunately, this meant nothing, as my situation developed into a comedic farce. Gleb made gesticulations to 'inform' us the room we were sitting in was bugged and we should be careful what we said or asked for. While Michael and I outlined our situation, Gleb listened and made notes and then he made a profound and somewhat ridiculous statement that I have never forgotten. "You must consider yourselves as bargaining chips. There will be negotiations and, when the price is right, you will be exchanged!"

With incredulity writ large on our faces, Michael and I looked at each other and Michael said, "What yo's mean? Like fucking slaves, we'll b'eet sold?"

Gleb nodded and said this was exactly what he meant and Michael who had been animated and loud when explaining his circumstances became quiet and morose. Gleb was polite throughout the visit but I think he'd formed an opinion about Michael.

During this first visit Gleb told us that he had visited Ian Richter, the last Briton to reside in Abu Ghraib, and so he 'understood' how the Iraqi departments responsible for us worked and informed us that he would apply for radios and single accommodation as soon as possible. This was marvellous, but I hoped I wouldn't be at Abu Ghraib long enough to enjoy the 'upgrades'.

I wasn't passed any of the mail that Gleb said he'd brought with him and the lack of contact with my family was driving me potty. I'd received more mail from total strangers, but nothing from my wife. These letters shared details of seeing Julie and William on TV talking about my plight which had compelled them to write and offer their support. This was amazing but it really hurt me not hearing from Julie.

RIDE TO HELL

Thursday, 24th September.

Three Swedish telecommunication technicians, Christer, Leif and Stefan arrived in Abu Ghraib. Christer was put in Section Three with me while Leif and Stefan were put in Section Five. When Christer 'arrived' it was mistakenly 'announced' that another Englishman was in our section. I rushed to Jabba the Hutt's cell thinking either Michael had been transferred from Section Five or another poor bastard had strayed a little too close to the Iraqi border!

At first I thought Christer was a Dutchman. Stereotypes eh! He had sandy-cloured hair, a moustache and was wearing working overalls and clogs. We spoke at length and then he was sent to bed in the 'big room' which by now I'd left for the 'comfort' of 'ghurfat sab-a' ('Cell' 7) in which I slept with 11 other inmates on six bunk-beds!

The Swedes were great lads and convinced they would be in prison for a short time when their government became involved – just like me! A couple of days later they were moved to a single cell in Section Three which they shared. This angered me as I'd been asking for a single cell for weeks and now I was seeing new Western arrivals being given a single cell almost immediately.

I questioned Major Abu Athier, a high-ranking Mukhabarat officer of curiously diminutive stature, who had responsibility for me in Abu Ghraib, "Have I annoyed someone? Who have I offended? Why am I being treated in this dismissive way, is it because I am English?"

He assured me that the changes were nothing to do with me, nor my behaviour, but instead they were due to orders from his superiors. The favourable treatment of other 'Western' hostages upset me and are a lasting memory. In my mind it was definitely down to me being English and coming from a country that drew enmity in this region. It was a bitter pill for an ordinary citizen like me to be treated as the personification of British leaders in a country blown apart by the people I was being being likened to – "You British!"

Prison is a place where even the most gregarious would struggle to keep the pace and quality of conversations going. Inside, your personal horizons reduce and the only source of news is contact with the outside world or the "word of truth" as I sarcastically nicknamed Iraqi news reports. New people coming into the system, as much as you didn't wish prison on anyone, were always a source of news and welcomed and the three Swedes were no exception to this rule and they would become a great comfort and help during the more difficult times I experienced at Abu Ghraib.

Thursday, 1st October.

I wrote to Julie and mentioned an interview she'd given in London for the 'International Guardian', 'Washington Post' and 'Le Monde', newspapers that Gleb Desyatnikov had just brought in. This was the first I'd seen or heard of her since my abduction and it was humbling for me to see the woman that I'd known as a housewife, housekeeper (her former job) and mother, speaking to international media outlets.

Gleb also brought with him 'British Army Compo-Rations' which I also raved about in my letters home. They really helped me to stay fit and well as harsher winter weather was already upon us and food was becoming more expensive. I asked Julie to thank whoever had arranged for them to be sent to the Russian Embassy; I was beyond grateful that someone understood our plight.

I wrote that we were well off with the arrival of the Compo-Rations and that, "Daily life in this country must be very tough, at the moment." I had been told that many ordinary Iraqis were selling off furniture to buy medicine and food. How did they cope in those years of harsh treatment under the dictatorial rule of Sadam Hussein?

In later letters I would also mention that, "The Swedish guys have never had to go without, and are laying into the Compo-Rations in a big way." At the time this upset me mainly due to my fear of having to go without again, but as I think back about it now I am filled with shame as so many people with very little of their own gave me half of everything they possessed. Prison was making me very territorial and greedy about my possessions and space. What little I had of both was everything to me and I would get very distressed if someone encroached on either.

Plenty of prisoners in the foreign section didn't, and never would, receive a visit of any sort. Some of these had been held in Abu Ghraib for years. Come visiting day, it was hard to witness the anguish of these poor sods. No doubt many of them were presumed dead wherever they came from.

In October, an American by the name of Chad Hall was seized by Iraqis in Kuwait near the Iraqi border as he cleared mines. He was released within 48 hours. I'd worked with Chad in Jahra, on the EHRT contract and knew he was ex-military. It made me wonder again why I got it so hard while other prisoners were treated like guests? Once again it hurt and I was offended that we British always seemed to be the last in line – if there was a line. I hoped that the speedy release of Chad signaled a softening of the Iraqis position – more straw clutching!

Sunday, 4th October.

Personal messages from my family arrived via the Red Cross. They were very short but they meant a lot to me. I had always been told "Bukra!" (Tomorrow!) no matter what I asked for since I'd been held in Iraq and my patience was exhausted so these notes were vitally important.

Towards the end of the morning Abu Athier came and said that I was expected to do a TV interview – "If you want to?" There was a question, but I had no choice. I had to do it. He ordered me to shave and,

"Put some smart clothes on." I replied that I didn't have any, all I had was the clothes I was stood up in. I'd actually aquired a change of clothes but given them to Christer. Abu Athier told me to borrow some!

Ranko, a Serb who'd been imprisoned for killing three people in a road accident, loaned me some clothes and nervously I paced my cell like a cat on a hot tin roof until just after 11.00am when I was told to report to Abu Athier's office in the administration building. For the first time since my imprisonment I was wearing clean, Western-style, attire complete with socks – the pair I'd been taken across the border wearing! It felt so good that I almost forgot where I was and what I was doing – almost but not quite! It rankled with me that the holiday camp, as opposed to prison, image I was now portraying was exactly what the Iraqis wanted.

Abu Athier escorted me to a car and informed me that I would be interviewed in the governor's office. Abu Ghraib was a vast complex. Each section had its own perimeter wall and between the sections were huge areas of scrubland which were also surrounded by huge, razor-wire-topped walls. As we set off I wondered why we were driving away from the main prison towards the external gates. Surely the governor's office was in the main section of the prison where I'd first been processed on my arrival. I'd seen a multitude of offices in the 'long section', as the main prison was known, and 'assumed' the governor was based there. As the main gates swung into view and I glimpsed the outside world I felt a surge of hope – perhaps the 'interview' was part of my release!

My hopes of getting out of Abu Ghraib were short-lived. At virtually the same moment I saw the 'outside world' the car lurched to the left and screeched to a halt outside a single-storey building. Abu Athier told me to get out and then escorted me into the building to wait – I spent my entire time in Iraq 'waiting'!

A few minutes later, a couple of men in Western clothes, but with an Arabic 'look', walked into the room. Abu Athier spoke to them and then they came across to me and introduced themselves as the 'crew' who were to interview me, "If you want to?"

There was that 'question' again. Abu Athier brought me here and therefore the Mukhabarat expected me to participate in the interview – I didn't see that 'what I wanted' really had anything to do with it and so I told the film crew that I was "happy" to do the interview and was then led into the governor's office.

Dressed in borrowed clothes and with my hair close-cropped, when I saw the interview later I was struck by my appearance which I felt was similar to that of mercenaries captured in Angola and filmed before their execution. This was a deeply disturbing and odd sensation!

The room was full of Iraqi officers; Prison? Police? Army? I wasn't sure, they all looked the same to me. There were also a lot of men dressed in plain-clothes who Abu Athier spoke to that I suspected were

Mukhabarat, which terrified me. I had already witnessed the brutality of these bastards and the hateful looks they gave me were not encouraging or reassuring.

When the interview started, I was nervous. Not even in the courtroom at Karrada had I felt so exposed or helpless. Whatever I said would be studied. I was terrified of saying something that would upset, offend, or insult the Iraqis. I measured everything I said to Beat Krattli, the Swiss interviewer. I didn't want to appear slow or guarded but as someone answering questions as honestly as possible. The interview was a sham and lasted about 20 minutes but it felt like bloody hours. I couldn't be honest. Held on a trumped-up charge in a country which made up and changed laws to suit itself, anything I said against the Iraqis or Saddam Hussein would have led to my already ridiculous sentence being increased. It would have put me in a vulnerable position liable to the arbitrary beatings many fellow prisoners endured. I suffered most of the indignities that my peers were exposed too, I wasn't brave enough to extend that to assault.

At the interview's conclusion I was led out of the room by Abu Athier and the film crew's chief. I had Beat at my side and I tried to tell him that actually I had lots to say but I feared for my own safety. "There is much more to tell," I said. "This is a very 'serious' country!"

He said he understood, and stated that the Iraqis required, "Some medical supplies." He told me that that Julie was trying to organise this and that I would be on the next plane home once the delivery was made!

I told him that I didn't know what was happening but I hoped it would work and he replied, "We will be doing all we can to help her. We will try to help in any way we can. We will try to get you some glasses and send you in some cigarettes. Okay Paul?"

I nodded and thanked him and asked if he would tell Julie that I was fine but to keep doing what she was doing.

Abu Athier came across to us and escorted me away from Beat towards the car. I climbed in shaking, knowing that in minutes I would be back in Section Three. Beat and the crew stood and watched us drive away. I waved but felt empty, alone and more frightened than ever. When we arrived back at the section I was dismissed by Abu Athier and found out that the Swedish lads had saved some lunch for me. By now It was it was almost 2.00pm and the food was cold but I ate it anyway. My fear and concentration associated with the interview had given way to voracious hunger.

I was asked by my fellow inmates about the interview. I hadn't had time yet to 'review' it myself, so I waffled. We all agreed that being interviewed was better than sitting on my arse and this was confirmed when Abet and Jiri, a Czechoslovakian imprisoned for a motor vehicle accident, said that Ian Richter had been put on TV prior to his release.

I already knew the Iraqis hardly ever did what was expected and predictably the interview was the prelude to nothing. Time passed by especially slowly over the next few days and my mind fogged.

In a letter I wrote to Julie I apologised that I didn't mention her and William by name during the interview and blamed the omission on my state of 'blind terror'. With the possibility of spending Christmas in prison, I asked Julie to arrange what she could in the way of creature comforts to be sent to me – a Christmas Hamper! Looking back I feel guilty and selfish at requesting this from my wife but at the time I wanted anything I could get!

Tuesday, 13th October.

Michael was transferred to Section Three. He brought with him some English newspapers that were a few weeks old. 'The Times' had an article about me which was accompanied by a photo of Julie. I asked Michael why he hadn't shown me this before and he told me that without his glasses he couldn't read the papers and hadn't 'seen' her! Even though it was now six weeks out of date it was nice to see Julie and read what she had to say.

Thursday, 15th October.

I wrote to Julie and the penultimate paragraph of my letter encapsulated the way I was feeling about my life at that present moment in time and how prison affected my mind-set. "As I close, let me just say that I thought this sort of thing only happened in books and films, but now I know that no matter what you think of your life it can get 100% more complicated and less enjoyable. Your worth is not what you have, but who you share your life with. Possibly the most important thing is freedom, without it you can't enjoy the rest."

Tuesday, 20th October.

A package sent by my Mum and daughter Rhian (from my first marriage) arrived with the Russians. It contained a radio which was immediately confiscated. Special permission was required to possess a radio! I saw neither sight nor sound of it again. During my time at Abu Ghraib countless items sent by family, friends and generous strangers were confiscated (stolen). It chipped away at my increasingly fragile patience.

Wednesday, 21st October.

The previous day, Gleb Desyatnikov said he'd brought mail the British Embassy in Jordan had been holding and as I hadn't yet received it I approached Jabba the Hutt and asked if I could have it. When he returned from the administration building he told me that I would get it the following week. The censor was not available and so no mail was being distributed. This was the catalyst to tip me over the edge. I lost control and began kicking cans around the Muster yard, spilling the contents all over other prisoners, shouting abuse at Jabba, the administration building, and other prisoners in the yard. I ranted for at least ten minutes and then went to my cell and abused the prisoners in there too!

There were some Kurds in my cell and they were always trying to get something from Michael and myself. This was really pissing me off and as I'd become even more territorial and needy I took the opportunity to also have a go at them. This went didn't go down well and by the time I'd finished blustering I'd already been 'sent to Coventry'. Nobody spoke to me for days – it was really peaceful in my cell!

As October drew to a close, the Russian Embassy delivered several big packages for Michael and myself. During the 'searching', make that organised thieving, process that prison officials conducted, the contents of these boxes had ended up being mixed and we received personal items destined for each other. Compounding the issue, letters explaining who had sent what from our families were given to us days later after we had both used some items. We got annoyed, blaming each other for the mistake. I tried to give Michael some of the items I'd mistakenly taken and although he grudgingly accepted he subsequently gave them all away.

It had started out well when we'd first met, but the truth was now that Michael and I didn't particularly like each other and after this episode we didn't trust each other either. Stupid I know, but prison provokes possessiveness and territorialism and I got them both badly. To avoid further confusion, I asked Julie to ensure that all items being sent in for me should be marked with my name. As if she didn't have enough to worry about!

I ranted about my treatment compared to the Swedes. They had weekly diplomatic visits and their Embassy was opened specifically for them. They received weekly supplies of food, magazines, papers and books. They had 'contact' with their families within two weeks of their detention. They had fax messages from their families in Kuwait and Sweden. I hated myself but I felt terribly bitter.

My unjust imprisonment was increasingly distressing me; denial of my human rights, the conditions of my detention, the treatment of the Swedes, refusal to pass my mail to me – everything drained me. The minutiae and daily grind of prison life hammered my spirit. I had always resented authority and struggled with it all my life. While imprisoned, I found it hard to bite my lip and not challenge the regime and the guards.

The following year when I was visited by Colin Cooper and Mark Le Goy, British diplomats from Amman, Jordan, I highlighted all these issues when complaining about my situation, but they were powerless to intervene or act. The Iraqis were in total control, the British impotent, and I was later told by Prime Minister John Major's office to take up my unlawful detention through the Iraqi courts – laughable! I was tried by a military court, or so I was told. Why waste my time trying to get justice through a legal system which I knew to be corrupt beyond redemption? Where the might of the British Government failed, I would be bound to succeed?

Once you have been the recipient of Her Majesty's Government's care and concern when held as a 'representative' of your country you start to understand Guy Fawkes' quote, "Desperate diseases require desperate remedies". 400 years later, bugger all has changed!

In late October I was told that Julie intended to visit Baghdad. I hated the idea and it preyed on my mind. This, along with all the other challenges I faced in prison, brought on insomnia. I lay awake every night and then felt awful the following day. Territorial, possessive, greedy, afraid, lonely – rather than admit that I had any emotions I shut them down. Seething hatred that I was unable to stop or direct at anyone or anything ate me alive like a cancer and as I grew more and more desperate it was increasingly difficult to remain rational.

I wrote to Julie and asked her about the planned visit to Iraq I'd heard about. While I was opposed to the idea, I still believed she would come if she thought it was the 'proper' thing to do. I felt hope building in me again and not to miss an opportunity, I suggested she should try and 'organise' an audience with Saddam Hussein! I understood that this would be terrifying, and a long shot, but I thought that if Julie was willing to risk coming to Iraq then going that step further to meet the madman wouldn't be out of the question! This might seem selfish but I would have said and done just about anything asked of me to get out of Iraq.

That evening I saw a programme on Iraqi TV featuring magician Paul Daniels who was a huge celebrity at this time and a prolific, annoyingly so sometimes, star of stage and screen back home. I was astonished! Even in prison in Iraq I couldn't escape him. *That's magic!* You had to laugh! Daniels performed a trick riding in a hot air balloon. There were lots of scenic views of English countryside around the Bath area. I remember getting really upset looking at aerial shots of 'our green and pleasant land'. It's often said that you never know what you've got 'til it's gone. It's true, believe me!

A VISIT FROM MADAM JULIE AND WILLIAM

Sunday, 1st November.

As October turned to November I felt sure that something had to change soon. Today was was a visiting day which meant two things. The regular diplomatic visit was cancelled and my cell filled with Kurds. Each family had three or four women, a couple of grandfatherly figures, a couple of brothers, and dozens of children. I wasn't happy about this latest visit because on the last occasion a Kurdish child had taken (stolen) pictures of Julie and William that a mate's wife had sent me. They didn't have any value to anyone else but me so it was upsetting. As it happened, on a subsequent visit, a Kurdish woman returned most of the pictures and thereafter I gave the Kurdish children sweets and biscuits – as a thank you and also as a bribe to stop the little sods from taking (stealing) anything else!

When the visitors departed, Section Three became a marketplace. Some of the lucky prisoners with food or other items to sell even had their own scales to weigh and price their merchandise!

Gossip was 'pooled' and became the main source of debate for the evening. Many of the stories were about amnesty but with the arrival of the Swedes who had a radio, a select band of us we were privy to lies and rumour directly from the BBC! We were above the hoi polloi!

I borrowed some 'listening time', which the lads were great about, and it was brilliant to once again hear presenters and football commentators I'd listened to for years on the BBC World Service while working overseas.

In a letter I wrote, I mentioned reports that the Swedes would be released soon. I grumbled that they had a vehicle full of cameras, lenses, and other electronic equipment, but asked Julie to wait until they were released before she told this story. I would be devastated if my moaning was intercepted and their release was cancelled.

Friday, 6th November.

Abu Athier called me to his office to collect a huge pile of mail that Gleb Desyatnikov had delivered at the beginning of the month. I felt great. Everyone, especially Julie and William, were that much closer. I was used to being apart from my family, but the last five months, riddled with threats, accusations and danger, had been so tense my nerves were shattered. In a reply I admitted that I felt scared, worried and anxious. I realised that even though it was a relatively short space of time, imprisonment had changed me.

Julie sent a box of my clothes from home and it was beautiful to smell her and my home in the box. The mixture of aromas was very evocative of life outside Abu Ghraib. The home-washed scent of the clothes was fresh and clean, a wonderful contrast to the stench of the prison that filled my nostrils every waking moment.

Abu Athier told me that Julie and my parents were trying to obtain visas to visit me. I didn't want my family exposed to the dangers of Iraq, however it would be lovely to see them. If five months felt long, seven years seemed like an eternity.

Monday, 9th November.

In the morning I sent a message via the Red Cross to Julie and William telling them that I loved them and then I was called to Abu Athier's office.

As usual he was solicitous about my health and conditions in my cell. I took his questions with a pinch of salt. Nothing ever changed. He then asked if Julie was in Baghdad? I struggled with the question. Thoughts went through my mind. *How would I know if Julie is in Baghdad, I've been in Abu Ghraib since the 27th of August. I don't have a clue where she is. Stupid bugger!* I said nothing, it was for the best.

Abu Athier persisted. "Mr Paul, is your wife coming to Baghdad to visit you?"

"I really don't know. There were reports, which you told me, that she and my parents would be coming but I thought that was cancelled."

After telling me that Julie and my parents would be coming Abu Athier had said that 'visa problems' were holding them up. Then I'd heard that the visit was not happening due to American attacks on Iraqi radar stations! I had no idea what was going on but the man in front of me thought differently.

"You see, a friend of mine was in the Al Rasheed hotel last night," he continued. "He thinks he saw your wife. Is she in Baghdad?"

"I really don't know. I was told nothing at Gleb's last visit."

"If your wife is in Baghdad, would you like to see her?"

"Of course I want to see her. If it is her, yes, of course!"

"Okay then! I will make enquiries of my friend and try to see if it is her."

"Thank you very much. What hotel is it again?"

"The Al Rasheed Hotel. Return to your cell, I will see what information I can find out."

I left with my head swimming and felt terrible for the rest of the day. I couldn't relax and felt sick and tense. Every time a name was called by a guard I ran to see if it was me they wanted. My conversations with everyone around me were nonsensical and of course, as per usual, nothing happened. I was distraught, stressed and edgy, and that evening the Swedes and I concluded that it was a case of mistaken identity. They'd been told that a female reporter was in Baghdad to interview them, it was probably her in the hotel! I was exhausted. Once again the Iraqis had taken me on an emotional roller coaster ride. Once again, when it all came to nothing, I struggled with hope, anticipation, worry and fear. I believed the Iraqis were taunting me.

Tuesday, 10th November.

For the second morning in succession I was instructed to report to Abu Athier's office. I was filled with suspicion not expectation. I shambled along there and Abu Athier advised me to smarten up as I was getting a visit. I asked from whom, and he said, "Madam Julie is here now with William!"

I thought this was all a bit too much and replied, "What? Here now?"

He assured me they were here and insisted that I should put 'proper clothes' on. I was in my daily prison attire which wasn't exactly presentable. I was readying myself to dash out of his office when with as much tact as he could he said, "Wait, these are yours I think."

He rummaged around in a drawer in his desk and under piles of other documents he found a pile of letters which he handed to me. I took them and ran back to Section Three. I dove at my bed space and began tearing at my clothes in my haste to get out and see Julie and William.

I examined the mail. I was stunned. He had handed back every piece of mail I had given to him since my transfer to Abu Ghraib including several to Julie, one to John Major, another to Ken Bates, (Chelsea Football Club's Chairman) and more besides. The bastard hadn't even given them to the censor let alone Gleb Desyatnikov. This should have angered me but I was so excited at the prospect of seeing Julie and William that I wrote the incident off and resplendent in my smarter change of clothing I rushed back to Abu Athier's office.

He told me to sit down and left the office returning a couple of minutes later with William whose hand he was holding! My emotions were overpowering and confusing. I felt deep joy and relief at seeing my son again after eight months and at the same time I was fearful in case he didn't recognise me, or wouldn't come to me. My fear was combined with a surge of loathing for the other Iraqis now present as they gathered around, trying to get William's attention.

Julie had kept William well aware of who I was and after a couple of seconds hesitation he came to me for a hug and a cuddle. What a wonderful feeling! All the fear and hatred of the previous months disappeared as I held my son. People say that we are alike – 'two peas in a pod' – and at that moment I felt as close to him as I have ever felt to anyone.

We were then led to the visiting room. To get to this room it was necessary to pass through the administration building. I took William by the hand and he walked with me through the twisting corridors – and then I saw Julie. I wanted to dash into her arms but knew it would be wrong to abandon my son after the traumas of the past months, so we kept walking together until we met and Julie leapt into my arms as William stood by our side. After a long embrace we pulled apart and I could see worry etched on her face tempered with the relief of the moment.

Julie's bags were taken and searched. A camera and cassette recorder given to her by the same Swiss film crew I'd met were confiscated. Ghassan, acting as interpreter while slyly watching everything that was going on, assured us that her bags would be returned quickly. I was seething. It was a stupid and selfish error by the Swiss crew to give Julie a camera and recording equipment to take into the prison. They had put my family at risk for the sake of a story!

Julie's bags were eventually returned and after excessive goodbyes from Ghassan and the collection of Iraqi officials present we were left alone to enjoy time together and to catch up. There were so many things I wanted to ask that my mind became a blur. We talked about how Julie was coping and how tough things had been. Due to my imprisonment, the associated media intrusion had been very unreasonable. Hacks were relentless in their quest for angles on the story which Julie was finding difficult to deal with. Bearing this in mind, I looked around the room we were in and the thought occurred to me that it might be bugged so I suggested we write notes to each other instead of talk.

I wrote, "I am sure that should the UK provide a consignment of humanitarian aid, (milk, food, medical supplies) that my release would be very swift. The people of this country (Iraq) are the ones really suffering."

And, "A quote from me would be. As John Lennon said, 'War is over give peace a chance' or is the West going to pursue Iraq 'til all inside it are dead? As castles were laid under siege in the dark ages or until another country (Iran) at present buying arms in the 'sale of the century', the break-up of the USSR, is seen as to be a greater threat."

And, "Did you get the letters telling you of the dates and where I'd been held etc?"

And, "Did the Swedish Embassy send you the faxes?"

And, "Just for your information. When I was in the Mukhabarat complex in solitary confinement, blindfolded and interrogated by the secret police I was asked if I would go back to Kuwait and 'do a mission' for them, if they supplied the weapons, to kill the Emir or any of his close family? I said I wasn't militarily trained and so I knew nothing about weapons or killing and was not about to become a terrorist. At the end of the session they said, 'we were only joking to lighten the mood and cheer you up!'"

While Julie wrote down her replies and questions I would play with William and run around the room with him and speak with him. This went on for a couple of hours, little boys have an enormous supply of energy, and it wasn't until he had a mid-afternoon nap that Julie and I were able to 'talk' one-to-one in hushed tones.

I told Julie more about the Mukhabarat and the verbal threats they'd made against her and William during my solitary confinement, and threats that should I go to the newspapers or TV this would, "be on my conscience", and would "lead to repercussions". Julie said that on her return she would inform the Foreign Office in London.

I asked her how long she was staying in Iraq and she said she was travelling with the Swiss film crew. Their plan had been to interview us together but the Iraqis had refused. She said that they would try to film us together tomorrow but if that failed they would be leaving Iraq soon.

Abu Athier then entered the room and in an obsequious and fawning manner, dialled-up whenever I had visitors, he said that Julie's time was up and that we should say our goodbyes. Julie said she hoped to see me the following day with or without the film crew.

Abu Athier took us to his office and Julie was given the camera and cassette recorder back. She asked if the film crew could take photos of us. He said no, so she asked him to take some and he took a family snap with Julie on my right and William in my left arm and then some more general ones – none of which I ever got to see.

We kissed and hugged and said our "see you tomorrow" farewells and then we were parted. I went back to Section Three and spent the rest of the evening with a stupid smirk on my face thinking that my ordeal would be over very soon as Julie had been extremely positive about the possibilities for my release.

She had brought large quantities of foods, medicines, toiletries, clothes and other items I'd asked for or thought I'd need. How she managed to travel with William and all his paraphernalia, her own bags and the supplies for me, I don't know. It was all very welcome though and made life a lot more comfortable for me.

Later I spoke to the Swedes and Filipino lads. They were delighted for me and I am sure they were relieved as my newly lifted morale had been disintegrating for weeks. I realised how lucky I was to have my family visit, the Filipinos in particular were never as fortunate.

That night I went to sleep knowing my family were close and well. Finally, at last, my worries about them were over!

THE TROUBLE WITH JERJES

I felt optimistic as I woke and after I'd visited 'hell' and Mustered I joined all the souls pacing up and down, as they did every morning, and every step I took seemed like a step closer to release. I hated joining in 'rituals' or 'custodial fetishes', but unable to stop myself I twitched and jerked in the prison dance. I was buoyed by twin hopes that later in the day I would see my family again and that Julie was right when she'd said I wouldn't spend much longer in prison.

I took my place on the 'treadmill of perennial being', a prisoner's lot, and returned to answer my mail with renewed vigour, writing letters back thanking people for their support. I have to admit that you can only say "thank you", and "I'm bearing up" so many times before the words mock their use and the necessity of writing them.

I also regularly spoke with the Maraheb in a bid to have contact with Abu Athier and an update on whether or not Julie and William would be coming to visit again, but was told that he wasn't available. As the hours passed, I realised that I was slipping back into the doldrums. It was incredibly frustrating.

Thursday, 12th November.

During the damp, dark days of winter I was devoid of energy and started going two or three days between showers. Hot water was provided between November and March from a single outlet in 'hell', but at this stage I hadn't found out who had the key and was still showering with cold water. I was miserable enough, cold showers in these temperatures really were the last straw, hence why on some days I didn't bother and apathy became the order of many days. Today was one of them.

To cheer myself up, as morning turned to afternoon, as I was still without an update on my family's whereabouts, I decided to write to Julie. It was a poor attempt to correspond with a woman doing her best to cope with a situation that was so far removed from her previous experiences. I thanked her for the supplies saying, "Someone up there likes me." I now had winter clothes, training shoes, and a coat. Luxury!

Julie had brought a selection of photos of William, and with pride and love I decorated my bedspace with the images. I had compliments paid to me about my son saying what a smasher he was, and what a nice temperament he had. I was very proud of him, he was growing into a great little boy and Julie was doing an excellent job of raising him on her own. I felt pride and comfort hearing the comments.

When we'd met, among the snippets of information Julie had imparted was some news she'd heard that the Russian's were trying to get Michael Wainwright hospitalised and his sentence commuted due to ill health. I had previously discussed this with the Swedes and we all thought that although Michael's behaviour was was 'odd' at times, he didn't deserve a stay in an Iraqi mental hospital. I decided to tell Michael what I'd heard so he could stop a very dangerous and, in my opinion, stupid decision being made.

Michael could be quite volatile, so I chose what I thought would be a tranquil moment after dinner to tell him what I'd heard. He went crazy and demanded to know why Julie and I were talking about him, barely mentioning the inference about his mental health! He accused me and the Swedes of trying to make him look foolish and laughing at him behind his back which was sad because nothing was further from the truth. We discussed the situation and thought that the idea of hospitisation was ridiculous, sinister, and unnecessary. I told him this but doubted whether he heard or believed me. He said that he would, "Take it up with the Russians on the 20th!" I thought, *Well, that's international diplomacy fucked!*

Concerned, I wrote a letter to the British Embassy in Amman, Jordan, informing them of the 'plan' for Michael and requested they sort it out. I also described his outburst when he'd been told about 'the idea'.

When Michael met Gleb Desyatnikov on the 20th he was furious. Gleb told him that Khalid Jerjes, an Iraqi consultant lawyer appointed to work on the cases of a number of foreign nationals held at Abu Ghraib including the Swedes, Michael and myself, had 'devised' the scheme. From the outset, I struggled with Jerjes and would end up perceiving him as a clown. He never gave me a straight answer when I asked questions or sought clarification about my situation and I got little satisfaction from him or the Foreign Office, which I came to dub 'the ministry for the retention of the status quo'.

Gleb's explanation didn't placate Michael who became increasingly difficult to have a conversation with after this episode. It also became apparent that the Russians, the Mukhabarat, the Abu Ghraib authorities, and Jerjes were 'blaming' each other and I was the 'piggy in the middle'.

Several days later, with the help of the Swedes, I sent a message to Julie by fax via the Swedish Embassy asking if she and William had arrived home safety. When I'd asked Abu Athier about them he told me he didn't know where they were. I was frantic with worry.

Monday, 16th November.

Khalid Jerjes came to the prison and I was called into Abu Athier's office. After the usual pleasantries were exchanged, I cut to the chase and asked Jerjes, "Can you give me confirmation that Julie and William have reached the UK safely?"

"You realise that there is a problem here?" he replied.

"What do you mean a problem?"

"Madam Julie was travelling with a film crew, yes?"

"Yes, as far as I know."

"This is the problem!"

"Why is that a problem," I asked, a shiver of panic coursing through my body. Jerjes' reply took my lungs and tied them in a knot. I couldn't breathe at all.

"The film crew had journalist visas. This does not allow them to enter the prison."

"So what does that have to do with Julie?"

Jerjes' reply was a hammer blow to heart. "Madam Julie was also travelling on a journalist visa. She was not allowed into the prison!"

My mind swam and as it did so I felt myself drowning as I tried to work out the permutations. "Where are they now? I asked trembling with fear for my family. "Where are my wife and son?"

I had already seen children in Iraqi jails and I felt physically sick at the thought of my family being put in conditions like those I was held in. *What are these bastards up to now*? I thought repeatedly as I was gripped by giddiness.

Jerjes paused and looked at Abu Athier before replying, "We don't know where they are now. Haven't the Russian Embassy told you where they are?"

"How could they," I replied quickly. "I haven't had a visit since they left here!"

I was sure Jerjes was taunting me when he replied, "This is very serious. To come to visit jail without the correct visa she could be put in prison, just like you, for seven years!"

My head started spinning and I felt bile rising in my throat as I stammered, "W-W-Why? S-S She is not guilty of a crime. Where is she?"

Smirking, Jerjes replied, "Really, I do not know, but I will find out!"

I then slipped into the grip of the psychological 'Stockholm Syndrome' phenomenon and throwing myself on the 'mercy' of my 'torturer', I replied in a pitiful voice, "Could you, please? Can you tell the Russians – so that I find out on the 20th please?"

"Okay. I will try to find out," replied Jerjes. "But the only reason that Madam Julie was let in to see you is because of the kindness of Major Abu Athier. You must thank him?"

In my anguish I now had to give thanks to Abu Athier! A man inflated beyond his pint-sized persona by the Iraqi regime! I hated giving thanks to a tool of the system that held me hostage and toyed with my emotions. I was none the wiser about my family. Were they at home or being held in prison by these despicable clowns? The demons were taking control of my head. I wanted to choke the life out of Jerjes. Now that would be worth doing time for! With as much conviction as I could summon, I said thank you to Abu Athier. As I looked at him I was enveloped by an all-consuming hatred for the bastards torturing me simply because they could!

I struggled with thoughts that terrified me and when I returned to Section Three I poured my heart out to the Swedes. Every thought I had was a nightmare scenario. I was so close to the problem, I was the problem. If I wasn't in prison, my family would not have been exposed to the lunacy of Iraq. I badly needed alternatives and reassurance.

Astounded that Julie could be imprisoned over an incorrect visa, the Swedes were marvellously supportive offering positive outcomes which were as likely as my negative fears but buoyed my mood which was exactly what I needed.

Over the next couple of days I wrote to Julie asking her to distance herself from Michael's case. I'd reached the stage in my thought process about our situations where I considered it best if I wasn't linked with him at all. If I distanced myself from him then he might recognise that I was not attempting to make a fool of him and understand we were being told lies by most of the sources we had.

I sought out Abu Athier and told him I wanted to be seen separately from Michael. He had entered Iraq voluntarily from Turkey, I had been abducted from Kuwait. We were thought of and spoken about as the "Two British" by everyone and I wanted to put a stop to that.

I'd been told to expect 'people' from the Foreign Office. They were due, I was told, on the 19th, but the visit never materialised and another aching day of fear, worry, and concern about my family passed slowly.

Friday, 20th November.

As planned, Gleb Desyatnikov came to see me. My priority was to establish the whereabouts of my family. "Gleb, have you heard where Julie is? Jerjes said you know where she is?"

Gleb hesitated before replying, "Well yes, the Foreign Office in London asked us to locate Madam Julie, and we conducted a search of every hotel in Baghdad!"

The fact that the Foreign Office thought it necessary to request a search troubled me. "So where is she now?" I asked.

"We searched every hotel. We failed, we could not locate her and we are trying to confirm from London her safety but have heard nothing yet."

This was madness! I was in prison for seven years for getting 'too close' to the Iraqi border. My wife had been brave enough to visit Iraq and now she and my son could be in prison. I was speechless! The rest of the meeting with Gleb was a blur, I hardly heard what was being said. I was devastated by what I'd just been told.

I shared my renewed concerns with the Swedish lads and they were able to help me send a fax to the Foreign Office asking for confirmation that my family was safe. I was grateful that they had visited, but was more worried now than before they came.

Sunday, 29th November.

Finally, I received confirmation that my family was safely back in London. The relief was enormous. For almost three weeks I'd been driving myself insane with worry. I had not been able to stop myself from dissecting every vacuous, vague, and noncommittal comment Jerjes and Abu Athier had made.

Monday, 30th November.

I wrote a letter to Julie which started, "I found out yesterday that you are home safely with William. It's a big relief. You can't imagine the type of things that were going through my mind, as a spell in isolation makes you paranoid."
    The reality is that I was never physically beaten, never tortured, and for this I am thankful. My mind however never stopped expecting negative outcomes while I was a hostage. It became my enemy. My health suffered, I lost my ability to be intuitive and any input became garbled, distorted, or felt like lies. Every conversation was dissected as I searched for hidden meanings. This hostage developed a bellyful of bile and a head full of twisted thoughts. I had enough time in prison to drive myself insane with distorted conclusions.
    I admitted to Julie, and myself, that it was looking doubtful that I'd be released for Christmas. Of course I still hoped that I might be allowed home and I tried to be as constructive and positive as possible but in truth I was falling apart at the thought of being in Abu Ghraib for the festive season.

GOODWILL TO ALL MEN, AND A TIN OF LUNCHEON MEAT!

Tuesday, 1st December.

Muster took place at 7.30am and then at 8.00am we were hauled outside for Remembrance Day, Iraqi style. It was a wild and bitterly cold morning and I gazed at the frost gleaming on the floor of the yard as we stood in silence for a minute. I prayed, not for the souls of the dead, rather that I didn't swell their numbers in the coming months and years!

Later in the morning, Abu Athier called Michael and I to a meeting with two emissaries from the Foreign Office, Craig Shelton and Heather Taggart. Heather was a quietly spoken middle-aged woman. Dressed in a woollen two-piece skirt suit, she wore sturdy, 'sensible' shoes, and was, I thought, the epitome of a country schoolteacher. Craig was missing the 'swagger stick' that would have made him the image of a retired British Army officer. To complement this he wore a heavy tweed jacket with leather patches on the elbows, crisply pressed trousers, heavy woollen socks and a pair of highly polished brogues. He had a clipped English accent and, in the diplomat-style I had now become accustomed to, issued forth vast amounts of verbiage while actually saying nothing!

I enquired about Julie and was angered to hear that she'd spoken to Heather the day after seeing me. "No one could confirm her safety," I stated but as I spoke I understood that the information I received was on a 'need to know' basis and that Foreign Office obviously considered it best that I didn't 'need to know' of my family's safety for three weeks!

We were then 'gifted' some "home comforts", as Heather termed them which included pots, pans, and various kitchen equipment, spoons, ladles, a chopping board and a knife for cutting and chopping! This was very welcome as the supplies we had been receiving were still being stolen and and I raised this with Craig and Heather who said that they would mention it in a forthcoming meeting they had scheduled with the Iraqi Foreign Ministry. We were also given some dog-eared English newspapers which were out of date on account of the fact our visitors had been made to wait two weeks in Amman for visas to enter Iraq! I was grateful. *Prisoners can't be choosers!* I thought to myself.

Craig then gave us an old calling card he'd used while he was stationed in Rangoon. Michael pointed at the address and with a look of incredulity asked him, "So like if ah wants to write to thee, I should send it 'ere?"

There was an element of humour about this which made me smile. Craig replied saying that all correspondence should be addressed to the

Foreign Office in London. The rest of the visit was small talk. "The Government are doing all they can within the current political climate."

This filled me with hope which I suspect was what Craig and Heather were aiming for. If you cannot give anything tangible, give hope!

Abu Athier insisted on showing the pair our accommodation displaying the "immaculate and luxurious" conditions we were held in! It was obvious to me that the clean-up that usually took place ahead of Red Cross visits had been performed. 'Trade' had been suspended, the floor scrubbed and disinfected and sleeping bodies ushered off the floor.

Heather walked around paying avid attention as Abu Athier pointed out the 'finer points' of the section. The toilet block, freshly scoured of course! The wonderful open-plan windows which allowed mosquitoes and flies in during summer and bitter wind and rain during the winter! The cells, with half the residents not being allowed to occupy their spaces!

The pride that Abu Athier had for this shithouse bemused me. Craig nodded approvingly while Heather gasped in awe! "Isn't it lovely and clean!" she said as she walked out of the section. "Things are very nice here!"

I was stunned. The truth was that Section Three was a quagmire of filth. Diplomacy obviously required the denial of reality! We then went to a room exhibiting the various trinkets made in the prison. As Heather remarked on the "beautiful things on display" Craig asked me a question that beggared belief. "What are you getting for Christmas then?"

I shook my head in dismay. "I don't want anything." I replied, continuing, "But the Swedes are getting the hell out of here for their Christmas present!"

"I don't know if that is the case," said Craig. "Their government has acceded to the demands of the Iraqis, but we feel it may still take them quite a while to get out of here."

"Well at least they've got some hope!" I countered, feeling my hackles rise.

"Don't allow yourself to become annoyed by the lack of activity," replied Craig in a patronising tone of voice. "We are trying, but the Swedes were not in the coalition during the Gulf War. They are neutral, it's much easier for them here at the moment. Be patient!"

"I'll try," I said, with a huge sigh. "But Christmas in here is not an inviting prospect."

Craig then made a statement that will be a part of me until I die. "With Christmas coming, is someone sending you some plum pudding?"

"As the Foreign Office is sending in my food I rather hoped you would!" I replied.

Michael and I had thanked them for the visit and for the information and supplies, and as I was walking back to Section Three I re-ran large sections of the meeting we'd had over in my mind. Craig's comment about the plum pudding caused me to stop in my tracks. I thought it a crass thing to say to a man facing seven years in prison!

When I got back into the section I went straight to the Swedish cell and told them what Craig had said about the plum pudding. Stefan looked at me and said, "That sounds like a request for dental work."

"What do you mean by that?" I enquired innocently, naively, honestly!

"I would have smacked him in the mouth so hard he would need to get dentures!" replied Stefan.

At this point we all fell about laughing. My anger dissipated as the Swedes, who'd met the Foreign Office duo on their 'tour' of the section, did impressions of Craig and Heather.

Saturday, 5th December.

The Swedes had lent me their radio and I tuned into the BBC World Service and listened to second-half commentary of a Premier League game. Tottenham Hotspur 1 Chelsea 2. Two late goals by Eddie Newton were good enough to see off Spurs. I could hear visiting Blues fans singing, "Chelsea, Chelsea, Chelsea" to the tune of 'Amazing Grace' and I smiled contently. A shred of normality in an unreal world.

Monday, 14th December.

As Christmas approached, the days seemed to be moving slower than previously. I wrote to Julie. "I really miss you. This is getting tougher instead of easier. I know you're trying your best and exploring every angle but I feel as if I am dying from the inside. My heart is slowly losing the will to go on. This place is more than I can stand, and half of it is the boredom. Day-after-day of the same routine, the same stupid regime, the silly roll-calls (that I really hate!) the lock up at 5.00pm, the constant cold, the waiting is driving me out of my mind."

I'm sure that Julie must have been fed up with my whinging and whining. During this difficult time for me I began to suffer with rashes and stomach disorders, and my irritability and insomnia worsened.

A couple of days later I wrote in another letter that the Swedish lads had been due a visit but it never happened and their disappointment had given me a horrible sense of joy. "This is going to sound terrible, but it is just an expression of my personal frustration with no real malice intended. Today the Swedish guys were due a visit, as they have been getting every week since they were imprisoned, but their Embassy didn't show up, and it gave me a strange feeling of 'satisfaction'. It left me feeling as if they had got their just reward, as by comparison, my time in prison for the same 'crime' has been a whole lot tougher. They are given everything they want at the drop of a hat. I must be honest, sometimes I've felt a little bit ashamed to be English, but, as Heather and Craig told me a couple of weeks ago, we are in a different political situation. 'Some men are more equal than others', springs to mind."

I believe the phenomenon is known as 'schadenfreude' in German. The experience of pleasure, joy, or self-satisfaction that comes from learning of the misfortune of others. It was probably fueled by the fact that Khalid Jerjes kept saying, "We will deal with the first case, and then with you!" The Swedes would be released before Michael and I. I highlighted that we were the first cases and had been imprisoned before the Swedes, which predictably Jerjes ignored.

I tried to warn Julie about being 'used' by film crews saying that if she found herself in trouble they wouldn't mind, it would just be another story for them to sell. I was starting to hate and mistrust everyone and everything.

On her visit, Julie told me an Iraqi businessman called Syed Uddin was negotiating for my release and that she'd been in touch and given him some items for me including thermal underwear which I needed as the temperature was decreasing rapidly. I had to make do without the thermals because Uddin never turned up. Julie had given him numerous things to pass to me. I received nothing!

In December 1992, Saddam Hussein banned the import of foreign goods. This inflated the price of goods already in Iraq enormously. Prices soared. Cigarettes became a sought after currency as good as money. Saddam had only just made the decree but its effects had been immediate. I wrote to Julie asking her to advise Heather Taggart of this development, requesting that the Russians brought us a good supply of food because there was no flour, rice, sugar, chickens and only a few vegetables available in the prison shop. The only meat we were able to buy was a Belgian minced beef which had offal in it and tasted awful.

In the week leading up to Christmas, a glut of mail arrived which lifted my spirits. Among the letters from family, friends and well wishers were cards from Chelsea supporters. This was a huge boost to my morale and I gleefully read about the team's performances and what was happening on the terraces at Stamford Bridge and beyond.

I am a poor example of an Englishman. I detest the cold and wet, and snow is the end of the world for me! When it rained, Abu Ghraib was dire. Shutters were put up to stop water coming through open window frames. Some were made of cloth and sacking, others, as in my cell were fashioned from steel. These were shoved into place as the rain began rendering the cell a dark, oppressive, humid, airless hole. At night, the shutters kept the biting winds and sub-zero temperatures out. When morning came, I would pull the rusty steel plates out of the window frames allowing the 'fresher' air in from outside.

I decorated my bed space with the Christmas card cards I received including one from the Chief Executive's Office at Walthamstow Town Hall. It was a nice to know I was being thought of in the area I lived at home.

Friday, 18th December.

A visiting day for the families and friends of prisoners. I wrote a letter to Julie. "I'm spending the day on my bed to ensure that more of my pictures don't end up in Kurdistan!"

Julie had sent out a pair of prescription glasses in November but they'd arrived broken and attempted repairs in Baghdad had made them unusable so I asked her to send another pair. I was certain Julie was sick of my continual requests but I was like an unborn foetus at the end of an umbilical cord. I was helpless, and if I didn't ask, and Julie didn't supply it, I didn't have, and with the dwindling food supplies in Iraq, and squinting without my prescription glasses, my situation scared me.

I'd noticed during her visit that Julie was still taking the pill for birth control. With a thousand and one things going on I wrote asking, "Something has been puzzling me. You got out of your bag a packet of contraceptive pills, why are you still taking the pill with me being away for eight months?" Then I piously added. "You know that continued use of the pill is not good for your health!" My _only_ concern was for her health! There was not a hint of suspicion in my mind. Forgive me. Negatives were always my initial thoughts.

Sunday, 20th December.

We'd been without water of any sort, bathing, cooking, washing, for 24 hours which was miserable and with this my hope for the miracle of liberty before Christmas Day had evaporated. Obviously it wasn't going to happen and I sank into a deep depression. I'm not a Christmas person. I like it as a holiday, but it has no spiritual significance for me. The thought of spending Christmas, and New Year in this filthy hole was something I didn't want to contemplate anymore. I thought I'd been 'brave' with a British stiff upper lip pretence in the letters that I wrote, but in reality I was petrified of extended captivity.

Water was restored at 9.00am and I was able to take a cold shower. I knew it was cold, as the water was turning to steam as it evaporated with my body heat – which was minimal to say the least! Dressing in a frenzy of shivering and chattering of teeth, I then dove into the Swedish lads' room as they'd been supplied with a heater!

Along with Michael, I was summoned to a meeting with Gleb Desyatnikov. He arrived and I gave him a huge pile of letters I'd written to be sent out. On many occasions I sent over 100 letters at each visit! We greeted him cheerfully and were depressed by his news. There was no news! Nothing! There had been no talks about us at all and to make matters worse, Gleb had brought with him a trifling amount of supplies and no mail. The Russian Embassy driver was on the road back from Amman but would not arrive in time to visit the prison.

I went down, like a deep-sea diver complete with lead weights, and sank into a morass of self-pity and hatred. Over the next couple of days I stopped eating with the Swedes, preparing myself the most frugal and unappetising meals. Sometimes I wouldn't bother to cook, instead I ate the diabolical Iraqi ration bread spread with margarine, jam or cheese from the Compo-Rations that were still to be had.

I sulked alone, not allowing myself to be drawn out of my depression by contact with other prisoners. The Swedish lads would come to my cell inviting me to eat with them but I refused pointblank, wallowing instead in my pool of misery.

I don't recall if I wrote any letters during this period, but if I did, they must have made dire reading. I sometimes wrote mail in a foul mood but usually had the good sense to destroy the rubbish I had written and start again, and I am thankful to everyone who provided me with blank paper to write on.

Wednesday, 23rd December.

Despondent, I taunted the soldiers manning the sentry towers around the 'sports field'. As I walked, it was too slippery to run, I drew circles on my chest, with a cross indicating my heart, inviting the sentries to shoot me. They never even picked up their weapons. I was warned by other prisoners about the danger I was exposing myself to. They didn't realise that I would sooner have died than spend years in prison, especially this prison.

I sat on the floor during Muster and an Iraqi officer asked me what my problem was? I requested with sign language that he put a bullet in my head. He would have none of this and sent me back into Section Three ahead of the other prisoners. For him, my state of mind was caused by the Muster rather than by my existence! This act ensured that the Swedish lads came round to see me. The other prisoners in my cell totally ignored me saying I was 'no good' and had a 'problem in my head' – and who was I to argue?

Thursday, 24th December.

A totally unexpected Christmas miracle happened. Gleb Desyatnikov made a special visit to the prison and delivered food, mail, and home comforts! Thinking back, the change this inspired in me was unbelievable. Momentarily, my state of mind improved radically. It really was bizarre but reinforced my notion that I was in a foetal condition.

The packages Michael and I received were nearly identical apart from personal items our families had sent. The 'Christmas hampers' contained an individual Christmas pudding, a 2.5kg tin of pork luncheon meat, some biscuits, and a box of eight miniature crackers!

Michael asked me what I wanted to do with the crackers and I 'generously' informed him, "Michael, I am not a cracker person, they will not go far between us, you are welcome to them!" To me it felt like a travesty to have a celebration, of any kind, in these surroundings.

Christmas Day.

There were no concessions made by prison officials. We woke, we Mustered – in the freezing cold. I spent most of the day with the Filipino lads who were full of stories of how Ian Richter had always been like Santa Claus to them, providing a virtual banquet meal on Christmas day. I had little to share around of a festive nature and in truth Michael made more of a gesture to the other prisoners than I did. He prepared a meal with all his 2.5kgs of pork luncheon meat, and cauliflower, in a huge casserole. He shared his meal with two Thai lads and five Romanians. At least he managed the spirit of Christmas. They all sat around in a circle in Cell 4 and pulled the crackers, each of them ending up with a paper hat on their heads. It looked a little bizarre to say the least!

I spent the evening with the Swedes which was an experience. Their families had arrived in Baghdad on Christmas Eve and they'd come to visit them on Christmas morning bringing traditional Swedish food for them to eat which the lads kindly shared with me. It was as unusual as it was delicious. I ate Rudolf! I had no idea that in Scandinavia they eat Reindeer! "How d'ya want ya reindeer? Fried or boiled?" I laughed. It was in fact smoked and tasted superb. Sorry, and all that, but when in Rome – or a Swedish cell in an Iraqi prison!

We watched a Christmas service on Iraqi TV. I didn't understand a word. It was conducted, I was informed, in Assyrian, one of the oldest known languages on earth. I thought it 'liberal' of Saddam Hussein to allow Christian festivals to be shown on Iraqi TV and then learned that there were over two million Christians living in the country! I supposed that even Saddam realised he couldn't afford to upset everyone!

HAPPY NEW YEAR! WELCOME TO 1993!

Friday, 1st January, 1993.

"Hi hon, Happy New Year! – this one has got to be better than 1992, for all sorts of reasons!" I'd written in a letter to Julie. Once again I hoped that a miracle would happen soon and I had mixed feelings when the Swedish Red Cross donated 62 tonnes of medical supplies to Iraq. It was a significant development for my friends Christer, Leif and Stefan, and the indications were that they would be released imminently. Nothing I'd been told so far suggested to me that the British Government would ever sanction such a deal. As far as I knew there was no dialogue at all going on between Baghdad and London.

Michael informed me that his sister, a lady called Susan Priestley, was going to stay with Julie and that they would come out to Iraq with a Sky TV crew. This worried me after the Beat Krattli episode with Julie in November so I wrote to her seeking clarification and asked her to be careful if the story was true. I was torn between wanting to see Julie and her safety. Safety won and I wrote her another letter telling her she should remain at home, safe, and never come to Iraq again.

Julie had sent me another radio in December but I had yet to receive it. It underlined for me once again how we Brits were treated and regarded in a vastly different manner to the Swedes, and it hurt. As a conseqence, many of the other prisoners were now totally ignoring Michael and me as they knew that the Swedes were much more likely to be able to help them. This reduced our status within the hierarchy of Abu Ghraib and we became the butt of some annoying comments by Arabic prisoners such as, "Your government forgets you, but the Swedish Government are very good for their people." And "Britain 0 Sweden 10." And "Little Britain, Great Sweden." My self-respect suffered as a result!

My Christmas mail had been opened and what was given to me were the remains after the Iraqis had filled their boots – and bags! Many kind people sent things in the mail, unfortunately nothing ever reached me. People asked about gifts I'd never seen and I felt 'guilty' having to apologise for the loss! I wrote and asked Julie to advise people about this and request that if they were sending things to do so via the Embassy in Amman rather than directly to the prison. At least that way they might have a chance of getting delivered.

I repeatedly asked Abu Athier where these missing items had gone and received in return expressions of contempt and sycophantic comments that really didn't help at all. I hated the thought of things posted to me ending up in Baghdad and eventually I would request that nothing be sent to me.

Saturday, 2nd January.

I was genuinely astonished and overjoyed to be given the radio Julie sent. This meant freedom! With this radio I could 'escape' the confines of the prison, with news and, even more importantly for me, music. I also realised, it was Saturday! I'd be able to listen to the football. In Abu Ghraib my radio was to be an absolute godsend.

Catering has its own trade magazines and a few weeks before Christmas I'd been contacted by the editor of a magazine called 'Catering Update' offering help and support for myself and Julie. I wrote back and accepted his kind offer and he used the letter I sent him in an article about my situation. This was another example of the kindness I received from total strangers while in prison.

I carefully 'measured' the use of the clothes Julie had brought out to me in November. This might sound ridiculous but I wanted to retain the wonderful 'home-washed' smell of the clothes for as long as possible. Everytime I opened the bag of T-shirts and jeans not only did the cockroaches in the bag dive for shelter but I was also given a chance to enjoy the rush of smells so evocative of Julie, William, and my home. Little pleasures which meant a lot as I didn't have many.

Over the next few days, news bulletins I heard on my radio informed me about increasing tensions between the United States-led coalition and Iraq. American, British and French aircraft patrolling the skies had been 'radar-locked', (a preliminary to attack) by Iraqi anti-aircraft missiles. In several cases the Iraqi hardware had been destroyed. The forces of the coalition finally realised that Saddam Hussein was taunting them with 'expendable' soldiers and logistics to ensure that to Arabic eyes they were seen as the aggressors. Both sides were posturing and I sensed that 'Gulf War Two' was about to begin. I wondered what that would mean for my chances of liberty. I sat and waited.

Michael and I had been told that when the Swedes went we would get their cell. I wanted them to go as it meant that I would not have to share a confined space designed for six people with 12 prisoners and Michael. The families of the Swedes had been due to leave mid-week but their departure was delayed by atrocious weather. The daily visits continued but given the scenario developing on the war front their release was looking less likely and they cursed John Major and outgoing US President George Bush frequently. I think they realised that while neutral, Sweden was still part of a much bigger picture.

When their families eventually left without them, deep depression set in for Leif and Stefan. Christer didn't seem to suffer as badly as the rest of us from mood swings. He had a dour countenance but a good attitude which while fatalistic, was totally realistic.

Julie wrote to me saying she intended to return to Iraq and she was campaigning to show that she sympathised with the plight of the country's population. Her intention was to change Saddam Hussein's attitude, a nice idea but she didn't stand a chance as hostilities continued. To her credit, she kept trying.

A Thai prisoner called Ong requested assistance from Julie. He was serving an eight-year sentence for a theft he denied taking part in and had got into enormous debt to the 'Egyptian Mafia' in the prison who were putting him under pressure to settle his arrears. He asked if Julie could bring him $1000 on her next visit! Passing money between prisoners was frowned upon, and I didn't want Julie, or myself, put on the spot. I learned later that this had been arranged through a link with Ong's sister in the United States and Jiri Foitek, a former Abu Ghraib prisoner who was married to a Thai himself. Leif's wife, also a Thai, had been warned off getting involved.

I wrote to Julie and told her that if she accepted the cash, she was to be careful bringing it into Iraq and not to change it on the black market as this was very dangerous. She should bring the dollars to Abu Ghraib and pass them to me if she had the chance. If not, then she could take them home with her again. She was to tell no one about the cash and not to give it to any third-party as Iraq was full of liars, thieves, cheats, and spies. I begged her not to take risks to get the cash to me, and then I waited and hoped.

Sunday, 10th January.

A huge batch of mail arrived. There were almost 250 letters, cards, and magazines posted from people all over the world. I had mail from America, Thailand, Botswana and Australia as well as places closer to home. It was staggering. My spirit soared, people cared! Ken Bates, owner of Chelsea Football Club, had asked supporters to write to me and flood the Iraqi mail system in support of my situation!

I will never know how much mail was sent to Iraq, but remember the comfort I drew from the contents of the envelopes received. I wrote and thanked everyone who put a return address on their letters but realise that not every person kind enough to support me will have received a reply and to them I would like to take this opportunity to say a public and grateful thank you!

Sunday, 17th January.

A cruise missile strike targeting the Zafraniyah Nuclear Fabrication Facility near Baghdad, relatively close to Abu Ghraib, was launched by the American 'Kitty Hawk' Battlegroup, and I subseqently learned that in the wake of this my family had requested information about my health and safety from the Foreign Office.

Wednesday, 20th January.

A report reached 'someone' that I was sick and when Gleb Desyatnikov arrived at the prison on his bi-monthly visit he was full of concern for my health. I told him the only thing I was sick of was Abu Ghraib! I had the strangest feeling that I was supposed to act as if I was having a good time and enjoying life in prison! Gleb took some photos of Michael and I to prove to the Foreign Office and our families that we were alive and well after the air strike.

Gleb was accompanied by the Russian Ambassador to Iraq and his aide and as usual the prison officials and Iraqi authorities made a complete pigs ear of the visit. Michael and I were told that Major Abu Athier was not at the prison and we would meet in another office.

Normally this would have been all right, but today, because the Russian delegation was three in number, Michael and I had to squeeze together on a scruffy sofa while Gleb perched on the edge of a bed – there was a bed in every Iraqi office. The Ambassador sat in a battered armchair and his aide hovered at his shoulder. The Iraqi officer who 'hosted' us in the room, I recognised as one of the prison's most sadistic bastards. I was in genuine fear of what he might do next, knowing he was unbalanced.

The visit was a total disaster, Gleb continually deferred to the Ambassador who knew even less about us than he did. Michael used comments made by the Ambassador to ask some very strange questions which prompted the Iraqi officer who spoke excellent English to continually give us all withering, suspicious glances. I was uncomfortable for the entire meeting and hugely relieved when it was over.

Later, back in the cell, the talk was mainly about the cruise missile strikes we'd heard about on the radio and concern about our vulnerability to stray missiles increased when the anti-aircraft gun batteries placed along the prison perimeter sprang into life! The noise was awful. Many in Section Three feared it would take a direct hit!

The Swedes and I knew that the missiles were unmanned, other prisoners in our section did not and they flashed the lights on and off in a frantic attempt at 'Morse Code'. We shouted at them that the missiles were automatic and to leave the lights on and were greeted with near-hysterical screams in Arabic that the guards had then ordered them to switch off the lights and so we sat there bathed in romantic candle light, in the middle of a 'missile attack', all four of us roaring with laughter!

The 'spy network' was on 'high alert'. They visited the Swedes and myself pumping us for information about the missile attack – as if we were party to coalition decisions, the bloody idiots! The Swedes were very open to the approach of the spies as they had befriended many of them in some way or another, virtually adopting them as 'pets'.

I'd seen this happen many times in the course of my work abroad with expats, especially Americans, who ended up treating Filipinos,

Thais, Egyptians, Indians and Sri Lankans as adopted children. Although at face value this was simply an attempt to be kind and friendly, I found it shallow and patronising. Each to their own.

It seemed to me that the prison had more 'spies' than an Ian Fleming novel. One of the youngest, Reziq, used my stove to cook on, so I asked him to move and I was greeted with a smile that spoke volumes. "I don't understand!" being the core statement. I really lost it, and shoved him away. I couldn't stand the near universal command of the English language when garnering information set against the total non-comprehension when requests or instructions were being given. It really wound me up.

On a far more personal level things took a turn for the worse in late January when my ex-wife, Delyth, wrote complaining about an article published in a woman's magazine in which Julie had supposedly made a statement which had upset my daughter Rhian. I wrote back and said that it was probably just a case of bad journalism. The article put my relationship with Julie overlapping my marriage to Delyth, and Rhian's birth. This was not true, but articles in magazines and newspapers and programmes on TV have extraordinary powers of persuasion and the hurt this causes is very real and deep for all those involved.

Delyth's letter would have been more welcome had it contained a question or comments such as "How are you?" or "Sorry you're in prison", however it was from beginning to end a list of complaints. I asked Julie to 'consider' her statements a bit more carefully, but in truth, what could she or I do if the media got it wrong. I mused that there were, *Lies, damned Lies, and newspaper columns,* and remember thinking, *I'm 4000 klicks from home in a foreign jail getting hassle about things I have no control or influence over.* This added, a smidgeon, to my increasing paranoia.

Most of the mail I was now receiving had comments praising the hard work and effort Julie was putting into her campaign for my release, advising me that I should be very proud of her – which I was, and I wrote back to every legible address provided confirming this.

Julie had generated such marvellous public support and I was extremely grateful for all her efforts. I'd been expecting another visit from her but I was still being contrary in letters I wrote. In one I would plead for a visit, in another I would use the missile strikes as a reason to stay away and then I would write 'shopping lists' hoping that it might lead to a visit or at least some more mail.

Wednesday, 27th January

An infestation of fleas and lice hit our section and to combat this some of the cleaner inmates insisted that the less hygiene conscious should immediately shower and reacquaint themselves with soap and water and jollied along those reluctant to comply. What followed was like a scene from a cheap comedy with screams of panic as the 'unclean' were dragged towards the showers. Those who refused to remove their filthy clothes were 'washed' wearing them. Those who refused to wash at all were forcibly soaped from head to foot. The prisoners with infestation problems had their heads and bodies shaved. It was a sad and sorry sight to behold.

The cells were emptied completely and scrubbed. Bed clothes were shaken, beaten, and hung outside in the cold, crisp winter air in the mistaken belief that this would eradicate the lice and fleas! Within a week, every cell in the section had been scoured though predictably it neither exterminated the offending parasites or improved the smell and appearance of the section!

Saturday, 31st January.

The Swedes got new diplomats, two were transferred from Islamabad in Pakistan and one from Helsingfors in Finland. They said this was because the initial low-level diplomats trying to expedite their release were being ignored. Their thinking was that higher-ranking diplomats would demand greater respect from the Iraqis. I pondered how this would play out.

I was also starting to think that the radio which I had been given was cursed. Since it arrived Chelsea had not won a game. They'd lost three Premier League matches and drawn one and been knocked out of both the FA and League Cups. I wondered if they were sliding towards relegation. I'd been here before were during the 1970s and 80s when The Blues had been up and down like Tower Bridge. The Swedish lads thought it hilarious every time they heard BBC World Service 'Sportsworld' presenter Paddy Feeny announce that Chelsea had been thrashed again.

I read a letter from Julie in which she commented that William was having tantrums when a film crew or camera appeared and that he was getting difficult to talk to when in company. I replied expressing concern. He was very young, a little under two at that time, and I wrote that I hoped that all this nonsense would be over before he realised that something was amiss. This worried me because he was always such a happy child and I became increasingly concerned that this episode would leave him with long-term psychological scars.

I had injured my knee in early December and hadn't exercised for over a month, but on the last day of January I went out on the sodden earth and started training again. It was wonderful to be able to get out of the stale cell block and into some fresh air and once more I found running to be a release, my only real release, from the tension bubbling away inside me.

A Lebanese prisoner in Section One called Noufal, who had previously been pointed out to me as being a spy when I'd been seen chatting to him, approached me suggesting that I run with him. When we'd spoken before we'd had conversations about food, films, and books, not danger areas. I'd thought he was okay despite the "he's a spy" allegations.

As we jogged and talked, the conversation started to embrace political topics and I began to feel uncomfortable. This went on for a couple of laps and then I really lost the plot and started to rant about the injustices I was suffering due to the Iraqis in the name of international politics. I stated that I considered myself to have been abducted from the DMZ (De-Militarised Zone) in northern Kuwait simply for being too close to the border and nothing more.

Noufal asked me, "So what do the British Government say to you about the position at the moment?"

"Not a great deal actually," I replied. "It appears that I'm just an embarrassment!"

"They must say something to you," continued Noufal. "I hear the Iraqis want the sanctions lifted and then you will be released?"

This vexed me. "Listen! So far I have heard that the Iraqis wanted the sanctions lifted, then they wanted them changed, now they are asking for huge quantities of medicines. I don't know what they bloody well want!"

Noufal smiled. "Well at least they are negotiating, this will be over soon I think! At least there are some exchanges. You should be grateful for this."

This vexed me even more. "Grateful! Are you fucking joking! These mad bastards have treated me like a spy. I've been interrogated and threatened while dressed in pyjamas and blindfolded. I slept on a concrete floor for over two months and I've been kept in conditions in which people in the UK wouldn't keep a dog, and you say I should be grateful. You're out of your fucking mind!"

"But what they do to you is no different from how they treat their own people," replied Noufal, unfazed by my anger. "These are cruel people, be grateful that you are still alive and healthy, no?"

Increasingly enraged, I'd had enough of Noufal's posturing. "I come from a civilised country where the type of shit I've been put through simply doesn't happen to ordinary people," I said, glaring at him and breathing heavily as we ran. "I will get out of here and then tell the world what mad bastards the Iraqis are. Just because they do shit like this to their own people is not a good enough reason for me to be grateful, I hate these bastards and will not forgive them for what they've put me through. This might be something which Arabs put up with, but these evil bastards are wrong and I won't forget! Now go and tell that to Major fucking Abu Athier if you want to."

Having concluded my outburst, I stormed off and hurried back to Section Three to await the consequences of Noufal 'the spy' grassing me up to Abu Athier. I felt pertrified as I contemplated what the Mukhabarat might do to me but also strangely euphoric that I had got some of my anger off my chest. I now understood why informers are despised. The actions of these low lives destabilise an entire prison. A difficult yet bearable existence with solidarity is twisted into a hell of intrigue and deceit with prisoners who should be helping each other dragging each other down in a desperate struggle to ascend the filthy heap.

I would like to make a point here that when I'm expressing my thoughts, talking, or indeed shouting, about the Iraqis, the hatred I express is linked to my captors, the majority of the guards, the system, the regime and the Ba'ath Party and not the ordinary people of Iraq.

YOU WILL PAY FOR EVERYTHING!

Sunday, 1st February.

In February the British Government ordered a 'media blackout' about my case, only health reports were released to the media. I didn't understand the need for this, the Iraqis were not about to let anyone see me. We 'heard' that Whitehall wanted to control information given to the media, to censor it so it showed the government in the best possible light!

Rumours hinted that Iraq was going to let five foreign hostages free at the same time, the three Swedes, a Filipino called Nicanor and myself. *I'll believe it when it happens,* I thought to myself. I also heard that the stupid plan, cooked up by Khalid Jerjes, about putting Michael in a mental hospital was in fact only half correct, the stupid sod had wanted to put both of us into a secure facility and get us both 'dismissed' as mentally ill! I was getting there!

I was called to Abu Athier's office where he and Jerjes ordered me to write a letter to Julie asking for her assistance in persuading the British Government to agree to partially release some of the monies seized by British banks for the purchase of food and medical supplies. The letter was short and sycophantic and I wrote it as I was aware that it would be monitored by the Iraqi authorities. This coincided with a request from Iraqi Deputy Prime Minister Tariq Aziz that the British Government act in a humanitarian fashion. I knew I was being 'worked' like a glove puppet and it sickened me.

I also asked Julie to send me out some 'dental fixer' as I had a false tooth and it had fallen out. It's possible my poor diet had caused my gums to shrink, that and metaphorically banging my head on prison walls meant I was finding it difficult to keep the bloody thing in my head and with no end in sight to my prison horror I wanted to prepare myself for some DIY dental surgery!

The same day I received a batch of mail and when I started reading the letters I realised the references were three months old as were the posting dates! I asked Gleb Desyatnikov about this on his next visit and he told me that the bundle had been given to an ITN reporter who tried to get in to see me, and when he'd failed he'd kept the letters until he remembered having them at which point he'd passed them to the Russians! Here we had another media clown purely focused on getting a 'story' about the hostage rather than the welfare of the hostage.

A lady who wrote to me regularly called Trina said that Julie had appeared on TV and when asked if she thought the British Government was doing enough to secure my release, William, who was sat next to her, shouted out, "No!" I thought to myself, *That's my boy!* What's that expression? *Out of the mouths of babes!*

Saturday, 6th February.

The morning was almost over when Michael and I were summoned to Abu Athier's office where he told us that our families were here and indicated that we should follow him to the visiting room!

Through the door I glimpsed Julie and some other people, among them two women. The only person I recognised was my wife. We embraced and it was obvious that she felt self-conscious showing emotion in front of the group. William was playing behind a settee and came out when he heard my voice. We had a nice cuddle and I was relieved he showed no reluctance to come to me as it had been three months since his first visit.

One of the men in the group introduced himself as Michael Whitlam, Director of the British Red Cross. Accompanied by an aide who was also acting as a translator, he was asking for clemency for us on humanitarian grounds. He was also here to examine the problems the UN embargo was creating for the Iraqis in respect of food, health, medical facilities, and medicines. He said he hoped to be able to build bridges between the British and Iraqi Governments and would be doing all he could to secure our release. He also told us that although he was channeling all his efforts into our case he didn't want us setting our sights on release that week. I found his candour invigorating, after eight months of being told that nothing could be done his comments were a breath of fresh air.

The two women in the group turned out to be Michael Wainwright's sister, Susan Priestley, and his mother, Iris Wainwright. After the Red Cross personnel departed for another meeting, Michael introduced them and we exchanged pleasantries and small talk. They were warm and friendly and for an hour or so we discussed the situation and the long-term implications of our imprisonment.

The atmosphere was strained at times, but the day passed off without any real problems. Michael did make a comment about William having a little tantrum. He was only 23-months-old and, not wanting to miss a thing, had become overtired. I thought Michael's attitude was a bit abrupt considering everything our families, especially my son, had been through in the past eight months and so I was delighted when Iris and Susan jumped to William's defence saying he was behaving extraordinarily well for a little boy of less than two who had endured the unsettling turmoil of a long journey. I felt vindicated at being vexed about the incident and Michael, who knew he was being told he was out of order, didn't say another word about William.

Julie brought me up to date on events as far as she was able to and Iris and Susan did the same with Michael. Our conversations would cross many times as the three women constantly sought clarification from each other about dates, locations and people.

Julie brought with her an enormous quantity of food, clothes, and other items all crammed into a huge kitbag. She said that this was only half of the items she had as she'd decided that as the visit was split across several days she would bring some in on each day rather than risk having a larger amount stolen. Given what had happened with supplies that had been brought in by the Russians, this was a sensible strategy.

Time evaporated, hardly had we said our greetings, before Michael Whitlam returned from his meeting to pick our family members up to return to their hotel for the night. There was no curfew in Baghdad but the Iraqis were not keen on foreign nationals doing very much in the way of travel after dark and in February darkness had already arrived by 5.00pm.

We said our farewells and, laden with supplies, staggered towards Abu Athier's office for the customary 'search' of anything coming into the prison. Julie had put an electronic handheld game in the kitbag which caused concern as Abu Athier inspected it. Ghassan was in attendance sniffing around in his usual ferret-like manner and I explained it was nothing more than a toy to pass the time!

That evening the Swedish lads and I swapped stories that our families and the Red Cross representative had told us. Things were looking really good now for the Swedes and I couldn't wait to see the back of them as I long since realised that until they were released I stood absolutely no chance of getting out of Abu Ghraib!

In the latest batch of mail I'd received was letter in a Foreign Office envelope. While my family was here I'd decided I would not spend time engaged in correspondence but curiosity got the better of me. I opened the envelope and in it was an undated letter from Heather Taggart, the Foreign Office diplomat who'd visited Michael and I at the beginning of December.

"Dear Paul,

It was so nice to meet you and Michael when Craig Shelton and I visited you in Abu Ghraib prison in December. As soon as I arrived back in the UK, I had long telephone calls with Julie and with Michael's family to let them know of our visit to you.

I know Allison Marriott has passed a message to you about the rations we are sending you, and I thought I would write to reinforce this. As you know, things are not easy for Julie financially and it is difficult for her to find funds to send you.

I am mainly concerned about the Compo-Rations our Embassy in Amman have been sending you and Michael. I appreciate that it must be difficult to cook up meals and not to share them with your fellow prisoners, however, our supply of rations is not inexhaustible and when they run out, I regret that we would not have funds to supplement prison fare. The financial burden will then fall on your families. So it is in your interests to use the supplies sparingly and, if possible, for you and Michael only.

My other concern is that you and Michael are running up bills with Khalid Jerjes which eventually you or your family will have to pay. We have suggested that if you have requests, you should ask Jerjes to inform the Russians, so they can keep an eye on expenditure.

I hope this doesn't sound like a lecture. It isn't meant to be. But I am concerned that your families here may be faced with bills that they will find very hard to meet.

I have spoken to Julie who sends her love. We usually speak almost every day and keep in close touch.

Rest assured that we shall continue to do everything possible to secure your release.

Best wishes

Heather Taggart."

I found it hard to comprehend a system that would send such a letter to a man being held by a foreign government as a hostage and a lever to extort resolutions to international political situations.

I was a novice at dealing with the Government and its agencies and its 'cavalier' attitude to British subjects held overseas in the international game of politics. The Foreign Office is not an institution designed, as the vast majority of British people think, to aid British subjects in difficult circumstances overseas. We are, if anything, 'flies in the ointment' and a bloody nuisance if and when we 'get into difficulty' overseas. In my opinion, the role of the Foreign Office is to maintain the 'status quo', where Britain is seen as a benevolent past ruler or a likely trade partner in the future.

It was a terrifying letter to receive eight months into a seven-year sentence. I had visions of my family ending up destitute and on the streets and myself resembling a concentration camp victim as some of the unfortunate prisoners with no outside help did.

Sunday, 7th February.

Burdened by this latest worry I hadn't slept well and as soon as possible after Muster I had a chat with the Swedes and explained that while I really enjoyed eating with them in future I was going to have to be more frugal in the use of the food I had and would eat on my own to avoid any future embarrassment. This was difficult, not only did they prepare a lot of the food, we had other people involved as well. The Filipino lads ate with us regularly and there was a social aspect to meals that I would miss too.

My Unilateral Declaration of Independence was an unwilling one, but the Swedes were very understanding and sympathised with me expressing their utter contempt for a government that would issue such letters (Michael Wainwright also received a similar letter from Heather Taggart) to men in detention for political reasons.

Later in the morning, Julie and William arrived with Iris and Susan and we enjoyed a second day together. Michael Whitlam and his aide did not attend as they had gone to meet Iraqi ministers to discuss the situation and hopefully our release.

That night I wrote to John Major asking for help. I asked as an innocent man trapped in a political argument for human compassion for Michael, myself, and the Iraqi people. Major did write back but his reply was political rhetoric.

Monday, 8th February.

In the company of Julie and William, again our chatter was mainly family-related and I played with William a lot. He was an active little bloke and I found myself exhausted at the end of the day.

Michael Whitlam arrived in the late morning informing us that he had been unsuccessful negotiating our release and that he and our families would have to leave shortly. The news wasn't a disappointment to me as I knew that until the British Government were 'willing' to play the Iraqi 'game' the outcome of any 'friendly' negotiations would be negative!

If Michael was surprised, he didn't show it and we were told that our families last visit would be a brief affair on the 11th of February, a flying visit before they were driven from Baghdad to the Jordanian border.

Thursday, 11th February.

The 'dreaded' departure day arrived all too quickly and after prolonged goodbyes we were allowed to accompany our families to the main gates of the foreign section and wave them off.

I was always euphoric after each daily visit from Julie and William and I'd been comforted by news about my family and the outside world but once they'd departed for home I was rapidly drawn back to earth by my situation and then a terrible depression would ensnare me.

That night I sat on my bedspace with the curtains drawn, trying to immerse myself in pleasant memories of the visit. I thought about what a lovely little boy William was growing up to be, and then a tear coursed down my face as I realised that it might be many months before I would be able to spend time with him again as a father should. My heart broke. I had vowed not to cry in prison but thoughts of young son whom I loved and missed so much brought me to my knees.

YOU SELFISH BASTARD!

I dangled like a puppet with the Iraqis jerking my strings. I hated my existence. I was living like an animal and began to despise myself for ending up in this ridiculous situation. Every day I questioned my luck and my role in this farce and concluded I was a fool!

Following the visit of Julie and William I felt vulnerable and weak. One evening while I was eating my evening meal, I heard the song 'You'll Never Walk Alone' by Gerry and the Pacemakers being played on my radio. It nearly had me in floods of tears. In Abu Ghraib I was never alone, but the truth was that I'd never felt more alone in my entire life.

I recall Michael Whitlam saying that he believed the situation would remain locked until the British Government changed their attitude towards Iraq, and I said to the Swedes, "Christ! I'm not too happy about being held here until the British Government change their attitude. Some countries have been waiting hundreds of years for that!" As you can tell, optimism was not a commodity I was overburdened with!

I wrote to Julie and asked her to contact BBC World Service broadcaster Paddy Feeny with a request that he mention her during his 'Sportsworld' show so that I could be sure that they had got home safely. I didn't want another agonising wait until I knew they were secure at home. She did and Paddy obliged. It gave me peace of mind knowing that my family were safe and it was also nice to hear my name mentioned in the same sentence as my team Chelsea! Julie had explained to Paddy that I was a supporter of the mighty Blues!

My release remained an unseen dot on the horizon and spending longer in Abu Ghraib was becoming more probable with every passing day. My employers, Taylors International, were still paying half my monthly salary but I knew that this was not enough for Julie to survive on. *How is she going to make ends meet? Will I have a home to go back to at the end of my detention? What will the future hold for me?* My head swam. I was scared by the possibilities

Nicanor, the Filipino prisoner who had previously been rumoured to be up for release soon along with myself, Michael and the Swedes was in a real state. When the Iraqis abducted him from northern Kuwait he had been driving a low loader carrying an earth mover leased to EHRT (Environmental Health Research and Testing) the mine clearance contractors. His employer, a Kuwaiti, insisted he was responsible for the loss. Financially, it was a bill that would leave him in penury and life-long debt.

The Swedes and I were aghast at the heartlessness of his employer and I asked Julie to forward Nicanor's details and situation to the proper authorities. I hoped that knowing someone was working to negotiate on his behalf would ease his fears.

Monday, 15th February.

I started to exercise properly again to keep fit and burn off the anger and apathy I felt. During my depression that followed the departure of Julie and William I'd found that the less I did, the less I wanted to do. I'd become intolerant and once again had been unleashing my anger at more and more of my fellow inmates. I had become 'isolated' by the financial threats in the letter I'd received from Heather Taggart and sitting in my cell with a swirling mist of hatred in my head was driving me insane.

Thursday, 18th February.

Two CIS (Commonwealth of Independent States) citizens arrived at Abu Ghraib. The CIS was formed following the dissolution of the Soviet Union in 1991 and the prison grapevine was reporting that they were Russians. I hoped that they might make a difference to the Russian efforts in negotiations for the release of Michael and myself.

As it transpired, the two men were not Russians but Georgians, and following the dissolution of the Soviet Union, the new 'Independent States' were now responsible for their citizens welfare overseas. This was a shock to the two men as they were expecting the Russians to represent them. The Russians did however start bringing them supplies as they had kindly agreed to do for us.

Listening to the news on the radio, I heard about a Liverpool supporter, Tony Bland, who had been critically injured in the Hillsborough disaster in April 1989. I'd attended games during the 1970s and 1980s and knew that this disaster could have happened to any team in the country due to poor standards of crowd control. He'd suffered severe brain damage that left him in a persistent vegetative state and was being kept alive by machines. His parents had applied for a court order to win the right to switch them off and allow Tony to die with dignity and I wrote to them via his hospital offering words of support. I understood their suffering would have been almost unbearable and my heart went out to them. I heard that my letter was later published as part of an article about the case in a national newspaper. (Tony Bland's life support machine was switched off on the 22nd of February 1993, and he died on the 3rd of March.)

The lads I'd worked with in Saudi Arabia organised a collection to help Julie through this difficult time. It was really very nice of them as I'd left there over two-and-a-half-years previously. I wrote to them and thanked them for their kindness and generosity. Similar collections happened throughout my imprisonment and I was amazed by the generosity of individuals who came from all walks of life and lived all over the world. It was impossible to thank everyone for this at the time and I would like to take this opportunity in print to do so now.

Alone with my thoughts I contemplated prison life and concluded that nobody 'benefitted' from a prison sentence. Prisons are cages, cages transform things. Take whales, if held in Aquaria they suffer from skin complaints, mental and dietary disorders, and it is no different for human beings – cages and prisons are contrary to thousands of years of human development.

A man's soul dies if it is locked up. People suffer when caged, animal instincts take over and the beasts inside everyone come to the surface. This is not to say that prison should not exist, but I believe that far more money should be spent on treatment, re-education, and life skills classes that will give a colossal percentage of the prison population an opportunity to address core issues that prevent many of them from becoming functioning members of society.

I'd been running away from situations I didn't like all my life but I couldn't run away from prison. If a job felt wrong, I would quit. If a location was not to my liking, I would move on. Now stuck in an environment I detested, I had no way out. I was helpless, this compounded my frustration. This could be why I ended up loathing zoos. I find the 'detention' aspect of them abhorrent.

I was sick to death of being 'nice and polite' and started to tell people that I wrote to the truth about my imprisonment. I ranted about the Government and the class-ridden society that controls the UK. My letters must have appeared to be the ravings of some political guru as I espoused opinions on every conceivable topic.

By way of an example, in one letter I wrote, "I think the best way to consider myself is, Cannon Fodder, as in another century I wouldn't have even received a mention in the media as millions of British people were used to fight, subjugate, and control far-off lands. If a few hundred thousand of them died, it was just too bad, the British elite don't give a 'monkeys cuss' about the ordinary man, we are still the most class, and worth, conscious country in the world – in a classless society – bullshit!

I feel sure the attitude of the Foreign Office, Government and the ruling class in society upon hearing of my situation said something like this. 'Oh the silly little bastard, but just sit back and wait, we don't want to rock the boat, otherwise we will not receive any contracts in the aftermath of all this Gulf War business and that won't be good for exports, or share dividends!' You don't think so, then why wouldn't Maggie Thatcher enforce sanctions upon South Africa?"

Saturday, 20th February.

Gleb Desyatnikov arrived with the rest of the supplies brought by our families earlier that month. It was a brief visit as nothing of any merit had been achieved on the diplomatic front in months. What was there to say?

Nothing!

Julie had told me that my supplies were in plastic shopping bags, easily identifiable from Michael's. This wasn't the case as everything that Gleb brought with him was packed in identical plastic bags. My first thought was, selfishly, *It's all for me then.* We took the supplies to be 'searched', watched more personal items being stolen by the Iraqis and, with the thieving over, carried the bags back to Section Three and our cell.

Michael started emptying the shopping bags and throwing the contents onto his bed. I was offended, Julie had said that the produce in the plastic bags was mine, so I explained this to Michael. He stared at me with a blank 1000-yard glare showing little comprehension. Eventually he replied that Susan had told him exactly the same thing. Fuck! There we were, both believing that all the supplies were our own, and resenting the implication that they were not.

My solution to this problem was to walk away from it. In my usual non-assertive style I told Michael he should, "Go through the bags and decide what you think Susan would have bought for you, then put the remainder on my bunk, Okay?"

Michael agreed to this with an obviously unhappy grunt and off I went to try to get the feelings of 'being robbed' out of my head. When I returned to our cell, I gazed at the, in my opinion, desultory little pile of groceries which Michael had decided belonged to me. Remembering the large quantity of food which had been in the bags, I lost my head, and shouted at Michael, "OI! IS THIS WHAT YOU DON'T WANT YOU SELFISH BASTARD?"

Michael then said that the food was available if I wanted it, to which I replied, "I don't want the leftovers, I want what my wife bought and paid for."

Beside myself with rage, frustrated at 'my lot', namely eight months of unwarranted, unjustifiable and animalistic captivity, my overload switch tripped and I screamed at Michael, "I WILL FIND OUT WHAT JULIE SENT ME, AND IF YOU'VE HAD IT I WILL DO YOU!"

Michael asked me to repeat what I'd just said to him which I did and then came the only occasion in our entire time 'together' that we nearly fought.

"DON'T FUCKING TALK TO ME LIKE THAT!" he shrieked at me. Leaping in my direction, he swung a clubbing left hand towards my head. I pulled out of range and the shot thudded into my right arm. Michael then followed up with a straight right which just touched my chest and a telegraphed left which barely landed on my right shoulder. At this stage the confrontation some of the other prisoners attracted the attention of Jabba the Hutt who with the help of a vast crowd came between us and propelled us in opposite directions.

Later, I wrote to Julie, "If Michael and I don't get out of here soon, one of us will be in for murder – and the other in a box. 60 million people in the UK and I'm stuck with Michael. God really hates me!"

Most prisoners in Abu Ghraib were Muslim and in a frenzy because it was Ramadan. This added to my abhorrence of the place. In this world each of us have enough to worry about without imposing our will or beliefs on other people and for this reason I didn't care if Muslims, fasting from dawn to sunset, wanted to sit up eating and chattering all night. However, in the close confines of a 16-man cell the resultant disturbance and associated lack of sleep nearly drove me out of what little was left of my mind.

News of the drama involving Michael and myself reached Abu Athier who told us that a repetition of the incident would see us separated with our 'privileges' removed. Punishment would also include being placed in solitary confinement. If the Iraqis thought being separated from Michael, Ramadan, or the prison regime would be a punishment they were far wide of the mark. All I wanted was to be alone – very alone!

News that I was no longer eating with the Swedes or contributing to the less fortunate prisoners' meagre food supplies swept through the prison. I was offered food by other inmates who'd heard that the 'British Government' had dictated that Julie was now responsible for me financially including my food!

I thought it ironic that a man from Britain should be offered charity from people considered to come from the 'Third World'. In a letter to Julie I wrote, "Don't worry, I am now considered a welfare case, people keep giving me food. All I want to do is get on alone, but everyone keeps giving me bits of rice pudding, vegetables, sweets, savouries etc, only last night I was invited for a Thai meal. Everyone thinks that being British means you're a charity case. The countries that these guys come from have all been asking for handouts, while their thieves, murderers, rapists, smugglers, and terrorists, know the truth about being an 'ordinary' British national. It's a total irony!"

Friday, 26th February.

I was called to Abu Athier's office and hurried there by my escort. No one kept the miniature major waiting, he inspired a level of terror in the prisoners that brought home the brutal nature and power of Saddam's regime. My fellow inmates realised that they were alive because of his 'benevolence' and they all understood that they could 'disappear' with just a word from Abu Athier.

He invited me into his office, bade me to sit down and after his customary small talk he said, "I have a video sent by your family. Would you like to see it?"

"I'd love to, yes!" I replied enthusiastically.

In a sad but concerned voice, without a hint of irony, he said, "The problem is that we don't have a video player in this section!"

The way he had said "this section" had me thinking he was going to say that a video player was available in another part of the prison which we could use and with this in mind I said, "Is there somewhere else we could go to watch it?"

I had learned that I was 'expected' to enquire if things were 'possible or available'. This game of 'cat and mouse' was performed to allow Abu Athier to 'offer' to arrange things.

His answer summed up the Iraqi regime's mentality. "No, there is nowhere at all. Videos are not permitted in the prison but you can have the video cassette if you want it!"

What he expected me to do with a VHS cassette I don't know. I told him to return the cassette. This farcical episode was typical of the mentality of the Iraqi officialdom I encountered. Seemingly full of generosity but brimming with boundless stupidity!

Sunday, 28th February.

I noted down the way I was feeling. "What I do here has no bearing on reality, I died on the 28th of June, 1992, and this is what Aborigines call 'Dream Time'. None of this is real, and I feel as if I'm a victim of someone else's crime!"

My writing became 'challenging'. I think the paragraph I used to sign off my latest letter to Julie summed it up. "Look after yourself and don't do too much. Tell the Foreign Office that I personally don't want another visit – I want out. I don't think I could be as reserved and patient through another visit which ends in platitudes that mean very little. I'm stuck here, no one else. Don't insult my intelligence with niceties about Abu Ghraib – it stinks."

With the fear growing once more that I had become a statistic, forgotten, brushed over, time marched on and February became March.

OI! BIRTHDAY BOY

I was angry; no that didn't fully describe how I felt, I was furious about the supplies that had gone missing. Thinking about the situation years later, I realise the letter from the Foreign Office was the reason for my fury. The prospect of being presented with a bill for the 'cost' of my unjust imprisonment was anathema to me. I wrote home denouncing them for my ongoing detention and the personal implications I'd been threatened with. I was frightened, confused, and annoyed that due to an international political situation I was being held as a British representative by the Iraqis but being treated like a vagrant by the Foreign Office and British Government. I was stupid, unlucky, and careless to be taken and held to hostage by the Iraqis; but if stupid, careless, and unlucky are all it takes, then I suggested that anyone in public office would have made, and will make, similar mistakes.

Gleb Desyatnikov had taken photographs to show that we were alive and well after the missile attack however the British media reported that Khalid Jerjes was the photographer. I tried to dispel this myth. We only saw him when he came to see the Swedes. Gleb was taking the photos when Jerjes happened to walk through the door and did a spot of photobombing. It was a cheap piece of self-promotion. I had developed a deep mistrust and dislike of Jerjes and was convinced he was working closely with the Mukhabarat, and 'fools' at the Foreign Office were giving him information about me which he used to put me in dangerous positions and destroy Julie's peace of mind.

I wrote a letter home about this very subject saying, "He (Jerjes) hasn't come to see us since well before Christmas. He is doing nothing for our cases and is only working for the Swedish guys. You could inform Heather at the Foreign Office that Jerjes shouldn't get paid for visiting us as he is being paid for visiting the Swedes, okay? He only sees us for four or five minutes. He is not coming to visit us, we just happen to be at the same site. On the day the pictures were taken he was luckily in the prison, to see the Swedes – and jumped into the pictures – okay?"

Saturday, 6th March.

A general visiting day. After the visitors left, the usual 'market' to sell the items they had brought in began and in the evening the monthly debt collection occurred. Prisoners living on 'credit' had money brought in to pay off the debts 'accrued' since the previous visit. In each section people provided services; tailoring, shoe repairs, laundry, ironing, etc. The system worked on a price per function, or a price per item, and so each man using these services would owe monies to three or four different people. Janitors, usually the dirtiest, deranged, or cunning of the prisoners, were 'paid' from the collection of one Dinar from every man in the section. The duty Maraheb visited each prisoner to collect, not easy when some prisoners had been there for more than ten years with no visits. These men had little chance of getting cash together to pay out twice in five weeks as visit days fell on Fridays and Saturdays alternatively on two-or-three-week periods. The cauldron boiled over every visit day about infinitesimal amounts of money, but to men trying to survive in Abu Ghraib the tiny amounts were of monumental importance. Demands, denials and accusations rang around the section as desperate men argued long into the night. In the tense and fraught setting of prison, this 'ritual' was something I dreaded, and I think in some ways feared, given the screaming and noise that occurred.

Due to my environment and on-going situation, the tone of my letters to Julie became increasingly negative. What was the point of writing letters like that to a woman who was doing everything she could to help me gain my freedom? I don't know for certain, but I do realise now that it's possible if I'd held my thoughts in and not admitted them to anybody I probably wouldn't be here today, such was the trauma and my state of mind at the time! Sorry Julie.

Michael 'sold off' most of the supplies the Embassy had brought in. I found it hard to deal with this as I knew he was selling off items Julie had paid for. As he sold off supplies, he was 'begging' for vegetables and other ingredients to prepare his food. Because of the negative impact this had on me, I found it difficult being linked with him given we were known as the 'Two British'.

Wednesday, 17th March.

My birthday! Falling on St Patrick's Day, I consider myself to be an honourary Irishman and I must confess I have little to recall about the vast majority of my birthdays as it's very difficult to have a 'quiet drink' anywhere in the world on the 17th. Usually I'd be swept along with the euphoria which the patron saint of Ireland engenders in many Westerners, but not today, not here in prison, in Iraq!

Being held captive accentuated my feelings of 'occasion' and the needy child in me hoped for some cards. There was nothing from Julie when Gleb had brought in mail at the beginning of the month so I didn't have a card from her which made me feel gloomy. However I did receive one she'd sent on behalf of William and there were others from family and friends which buoyed my mood as did the Swedes and Filipinos whose company I enjoyed in the evening.

It was difficult to be objective though as the paranoia clawing at my head made me think that instead of it just being a cock-up, maybe there was something sinister about not receiving a card that Julie had surely sent me. Perhaps it was a plan by the Iraqis, or the British, or, my biggest fear of all, was Julie trying to tell me something?

Thursday, 18th March.

I was called to Abu Athier's office and advised that Gleb Desyatnikov was in the visiting room. Gleb 'wore' his 'serious Russian look', giving little away, so I didn't have a clue what was going on. He rose, shook my hand, and pointed at a pile of supplies on the floor by the door saying, "I have been asked to come to the prison early and give you these supplies, letters and birthday cake!"

As he spoke, he handed me the cake. Flabbergasted, I couldn't think and stood there with an inane grin on my face until he spoke again, saying, "Your wife sends her regards with the cake and says she is sorry that she cannot be here to share it with you, but she hopes that you and your friends enjoy it."

I thanked him for his efforts in bringing the supplies to me and went back to my section feeling thoroughly ashamed that I'd had such negative thoughts the previous day.

Khalid Jerjes came to the prison later the same day and saw Michael and myself and enquired about our health and general wellbeing. It was a box-ticking public relations exercise. If we requested anything, we were told, no matter what we asked for, that it was unavailable due to the sanctions but the Iraqis could say that we'd been asked regularly.

Jerjes did tell us we would be given a two-man cell shortly if we didn't create any problems. "We will inform the Russian Embassy if you create trouble!" he said.

What a load of old bull. After all, what could the Russians do, they could hardly put us in detention like naughty schoolboys! Jerjes' threat was so hollow that I almost laughed as he said it. He told us during this visit that we should expect to receive his bill for the work he had carried out on our behalf upon our release!

Later I wroted to Julie saying, "I will be asking the United Nations to help with my bill. As they didn't do a good job of observing, I hope they do a better one of paying."

I realise that this sounds like sour grapes, but the UN had an image, at least in my mind, of being a crusading defender of rights. I have to say, in my experience, it is not. It is poorly run, ill-prepared, and answerable in the main to the United States of America. I and many of the hostages in Iraq felt let down by the UN. I think the main criticism was that they are above reproach or should I say, *They answer to nobody!*

In the evening I cut the cake into small pieces and distributed it as far as I could. I offered Michael a piece which he refused so I divided it among as many in my cell as it managed. We enjoyed it, and I received many compliments about Madam Julie's coffee gateaux!

Among the items Gleb delivered was an assortment of strange foods. I had asked Julie to provide some variety instead of the usual produce I had been receiving, however much of what turned up was 'like' but not what I'd requested. I'd asked for yeast and flour to make bread and received dried pancake mix! I'd asked for assorted drink powders to disguise the foul taste of the water, I received 12 litres of 'out of date' grapefruit juice. Pretty much all of the delivery was like this. It was all 'nearly right', but almost all wrong!

How could this happen? My initial request was made to Gleb who contacted the Russian Embassy in Amman. The list was then passed from the Russians in Amman to the British Embassy in Amman who then contacted the Foreign Office in London who passed the message on to Julie in Walthamstow, London. This 'network' then worked in reverse before the items reached me. With so many personal interpretations involved along the way it was of little surprise that I received pancake mix instead of bread flour and yeast!

At the end of a 'memorable' day which included a 'wonderful' contribution from Gleb, and the usual nonsense from Jerjes, I was kept awake by a religious service on the TV which started at 11.00pm and drew enthusiastic vocal participation from the majority of the inhabitants of Section Three! It was late and I wasn't in the mood. I tried everything to get to sleep including counting to ten, counting sheep, and sitting up and reading. Finally I capitulated, climbed out of bed and sat up smoking for hours until the service concluded.

Towards the end of March, the Swedish families arrived back in Baghdad with an envoy from the Swedish Prime Minister travelling with them in an effort to secure the release of the three lads. During the visit they became reticent about getting our mail out via their diplomatic visitors. They said they had been advised that to continue passing mail at this stage could damage their 'imminent' chances of release.

The Swedish Government had, from the outset, 'dealt' directly with the Iraqis for the release of their three citizens being held hostage. It became obvious that something had stopped their release. It emerged that despite having previously received a large shipment of medical supplies from Sweden, Iraq was now demanding more. Diplomatic discussions were on-going, however with Sweden stating that it had honoured the original request and that Iraq was now trying to 'up the ante' there were fears that any proposed release would be further delayed as more demands were made. I heard that this was reason for the reluctance of the British Government to enter into negotiations.

Friday, 26th March.

Michael was sent to the punishment cells which were located in a freestanding block. He'd had a fever for two days, his sheets were wet through and he'd not been out of his bed a great deal at all. A sadistic young officer ordered him to be taken to the punishment block for failing to get up for Muster. It was outrageous, but I realised that trying to help Michael would be unproductive. He would have spurned the help and for this reason I didn't bother. I think his harsh treatment was posturing on the part of the Iraqis to show the section that they were serious with their threats about punishing any behaviour that they considered to be insubordination.

Later that evening Michael returned and was greeted like a hero by the other prisoners. He enjoyed this, repeatedly exclaiming, "The bastards aren't going to get the better of me!" He stripped his bed and someone gave him food. After eating he leapt onto his bed and lay there muttering until he fell asleep that he would, "Sort these fuckers out!"

Michael was a pain in the behind. He had a strange sense of pride and honour which I considered to be warped and misplaced. He was off the wall but would always defend his position regardless of who he was talking to or what was at stake.

Before he fell ill, I'd heard Michael talking about the amount of canned food I had and I found his comments annoying. After the letter from the Foreign Office I'd used my supplies carefully and kept myself to myself. Michael, as far as I could tell, was using the same amount of food as before the letter and selling off anything he could! This gave him a huge amount of useless Iraqi Dinars on his hip and a rapidly dwindling supply of food. I couldn't work it out and I did wonder if he knew what was happening around him!

The BBC news bulletins I heard on the radio were grim. The Provisional IRA had carried out two bombings in Warrington. The first on the 26th of February, the second on the 20th of March. The second bombing, in an area crowded with Mother's Day shoppers, killed two children and injured many more innocents. The abduction and murder of Jamie Bulger, a two-year-old boy from Kirkby, Merseyside really got to me. I could imagine my hurt if either of my children were involved in crimes like these and as I sat in my cell I felt sad and my despondency worsened when I realised that I was really feeling sorry for myself.

In my initial months at Abu Ghraib I'd run short of food and money and had ended up borrowing the latter from Khalid Jerjes. I'd recently been informed by the Foreign Office that I would have to repay this myself. I wrote to Julie asking her to send the sterling equivalent of 5000 Dinars to the Foreign Office to pass to the Russian Embassy to settle my debt. I hoped that this would reduce the bill he'd threatened me with. I said to Julie, "I shall not be taking any more cash from Jerjes, so this is a one-off payment and it's better to do it through the Russians who will buy 'black market' Dinars rather than through our Government who will pay top price for Dinars."

5000 Iraqi Dinars was a lot of money (approximately £1250) at the start of my detention, but inflation had destroyed the currency's value and so paying the money back like this would be far cheaper than going through official channels. That was how I looked at it and how I justified it in my head.

I repeatedly requested Julie sent me clothing. When I'd arrived at Abu Ghraib I had nothing and had to beg and borrow clothing to wear. Some of the clothing sent in I gave away to cover my debts. I didn't for a minute resent this however it felt a bit strange as they were from my own wardrobe in London. Most of these clothes didn't actually fit me anymore so maybe realising value for them wasn't such a bad idea, but the fact I'd lost several centimetres from around my waist and I'd 'shrunk' due to losing over 25 kilograms in weight was deeply worrying. My clothes hung from what was left of me. I'm sure that Julie was exasperated by my continual demands but I was trying to keep body and soul together!

My Grandfather had passed away on the 4th of January and in my reflective mood I considered that even though I'd not seen him in years it saddened me that I had not been able to mourn his death with my family. I started to wonder if I would always be missing this part of my life. It felt as if my family and friends were moving on but I was in limbo. Would part of my life always be missing? The question haunted me.

I had the notion that Julie was presenting an inaccurate image of my detention to the media, principally that things were easier for me than they actually were. She wasn't misleading people but being careful that her comments would not give the Iraqis reason to take offence. She tried to convince the Iraqi regime that she was on its side and hoped that having a good relationship with them would help my situation. How could I argue?

Family and friends upset with some of Julie's comments wrote and told me that she spoke as if I was on a 'Club Med' holiday. I replied to their angry letters assuring them that Julie was building bridges, and if the facts had to be 'stretched' to create the 'truth' the Iraqis wanted then that was what she was doing. I understood Julie's reasons for her 'presentation' of my situation but the criticism from my family got me thinking. My fear of being underplayed, exacerbated by a fever encouraged me to write a horribly negative letter to Julie. I don't think it was rude, but I ranted about Abu Ghraib and Iraq. This didn't change my situation, but getting it off my chest helped me.

Sunday, 28th March.

I listened to the 'Vintage Chart Show' on the radio while replying to some letters. The DJ was playing old classics from March 1967 and I laughed out loud when he played the big number one from back then. 'Release Me' by Engelbert Humperdinck! The Iraqis didn't and my captivity continued as did my letter writing!

Monday, 29th March

A couple of times a year the Turkish Embassy visited Abu Ghraib and spoke with each Turkish prisoner. The Turks were held on various charges ranging from extremely criminal to mildly ridiculous! Smuggling was the most common charge, then theft, and of course there was a fair quota of unfortunate 'spies' in the camp; people like me, jailed for many years for insignificant crimes.

There were over 170 Turks in Abu Ghraib so it took several diplomats two or three days to see everyone. I was sitting in my cell on the second day of their visit when my Turkish friend Abdul Baki entered.

A small intelligent man who'd outwitted the Iraqis in business on a few occasions had been tricked at the border and was now serving a five-year sentence for illegal entry. He had a visa for Iraq in his passport and had handed it over at Habur, the 'official' customs border point between Iraq and Turkey. The border guard failed to stamp his passport with an entry visa and later at his hotel this had been noticed and he'd been reported to the police. He'd spent time in the Mukhabarat complex and Al Alwiyah with Michael and me and was then jailed on the trumped-up 'illegal entry' charge. When he'd appealed, his passport, bearing numerous entry and exit visas that demonstrated his long business association with Iraq, was conveniently lost by the unforgiving, merciless bastards masquerading as the police.

Abdul Baki had a huge smile on his face and was waving a Turkish newspaper at me. I guessed that this had something to do with his case. He sat on my bunk and said he'd seen an article he thought I'd be interested in. I asked him what it was about and as he unfolded the newspaper he said I could see for myself. The words and print made not one iota of sense but at the top of the page, in the sea of Turkish script, I saw a picture of Julie and William. It was a surprise to see them in a Turkish newspaper. I asked what the caption said and Baki explained it told of my family returning home after a humanitarian attempt with the Red Cross to secure my early release. He told me that I was welcome to the picture as soon as he had finished reading the rest of the newspaper!

While chatting to Abdul Baki I'd glanced at Michael who was building model ships, something he was spending an increasing amount of time doing to earn money and also no doubt to fritter away the hours. This wasn't a popular development with other prisoners. There were several 'boat builders' in our section who'd been making models for many years. They shared a routine of sawing wood and carrying out the noisy jobs during the mornings when the other prisoners were out of bed, Michael however sat directly outside our cell and sawed wood while other prisoners were trying to take a siesta! There was growing discontent and complaints about Michael's burgeoning flotilla and the noise he made putting it together! I thought it served the ignorant bastards right for keeping me awake every night with their arguing, playing noisy games, and watching the TV at full volume. The strange thing was that despite the moaning, nobody ever took up the problem with Michael directly!

Tuesday, 30th March.

I woke early due to the noise being made by inmates observing Ramadan. I couldn't get back to sleep so I continued a letter that I'd started the previous day writing, "It's 4.25am and these arseholes are all up laughing, eating and walking about. It's like a sodding circus in here, and I can't sleep so I thought I would jot down a few lines to you. As I tried to explain to them, I am neither a Muslim nor a Bat, but what can you do!"

After a pause I continued, "Now prayers have started at the local Mosque! It's 4.45am – what a life! I read a good, and apt quote this morning by Roman poet Martialis; 'Life is not just to live – but to be well', well I ain't well!"

Later in the day I explained my issues with the Foreign Office to the Swedes and started to remove food I'd taken to their cell for community use. This was very difficult. It sounds remarkably simple, but I was totally isolating myself and putting invisible barriers up hoping I could survive. After almost six months of sharing everything with these lads, including their incredible Christmas food, I was unhappy about altering the status quo but I had to do it because the Foreign Office in London said so!

Wednesday, 31st March.

I received a letter from Julie in which she asked me to give her regards to Abu Athier. Given my mindset the last thing I felt like doing was being polite to an Iraqi and so I replied succinctly, "Fuck Abu Athier!" I hoped this would indicate how I felt about the situation. In the next sentence I turned my vitriol on the Foreign Office saying, "Tell the British Foreign Office to stick their bills, and requests, where the sun don't shine! I'm sick of the posturing bastards – 'please don't feed everyone with your food' – fucking Rule Britannia! What about all the overseas aid we hear about? Where was that regarding feeding victims of Saddam Hussein's regime? Perhaps the Government or Foreign Office felt that it wouldn't get good exposure in the media, sending food to a location where cameras can't capture the crowd thronging to collect their rations – or have I been made cynical by my experiences?"

Ranko, the Serb who'd loaned me the clothes I'd worn to do the interview with the Swiss TV crew, had mentioned that he wasn't able to correspond with his family at home as a consequence of the on-going Yugoslav Wars. As there was no chance of getting mail from Baghdad to Belgrade I'd got him to write a letter which I incorporated with mine and asked Julie to get it to the Yugoslavian Embassy in London so it could then be delivered to his wife via their diplomatic pouch.

One of my cellmates, an Egyptian called Mohammed, was a virtual pauper living or trying to live on the meagre earnings he generated by making crochet purses, pictures, key rings and many other attractive little objects. To do this he sat for hours with spools of nylon thread, surrounded by thousands of tiny multi-coloured balls which he crocheted onto any article he was making to produce fantastic designs and patterns. They were sold to other prisoners or to visitors who arrived with Dinars to spend.

Like many of the inmates Mohammed existed on food supplied by the prison supplemented with additional rice, bread, and vegetables. Later in the day, when I was cleaning and re-packing my food supplies due to a cockroach infestation, he asked what was in a tin I was holding. With my index fingers against my head raised as horns I made the moo moo sound of a cow. Understanding this he said, "L'ham" (meat), followed by, "B'gra" (beef), and I agreed. I felt compelled to offer him the tin. After the obligatory polite refusal he took it and then sat down on his bed and started to cry. I spoke to another Egyptian in the cell later and asked why he'd cried? He explained to me that Mohammed had not tasted meat in all the time he had been in Abu Ghraib – over six years!

AMNESTY, WHAT AMNESTY?

Wednesday, 7th April.

Ranko came and told me that Julie was a hero for passing his letter to the Yugoslavian Embassy in London. It had been delivered to his home in record time and he'd already had a reply and was over the moon to hear from his wife. I was instructed to pass on praise, thanks, and best wishes to Julie.

I gave Michael some tinned food. He managed to make me feel guilty for having more food than he did even though I knew he was selling his food! It was perverse, but I couldn't let him go hungry. Finally, I forced myself to stop being concerned about Michael when he started bothering Arabic prisoners for raw ingredients to make his meals. I thought that anyone who could take food from people in dire need of the basics of life themselves was not worth worrying about.

The section learned that Abu Athier's son had been killed in a motoring accident in the first week of April and while my heart went out to the human being, I had problems showing sorrow for a man who, due to his position, was overseeing the suffering of others. Abu Athier could be kind and compassionate, however, his alter ego held me balanced between respecting and loathing him.

Julie read out on TV a letter I'd written to John Major. I was worried she'd read it in its entirety as it contained a lot of anti-Iraq sentiment and, while I believed it, I didn't want the Iraqi regime to know I held it in contempt! I had faith in Julie's judgement, but I was aware the media did not give a damn about people, their safety, or wellbeing. The only thing in the head of a media person appears to be sensationalism and getting an exclusive. I didn't want a hack to win the Pulitzer Prize at the cost of my freedom, or life!

Julie had also told me she'd provided information and a photo for an article to be printed in 'Onside', the Chelsea Football Club newspaper.

During their visit in February, Abu Athier had given Julie, Heather, and Iris some 'jewellery' crocheted by inmates. Julie hated the bloody stuff and she only took it because the Red Cross was having an auction shortly after they returned to the UK and they hoped that the items, subsequently pictured in national newspapers, would raise a bit of cash.

One of the Kurd's in my section told me they'd heard a report, on a secret radio, that Julie and Michael's mother, Iris, were coming to visit us again and it was believed that our release had been agreed. I thought this strange as my impression was that the Iraqis were not even considering our release – but my hope sprang eternal and I was willing to believe that anything was possible. I tried to discover if anybody else had heard the report but no one could confirm the story. I went back to the Kurd who'd told me the 'news' in the first place and he again confirmed that he'd heard the report.

I decided to consult with Adel Mansoor, the top informant in the prison. Adel had been in Abu Ghraib for seven years and had the connections to be able to find out if the Kurd was telling the truth. Adel was holding court and eating not in his own cell but that of Hamo who helped run the Hanoot. I wasn't sure why this was, but it was the norm. Maybe he didn't want his own cell full of people. I engaged in small talk until the moment seemed right for me to ask the questions which were eating me up, "Is 'Madam Julie' in Baghdad? If she coming to see me?

Adel's response should have started alarm bells ringing but I was blinded by the need to confirm the Kurd's story. He asked why I thought that 'Madam Julie' was in Baghdad and I replied in a throwaway manner, "Someone told me!"

Like the snake he was, Adel immediately launched into a series of questions to discover the identity of my informant. I immediately realised that I had just placed someone else in danger by my need and thoughtlessness. I squirmed and tried to move the conversation away from the Kurd back onto Julie. It was no use. Speared like a fish in the claws of a huge bear, the more I wriggled the tighter Adel clutched, until stupidly and selfishly I blurted out the identity of the Kurd.

Adel dispatched Hamo to fetch the unfortunate Kurd and when he arrived he interrogated him about where he'd heard the story. The Kurd was far smarter than me and managed to fob Adel off with a cover story. I didn't have a clue what had been said as the whole conversation was in Arabic but at its conclusion Adel dismissed the Kurd and resumed being gracious and friendly, advising me not to listen to the Kurds as they were stupid and always starting rumours. I went to bed that night dreaming of what might have been. Freedom!

Thursday, 8th April.

I awoke to the usual filth, stench and din of Abu Ghraib and had already forgotten the incident with the Kurd when at 9.00am Muster he was escorted to Abu Athier's office and I didn't see him for the rest of the day. I was very worried about him and mightily relieved when I saw him reentering our section. A crowd soon gathered around the Kurd and began asking him questions about his visit and it was only when this 'court of enquiry' had finished and the prisoners around him had left that I noticed the fear in his eyes which was bordering on panic.

One of his friends eventually told me what happened. The Kurd had been interrogated about how he had heard that Julie was in Baghdad and when his answers had not been suitably forthcoming he'd been taken into one of the solitary confinement cells and beaten. This was a painful rather than damaging beating but I still felt ashamed that my stupidity had caused this.

In the evening during the last Muster of the day, the officer performing the lock-up ritual made an announcement to my section. He said that the 'other' prisoners were to have no further contact with the 'Western prisoners'. They were not to ask for, or take, articles from us. They were neither to talk nor pass information or rumours to us. He warned every prisoner to stay away from us with the threat that if his orders were not adhered to, those 'guilty' would find themselves severely punished.

Following this announcement, the other prisoners ignored me and who can blame them! This 'stand-off' only lasted for a few days after which the threats were forgotten by both prisoners and guards. This was perfectly normal in Abu Ghraib, however I also saw unsuspecting prisoners swiftly and brutally punished for breaching 'orders' that had been set weeks or months previously by guards with a selective memory.

Saturday, 10th April.

I'd been invited by my Turkish friend Abdul Baki to go to his section and have lunch with him. I'd asked for permission to move between Section Three and Section One where he was 'housed' the previous day which had been granted and so off I went.

Although I was able to give him little in return, Abdul Baki had been very supportive and kind to me, and one time when his associates appeared to have abandoned him I'd been able to pay back a tiny part of the generosity which he'd showered upon me, by the simple act of giving him some coffee when he'd run out.

I was astounded by the amount and variety of food which he offered me. There was a huge amount to eat; soup, chicken, rice, vegetables, assorted breads, desserts and sweetmeats. It was fantastic and I was encouraged to stuff myself so-much-so that I thought I might pass out! All of this was arranged to thank me for the jar of coffee which I had given him a few weeks earlier. I was truly humbled by this as in the past Abdul Baki had been my greatest ally, especially when arranging for the first of my letters which reached Julie to be smuggled out of Al Alwiyah, and Iraq. All I had done was give him some coffee, and in return he treated me like a king. In an environment of dire want and need it made me feel greatly honoured and deeply grateful.

Friday, 16th April.

Visiting day. A Tunisian called Mohammed, known as M'hmd al Tunsi, or Mohammed the Tunisian, was thrown into the punishment block and heavily beaten. This was after the father of a little girl visiting the prison had complained that he had 'abused' his daughter while he'd been with the prisoner he had come to see.

Mohammed the Tunisian, a policeman in his own country, was a known child molester, and this did nothing to endear him to me. As time passed and I learned 'the system' in Abu Ghraib, he was repeatedly pointed out as a monumental spy and a liar, to be avoided at all costs. It had, until the abusing of the little girl, remained in my mind as prison gossip but now I realised that some 'rules' for future behaviour had to be established. I told Adel Mansoor that if I ever saw Mohammed the Tunisian around William, if he ever came to Iraq again, I would without hesitation kill him! I asked Adel to pass this promise to Abu Athier so that an unpleasant scene could be avoided in the future and I wrote to Julie explaining all of this saying, "I don't want my seven years for 'illegal entry' extended to 25 years for murder!'

Saturday, 17th April.

I'd woken up feeling grouchy on account of having an ache in my flanks which wouldn't shift and was depressing me and Chelsea Football Club didn't help my frame of mind. A run of shocking results had seen manager Ian Porterfield sacked in February and replaced by David Webb. Blues legend Webby had stopped the rot but was no miracle worker and in the afternoon I'd tuned into World Service to listen to commentary of Chelsea's away game with Manchester United. A 3-0 drubbing wasn't the tonic I was hoping for.

I wrote to Julie, "I'm off to bed now. I'm on a mild downer as not only am I missing you both terribly, but The Blues got stuffed, (and I do mean stuffed) at Old Trafford. What a life!"

Sunday, 18th April.

I went to the prison doctor who examined me for the continual flank pains which I presumed was related to my kidneys. He told me I wasn't ill and that I should increase my fluid intake. I realise that doesn't sound very difficult but the water supply went off sometimes for hours or days at a time! He gave me some pills and recommended I should get more exercise which I would have been happy to do but a block punishment had kept our section on lockdown for the previous two days for a 'misdemeanour' that would remain a mystery to me.

The political situation was very tense during April as the USA had been posturing again and, never one to refuse a challenge, with his obviously expendable army, Saddam Hussein appeared to be picking up the gauntlet. I'd heard via the Swedes that Julie was not in the Middle East and with tension growing in the area this was great news. I remained ignorant about developments at home because mail from Julie had stopped altogether. I sent letter after letter with virtually the same set of questions but received no reply.

RIDE TO HELL

Monday, 19th April.

Ghassan told me that I was going to the main prison for an X-ray on my kidneys which was a surprise given the doctor's comments the previous day. I was ordered to the administration building and told to stand alongside four other prisoners who were waiting in a corridor by the door. As I took my place with them they cast me furtive glances, unsure why I was a part of the group. This unnerved me slightly. Next I was manacled to one of the men for the walk to the main prison and the hospital. I remembered the first time I'd seen the 'Hiatt's of England' stamp on the handcuffs used by the Iraqis to shackle prisoners and I laughed again.

It felt strange to be walking into the 'reception area' using the same route I'd used on my initial arrival at Abu Ghraib and I wondered where the hospital was as we appeared to be heading toward the administrative section of the prison. Momentarily our path was blocked by a throng of Iraqi prisoners who were slapped and beaten by our guards to allow us through. We turned off the main corridor into a side annex. The scene that greeted me could have been from a horror movie. Hundreds of 'bodies' stood, crouched, sat, or lay along the passageway. Strutting Mafiosi-types, complete with henchmen, competed for space with sightless beggars. Of those prisoners who were sitting, some cowed like beaten dogs while others sat staring and unseeing in a dream world of their own. Several men who were lying down on the dirty floor appeared to me to have breathed their last until a guard kicked them and they dragged themselves into upright heaps of humanity. Uniformed guards impatiently patrolled the corridor while medical staff in soiled white linen moved through the throng, occasionally pulling somebody into a side room for closer inspection.

When it was my turn, a guard removed my handcuffs and I was 'shown to' the X-ray department which, like the rest of the place, was filthy. I took my top off and within seconds was back in the corridor waiting for my 'companions'. I asked a guard if I could visit the toilet and he nodded and pointed out directions. I set off down the corridor, rounded a corner and went through the wrong door into a 'ward' that resembled a filthy butchers shop. Blood was smeared across most surfaces including beds and bedsheets which looked little better than rags. The floor was uneven and soiled and the patients looked like the ematicated prisoners of a Nazi death camp, equally resigned to their fate! I shuddered, turned on my heels and saw I was facing a toilet door which as I was about to find out should have been signposted 'welcome to hell'.

The 'facilities', brimming with excrement which had pooled around the floor and into hollows caused by its unevenness, were the most disgusting and unsanitary I'd seen in all my time in Iraq. The smell was indescribable. Later I learned that these were the toilets that hospital in-patients were forced to use. I hurriedly did my business and then carefully threaded my way around the deepest pools of faeces to the door. I rejoined the guards and waited for the other prisoners to return and when we were all present and correct we were paired off and handcuffed for the return journey.

Tuesday, 20th April.

The X-ray indicated there was nothing visibly wrong with my kidneys while a urine sample I'd given showed I had a 'slight infection' which was probably due to sand or dirt in water I had ingested. I was glad that 'something' had been diagnosed as I'd been in a lot of pain which thankfully had now eased.

In April a new Russian Ambassador had arrived in Iraq. This should have made no difference to Michael and myself, but today we'd expected to receive food supplies and been disappointed. I had enough for a further four weeks but I knew that Michael was very low. Out of self-interest but also concern for another human being, I asked Julie to contact the Foreign Office to ensure that the procedure for our supplies was known and acknowledged. I asked for a system of individual lists for us because the incoming search (theft) continued to mix articles from differing boxes. Things would improve but never became fool proof!

Mail arrived again and I received many letters from people in the UK who were contacting their MPs lobbying for our release. I was very glad that the British public were behind us and hoped that it would make a difference.

Wednesday, 28th April.

Saddam Hussein's birthday! For weeks there had been an expectation that the dictator would grant an amnesty. These amnesties had been regular events with two or three different groups, variously comprising of thieves, sex offenders, drug dealers, rapists and murderers, being released but the harder things became for Iraq, the more unforgiving Saddam and his regime had become. Since the imposition of the latest sanctions there had been no amnesties at all. The birthday was another 'maybe' pencilled in on calendars; long shots, but days of hope and anticipation.

I regarded myself as separate from the majority of prisoners believing that I would be free before most of them but it was difficult not to become involved in the 'hype' before a possible amnesty.

Stories were recalled by some of my fellow prisoners of previous amnesties. One of the Filipino lads, Abet, explained he had been about to climb on a 'freedom bus' when a guard grabbed him and said he was not eligible for the amnesty. Then in an uncharacteristic moment of spite he said, "As you are a political prisoner, even if there is a general amnesty you probably won't be released but held by the Iraqis until they have profited from you!"

In my usual style I laughed this off but inside I shuddered with fear at the prospect of continuing to be held hostage in Abu Ghraib as the diplomats maintained their stand-off positions.

Saddam Hussein's birthday was a marvellous opportunity for Iraqi TV broadcasters to rerun the millions of metres of film they had of the madman already in the can. The poses Saddam featured in beggared belief. On a white charger dressed in 'sultanesque' robes. The battle-hardened military leader in his greatcoat, a tactician poring over maps planning the next move. The man of the people with huge crowds of Iraqi citizens cheering his every gesture. The man of God on his prayer mat with a gun, which he is never without, in his side holster. The Tyrolean gentleman in lederhosen with a 'brush hat'. The family man surrounded by packs of adoring youngsters. Roars of agreement for the sycophantic praise showered on Saddam by the TV presenters rang around the section. As the time approached for the man himself to make the speech which was hoped and expected to contain the amnesty the tension became palpable.

The section hushed and many prisoners sat in front of the TV as the voice of the supreme power in Iraq boomed from the set which was mounted high up on the main corridor wall. Each of his comments were met with a ripple of discussion which was quickly hushed less a vital word be missed. The mentally ill wandered around unconcerned by the expectations of everyone else. Their personal prisons would never be opened; their family's murdered, bodies tortured beyond endurance, heads beaten until the ringing would never stop, prisoners for life in a world created by a brutal regime. Unseeing, unhearing; the walking dead had no interest in the TV and its issue.

I had been in Abet's cell all afternoon discussing an amnesty. He told me that his loathing of his captors was a driving force which carried him on, but now only the thought of an amnesty and early release buoyed his spirits. He confessed to me that he didn't think he could remain in Abu Ghraib much longer and his eyes filled with tears as he spoke with great bitterness of the unfair sentence which had already stolen more than six years of his life.

There was a huge roar from the corridor and Abet and I rushed to see what the reason for the commotion was. As we rounded the corner we were met by a smiling, hugging, shouting crowd surging away from the TV. Abet spoke fluent Arabic and asked what the news was. He was assured that an amnesty would be taking place and so I dashed to the Swedish cell and repeated what I had just heard.

Leif was the first to react enquiring who'd told me. I replied that the news had just been announced on TV and that someone had told Abet in the corridor. Stefan, Leif, and I went to find out about this pardon. Was it true? Would it include us? And, most importantly, when would it be taking place?

We went into the main corridor, which was full of shouting, dancing, laughing prisoners and caught sight of a dejected looking Ghassan. I knew he would never get an amnesty and I guessed his morose expression was due to the 'suggestion' that others would. As we approached, his gloom lifted and we asked him about the amnesty. He said that to his knowledge there wasn't going to be one, explaining the euphoria was due to a suggestion that if the UN eased the sanctions Saddam 'might' release prisoners.

As they heard this, Stefan and Leif gave me a withering gaze speaking volumes without uttering a word. What could I do? I simply looked back at them and gave a small shrug which I hoped would be understood as, *Sorry lads, it's not my fault. I heard we were all out!*

I had been misinformed so often in the past by inmates with half-baked ideas, I should have asked some proper questions before joining the unwarranted hysteria. The truth is I think I wanted, or needed, to believe it if only for a few minutes. It was a simple case of self-deception!

In celebration of Saddam's birthday, a football match had been arranged between the Iraqi section and the foreign section. Our best players were a mixed team including Egyptians, Sudanese, Romanians, Turks, Jordanians, and Palestinians. The game was a closely-fought affair and well-supported, drawing a large crowd from each section. Most of the action was in midfield interspersed with galloping surges by both sides which faded as the goalposts came into view. It was evident that the poor diets endemic in Section Three in Abu Ghraib were responsible for quickly sapping the energy of many of the players, and 'our' team in particular soon looked very tired. As I watched, I was reminded of the World War Two football-come-prison-escape film 'Escape To Victory'. Similarly, the will to win was enormous. There was however one key difference, there were no plans for an escape. Men who were dizzy from dietary deficiencies ran until they were in a state of collapse. They wanted to be part of the side which defeated the 'well-fed' and strong Iraqi team on Saddam Hussein's birthday!

There was plenty of vocal encouragement and chanting for 'The Foreigners' team and the guards from our section were obviously proud of the effort of both the players and supporters. 'We' scored first, and the noise from the crowd rang around the pitch. Joy didn't last as just before half-time the Iraqis equalised. During the break, both sets of players were harangued and scolded by their respective 'coaches' and following much yelling and waving of arms the game was soon back under way.

The second-half was much the same as the first, but the Iraqi team began to win the war of attrition. As 'the clock was running down', they pushed forward and started to control possession. Against the run of play our lads won a corner. This was poorly taken but not cleared well and the ball was driven out onto to the wing. Our man on the right found the energy to run at the Iraqi defence, slip the tackle of a lunging defender, and put a wonderful ball into the middle. One of our Sudanese players picked up the pass and attacked the goal with a probing run. The Iraqi goalkeeper sensed danger and came out of his area to try and intercept him but with neat footwork the Sudani side-stepped him and placed a magnificent shot high into the net.

As the net bulged the spectators went into a frenzy; screaming, shouting, and embracing on the side-lines. The watching Iraqi senior officers looked crestfallen and the Iraqi supporters and coaches screamed at their team to redress the balance. The pressure, which was absorbed by the foreign team, was incredible. For the remainder of the match the Iraqis tried everything to score a goal but they failed in their endeavours and, when it came, the final whistle was met with roars of approval by the foreign prisoners, myself included. Our team had been victorious over the far stronger Iraqis. It was Saddam's birthday and as he had not granted the pardons everyone had hoped for, the consensus was that justice had been done!

Once they had been counted, the Iraqi prisoners, both team and supporters, were marched out of the area and as they passed the foreign prisoners they were given a sporting round of applause that showed respect for their effort. The players on the foreign section team were given a word of praise by the officer who conducted the Muster at lock-up time and we returned to our section applauding the valiant team.

I wrote to Julie and informed her of the day's events, I'd not had any replies to my recent clutch of letters and was becoming sick with worry about why she was not writing to me. Trying to hold a conversation by mail is possible, but if the dialogue suddenly becomes one-sided it is difficult to maintain. Other mail slackened off quite considerably also and the more time I had on my hands, the more I worried. At night when alone, locked in, captive with hundreds of others, demons would drive my thoughts into the abyss and back. I felt as if I was on a huge beast that I had no control over. I would be dragged along and become metaphorically ripped and torn by each successive situation raging through my head, each growing in complexity.

I continued to write my letters and in one I complained bitterly about the number and size of the mosquitoes which with late April's warmer weather were reappearing around my bed in vast numbers. I felt especially persecuted by these little swine and wrote, "I think some of these bloody mosquitoes must be hybrids mated with seagulls. They are huge, vicious brutes! Put a saddle on one and I could fly out of here!"

It seemed to me that I was the only person bothered by these horrid creatures. If a portion of my flesh was uncovered overnight, in the morning I would be covered in angry red welts.

I also wrote about the depression which had seeped through the entire section since the amnesty failed to materialise. It appeared to be both mental and physical. The men with huge sentences looked 'pained' as a pardon was their only hope of getting out of Abu Ghraib alive. Some of the prisoners were old and the terms they still had remaining to serve were so long they were a virtual death sentence, unless a pardon said otherwise. Little did I realise how true this was, until the very next day!

Thursday, 29th April.

Crazy Mohammed, a Kurd with some strange habits, was walking about after lunchtime Muster and as it was a 'special' visiting day the section gates had been left open so that people could go about their daily routines a little later than usual. Nothing could be done when visitors were in the section, so food preparation and all other daily events that made up our routine were held up.

I went to get some soup and passed Mohammed on the way. "Kiefak enta?" (How are you?), I enquired politely. He was muttering under his breath as he always did and so I walked on not really expecting an answer. I laughed internally, thinking to myself, *Mohammed – as crazy as ever!* I collected my soup, took it to my bunk, ate it and fell asleep. When I woke I could 'feel', call it a sixth sense, that something was wrong.

I walked into the main corridor and saw a crowd outside Cell 1. *What's wrong?* I thought. They were all so quiet! As I progressed toward the cell, I heard hushed whispers that Mohammed was dead. The shock chilled me to the bone. I had only walked past the man 90 minutes or so ago. How could he be dead? I pushed my way through the growing crowd to the cell and through the bars saw his body lying on the floor. The inhabitants of the cell were standing and sitting around the corpse. My shame was overpowering. I might have been the last person to see him alive! I might have been the last person to speak to him. This, and the memory that I had actually laughed at his antics stung me deeply and I dashed away with shivers running up and down my spine.

Mohammed's death had been caused by a massive heart attack killing him instantly, or so I was told. His body lay on the floor of the cell most of the afternoon until finally the authorities arranged a van to remove his body. *No! This is beyond belief!* The vehicle the bastards had sent was the same one that delivered our vegetables! I was staggered, and very nearly sick. The anger brought bile to my throat and tears to my eyes.

Although Mohammed had been the butt of numerous jokes, every Kurd wanted the 'honour' of carrying his corpse to the waiting 'hearse'. A party of 'pall bearers' was chosen and after much Kurdish drama the body was taken, in my opinion without a great deal of dignity, to the van. Prisoners from every section stood clinging to the chainlink fencing gazing pitifully at the body and then at the van as it drifted out of the section gates. Each of them I'm sure was pondering their own mortality. I know that I was and I struggled with it.

It was a subdued and frightened place that saw the swift return of the delivery van which came to a juddering halt in the space between sections Three, Four and Five. Silently, prisoners began to congregate, clutching at the chainlink fences again and soon every inch was draped with hundreds of bodies, each with an expressionless face. I had a flashback about a TV documentary concerning the Holocaust in which I'd seen doomed faces clinging to life. The hopelessness of what I was witnessing now sent a shiver through me as whispers questioned why the 'vegetable van of death' had returned. The awful truth was soon revealed, Mohammed's corpse was still on board.

The 'mortuary vehicle' sat in deafening silence as more and more prisoners gathered in what was becoming an increasingly desperate crush to get a view of it. I heard a low moan, akin to an animal in pain, rising from part of the crowd that seemed to be willing the corpse to rise up and exit the van. I felt as if I was attending a religious event.

By the time the authorities eventually removed the van, it seemed as if every prisoner in Abu Ghraib was stood clinging to the fences or filling the yards behind them in a swelling sea of humanity which moaned or sobbed involuntarily. Many seemed unable to draw themselves away from the vigil until finally the van exited the prison and the spell was broken. A thousand prayers escaped a thousand lips and I guarantee that many were for the prayer giver themselves and not the recently dead, gone, and now departed, Mohammed.

Relief, release, and recovery swept us all along as we returned solemnly to the daily routine of staying alive, sitting around the yard, cooking, pacing up and down, and generally attempting to rid our memories of the event that had just occurred. There were hushed conversations and furtive glances among the small huddles of frightened men that formed. The shock was palpable, the cold hand of death had touched us all. Mohammed wasn't old and the realisation that a man in his late 40s or early 50s could be 'snuffed out' like a candle terrified the section.

Understandably the Kurds were the most affected and prayers were said for Mohammed's soul, while the evening saw the start of an all-night vigil in the prison Mosque. This did little to remove the horror and trepidation from the eyes of everyone I spoke to. Fear is a communal emotion, and grown men were reduced to hunting for the 'bogey man' that night.

In subsequent days I heard that the van and its cargo were returned because Saddam Hussein had not granted the corpse a pardon! Without proper authorisation the guards at the main gate had not been allowed to let it leave the prison. They say that fact is stranger than fiction, and most things I heard and witnessed during my time in prison confirm this!

I wrote to Julie saying, "Poor old sod. I felt very mixed emotions. Pain that I'd thought poorly of a man about to die, but a strange kind of relief that he is now out of this terrible place. (But as you can see, even when dead, it's tough to get out of Abu Ghraib!)"

WE'VE GOT A NEW SEPTIC!

Saturday, 1st May.

Visiting day. Unusually, the number of children in attendance was minimal. Because of this I relaxed a bit more than normal, opening the curtain around my bed and sitting doing a crossword. Early arrivals were two, very obvious, prostitutes who came into the cell and sat with one of the new men who was sleeping on the floor. Eventually this prisoner, an Egyptian, introduced me to both the women, informing me that they were his wives. I greeted them politely and got back to my crossword. A short while later another woman entered the cell wearing full Arabic dress complete with a veil. Once again, I was introduced to the woman and told that she was also his wife! She unpacked a basket full of food which I desperately tried to ignore. The smell was divine – hot, oven-roasted food! Dear God! I was salivating.

The Egyptian offered me some of this deliciously aromatic food and at first I refused, but a plate was thrust at me and this time I accepted it gratefully. The taste complimented the smell. The food, a concoction of large beans and rice, was superb and with genuine thanks I wolfed it down and left to wash the dish I'd used.

When I returned to the cell, the woman, his 'wife', had taken off her Yashmak (veil). It was obvious that the Egyptian was this woman's pimp and the 'wife' statement a convenience. She took a cigarette from her purse and began to search for a lighter. I offered my lighter and she, quite unnecessarily, cupped my hand and lit the cigarette. As she was 'holding' my hand she started to stroke it. This was strange, and a bit frightening. Not only because I'd been in jail for nearly a year and had no dealings of this sort with women, but also because the room was full of people and Arabic women are very careful not to arouse suspicion by their actions. Her behaviour really threw me and I sat amazed and slightly shocked at her daring!

The situation in Iraq had become so serious that women were becoming 'desperate' to feed their families. The strict Islamic moral codes were becoming eroded as the oldest profession in the world took a nation under its wing. I had a conversation with a guard a few weeks after this and he said that families who would not normally have allowed their daughters out after a certain time of night were now actively forcing them into prostitution to bring in much needed cash. Ordinary people were sliding rapidly towards ruin as inflation and prices rose at alarming rates. The guard said that the whole moral infrastructure of Iraq was being destroyed by Western sanctions and brazen prostituition was a by-product of this.

Saddam's birthday celebrations had been muted in the section by the death of Mohammed and the fact there had been no amnesties granted. Outside prison however, they continued for days and the singing, dancing, and cheering was shown night after night on TV. It was grinding my gears and the final straw for me came when I was asked to contribute to a party being held in the prison 'school' on Sunday. The collection was being made by the head spies from each section and the 'responsibility' in Section Three lay with Ghassan.

"Will you give anything towards Saddam's birthday party?" he asked

"No, I fucking well won't!" I replied angrily. "The Bastard is keeping me here for nothing. FUCK HIM!"

Ghassan gave me a look which suggested that I was suffering from a mental illness and said in a most worried manner, "Be careful Paul. This is a very dangerous way to speak. Do not let anyone else hear you talking in this way it is a very serious crime to speak against Saddam Hussein. Be careful!"

I hoped, stupidly I realise, that my feelings would be passed on to the Mukhabarat. I wanted a change in the situation and believe me I meant it when I say that I would sooner have had a negative reaction than the total vacuum I was getting.

I remember Jiri Foitek had told me that two years previously Saddam Hussein had made a personal appearance at the prison. The prisoners had believed that if they showed the tyrant that he was a just and benevolent ruler he might grant them amnesty. Jiri said that the prisoners worked themselves into a frenzy during his visit, leaping and jumping about in the same way that the 'spontaneous' street gatherings did wherever the madman went.

Amnesty was clearly not one of Saddam's thoughts as he'd gazed at the pitiful leaping, thrashing, writhing mass of humanity locked inside Abu Ghraib. Since his visit only prisoners who had completed their sentence or died had departed the prison.

Monday, 3rd May.

I received a letter along with a large envelope advising me that I had been subscribed to the BBC World Service magazine 'London Calling'. The letter explained that someone had kindly put me on their mailing list! I was elated, 'London Calling' would give me the ability to plan my radio listening however there was a problem. When I opened the envelope, the magazine had been stolen!

When I enquired about the empty envelope, Abu Athier said that his own mailman had delivered it empty to him while he was about to leave for the prison in his car! I felt like saying to him, *For God's sake grant me a little intelligence,* but by now I was unfazed by the continual lies and stupid things I was expected to believe. The Iraqi mentality considered that it was better to say something, no matter how ridiculous. Saying nothing was considered rude!

I held a perverse hope that if I didn't begin a diary this would protect me from a lengthy term in prison. Now, like a bloody fool, I opened my eyes and realised that ten months had passed and if I was going to be able to recall the salient facts and details of my experience I would need to start making some proper notes instead of just writing letters.

Another reason for not wanting to start keeping a diary was my steadfast belief that my sentence was a 'mistake'. I hoped that someone would realise that I was not a government agent, not a spy, not Jewish, and presented no threat to the Iraq's security. Then I would be released. I couldn't understand why the Iraqis believed I was a spy. Every intelligence device in the Western world was being used against Iraq at that moment so, what difference would one person, especially a chef, make to any unfolding events. Why couldn't these mad sods grasp that?

I hated Abu Ghraib. I knew I was being held here unjustly and informed the prison's spy network of this regularly, hoping that they would pass the information to the Iraqis. I didn't fear the spies. In my fantasy world I thought that if the authorities here knew how I felt then it would strengthen my resolve and position!

Thursday, 6th May.

A single cell was cleared for a new prisoner – an American! His name was Ken Beaty and his arrival infuriated me. Single cell aside, I also learned from Ken when we spoke that he had been 'processed' in a comparatively short space of time. We'd been treated like spies, put into the Iraqi criminal system and dealt with appallingly. Now it seemed the Iraqis were treating their hostages in a more humane way. The speed which people were getting from the 'border' to Abu Ghraib was becoming ridiculous. Ken had made the trip, which took me 54 days and the Swedes 21 days, in nine days!

Ken had a great deal to say about the way the Iraqis had whisked him over the border, as had we all, and expressed surprise about his single cell. "Surely, I am an American, which makes me the big enemy in this whole situation." He said to me. "And yet here I am being treated better than you British guys!"

He didn't understand it at all and, to be very honest, neither did I. It was quite simply a big slap in the face. I was furious, not only because since the arrival of the Swedes I had been told that no single cells existed but also that an American should be given such special treatment. Clearly Iraq was shitting itself about the USA and was putting Ken in the 'VIP' category. For me it was an ignominious defeat and I felt really belittled. The Swedes and Ken were getting 'five-star' treatment while I was put through the mill and had been forced to live in appalling conditions in the Mukhabarat complex, in Faisaliyah, and in Al Alwiyah.

I was a man who had been 'important' enough to abduct and

imprison, but now bigger fish had been hooked I was just small fry still significant enough to hold as a hostage, but not as important as other hostages. It hurt my pride, never had I felt so used and abused. I had a strong sense of self belief, but this was being stripped in Iraq. I began to feel that I didn't count and this ripped the heart out of me because I thought that the more numerous the special cases became, the lower down the pecking order I fell. The other prisoners recognised this and I remember Abet cruelly mocking my situation and recall the nodding looks from other prisoners which made me feel immeasurably small.

Ken was an 'oilman' who'd been in Kuwait since April 1991, and while being held at the Mukhabarat complex he'd been given a camp bed to sleep on and extra food rations, as had the Swedes. He'd been permitted to take his blindfold off during interrogations and had not suffered Faisaliyah, Al Alwiyah and Tasfirat. He also managed to avoid the delightful 'reception' cells in the Iraqi section of Abu Ghraib. This felt like more skins peeled from the onion that had once been my self-esteem.

A Palestinian who'd accused me of being part of a group trying to 'control and run' Al Alwiyah arrived at Abu Ghraib. He was vile and openly informed on the other prisoners at Al Alwiyah so he could form a power base. I didn't 'hate' many people who I met as a hostage but he attempted to include me in his grubby power games and of all the spies I came into contact with, I despised this pig with gut-wrenching intensity!

Friday, 7th May.

An Egyptian and a Kurd were put in the punishment cells and beaten after they were caught have sexual intercourse. Many inmates at Abu Ghraib were having homosexual relationships and the unwritten rule was do not get caught!

Ken's treatment, plus lack of sleep fed my foul mood. I lay awake at night struggling with scenarios created by my own imagination. An entry in the diary I was now keeping read, "The Palestinian 'grass' is talking about me. I'll find out what he said from Abet later. I really can't handle this, I think I may be cracking up."

Sunday, 9th May.

Abu Athier called me to his office and told me that Julie would be coming to Abu Ghraib with one of Michael's relatives, probably in June. When I returned to the cell and informed Michael of the news he thanked me. This was the first time I'd heard Michael use the words, thank you, when speaking to me. It was nice.

Abu Athier also told me to ask Ken if I could share his cell! Surprised, I willingly followed orders and and went to see him. "Hi Ken, Abu Athier has asked if you would be willing to let me share your cell," I asked politely.

Ken raised his eyebrows and smiled as he replied, "Hi Paul, the truth is that my wife is sending me a 'care package' and I just don't want my cell getting too crowded, so I'd rather not share if that's okay with you?"

What could I say? It was fine that I slept in a cell with 16 people in it while Ken had a cell to himself; I mean, *Who the fuck am I to get upset anyway?*

I wrote in my diary, "The Septic (cockney rhyming slang – Septic Tank = Yank) doesn't want to share – he should live as I've had to for a few weeks, it would open his eyes. Another Western hostage treated with kid gloves."

I tried to get rid of my rage by running. I ran for as long as I could every day. The distances grew longer but the bile and venom never left my body. I seethed. I was on the brink of a meltdown again. I desperately wanted vindication, justice, equality, and my freedom!

Things I took for granted as a 34-year-old were not so for men from Muslim backgrounds. An Iranian Kurd by the name of Tahir had been telling me things about himself for months. He made it clear he had been forced to leave Iran due to connections with a terrorist organisation. He said he was a wanted terrorist. I noted in my diary, "Tahir has just told me that he has never made love to a woman or seen a naked woman in his life – he is nearly 26 – the poor son of a bitch wants so badly to come to the West, he doesn't know what he's letting himself in for, he is a child with the mind of an anarchist."

Tuesday, 11th May.

The Swedes joined the Abu Ghraib rumour mill, informing me that the Foreign Office was sending a delegation to negotiate our release. My problem with rumours was that try as I might to ignore them, because they were usually unfounded, they invaded my head space. The ride up the roller coaster saw my emotions soaring until I realised that the promised outcomes were never going to happen and then the stomach-churning downside of the trip kicked in!

Michael had developed a fever and the following day a doctor was called at 2.30pm but he didn't arrive. At 8.30pm Ghassan arranged for him to be taken across to the hospital. A short while later he returned, supposedly fit, but still looking very ill. Michael later informed people that his problem was a migraine, and bed rest usually cleared it.

Thursday, 13th May.

The deputy governor, well-known for being a sadistic bastard, conducted the 7.00am Muster. Iraqi officers liked to have all prisoners crouching and waiting when they arrived to count but unfortunately some heavy sleepers arrived late and the deputy governor arrived before they assembled. He stood and waited as they emerged bleary-eyed into the bright morning light and as they closed their eyes against the sun he beat each of them with a length of 'three-phase' industrial electrical cable. The cable was heavy-duty, several centimetres in diameter, hard, flexible, and painful when it struck, and the screams of the late arrivals rang out in the still morning air. Anyone unwilling to leave the section 'voluntarily' was given a longer beating for their impudence. Witnesses crouched and hoped his fury would have run its course as he entered the yard. We feared this madman, he was insane, irrational and very violent.

Events like this were commonplace. Regularly senior officers would pick on a prisoner, or anyone stood near them, and for no apparent reason slap, punch and kick them or force them to perform debilitating and humiliating tasks such as running in circles with one finger held against the floor. When the victim became dizzy and fell to the floor, they would be kicked and threatened until they dragged themselves to their feet and continued with their 'punishment'. All of which was much to the amusement of the screeching guards.

Friday, 14th May.

Visiting day. In our cell we had such a range of illnesses that I nicknamed it 'The Plague Pit' and increasingly I tried to spend as much time out of it as possible. Given the problems with light-fingered visitors, I decided to stay in the cell until the visitors departed, only leaving to go to the toilet. When I came back, Adel returned a magazine which one of the Kurdish kids had taken, I also lost a teaspoon and a lump of cheese! How low can you get? Stealing from a man who is in prison! I now viewed this as a reflection of the desperate situation the Iraqis were in. I should also say that many honest visitors, who had very little of their own, insisted that I accept some of the food they had brought to eat with their detained relatives.

I heard on the news that Saddam Hussein was acting to plug holes appearing in the Iraqi economy. He sealed Iraq's borders and withdrew the country's old 25 Dinar note, reissuing a new version. Nothing sinister about that you might think, but this was another act of a wicked tyrant. The old Iraqi 25 Dinar note was printed in Switzerland and had been in use since UN sanctions had been imposed. It had been used to purchase goods from all the countries surrounding Iraq especially Jordan. The sealing of the borders meant that traders from outside Iraq could not get into country during the specified period to exchange millions of dinars worth of the 'old' currency they held while conducting business with, and supplying goods to, Iraq!

Saddam's regime announced that for four days the Iraqi bank would exchange the Swiss note for the new note printed in Iraq. This was the same period during which the borders were shut! In doing this a huge debt which had built up in countries trading with Iraq was wiped off! What a really nice way to repay the humanity shown by the Jordanians during a period when the rest of the world had turned its back on Iraq! I heard stories of businessmen being ruined by the move and committing suicide rather than face poverty. Some were holding hundreds of thousands, perhaps even millions of the Iraqi notes. This was a terrible blow to the struggling Jordanian economy. Saddam was a shining star in the theatre of Arab unity!

Saturday, 15th May.

I got a bout of the Gastric flu and had been up all night in the toilets where I shivering with fever! It was very unpleasant, but fortunately short-lived!

The Swedes families arrived, a reminder of the fact nothing seemed to be moving forward in respect of my own situation. Christer's wife brought a letter for me, the first in many weeks, from Julie! They had been due to arrive a week earlier but the border closure had delayed their entry to Iraq! There was some good news however in the afternoon when I was summoned to Abu Athier's office and told that a delegation of British Government MPs would be coming to see Michael and myself on Monday.

In the evening I listened to The FA Cup Final on my radio. Arsenal v Sheffield Wednesday. The game which was bewilderingly boring finished 1-1 after extra-time. I would not bother with the replay!

Monday, 17th May.

As summer approached, the outside temperature was rising and sleep once more became a hot sticky affair. In the small hours of Monday, under sheets and blankets I'd sweltered, tossed and turned in semi-delirium and then while uncovered atop my bedclothes I'd fallen victim to the juggernaut mosquitoes. I couldn't win. In all my time in prison never a day went by when I didn't have a head full of spanners about something or another. The heat, the mosquitoes, the cold, the food, the guards, the prisoners, the conditions, the Mukhabarat. The list was endless!

At 9.00am Muster, Michael and I were ordered to Abu Athier's office. Two British MPs had arrived to see us, just as I'd been told they would! A first time for everything! Abu Athier sent us into the visiting room where five men were waiting. Two Iraqis, from the foreign ministry, a reporter from the BBC, and two British MPs who introduced themselves as Tam Dalyell (Labour MP for Linlithgow) and George Galloway (Labour MP for Glasgow Hillhead).

My diary expresses how I felt. "Had a very good meeting with the British MPs, they didn't promise anything but spoke sensibly about the poor relations and took a promise from the Iraqi authorities that we would get a small cell in a week to ten days. The meeting lasted an hour-and-a-half and I made a statement to the journalist saying that as well as being held here for political reasons with the Iraqis being the initial cause, now the intransigence of the British Government was keeping us in prison."

The MPs left with no promises being made, stating that, "The kind and considerate Iraqi government had granted them permission to come and visit us." I took this comment with a pinch of salt. Surely, they were paying lip service to the hidden microphones in the room. I didn't believe the Iraqis were kind, or considerate. I went along with the 'charade' for the sake of the two MPs. I didn't want to embarrass them in the way Michael and I were being embarrassed daily.

I wrote to Julie on the day of the visit saying, "It was very good. Before we started the meeting they stated that they hadn't come out to free us, and we were not among the main priorities they wished to get in motion," which I thought was both very honest and a good thing to say. That way there could be no misconceptions or misunderstandings. They went on to say how much they opposed the war and they now opposed the sanctions as they said Kuwait had behaved in a very bad way towards Iraq before the whole thing started. They said that they hoped the reconciliatory nature of their visit would bring some definite actions and changes in attitude."

I'd told the MPs about how I'd been forced to live during the initial months of my detention and compared it with the treatment received by the Swedes and now the American. The truth upset the Iraqis, especially Abu Athier who called me into his office later and gave me a very hard time about my comments. He said that I should have spoken to him about it and not made him look bad to the MPs. I stated that when I spoke to him, I was informed that no cells were available for Michael and I and that I had to use every means to improve our position which meant speaking to the British MPs about our treatment.

I'd stuck my neck out, but in that sort of situation things are black and white and right now I thought that they couldn't get any blacker. Abu Athier assured me that in a week to ten days I would be put in a twin cell with Michael but he wanted a signed statement that promised good behaviour from us!

I want to clarify my feelings about the situation here in repect of my comments about the Swedes and the American. I felt no personal animosity towards them or any of the individual Western hostages whatsoever but I did feel great deal of anger that other 'Western' nationals, held for the same reason as myself, were being given preferential treatment. It made me boiling mad, but the people involved were all okay with, and for, me.

Tuesday, 18th May.

An air conditioning unit was installed in our cell! Far from being modern, this was a monolithic piece of kit that was not only ancient but also totally filled the cell window it was fitted to. Our environment changed immediately and not for the better. Natural light was reduced and when switched on the blast of air delivered was a veritable typhoon. We became cooler but the air-con affected me personally as it blew directly onto my bed space and turned my ordered world into a disaster area!

Thursday, 20th May.

Today was the day Michael and I had been due to move to a smaller cell but there was no contact with anyone in authority and nothing happened.

Ken was given a meal in the governor's office and apparently all the prison hierarchy were in attendance. More evidence of the differential treatment prisoners received. It filled me with a determination that people should know the truth about the sycophantic bullshit the Iraqis got up to.

Khalid Jerjes became an increasing problem for me. Due to Ken's arrival Michael and myself had dropped further down the 'pecking order' as Ken was politically more important. Jerjes appeared to be doing all the legal work in Abu Ghraib. People on similar charges such as my Turkish friend Abdul Baki were being told to switch to his services. It didn't seem logical that one lawyer would handle all high-profile cases, was he the only lawyer in Iraq?

It made no sense unless the 'lawyer' in question was an agent of the Iraqi authorities or someone they could control, either way I was increasingly concerned with his attitude, omnipresence, and inability to get results. The Swedes were still in prison five months after their government complied with Iraqi demands. The question that continually went through my mind was, *What is this clown Jerjes up to?*

I was not alone in thinking Jerjes was inept. In an article printed in a British newspaper, George Galloway described Jerjes as, "The bungling Arab in a Whitehall farce." Galloway had said to me in our meeting that, "He should be changed, he's useless. Who appointed him?"

Julie wrote and said I'd been called up for jury service at the Central Criminal Courts (Old Bailey in London). She'd replied to the Clerk of the Court, "If the Foreign Minister, (Douglas Hurd), was willing to secure my return to London, she was sure that I would be glad to attend!" I thought it bizarre that someone held as a hostage in Baghdad should be called up for jury service.

Julie mentioned a Doctor Paul Kane. He'd told her he was well-connected internationally and politically and was willing to help negotiate my release. She'd also heard he was a name-dropper, possibly connected to the US security services, who used 'senior figures' he met to introduce him to other political figures as a friend and worthy contact. He told Julie that he could arrange an Iran-style helicopter assault on Abu Ghraib to secure my freedom!

Julie contacted the Foreign Office and stated that Kane's attitude might extend my time in Iraq or get me killed. She wanted to know if Kane had any official links. The Foreign Office denounced him as a maverick and told Julie to have nothing to do with him saying that he was a "self-serving independent".

Prison rumours indicated that it was actually Ken who was the likely candidate for a helicopter trip out of Abu Ghraib! I knew it was probably bullshit as usual but I said to the Swedes if the story was true then the only place to 'spring' Ken would be from the exercise yard. For weeks I stuck to Ken like glue saying to myself, *If he's getting out of here in a helicopter, then I am going to hitch a bloody ride!*

I spoke with Ken about the possibilities of being 'broken out' of the prison and while he never said he'd heard of the rescue plan, he never denied it either! Was I growing more desperate believing Iraqi claims that I was a spy, or was I simply losing my mind?

Saturday, 22nd May.

Football! The foreign section versus the Iraqi section 'series' continued. I watched enthusiastically as 'we' played well and won 3-0. The deputy governor of our section got a game today which I felt was unfair. He was an evil bastard and wasn't tackled properly once! I enjoyed these matches enormously because I had no other way of 'seeing' us foreigners beat the Iraqis even if they were fellow prisoners!

I heard from Abdul Baki that the Mukhabarat were very upset that I had spoken out against my treatment during the MPs visit. I told him what I had told everybody else, "If they treat me like a prick then that is how I will act. I've spent months in this shithouse going along with all their lies – no more!"

Tuesday, 25th May.

The Swedish families had gone home at the weekend and the lads were already distressed. For weeks they'd been told 'soon', and for weeks nothing had happened. Their Embassy kept repeating it would be a matter of days and that all that was required was patience! Easy when you visit once a week and return to the luxury of an Embassy compound!

I received 80 pieces of mail delivered via the Iraqi system! This ended a lengthy period without letters to read which had depressed me. The Swedes were depressed, this depressed me. Ken was treated like royalty, this depressed me. I upset Abu Athier with my revelations to the MPs, this depressed me. Iraq was being 'attacked' by the West, this depressed me. Michael was Michael, this depressed me. I wasn't happy and the mail distracted me and lifted my spirits.

I had a chat with Ken who told me that he'd seen Paul Kane, who'd been refused permission to see Michael and myself. Kane had also met Saddam Hussein and with Ken now being a hostage and having a history of heart trouble he was the doctor's priority. I wasn't surprised!

The Polish Embassy represented Americans in Iraq, and therefore Ken. They were really pushing the heart problems and illness angle at the Iraqis pointing out that should anything 'injurious' happen to Ken while he was a hostage then the US response would be swift and damaging.

I wrote to Julie, "Let me tell you that the Septic is an ill man with blood pressure and heart problems. If he gets out because of his illness I may develop a broken heart!"

Wednesday, 26th May.

Iraq were competing in a World Cup qualifying competition for the finals to be held in the USA in 1994. Qualification was a two-stage process. To qualify for stage two, Iraq had to win a group that also comprised China, Yemen, Jordan and Pakistan. Most of the games were shown on TV and while not comparable to European standards, the dedication and commitment shown by the players was phenomenal. They looked as if being picked and playing for their countries was the greatest honour ever. They didn't play in an aggressive or cynical way but contested every ball, fought every tackle, and never gave up.

In the evening I watched Iraq beat Yemen 6-1. Lots of the prisoners openly supported the 'other' side when Iraq played and there was plenty of frustration as the Iraqis played well and scored plenty of goals. The 'spies' were 'watching' people as they 'disrespected' the country responsible for the filth and squalor in this dreadful hole. I enjoyed the football and even though sitting on an old milk powder can converted for use as a stool amid a nightmare wasn't the same as being on The Shed terrace at Stamford Bridge cheering on Chelsea, it was a good diversion to 'life' in Abu Ghraib.

As I lay on my bed, my thoughts were drawn to the fact it was my sixth wedding anniversary and I drifted into a twitchy, nervous sleep thinking about Julie.

Thursday, 27th May.

The Iraqis went insane, placing an ambulance in our section 'in case' Ken was taken ill! What a load of bullshit! If they were that worried about him dying, why didn't they release him? Intransigence ruled. Saddam and Iraq would not budge an inch! I felt sure that the activity surrounding Ken was a prelude to his release. It both annoyed me and made me wonder if I'd need to become 'ill' before I was released.

Mail Julie had brought in February contained a letter from Sky TV journalist John Cookson asking if I could phone or fax him! In a scruffy reply I said I'd forgotten how to use a phone and had not seen a fax in months adding that we had several pigeons I would try to get a message out on. He never replied, but I heard that the note was used in a Sky News report.

The media had no concept of conditions in jails and prisons they described as 'infamous', 'notorious' or 'feared'. They spouted rhetoric for public consumption with no idea of the reality of which they were speaking. Abu Ghraib is in an Arabic, Islamic, state which means for committing a crime you need to be punished, and to be punished the hell hole you will be placed in must be so degrading and so inhuman that you will at times think yourself dead. I would need to act swiftly to get messages out on the pigeons as due to the food crisis they were being eaten!

Friday, 28th May.

More football! In the afternoon I watched Iraq beat Pakistan 8-0 and in the evening saw Yemen beat China 1-0 which didn't leave much time for anything else apart from writing an entry in my diary which read, "It's like a bloody zoo in here and it smells like one too. That MP Dalyell said my cell looked reasonable. I'd like to see him put up with one night in here, days and nights are like chalk and cheese! I am losing it, so I will stop, count to ten and have a cigarette!"

I'll mix with all classes, cultures, and backgrounds, but I struggled in the pressure cooker environment of Abu Ghraib. When I use terms such as, *I thought I was losing my mind* or *I wanted to kill him!*, believe me that this was exactly how I felt. The thin veneer of civilisation had been flaked off leaving an open wound which screamed self-preservation. At times I exploded with a rage so powerful that it scared me.

Saturday, 29th May.

Still full of bile, angry and bitter towards my captors and the grey politicians who prolonged my stay in Hades I wrote, "John Major said he was going to listen to the people. Ask him why we maintain a costly embargo while donating millions in aid. We have a broken economy but ban Iraq from selling its own oil to buy food. It's ridiculous, a high-handed stance which we (Britain) simply can't afford. It's 1993 not 1893, wake up!!" I realise a lot of my feelings were fuelled by anger, which distorted my view of situations.

Ken had a visit from the Polish Embassy and was given a radio the size of a jukebox! I hadn't seen a radio this big for a long time, it required a dozen batteries for Christ's sake! Less than a year earlier a small portable set I'd been sent had been deemed "too big" and confiscated!

Sunday, 30th May.

An Iraqi guard told me that he would gladly 'exchange' fathers, trading his for Ken. When I asked why, he said Ken was given better treatment in prison than he had ever seen before. Ken was regularly driven to Baghdad for medical treatment, no handcuffed route marches to the prison hospital for him then. The sad moaning bastard inside my head was making my life hell!

In the afternoon I watched Jordan beat Pakistan 1-0 and looked forward to the China v Iraq match that evening. It turned out to be the best game of the series and although it was only 1-0 to Iraq the standard of football was excellent.

Monday, 31st May.

In the evening as I was going to the toilets to brush my teeth I passed Ken's cell and had a major surprise. The Iraqis had put an oxygen cylinder in there! I had to laugh. "I wonder if he has one in his car in Kuwait!" I wrote in my diary later.

This sounds very callous, but it was how I'd become. I was angry and upset that everyone arriving since my imprisonment had been elevated above me in every respect, including legal representation and consideration for release. I was now totally switched off to the plight of others and cynical and sarcastic about everything.

ONE TRIP AROUND THE SUN

Wednesday, 2nd June.

As I had come to learn, prison can be a bore for days and weeks at a time. I had been held hostage for almost one year! If a fortune teller had predicted this as my fate I would have laughed and dismissed the idea as too fantastic to even contemplate!

News, whether developing in the prison or heard on the radio, was more-often-than-not the only thing that livened up the drudgery of my existence in Abu Ghraib, and today was one such day.

At the 1.00pm Muster, all the spies, forgers and killers were dismissed and sent into the section. Those remaining were informed that a special one-third amnesty was to be granted to us! A cheer rang out and questions, opinions and hopes were uttered as we returned to our cells. Nobody had a 'siesta' as prisoners dashed around consulting with each other and trying to work out their new release dates. Some were sure they were eligible for immediate release as they had less than a third of their time to serve. The panic, furore and excitement caused by the announcement was amazing. Following the initial euphoria, an exhausted peace descended upon the section as individuals withdrew into themselves and dreamed of their futures.

At 5.00pm, as I cooked my evening meal, an early Muster was called. This caused panic. Everyone thought we were being locked up for the night. This Muster was for an announcement! We were informed that the 1.00pm announcement was incorrect, the amnesty still existed but it was only for prisoners with over eight years already served. While there were many eligible, there were many more who were not.

The disappointment was palpable. Bodies sagged, eyes glazed and vacant expressions replaced hopeful enthusiasm. The Filipino lads had said previously that amnesties were announced, altered, and denied at will by the prison authorities and here was confirmation. It was brutally cruel. The Filipinos complained that on a few occasions they had been ignored and passed over when many other Arabic prisoners had been released, only to be returned for subsequent crimes committed while they had languished behind bars, forgotten in Abu Ghraib.

I was called in to see Abu Athier and Khalid Jerjes. I was still being reprimanded for speaking out to the Labour MPs and also being told that Michael and I would be in a single cell within a week. I thought, *We'll see!* Or as Michael was fond of saying, "They'll say 'owt' barring their fucking prayers, this lot!"

Michael had his faults, but he had the Iraqis worked out from a very early stage.

Friday, 4th June.

I spent the afternoon in Section One which was also known as the 'Spies Section'. Noufal, the Lebanese prisoner I'd had a heated exchange with while out running in January, had been nagging me to go over and bake him some bread! One of the spies said I would be getting the cell 'belonging to' an Egyptian called Maahes. This was seemingly confirmed by him crashing around the section in the evening in a terrible mood. I got very little sleep that night, excited at the prospect of being in a two-man cell with Michael!

Sunday, 6th June.

Michael and I were transferred to a cell on our own but not before he had put the long-desired move in jeopardy. I was summoned to see Abu Athier and told that Michael and I could move into a twin cell, "Vacated at considerable disruption and inconvenience especially for you."

I thanked Abu Athier with as much sincerity as I could gather, while thinking to myself that it was, *About bloody time!*

I raced back to Cell 7 to tell Michael the good news. He was lying on his bed twiddling a piece of paper and was less than impressed. "What do I want to move for? I'm not going in a cell with you!" he said with more than a hint of scorn in his voice.

I thought this was farcical. We had been sharing a cell for eight months albeit with many other prisoners. After a few attempts to reason with him I gave up and returned to Abu Athier and informed him of Michael's position. He said that if Michael refused we would never get the offer of a single cell again. I asked if I could move independently of Michael and was told that the move included Michael or it was off, for both of us! I was sick with fear, Michael would be pig-headed simply to spite me. I was sure he hated me, and now he held all the cards!

I returned to our cell and tried to force words out that would persuade the stubborn 'Yorkshire Dry Stone Wall' to move. At first I stammered as I didn't know where to start. I wanted to beg but choked on the words. Finally I said, "If you don't move then neither of us move. Are you going to stay here?"

Michael said nothing. He simply sat up, climbed off his bunk and started to walk out of the cell. When he reached the gate he muttered, "Where is this cell then? I'll take a look?

I dashed after him, fumbling with my sandals to point out the cell we were being 'given'. Michael 'toured' the vacant cell as a homebuyer might a house saying what he considered it required before it would be habitable. This was ridiculous. The cell measured two by three metres! My stomach flipped over in case the silly sod refused to move. Like a film star Michael swept from the cell, saying, "Tell Abu Athier I'll move!"

I went to see Abu Athier and told him we would move to the cell once we had cleaned it to Michael's satisfaction! As I spoke he stared at me with his mouth hanging open and then screamed that we would make any alterations after the move. I nodded and returned to the section hoping Michael would not veto the move. On arrival, I thanked God! He was already packing his personal effects into boxes. This change of heart meant that we were getting out of the over-inhabited circus that Cell 7 had become.

Our 'new' cell was filthy. We piled our possessions outside and the Filipino lads disinfected it thoroughly for us. Once we had 'moved in' I relaxed in the 'sanctuary' of my new abode. It wasn't perfect by any means, but it was a vast upgrade on the cell we had just left.

The move was the catalyst for Khalid Jerjes to demand I write to the British authorities and tell them that even though we had insulted the Iraqis in front of the British MPs we were getting wonderful treatment. I wrote the letter, and another informing Julie about Jerjes' 'request' and how I thought he fitted into the bigger picture. "Tell her (Heather Taggart) please not to contact Jerjes. This is a very complex web and I believe Jerjes is 'very close' to the authorities here. What he is told goes straight to them."

During the evening, there was a loud roar and much clapping and cheering from the prisoners watching TV. An announcement had been made that a general amnesty was going to happen! My immediate thought was, *Bloody typical! We move our gear then they let us out!*

As usual, the news brought with it false hope. It was not a general amnesty but a week's home leave for Iraqi prisoners only. How this could be perceived as an amnesty I'll never know, but in Abu Ghraib anything was possible!

Monday, 7th June.

I spent most of the day baking a batch of bread. Previously, I'd not been able to do any 'food preparation' but now my new cell allowed me to indulge my culinary creativity! I split the bread among my fellow hostages and the Filipino lads whom I thanked graciously for their help. I remember the bread made having a sandwich a pleasure! I don't know how the others felt but I hope it was something similar. I enjoyed how it made me feel.

The Swedish Embassy diplomats were changed again and an obligatory tour of the section followed. I kept a low profile. I didn't want to offend the authorities again. They toured the prison mouthing platitudes. Heather Taggart had done the same, as had Gleb Desyatnikov, and I now knew that the politicians saw exactly what 'the hosts' wanted them to see and nothing more! God! It made my blood boil!

Over the next few days I noticed that being in a 'single cell' increased visits from people telling me to "watch" certain prisoners, who were spies trying to cause problems. In this Nazi-style environment everyone was informing on everybody else. Many came with reports of spies denouncing me.

I had something to lose now – the cell! Losing it to a grass terrified me and once more I was gripped by fear and paranoia. My every action was being watched and reported on. I can't describe the anxiety I felt at the possibility of unwittingly falling foul of Abu Athier, or even Jerjes who was clearly a lot more than a lawyer. Which Judas would betray me and destroy my world? Thoughts of being returned to the degradation of a squalid multiple cell tortured me.

Prison, if it gives you anything, grants you the time to expand tiny acorns of suggestion into mighty oaks of doubt. Every second unoccupied is prey to negative thoughts so I worked, exercised, cooked meals, and wrote letters in earnest to block the fears and worst-case scenarios that were hiding in my sub-conscious.

Wednesday, 9th June.

Ken had a visit from Polish diplomats and predictably, in advance of this, the floor of his cell was given a scrub. Double rations of soap powder were used and the corridor outside resembled an indoor 'Cresta Run' with mountains of white soap suds replacing the ice and snow.

I caught sight of Abu Athier peeking through the 'net curtains' used to repel mosquitoes that were hung across the gate to our cell so I got up and opened it. Abu Athier marched in followed by Khalid Jerjes who told me that another Brit and a German were 'being processed' and would soon be in Abu Ghraib.

30 minutes later Simon Dunn and Kai Sondermann were in our cell. Initially you're elated that 'new' people have entered your world. Simon was 23-years-old and Kai a very youthful 27. They looked like a couple of students on a beach holiday. The 'relief' of ending up in Abu Ghraib with us was apparent. They didn't have a clue what was going on – just as I hadn't a year earlier. I was delighted to meet them but sad and angry that people were still being abducted from the border area.

Having been told that they would be found a cell the following day, on their first night at the Hotel Abu Ghraib, Simon slept on the floor of our cell and Kai slept on the floor of an adjacent cell shared by a pair of Sudanese lads.

There was no mention of Kai or Simon on the BBC news bulletins I listened to on my radio and I assumed that their story had not reached the world's media yet. I hoped their detention would rekindle interest in our case. For a while now I'd felt that Michael and I had been forgotten by the journalists who had been so keen to find 'exclusive' angles on our stories in prior months. Had we become yesterday's news?

Kai and Simon were given a twin cell the next day and I wrote about it in my diary – but was I right or accurate?

Thursday, 10th June.

"The two newcomers got a single cell today – quick eh! I saw Jerjes. I don't think the bastard has informed their parents, but he did tell the Russians so hopefully it will get sorted out. I really don't trust Jerjes. I believe Michael and I got a room as Kai is a neutral German and he and Simon would have had to go in a single cell due to this and it would look bloody funny if newcomers were looked after while we still slept in a 17-man cell. This place is horrible. Distrust, arguments, fights. It really is too much. Was I always like this, always arguing and doubting?"

Jerjes came into the section and claimed to have arranged their cell. He said he'd contact the Foreign Office on Saturday and inform them about Simon. I said it was pointless to wait until then, the information should be passed today, or even better yesterday. To my surprise, Jerjes agreed! That was a first!

Friday, 11th June.

I developed a fever which turned into delirium. I felt so awful that I feared I was dying. I am usually in good health and so when I develop an illness I let everyone around me know!

Ghassan the 'spy' who 'worked' at the clinic came by and paid me close attention and to be fair to him he did a good job regularly taking my temperature which stood at 39.4 Centigrade all day! He called the doctors at 9.30pm and they said I should be taken for a full medical in the prison hospital. I was shivering uncontrollably while simultaneously sweating profusely. I was in a lot of pain, I felt cold, I ached all over, and my sheets hurt where they touched me. I didn't want to die in this dammed place. I didn't object to death, but felt dying here would be an Iraqi win and I didn't want to give them that pleasure.

I lay on my steel platform, such was my bed, soaked in sweat. The doctor came to see me and instructed Ghassan to sponge my body down – a job that he delegated to a young Sudanese prisoner called Hassan who looked like a child in a man's body. He was one of the nice people in Abu Ghraib, but his innocence was often the target of numerous jokes. As he was well-liked, none of the jokes were malicious, as they often were when about other prisoners.

Hassan was a driver who had been delivering a consignment of televisions and videos close to the Kuwait/Iraq border. He too had found himself charged with entering Iraq illegally however at his court hearing he'd been discharged but told that his lorry and its load would be confiscated. He protested that the cargo was not his and demanded they should be returned to Kuwait with him. As a consequence of this he was taken to another police station, charged again, tried and this time sentenced to 15 years in prison! This bizarre sentence caused sarcasm within the section while his naiveté 'embarrassed' his fellow Sudanis in

Abu Ghraib. I felt truly sorry for him. His kindness was a breath of fresh air in a fetid, cynical hole.

Saturday, 12th June.

Still in the grip of fever I was lying in bed at 10.45am when Ghassan called me to the hospital. I felt ill and expected to be driven there as I didn't think I could walk as I'd had serious trouble just getting to the administration block. I began to worry as soon as I staggered in and there stood three other prisoners. I wanted to refuse to walk but I was so confused that I lamely held out my arm and allowed the cold steel of the handcuffs to sting my wrist as they snapped shut and I was manacled to a Sudanese prisoner I didn't know from another section and we were shoved on our way to the hospital – on foot!

Walking in the blazing sun at 11.00am in June is not easy. I remember very little of the experience except I felt as if it lasted several hours. I staggered along with imploring glances and encouraging words from my 'partner'. Why couldn't a car have been provided? I bet Ken Beaty wouldn't be expected to do this? Are they trying to kill me? Do they know how I feel? Thoughts careered around my head as my vision blurred and the horizon bobbed and rippled in front of my eyes. The other prisoners were solicitous throughout the long walk to the main prison, probably from fear that I might collapse and they would be forced to carry me, an onerous burden they could do without.

We reached the hospital building and once inside the relief of cooler air upon my sweat-soaked clothes was a delight and I walked a little faster. I had slowed the group considerably as I'd struggled along in the heat outside which had angered our guards who enjoyed the walk no more than we did.

The doctor I'd seen the previous night said that I should have blood, urine, and stool tests as well as X-Rays and a full physical exam. Some of this was lost in translation. I received an X-Ray and a check with a stethoscope. The doctor pronounced my heart and lungs "fit and well" and soon we were on our way back to our section of the complex. I was given an assortment of capsules, what they were for I couldn't say, but if this was how a fit and well man felt, I thought I certainly didn't want to get ill!

I made the return journey to Section Three handcuffed to an Egyptian and climbed straight back into bed when I reached my cell and drifted off to sleep. Waking a couple of hours later, I was soaked to the skin again and shivering. After a brief respite, my fever was raging once more. During Saturday evening I had my clothes changed five times in an effort to stop the fever 'feeding' on itself and Hassan sponged my body off on each occasion to remove the sweat still seeping from every pore.

I prayed that my fever would soon pass as I honestly didn't know whether to lie in bed, go to the toilet, eat some food, or stay on the liquid diet that I'd been on since my illness started. For several days I felt intermittently hot, cold, flushed, sweaty, dry, or nauseous. My ability to concentrate vanished. I couldn't write letters and those I did scrawl were not legible and I burnt every meal I cooked. Ruining food annoyed me. Whether it was down to my professional pride or the waste of precious ingredients I wasn't sure, but it wound me up.

Monday, 14th June.

I got out of bed and felt better than I had over the weekend. I decided to have a shower, but there was a problem with the water supply to Section Three! Adel Mansoor said I could take a shower in the Hanoot which he 'oversaw', as the shower there was fed from a different mains supply. This was decent of Adel and after I'd showered I felt fresh but, considering the time of year, cold! I wasn't better yet!

Ken Beaty returned from a hospital clinic in Baghdad he'd been taken to and told me that it was a horrid place with armed guards, locked doors, and no medicines. He'd insisted on returning to Abu Ghraib! If Ken preferred Abu Ghraib, the hospital he'd visited must have been rough! He also said that Khalid Jerjes had told him a "big British delegation" was coming. I chuckled and told Ken that time would tell and I wasn't going to put the flags out just yet.

Tuesday, 15th June

I had not been aware of the nauseous smell the fever had left on my sheets. My illness had blocked my senses and so when I woke up I'd nearly gagged. I stripped the bed and had the sheets washed.

Tahir, the Iranian Kurd who'd told me he was a terrorist and another Kurd, Omar, were put in the punishment block. I wasn't aware of the circumstances surrounding this but when Tahir emerged a few days later his feet had been so badly beaten they were double their normal size and grotesquely discoloured. For weeks he limped about in pain and while I was at Abu Ghraib he never appeared to regain the full use of either foot.

An Egyptian who was making homosexual advances to me came on strong while I was taking a shower. He spent hours each day in the toilet, leering at men urinating and taking a shower. As I washed myself he kept watching me and I saw he was masturbating. I grabbed my towel off the wall and dashed out into the corridor roaring, "If someone doesn't do something about this stupid fucking Egyptian, then I will kill him."

He was a pathetic, mentally unstable, creature but my fear of letting him get away with his behaviour and the escalation of it demanded action! The corridor filled with people all shouting at once. The Maraheb's tried to calm things down as I stood in the corridor, dripping wet, wrapped in a towel shouting at the Egyptian who was stood nearby still rubbing his genitals! At the sight of his openly homosexual display the Arabs went berserk and dragged him out of the section.

I was told that he had been placed in the punishment block and given a beating for his actions. Truly, I hated being a catalyst that caused him to be punished, but if I discovered one thing in prison it was self-preservation.

Thursday, 17th June.

Abu Athier asked me if Michael was, "behaving himself". I hated having to decide if he was behaving himself. I was being asked to spy on Michael so I always answered, "Yes. No problems."

Simon had yet to have a supply of food brought in by the Russian Embassy and so I prepared meals for the both of us while Kai who was also in the same boat was eating mainly with the Swedes. I wrote home to Julie and commented on the eating arrangements. "Simon is eating with me most of the time. Like myself he arrived here with nothing. I've got enough food to last a couple of weeks but I am using a lot more than usual as he has a good appetite! Could you mention this to the Foreign Office. I don't want to be accused of giving food away."

I didn't want to receive another letter from the Foreign Office commenting on my food consumption as the previous one had really upset me, so I thought that due to the change in the situation the best method of defence was attack.

Much of the food, clothes, and equipment Julie had brought or sent me had been either used, worn out, or broken. From mid-June my letters home contained requests for replacement goods. The harsh prison environment was hard on things such as buckets, bowls, and jugs which had been purchased locally and were of poor quality. I worried about the financial strain for Julie as the rate at which things broke or became unusable was staggering. Most of these items were available to borrow, but this put me in others debt which I viewed as being an unhealthy position. I preferred to be self-sufficient.

Monday, 21st June.

Gleb Desyatnikov visited Abu Ghraib. Simon had been hoping for a positive development in his case and his disappointment after the visit was obvious. With a 'been there, got the T-shirt' stance I tried to explain this was normal and no slur against him. It was just more of the same for all of us. Just as I had, Simon hoped he would be the person who inspired the British Government to act. The shock that, like Michael and me, he was a non-negotiable item was a bitter pill for him.

The only comments Gleb made which could be interpreted as positive were the statements, "The worst-case scenario in a hostage situation like this is a duration of half-sentence! Then, in case we were unable to do the mathematics involved, he added, "That would be three-and-one-half years for you both!"

I received a copy of a letter from Parliamentary Under-Secretary of State for Foreign and Commonweath Affairs, Mark Lennox-Boyd, to Peter Lilley, Secretary of State at the Department of Social Security, which implied that Michael's family and Julie had been in receipt of government donations to travel to Iraq. This simply wasn't true and I wrote to Julie saying, "You really should tell Mark that he shouldn't make statements that can be so easily misinterpreted. One doesn't want to look a ninny at a later date does one?"

After our less than satisfactory diplomatic visit, Abu Athier and Khalid Jerjes sat in the office and asked me, "When is Madam Julie coming out next?"

Abu Athier then asked if I wanted a scotch or a beer! I replied, "I've done a year without a drink, so I can do without a drink today!"

He didn't labour the point and Jerjes launched into another attack on the Russian Embassy. Something would happen in a couple of cases soon, and then he would look at my situation. I treated this comment, as I did everything he said, with contempt.

I was about to leave when Abu Athier questioned me again about Michael and his behaviour. To tell them the sort of things they wanted to hear would have been a lie and counterproductive. The twin cell worried me at first, but Michael and I hardly spoke so it was just like being in a single cell! It seemed to me that Abu Athier was looking for an excuse to put Michael in solitary confinement. He told me several times that he disliked him calling him "a very bad person". Why? He never said. Here I was, 'piggy in the middle' again. As if I didn't have my own problems!

Abu Athier concluded by saying that on Julie's next visit he could arrange a special 24-hour-pass so we could spend a day together outside the prison! This was brilliant news; however, I think the best way to describe my thoughts about the statement was, hopeful while not entirely convinced.

Tuesday, 22nd June.

Everyone in the section was ordered to visit the Hanoot where we were photographed to update our files!

Wednesday, 23rd June.

Things were plodding along when Abu Athier and Khalid Jerjes arrived and said that a delegation from the Foreign Office would be arriving on Sunday. *More visitors coming to the zoo?* I wondered. *I hope they have plenty of peanuts!*

Jerjes then started to question me about the Ministry of Defence in

London, saying, "Paul, you remember the office which you had to go past while you worked in the Ministry of Defence (MOD) in London?"

I was astonished and with my jaw hanging open asked for confirmation of what he'd just asked, "Sorry, did you say the Ministry of Defence?"

"Yes!" nodded Jerjes. "While you worked at the MOD in London, you went into a section with offices on your right. Did you go into these offices?"

With as much bravado as I could summon, I replied, "I could draw you a map and show you where the MOD is in London, but what it looks like inside – I haven't got a clue!"

"This is very useful information. Are you sure you are not a spy?" retorted Jerjes in a joking manner. "With this information you could make lots of money, no?"

Flippantly, I replied, "No! I am sure that everyone who wants or needs to know where the MOD is are aware of its location, even the tourists!"

I tried to appear as offhand as possible, but was flabbergasted by the questions from Jerjes. This was the straw that broke the camel's back as far as my trust of him was concerned. I seethed that the Foreign Office in London should be so casual with very dangerous information that Jerjes had used to put me in an invidious position. I'd worked at the MOD during the Gulf War. I started on the day before the outbreak of hostilities and had kept this a closely-guarded secret as I feared it would be used against me by the xenophobic and illogical Iraqi regime. My fear was driven by a recollection of UK-based Iranian freelance journalist, Farhad Bazoft, who'd been arrested at Baghdad International Airport, accused of being an Israeli spy, and subseqently executed. I was terrified that Jerjes knew my work history. I never saw or heard anything that might be considered 'secret' while working at the MOD, but realised that this would have been of minor importance had the Iraqis believed otherwise.

Sensing my rage, Abu Athier then repeated his statement that he would arrange a 24-hour-pass for me, so that Julie, William, and I might spend some 'normal' time together. Both Abu Athier and Jerjes said how they enjoyed a trip into Baghdad with Julie when she had visited in February and suggested that Julie had been talkative and had a wonderful time. If this was designed to plant seeds of doubt in my mind, it failed. I knew how Julie felt about my detention, and any notion that she sympathised with the Iraqi regime was an act to influence my situation.

Until the Foreign Office arrived, I spent the days exercising and writing angry letters. Knowing their representatives would soon be here made me angry. The Iraqi regime had put me in prison and in doing so broken international law. I'd committed no crime and visits from Foreign Officials mouthing platitudes were more than I could bare. I found the dialogue patronising and wished diplomacy would stop and the truth be told.

Friday, 25th June.

I'd gone to bed at 11.30pm on Thursday evening and at midnight the prison became a noisy active cauldron again. Two Frenchmen arrived in the section which was becoming more and more like the United Nations! We put them in a cell and let them sleep, I was too tired for a big discussion.

In the morning, Michael and I gave our cell a good clean out as cockroaches were multiplying at an alarming rate and where one sort of vermin gathers others, like the disgusting prison rats, were sure to follow.

Later in the day I met the two Frenchmen properly. One was a bespectacled 25-year-old called Jean-Luc Barriere, the other a French /Moroccan aged 28 called Ali Autout.

"Nice blokes, day trippers. Looked a bit choked when I told them I'd been here a year!" I wrote in my diary, summing up the situation with perfect irony. The bemused look on their faces when I gave them this snippet of information was priceless. They looked at each other, had a double-take at me, and then back at each other. It was comical they resembled Thompson and Thompson, the incompetent detectives from 'The Adventures of Tintin' books!

Saturday, 26th June.

I cooked for Jean-Luc, Ali, Kai, Simon, and myself. We were trying to help each other through this lunacy. Jean-Luc and Ali had made it from the Iraqi/Kuwait border into Abu Ghraib, via the Mukhabarat complex and the courts, in six days. This was a record, one I'm sure they would rather not have had! They were the last people, I know of, to be abducted from Northern Kuwait.

Sunday, 27th June.

I was rudely awakened at 2.00am by the Swedes. There was a major air strike going on and I was sleeping through it! An air of hysteria came over me during the attack, not panic, but a feeling that, *This is it! We are about to die!* My thoughts were accompanied by manic laughter! These emotions combined with everyday fatigue, the sort you live with after time in prison, left me quite giddy and breathless.

During the air strikes, as happened previously, lights flashed on and off, playing a sardonic duet with the anti-aircraft guns. I laughed till my sides hurt, other prisoners were screaming and panicking, they weren't listening to the Swedish or BBC news carrying reports on the launch of over 20 cruise missiles at Baghdad. The computer-controlled missiles were flying so low the Iraqis couldn't hit them.

The launch had been simultaneous from American fleets in the Gulf and Red Sea. As the radio broadcasts explained the details for the rest of the world, I was sat with half of the missiles flying over my head – lovely! With little to stay up for, other than the discotheque light display, I went back to sleep, surprisingly without any difficulty, at 2.45am.

Later in the day I heard a radio report claiming the attack was retaliation against Iraq for their attempt to assassinate former President George Bush during his visit to Kuwait in April. As I have mentioned previously, the Iraqi Mukhabarat sent agents to carry out the mission, yet when I'd reported the same thing, about the request made to me, the Foreign Office dismissed it as fantasy. I'm still convinced that the offer was legitimate and, had I taken the Iraqis up on it, God only knows what would have happened to me.

I'd experienced a missile attack in January but this was new territory for Simon, and he worried about the negative implications of the attack. He said the size of the attack was overkill, which it probably was. He disregarded the fact that the United States takes an attack or threat to the President very seriously, as it does an attack on all US citizens. Here in Britain we are 'regarded' as subjects of The Crown and eminently disposable

Abu Athier claimed he was injured in the missile attack! He said he was at a drinking club near the Mukhabarat complex when the attack occurred. I knew it was a lie. He probably realised that I knew it was a lie, but there we stood, captive and captor, I could hardly call him a bloody liar – could I?

Abu Athier used me as a 'messenger' between him and Michael. I regularly went to the office to listen to the latest complaints about him. It was bloody ridiculous. Michael contradicted every word I said to him. Using me as a messenger was the most negative approach. I knew it, and wrote in my diary, "I don't have problems with Michael. I hope to get him told by the Foreign Office guy just what he is doing to annoy the Iraqis. Today I asked Jerjes to make sure Abu Athier tells this guy just what he wants Michael to do. He thinks the things I say are all wrong, so hopefully he'll listen to the official – but I doubt it!"

Monday, 28th June.

Unhappy Anniversary! It was exactly one year since I'd been taken hostage and for the first, and last, time I heard Julie on the BBC World Service. She featured on many programmes while I was being held, but I was without a radio for one third of my sentence and besides I never knew when she'd be on so I missed them all except this one. Julie was asked to comment on the attack on Baghdad and she was vociferous, accusing the Americans of using a hammer to crack an eggshell.

"The USA attacked a site in Iraq and Britain morally supported them," I wrote. I heard the full brief on the World Service, and later the obedient tail-wagging of muted praise for an unwarranted attack both from our Foreign Minister and Prime Minister.

I was made aware of an article George Galloway, the MP who had visited in May, had written for the 'Mail On Sunday' in which he'd stated that I'd reported a physical attack on myself by Michael to the Iraqis. Galloway claimed that many witnesses, other prisoners, were present when I spoke of the assaults, with Michael sat alongside me. I recall I sat opposite Galloway and Tam Dalyell and that to their left sat a BBC reporter, then Michael, and on the MPs' right sat two Iraqi 'minders'. To say Michael and I sat together was a lie, there were two empty seats between us. We never sat together and hadn't since the new ambassador came with Gleb. Every letter evidencing the entire article was inaccurate.

The plain-faced lies stunned me and I decided to write to the editor of the newspaper and obtain a retraction or at least an apology.

"To whom it may concern,
I would like to express my horror at the amount of letters I am receiving from concerned people in the UK about an article printed in the 'Mail on Sunday', so I am informed, shortly after the visit of two Scottish Labour MPs to Iraq in May.

I don't know who gave Mr Galloway his information concerning the alleged problems between myself and Michael Wainwright, but I wish to state in this letter that in nearly a year of imprisonment together we have had one argument, that was on the 20th of February this year in which punches were thrown.

Michael does not 'physically abuse me on a regular basis', nor do the 'other prisoners have to pull us apart on many occasions', this I think is part of the 'spy network's' wonderful stories. The way to 'work your ticket here' is to inform on your fellow prisoners, which all inmates do in varying degrees, and then the lies are expanded on and developed until there is a neat package of lies, and I believe myself that Mr Galloway was 'spoon-fed' the story to blacken one or both of us.

Now I don't mind what is written about me, as I am hardly in a position to defend myself, but I do object to my wife, my parents, my brother, my family and, just as importantly, Michael Wainwright's mother Iris and his family, being made to read this fabrication in a newspaper which I had always considered a slightly more sensible issue from the British press. I would ask therefore that the proper apology is made to both my family, and Michael's family as there is no truth in the rumour whatsoever, and I do know from my mail that there was considerable anguish from my side of the story, this is from people already under a terrible strain due to the very nature of this episode.

I won't comment further as I haven't actually seen the article, but I do know that the rumours I'm getting lead me to believe that vast tracts

of the article were ill-advised and extremely un-informed – if you want to know the truth wait and I know it – please don't print wild guesswork or at best ill-informed rumour, as it serves no purpose, other than to muddy the already turbulent waters.
Your Sincerely
Paul Ride"

I also wrote an accompanying letter which I sent out to Julie with my letter to the 'Mail'. In it I said, "I was bloody annoyed that you thought I'd been keeping things from you. Please get on to Iris and give her my greatest regrets that this lie should come out at this time. It was in no way inspired by me."

I had little contact with the British media at this time and failed to understand that they publish what the hell they like, truth or not, and have no regard for the consequences. Like a runaway juggernaut, newspapers plough on 'crushing' individuals in the 'public interest' – it's their raison d'etre.

The Foreign Office coming to Abu Ghraib was not going to make a difference to my situation and I began to regard the visit as more of a hindrance than a help. I started to feel as if I should carry out some low-key protest about the lack of will to alter the status quo and I told Simon, "I don't want people coming in here mouthing platitudes and then going away and saying how well we are. I want someone to come and get me out of this fucking place!"

I thought about refusing to attend the visit but realised this would offend the Foreign Office officials and Abu Athier would be furious of dissent on that scale, so I decided that it wouldn't benefit me to rock the boat that hard!

At 11.45am, Ghassan came to tell us that Stephen Howarth, head of the Consular Department of the Foreign Office, and Mark Le Goy from the British Embassy in Jordan, had arrived. They brought with them much-needed food. Despite my cynicism, my diary reflects it was a good visit and although nothing new was said, the quality of food was excellent.

Simon asked Stephen Howarth about our detention to which Howarth replied. "Well, we have let the Iraqis know that I am in Baghdad, (I thought this idiotic, as the Iraqis knew he was in Baghdad – they had granted his bloody visa!) and we are taking the softly, softly approach to all of this."

I then asked him, "So you haven't arranged to see anyone?"

"No!" replied Howarth. "We thought that if the Iraqis had anything new to say then they would call us to a meeting and advise us of the facts there."

Simon's disgust was obvious. For me it was further proof that comments such as, "We are doing everything we can," should actually be, "We are doing all we are willing to do!"

I found it outrageous that the British Government would send an official to Baghdad with instructions to contact nobody at all within the Iraqi regime. It was little wonder that with this sort of autocratic, superior attitude, it took as long as it did to get me out!

Howarth told me that Julie was working incredibly hard and he had a multitude of little stories to tell me about her. Most involved her 'slagging off' the Foreign Office or passing comment about his department in the media. As he was telling me this, I kept thinking, *If the cap fits, wear it!*

When the meeting was over, I pulled Howarth to one side and asked him to tell Khalid Jerjes to stop the MOD questions and to not be so bloody stupid in front of Abu Athier. I didn't expect to be placed in an awkward, and dangerous, position by someone supposed to be 'on my side'.

Abu Athier told Howarth, about my 'day pass' on Julie's next visit. He didn't look comfortable about this but remarked that it was a very nice gesture!

When the diplomats had departed I spent the rest of the afternoon unpacking and reorganising my stores to include the new articles which I had just received. I made a short entry in my diary about "fending off the scavengers" noting, "It's like a bloody carcass when anything new comes in."

This was true of every visit I had. Ghassan would be present to 'advise' Abu Athier what certain items were. He would then tell the 'spy network' what new articles I had. All afternoon and evening following a visit there would be a stream of prisoners attempting to extort my newly delivered supplies. I should make the distinction that the people attempting to get my supplies were not the poor and needy, but the greedy and relatively affluent prisoners who formed a clique within Abu Ghraib. I think this pillaging by the Iraqis and prisoners pleading for gifts fueled my selfishness.

A woman from a village in North Devon sent Michael and I religious pendants. She claimed that they would protect us. Abet made me a length of cord and I hung mine around my neck and was 'ready' to be protected!

A book that Mr Neil Gerrard, my MP in Walthamstow sent, arrived. It was a history of Chelsea Football Club filled with facts, dates, and figures. I trawled its pages for hours learning things I'd never known and getting misty-eyed over events I'd been part of.

Neither Jean-Luc or Ali had any toiletries; towels, soap, shampoo, toothbrush, paste or even a comb, so I provided what I could from my boxes and then went around foraging from the other Western hostages to get them a set of toiletries each.

Tuesday, 29th June.

I went to the 'sports field' for exercise and fell head over heels on the damp, sticky, surface. I went into paroxysms of rage shouting about being totally fed up, and 'over' Abu Ghraib and everything in it. My outburst must have been audible throughout the establishment. As I trudged back, dripping with sticky, cloying mud, many of prisoners were hanging from the fences of their sections looking on and the guards gave me bemused glances.

The 'Crazy British' returned to his section, had a shower and listened to the radio for the rest of the day. I heard United States President Bill Clinton mention Ken Beaty and say that he should be released unharmed, or else he would flatten Iraq! I wished the simpering John Major would use language like that, it would sound as if he cared – even if he didn't give a monkey's!

When Britain spoke about 'Iraq hostages' it spoke for British, American, Swedes, Germans, French et al. Other countries requested their nationals be released – singularly. My diary entry reflected this. "What about us? Are we not part of the coalition, or is that only for the war – not the dubious peace?"

Wednesday, 30th June.

The occupants of the cell adjacent to mine and Michael's were ordered out to make way for Jean-Luc and Ali. Amin, a Palestinian falsely accused of spying and tortured until he'd admitted the accusation, and another guy called Omar, had been in the single cell for many years. Omar went ballistic, running around the section shouting, screaming, and banging doors. Finally, he went into his cell and slashed his body all over with a razor blade. This sounds suicidal I know, but in Iraqi prisons inmates inflict self-mutilation with blades knowing how deep to go and ensuring the maximum amount of blood with the shallowest of slashes. When he had finished, Omar looked like slab of meat on a butcher's block then, rather than laying down in agony, he continued to parade around the section shouting and denouncing his unjust treatment. Within minutes the guards hauled his sad arse off to the punishment block where he would spend the next three months – all of this for arguing with Abu Athier's decision!

I saw Khalid Jerjes later on and he told me that he hoped my situation would be resolved in four months, and later I heard he'd told Simon and Kai three months. There was something bloody funny going on, and I couldn't see the joke. My paranoid delusions were being bolstered by these events which were becoming more common place. He also told them that he and the Iraqi regime were not happy that Kai's father had appointed another Iraqi lawyer. He intimated that this was not helping. How surprising! Jerjes wanted no outsiders muscling in on his case(s). One lawyer means singular control. One lawyer means maximum publicity. One lawyer means no awkward questions. I could be wrong, but I don't think so!

There were reports of American aircraft destroying an Iraqi missile battery on the radio. I was hardly taking any notice of these events now. I thought, *What the hell can I do?* It's said that familiarity breeds contempt. Well, in my case it did!

Ghassan came and spoke to all the hostages telling us that we had to watch the news on TV that evening. I asked him why and he said that Abu Athier had informed him that there was going to be something on about us. We had all become so hardened to the lies that we didn't really give it much thought.

At 9.45pm Ghassan came to our cells and told us to make our way to the corridor with the TV in it. Spaces were cleared for us, everyone had their own jealously-guarded spot, and we sat down to wait. First off, Saddam Hussein was shown in various locations and situations. The local populace were shrieking and prostrating themselves in front of him wherever he went. Then came the bulletin we'd been requested to watch.

Pictures showed the site of the recent missile attack. The cruise missles had been aimed at the Mukhabarat complex where I had been held. The pictures didn't show the complex but a typical suburban scene. Palm trees lined the streets, high walls surrounded each house. The semi-detached houses were two storeys, sand-coloured and as the camera panned away from the image of undamaged houses, it zoomed into a vision of carnage and destruction. Many houses had been hit and residents and medical personnel were pulling corpses out of the rubble. One of the houses which had taken a direct hit was that of a celebrated Iraqi female artist. There followed a brief biography of her life and work, and then we saw pictures of people breaking down in the streets as corpses were carried away. Following this came the part we had been called to witness, the denunciation of the coalition forces that had carried out the murder of innocent Iraqis in their own homes.

We were wondering why weapons so accurate and deadly during the Gulf War were now striking civilian targets and arrived at the conclusion that so many missiles had been fired at the Mukhabarat complex that by the time the last few had reached their target there was nothing left standing and the missiles flew on until they hit something else – in this case, suburbia, Baghdad style. I felt great sympathy for the civilian victims and realised I could easily have been among them.

The reason for our on-going detention was glaringly obvious to me now. We were nationals of countries which attacked Iraq daily, and since the Iraqis couldn't get their hands on the elected leaders of our nations – we were the next best thing!

RESEARCH STUDENTS, RUMOURS AND RHETORIC

Thursday, 1st July.

July started with the Swedish families finishing their fifth visit since Christmas and me being chastised at Muster for not shaving. There was a new normality to both these things which was slightly annoying, as was the fact that the new crowd of hostages surrounding me, who had all arrived since Julie's last visit, made me think that my imprisonment was going to drag on even longer.

Stephen Howarth arrived at Abu Ghraib for a second time, a good opportunity I thought to get a model boat I'd had made for William taken home. I thought Howarth would be as good as anyone else when it came to transporting the 30-centimetre-long model home. He appeared a little taken aback by my request but agreed to take it. He was worried, possibly, that a senior British diplomat carrying a wooden model boat might be ridiculed. He really had no fears there I thought to myself, because as one of the senior men at the Foreign Office he must have the hide of a rhino!

As far as my situation was concerned, I received the full benefit of Howarth's years of 'diplomatic speak' – he said a great deal but in truth, nothing. It was waffle. Everything he said, Michael and I knew already. We were going to remain here until the Iraqis changed their attitude because the British Government certainly wasn't about to change its position. Lovely! I felt so refreshed!

Julie had written and told me that William kissed my picture goodnight before he went to bed and said that she might take him to 10 Downing Street and have him shout at the Prime Minister that he wanted his Dad back. My reply, via a letter that Howarth carried for me, said, "Put him right outside so John Major can hear that he wants me back. It won't budge the hard-hearted twat, but the publicity will be good!" I also added, "As it happens, I want my wife and son back too – but no one will listen to me either!"

I asked Howarth if he could please tell Julie and William that I love and miss them both, and to tell William that his Dad was 'doing some work for the Government' and that I would see him soon.

He said that my statement wasn't exactly true and I agreed but said that I was here as a direct result of British Government policy and its actions or inactions – whatever the case may be!

I'd previously written and spoken to Julie about a Thai guy called Ong, who like many others was in dire need of help. I mentioned the situation to Howarth who said that unfortunately this was often the situation the world over and that he didn't think it would be possible to assist as it "might set a precedent". *God forbid*! I thought! Later, I advised Ong about the 'official line' and told him I would try to set something up with Julie and I advised him to get his family to liaise with her directly.

During my conversation with Howarth, a Tunisian called Hadi, an associate of Mohammed the Tunisian, who like him was also a spy and a child molester, had been trying to eavesdrop on what was being said and was pathetically obvious about it. I have no idea what he hoped to learn as he spoke only the most rudimentary English. I should have remembered however that it really didn't matter if this scumbag understood or not because in true Abu Ghraib fashion, what he didn't hear or understand he would fabricate – just like the British press!

In excellent French, Howarth spoke to Jean-Luc and gave assurances that every effort was being made for them and the other Western hostages. He also said hellos and goodbyes to the Swedes, Ken, and Kai, and then he went on his way. Lucky sod!

Abu Athier asked when 'Madam Julie' would be coming again, I told him I'd heard she may try in August. He said I could be released by then. I didn't laugh at him but thought, *Some bloody hope!*

Abu Athier also allowed me ten minutes to say thank you to the Swedish families. In the visiting room I wished them a good trip and said that the next time I saw them I hoped it would be as a free man. I have still not seen them and thanked them for their kindness during my imprisonment, but one day I hope to.

Christer's wife, Liisa, said she would be in touch with Julie when she got home and the fact that I knew Stephen Howarth was also going to see Julie and William in the next few days upset me and I spent the rest of the day feeling low. The Swedes also became dejected as their families left Iraq without them. Even the calm and rational Christer had a rant about the coalition air strikes saying that he and his friends, despite coming from a neutral country, were being held in prison due to the aggressive actions of UN forces.

Friday, 2nd July.

A typical Abu Ghraib day – boring and repetitious – began with me being reprimanded at Muster for not having shaved which was becoming very tedious! I prepared lunch for Ali, Jean-Luc, Simon, Kai and myself and also had a visit from Abdul Baki. As we sat on my bed drinking coffee, Michael made a comment about greed which was probably aimed at me. It was perverse coming from a man who wanted everything and then, not knowing what to do with it, gave it all away!

Saturday, 3rd July.

Simon and Kai were with Abu Athier and Khalid Jerjes most of the afternoon. When they returned, they said they'd been told to drop the

Iraqi Lawyer that Kai's father had appointed in London. Ominously, Jerjes had used the words, "Or else you will have to suffer the consequences if you continue to use his services."

What a piece of work Jerjes was! An assassin dressed as a Good Samaritan! As long as hostages played along with Iraqi wishes everything was fine – any deviation was immediately attacked with threats.

Sunday, 4th July.

Vermin control operatives came through the section and sprayed the entire place. For hours the air was thick with fumes and chemical dust and when it cleared there was a flim of white powder covering the ceilings and walls. This was designed, we were told, to get onto the bodies of the cockroaches and kill them in their nests. It felt as if it nearly killed me!

In the afternoon Abu Athier came into the section and said that some university students studying the effects of imprisonment would be interviewing us. Nothing surprised me in Iraq but this was very odd. Now we were specimens.

I was asked to disclose my date and place of birth and details about my family, my interests, my career, and my diet (food preferences both before and during detention were scrutinised). I was asked if I drove and if I drank alcohol and then my dreams and nightmares were examined in some detail! I was asked what kind of nightmares I had experienced, and I told them that a regular one was a situation where I became helpless and kept being molested and manhandled by the many lunatics in my section, not sexually, just continually touched and harassed.

I was also asked what I felt about the back-up from London and I lied and said that I thought it was fine, why I don't know! I was asked what could be provided to help me cope with prison better? I said music. When asked about my detention I said that had been very agitated when hopeful of an early release six months ago but had become calmer and more relaxed lately, realising that release would take a long time. I added that to excite myself about probable scenarios was detrimental to my state of mind and I tried to ignore rumours and avoid getting my hopes high about possible amnesties. Getting wound up did not help, nor did it give me great satisfaction to be continually disappointed.

They asked about my feelings and personal state of mind when I had been brought from Basra to Baghdad on the 30th of June, 1992. I felt a shudder run through me as I remembered the journey and stated I'd been terrified which wasn't a million miles from the truth! They thanked me for my answers, and my time – a commodity which I had in abundance – and said they hoped I would be released soon.

That evening we all questioned what the 'interviews' had been about and who exactly were the people conducting them? I suggested that they were not university students but a psychological branch of the Mukhabarat checking on answers we'd given them when we were in solitary confinement and comparing them with our answers now.

Monday, 5th July.

I went for exercise and met Noufal. He was a very intelligent man who used constant double entendres to prevent anyone turning conversations with him into anything more dangerous, and he never dropped the pretence! I learned that the Iraqi media had been used to ask the West for a supply of humanitarian aid in return for hostages. (This didn't stop the British Government from denying that I was a political detainee.)

I visited Abdul Baki in Section One and saw the results of a gas bottle fire. A couple of prisoners in bandages didn't look too badly injured but I saw another guy whose upper torso covered in horrific, suppurating burns. He had been heating some food when the worn seal of the cooking ring he was using had split allowing gas to escape and explode into flames. He'd been wearing a nylon shirt which burst into flames which he nor any bystanders could extinguish. The shirt adhered to his skin burning it. he looked awful, and I sympathised. I lost track of the times in prison that I thought, *There but for the grace of God go I*.

Kai and Simon were expecting their parents to arrive in a few days and the wait was bringing out the worst in them. Kai had been left disappointed when a previous promised visit had not taken place and the thought this might happen again was haunting them both. Comments were replied to in monosyllables or shouted down. The pair were eminently avoidable all day.

Expectations often led to disappointments. Men do not get upset, men get angry and with no outlet to express feelings we niggled at each other. In times of stress, when we should have been more supportive, with empathy and sympathy removed, we pilloried! I found pity rare in Abu Ghraib, it was as if another's disappointment bolstered your own fragile confidence.

Friday, 9th July.

I made pizzas, a selection shared among us for the evening meal. Were they good? They were edible, but none would get an award. The dough and toppings took all day to prepare. Among the topping ingredients were some foul sardines that had arrived in a box brought in by Stephen Howarth. They didn't improve the pizza but it got them eaten 'disguised' among a variety of toppings! Whatever I prepared, I always felt as if I could, and should, have done better.

Howarth had also brought some liquid washing detergent and I used it on my bed clothes. The results were excellent and the 'homely' smell fantastic. I realise this may seem trifling given the context of my situation, but it meant a great deal. It linked me to real life. Prison life wasn't real it was existence and I needed things to cling to.

Sunday, 11th July.

Simon and Kai were still waiting for their families and the tension was now greater, if that were possible, than it had been during the previous week. Tired of the trauma, I kept out of their way.

I was sitting on my bed after lunch reading when Ghassan walked into my cell. As 'head spy' he went wherever he liked, coming into my cell whether I'd invited him or not! My diary reads, "Ghassan was hugging me and biting my chest! The guy is a sad case. Seven years in 'nick' and he is on the verge of becoming homosexual, but I'm adopting the attitude that if prisoners want to talk about sex, mostly homosexual sex, and touch me – in a purely harmless way, I will not react. While it bores me, the situation would become volatile if I was to start getting 'huffy' about it so I ignore it as harmless and they are satisfied."

I decided that with Ghassan making such obviously sexual advances, as long as it did not go beyond stroking my hair or touching my arms, legs, etc., then I wouldn't react. Reading this now, decades later, feels very strange, however I was never compromised.

Listening to my radio in the afternoon, I heard that the UN were sending in teams of experts to dismantle armaments factories and install surveillance equipment. One of these teams had returned to Bahrain accusing the Iraqis of refusing them entry to key sites. I could almost hear the sound of cruise missiles and anti-aircraft fire again!

The radio talk about Iraq and UN sanctions depressed me and activity in the cases of other Western hostages disappointed me. Negative letters in and out upset me and the loss of three games of chess to Kai annoyed me! I lay on my bed and wondered, *Why is this still happening to me? Isn't a year of this sufficient? Doesn't God think I've been through enough? Obviously not!*

Jabba the Hutt was thrown into the punishment block today. I wasn't aware of his 'crime' but I saw Abu Athier in the Muster area, the only time I ever saw him there, giving Jabba a slashing blow across the face before storming off towards his office. Jabba was then dragged off and I wouldn't see him again for a month.

Monday, 12th July.

Iraqi and Iranian Governments had come to an agreement about the exchange of prisoners. Figures suggested 20,000 Iraqi soldiers were being held in Iran and Saddam wanted, (needed), them back.

With this in mind, the Mukhabarat turned up and began interviewing Iranian prisoners held in Abu Ghraib. Many of the Kurds in the prison carried Iranian nationality and this sent shock waves through the prison as many political prisoners and asylum seekers screamed that to be returned to Iran, and the Iranian Government, meant certain death. Now this appeared to be a very real possibility, the panic was awful, the fear very real. The Iranian Government were not a forgiving bunch!

Iranians gathered in small huddles to discuss their situation. Kurds knew whatever happened they were in a lose-lose situation. Whether they were returned to the Iranians or not, they were stuck between a rock and a hard place.

I learned that Jabba the Hutt had been trying to extort cash out of a Turk with details about illegally held US dollars. The prison authorities used the domino principle, with endemic informing pervading every section, and soon inmates were pointing accusing fingers at dozens of people guilty or not. In Iraq people were guilty until they could prove their innocence. The Iraqis never, to my knowledge, punished people who openly lied. It seems that lying was accepted within the penal system, and if people were beaten for no reason because of lies then that was just too bad!

Tuesday, 13th July.

Kai's father and sister arrived in the early afternoon and he was out with them until 7.30pm. He returned with a huge bag his family had brought for him but as it hadn't been 'customs cleared' by Abu Athier yet he he was instructed not to open it.

Kai was a member of a group of rich young men from Dortmund. Hearing of his plight in Iraq, his affluent friends banded together and put 20,000 Deutchmarks into a special fund for his use upon his release! Pure jealousy made me think, *Here I am sat in nick for over a year, with bugger all to look forward to, and he's been here a month and has got 20 grand in the bank already!*

I wrote to Abu Athier requesting assistance in recovering my personal effects 'taken for safe keeping' in Baghdad in July 1992. The head of the immigration bureau had advised me that I would be in prison with many 'bad men' who would take my possessions. The only 'bad men' who took things were the Iraqi authorities! I still hoped to get some of them back – stupid boy!

Wednesday, 14th July.

Kai's family were shown around the section. This was preceded by the usual clean-up. Almost imperceptible changes in the situation were beginning to concern me, my diary illustrates why. "With rumours that Kai and Simon won't be on the same case I am worried that this is turning into an international circus with some countries trying to gain the freedom of their hostages more than others! I asked Jerjes what rank our case was now and told him that I was starting to feel a bit strange and strung out. He just looked at me as if I was a nutter. I asked Ghassan to give me a sleeping pill. "I need out, I think!"

Thursday, 15th July.

I tried exercising, but felt awful realising that I would have to stop running or become ill. I now felt drained when I did any form of physical exertion.

I aplogised to Kai as I had avoided his family when Abu Athier and Khalid Jerjes brought them in yesterday. This was not bad manners or ignorance, rather a realisation that 'we' Western hostages were reacting exactly the way the the Iraqis wanted us to. We were polite, gracious, and ultimately dismissive of our surroundings and forgetful of the injustice of our captivity when meeting the families and diplomatic representatives of our fellow hostages. I wrote in my diary, "I tried to avoid yesterday's stage-managed circus. If I couldn't influence the outcome of my predicament, I wouldn't take part in condoning it!

Jean-Luc and Ali said that they had heard reports of an amnesty. "Inshallah!" (God willing!) I proclaimed with a cheer. Ali laughed, but the irony was lost on Jean-Luc.

It was Kai's birthday and a spy who was a part of Adel Mansoor's network baked him a cake! We had no problem with Mansoor's 'spies' and a 'you scratch my back, and I'll scratch yours' situation had developed and was maintained throughout my time in Abu Ghraib. The birthday cake was part of this!

Hadi, the child molester, was in trouble again. He had been caught with smuggled whisky and had attempted to bribe the guards when caught. He was given a good beating and thrown into the punishment block. In my opinion it couldn't have happened to a more deserving man!

Saturday, 17th July.

Friday and Saturday were both open visiting days. Friday had been a part of the twice monthly visits which were the 'norm'. The 17th was an extra visit to mark 'Revolution Day' of which Iraq appeared to have had quite a number!

Kai's family had left on Friday evening. He couldn't deal with it and as soon as they went he'd climbed into bed and stayed there and I didn't see him for 24 hours.

In June, Michael and I 'leased' an air conditioning unit for our 'new' cell but it was in a shocking condition and after a couple of days the motor failed. The Swedish Embassy had offered to get replacement parts and a new motor had been brought in today. A Sudanese handyman called Moomin replaced the motor and then we attempted to get it connected to the power supply. When we switched it on the entire section was plunged into darkness! With the circuit breaker reset and some adjustments made, we tried again. Darkness! For an hour we attempted to cure the electrical fault without success. It was infuriating. As I lay on my bed sweating like a Grand National winner I decided I could live without air conditioning and asked myself why I had wound myself to the point of almost having a seizure in an attempt to keep cool!

The Swedes started shouting abuse each time their cell was plunged into darkness. I hollered back at them, "So long as you're comfortable, cool and well fed, the rest of us simply have to put up and shut up." This was greeted with hoots of derision which reflected how we all felt – a bit niggly, selfish, and self-absorbed. We all wanted out and were getting ragged.

I was given a case of Compo-Rations by Abu Athier as several boxes we couldn't accommodate in the cell were kept in his office for 'safe keeping'. As a 'thank you' we told him to take some of the boiled sweets and biscuits in the boxes for his children and so it was now the norm for all the boxes we received to be bereft of sweets and biscuits!

Kai reported that the German Government were saying the same as their British counterparts which wasn't encouraging for him. Khalid Jerjes had assured his father that Ken Beaty and the Swedes would be released soon, then one of the Brits and eventually all the other Western hostages by Christmas. The timeline was constantly slipping and with a rumoured Revolution Day amnesty also failing to materialise my confidence in the reliability of information related to my release took another knock.

I met Abdul Baki and Noufal on the exercise pitch, and release rumours were the topic of conversation. They said the Iraqis had suggested they were going to release some or all of us the previous day but had changed their minds at the eleventh hour! I didn't rubbish this idea out of hand as the pair had been very good to me and they would have lost face had I done so. The Revolution Day amnesty fiasco left people subdued and even the Swedish Embassy kept a low profile, saying nothing!

Later in the evening, Ranko the Serb came into my cell jabbering and using hand signals in the form of clenched punching fists to try and tell me something. Communicating with Ranko required calming him and then trying to filter his point from the barrage of signs, words and expressions using Russian, Slavic, Arabic, and pidgin English. Finally, I gathered that boxing legend Muhammad Ali was in someway connected to the latest efforts being made to secure the release of Western hostages!

I knew that in 1990, Ali had travelled to Baghdad and met with Saddam Hussein to discuss the release of 15 US hostages abducted by the Iraqis before the Gulf War who were subsequently being used as human shields against missile attacks. In exchange for promising Saddam he would give 'an honest account' of Iraq, Ali secured the release of the hostages and with this in mind I kept an open mind on this latest gem out of Ranko's never ending bucket of hope!

Monday, 19th July.

Maybe Ranko was onto something! I heard that Mohammad Ali was here to act as an intermediary in the Iraq/Iran prisoner of war exchange and that he might also be talking about Ken Beaty's release.

I sent out another letter for Ranko who'd aged ten years in the ten months I'd known him. Not only were the conditions in the prison affecting him, the situation back home was still making it almost impossible to communicate with his family. It wasn't much, but I did what I could to help the poor bloke.

Simon borrowed copies of the 'Wisdens Cricketers' Almanac' from Abu Athier who had inherited them from Ian Richter. He proudly showed me his name in his school's entry in the 1986 edition. He had a batting average of 11.4 – being a football man, I wasn't sure what that meant.

The whole of the section felt to me as if it were on edge and this was confirmed when a fight among the usually lethargic Arabs housed in cell number five broke out. I learned that they too had become enraged by the constant false dawns.

Tuesday, 20th July.

The night Maraheb pounded on the gate at 6.30am getting everyone ready for the retribution for the previous night's angry outburst. Muster took place at 7.30 and nothing happened. I felt a little cheated to be awakened early in preparation for a beating that never materialised.

I went to collect my mail and encountered Khalid Jerjes who in a brief discussion implied that I'd been in custody for nine months! He appeared amazed when I informed him that I had been a hostage for 13 months. If he was trying to wind me up, he succeeded and I spent the day in a foul mood cursing him, the Mukhabarat, the Iraqi judicial system, and anyone else whom I decided was entitled to some vitriol.

My mood oscillated between mild elation and deep depression and I dealt with people accordingly. Arguments were commonplace and once again I found myself being 'sent to Coventry'. I wrote in my diary that this did not worry me, the truth was though that because I enjoyed the company of others, and maintained good relationships with those around me, it was hard when I was ostracised and it fuelled my paranoia.

Saturday, 24th July.

Ghassan came to my cell and told me he'd heard that all Western hostages were being released on the 30th. Even though I took all rumours with a large pinch of salt I knew Ghassan was privy to the most sensitive conversations and so this gave me hope that what he was saying might actually be true.

Sunday, 25th July.

When I got up I switched my radio on and listened to the latest World Service news bulletin to hear if any official statement had been made about our situation. "Bastards!" I exclaimed as I heard details about an American attack on an Iraqi missile battery in the exclusion zone. This would put paid to our release – yet again!

Monday, 26th July.

At first Muster my head was throbbing, my throat felt dry and sore and I felt sure I was about to pass out. A slightly raised temperature and normal blood pressure suggested that I was dehydrated so I ate a melon sprinkled with salt to rehydrate myself. This was a trick I'd been taught when I'd worked in Algeria.

Tuesday, 27th July.

I was summoned to Abu Athier's office and ordered to write an account of 'crossing' the border and that there were no warning signs from the Kuwaitis or the United Nations that I was entering a prohibited area. As this was true, I gladly wrote an account of what happened. As I finished, Michael joined us and we were informed that the hostages taken from Kuwait would be released soon while those from Turkey would be held longer.

In my diary I wrote, "I hope this isn't true, but stranger things have and do happen here. Michael took it all philosophically – but I just hope it's not true. I don't think I'd have been able to cope if the situation had been reversed with Michael and the others getting out, while I remained. If I have to praise Michael for one thing it is his stoicism, he appeared unfazed."

Eventually, all the 'Kuwaiti hostages' went to the office and wrote accounts of crossing the border along with condemnation for the Kuwaitis and the United Nations. Kai, Simon and myself felt that the Swedes knew more than they were saying and this caused a rift with them for a while.

Wednesday, 28th July.

Khalid Jerjes took new statements from Jean-Luc and Ali. In their original statements of the previous day they'd insisted they were 50 metres inside Kuwait, as were we all, when abducted. They said they were struggling with their consciences, not wanting to lie, in case this caused them problems on their release! Personally, I'd have said the moon was made of cream cheese to secure my release!

I virtually screamed that they should say day was night or black was white if that was what the Iraqis wanted. When released they could tell the truth and everyone would realise that the statements were extracted under duress. After many Gallic shrugs and much sighing, Jean-Luc did alter his statement and we breathed a collective sigh of relief as we'd been told that all the statements must indicate similar events or there would be no release for any of us.

Thursday, 29th July.

Ken Beaty was taken to Baghdad for what we were told were 'pre-release' examinations. Lucky Ken!

Jabba the Hutt came out of the punishment cells and I learned the reason he'd been sent there was because he'd claimed that Haji Salim, a Turkish smuggler, had paid bribes to secure a Maraheb position. Not a shrewd move!

Simon told me that Khalid Jerjes had asked him during his 'border letter' writing session if I had come from Turkey or if that was Michael? This from my lawyer! My God! "Stupid Bastard! The man's representing me!" I wrote in my diary.

There were mutterings about military action between Lebanon and the Israelis, and another missile attack on Iraq which was now almost a daily occurrence. I worried that things would blow up in the Middle East removing interest in Iraq where we'd remain – forgotten!

Friday, 30th July.

I woke up to the news that the Conservative Party had been trounced in a by-election held in Christchurch, Dorset following the death of Tory MP Robert Adley. The Conservatives lost a 23,000 majority to the Liberal Democrats who won with a majority of 16,000, and I thought, *I am, apparently, not the only person unimpressed with the way that the Government are running things!*

I considered writing to John Major suggesting our freedom might boost the Tory poll percentage a bit, but the poor sod clearly had enough on his plate!

Simon and Kai became more depressed with every passing minute, as it became apparent that none of us, not even Ken or the Swedes, would be released that day. I should confess that my attitude, which resembled a verbal prophet of doom, didn't help. No one likes to hear "I told you so" at a time like that!

The United States admitted the previous evening's attack was a mistake caused by 'pilot error' however no apology was forthcoming and Iraq denied the attack had ever occurred. This situation had the makings of a 'Catch-22'-style satirical war novel complete with unlikely scenarios and characters.

I received a nice letter from my daughter Rhian which was both a

RIDE TO HELL

very pleasant surprise and a boost to my flagging morale.

When I replied to letters I tried to escape mental constraints leaving my fellow hostages to grapple with the enigma of our ongoing detention.

Predictably there was no 'big bang' to herald the end of July, it simply fizzled out with no release and no general amnesty. The only things going 'bang' in ever-increasing numbers were the Iraqi missile and radar sites which didn't give me any cause for optimism of a 'friendly' resolution which would bring about my release.

PSYCHO

Monday, 2nd August.

August began with a strange Embassy visit. Gleb Desyatnikov seemed reluctant to speak to us and every slither of information had to be drawn out of him. The conversation was stilted. Nobody wanted to disclose or discuss the rumours we'd been hearing recently. My reason was the fear of Gleb scoffing that I'd be gullible enough to believe such rumours. It was like a game of cards. *Show me yours and I'll show you mine!*

Eventually Gleb showed his hand and there was real optimism in his voice. "This is a very good development for your situation," he said, with a smile. "I hope most heartily that you will get released very soon."

We expressed optimism that this would be the last time Gleb would make the journey to Abu Ghraib but added that should it not be the case we would be glad to see him on the 20th! Don't burn your bridges was our attitude, recognising we were still at the end of the umbilical cord.

Mike Dunn, Simon's Father, had arrived with Gleb and when he announced he was leaving, Michael and I were ordered to return to our section. Visitors were always fabulous and so being told to leave robbed vital moments of sanity in the information-void of Abu Ghraib. This distressed me and sullenly I went back to my cage with hatred coursing through my body. At times like these the helpless hostage in me woke up and I felt like screaming that I wasn't an animal, or a carcass that these idiots could toss aside, but a human with feelings.

On the upside, Simon's father had brought in the quiz/board game 'Trivial Pursuit'. This was a blessing for me and I would play it often, especially with Kai, but it was unfair as it was an English edition and I had an advantage. It was fun to beat Kai as he was very competitive and hated to lose, especially to me.

Tuesday, 3rd August.

All of us Kuwaiti hostages were taken as a group to meet a man introduced to us as a 'Major' from the 'Ministry of Justice'. I was sure he was not from the Ministry of Justice, thinking, *'Justice' has nothing to do with the 'legal' system in Iraq.* To further underline this, Khalid Jerjes was also present!

The meeting was about the statements we had written the week previously and the 'Major' asked each of us the same questions in Arabic with Jerjes acting as translator.

"Did you write it?"

"Were you prompted?"

"Do you agree with what you've said?"
"Do you have anything to add?"
"Do you have anymore to say about any of it at all?"

Of course we all lied and told this self-important fool from the Ministry exactly what he wanted to hear.

At the end of the meeting, I went to Abu Athier's office and he passed me a box of American clothes. I figured the box must belong to Ken Beaty and then I noticed, near the bottom of the package, a tiny note from the sender, Mrs Vilawan Kelly. The box was for Ong, the Thai prisoner who'd requested help from Julie at the start of the year. I recognised the sender's name as Ong had mentioned her in conversation. Vilawan was his sister and the the box had been sent via the British Embassy! As the penny dropped, I realised that Ong had organised this before he had even spoke to me! I didn't know whether I should be angry that Julie and I had been taken for granted, or happy that we were trusted to such a degree. I chose to be happy.

I informed Ong that the box of clothes had arrived and asked him to be discreet as I didn't want the spy network informing the authorities that I was smuggling items into the prison for distribution. Ong went to his cell and returned with a bag which he loaded with items from the box. It took three repeat journeys to transfer everything to his cell and as he scuttled away for the third time I worriedly thought, *People will need to be stupid to not understand what is going on.*

In the evening, Abet, Ronnie and myself ate 'fried rat', as Abet called it, which was aubergine, blanched, skinned, and coated with beaten egg, then shallow-fried until it browned. It was really nice. Abet was a good cook and he still invited me to eat with him and his Filipino compatriots now and again and I would give them tins of stewed meat from my Compo-Rations to 'pay' my way just as I always had done.

The Filipinos had heard a rumour that Adel Mansoor would be released soon. The 'Godfather' of Abu Ghraib, Adel was hated, feared, and treated with respect by every inmate. He was a real snake and so if the story was true, even though there would be envy at his release, no one would miss him.

Wednesday, 4th August.

Prisoners were watching TV into the early hours of the morning and some were failing to get up for Muster. This morning I was late due to having stayed up playing 'Trivial Pursuit' and a guard delighted in reprimanding me in front of the section. He went on and on. I do not respond well to petty bureaucrats and it took real effort not to reply with my own tirade of bullshit!

Sometimes I ignored the guards, pushing them as far as I dared. I knew the younger guards would never harm a Western hostage so taunting them brought me very little satisfaction.

A joint of pork which arrived with Stephen Howarth went missing. I'd been saving the pork for a 'special occasion' – what the occasion was going to be I had no idea! Some thieving oaf had stolen my pork and I was homicidal until someone pointed out that it was probably an act of ignorance by one of the Arabs! I wondered, given that Muslims do not eat pork, how he would explain that to Allah at the gates of Jannah! (Heaven)

Christer, Leif and Stefan had a visit from their employer, Swedish telecoms giant Ericsson. What was said or discussed we never heard.

Thursday, 5th August.

Adel Mansoor invited all the Western hostages, except Kai, to have a meal with him. I had no idea why, but Adel would have nothing to do with Kai, and vice versa. The rumours had been true. This was a 'last supper' for Adel who would be leaving Abu Ghraib on Monday. For me, Monday could not come quickly enough!

Friday, 6th August.

Visiting day. I whiled away the hours by sleeping in my cell with the lights out! Later, I had a dig at Abet who 'dressed up' for visits and 'posed' for female visitors. Taking my frustrations out on him was unforgivable. He had spent six years in prison and with another five to serve it was little wonder that female visitors cheered him up, and here I was destroying the illusion by pointing out the futility of it all!

Saturday, 7th August.

A national holiday. 'Victory Day'. I wasn't sure which victory was being celebrated as there seemed to be so many holidays related to 'revolutions' and 'victories' that I'd lost interest.

Adel was leaving the prison and fellow Egyptians were using his departure to try and send mail and messages or get favours from him. I don't think he was very forthcoming as in my experience the trait of a person's character that develops most in prison is selfishness and, in my opinion, Adel was living proof of this.

Adel had been jailed for embezzlement. I hadn't realised that Mohammed Mimi, another Egyptian whom I'd known for 11 months as the 'Ironing Man', had been jointly convicted of the same crime. Adel used his money from the Hanoot to pay his way out of prison. By repaying the monies he'd misappropriated the system had agreed to free him! I asked Mimi was he being released? Surely Adel would take care of all the monies, after all he did run the shop. With a sad but dignified shrug, Mimi informed me that Adel had only taken care of his own debt. I asked how much he had to pay to secure his release, he said 5000 Iraqi

Dinars. I did some mental arithmetic. Mimi charged half a dinar for ironing one item so without eating and surviving in prison he would need to iron 10,000 pieces of laundry which amounted to 27 pieces a day for a year. If I'd had the money, I would have given it to him. It all seemed so unfair, but the truth is that the world is a harsh place!

Ong provided lunch which I shared with Simon. He prepared a bowl of chicken in a marvellous stock and fried eggs on a bed of rice. This might seem like an odd combination, but it tasted wonderful.

Sunday, 8th August.

Abet was ordered to move to Section Two, the filthiest, most troublesome section in the prison. He was in tears. In his time in Abu Ghraib, Abet had upset a lot of people and this was probably retribution for crossing a prisoner who had influence. I later recalled that Abet had given the weasel Ghassan a 'mouthful' a few days before and wondered if this had anything to do with his transfer.

Abu Athier came to the section and spoke to Abet's cellmate Ronnie and then he came into our cell and asked me about a picture of some pigs which I had stuck on my wall. He enquired what it was all about? I gave him a bullshit story to cover the truth which was that it was there to to annoy the Iraqis who despised pigs and would pull disgusted faces and leave the cell when they saw it. I also had an advertisement featuring the English Rugby Union team stuck to my wall. This gave me a sense of national pride and it also wound up the Iraqis. I delighted in finding ways to metaphorically poke my tongue out at them!

Iran admitted it had bombed northern Iraq destroying a Kurdish rebel camp. There wasn't talk of a response from Iraq, but having the Iranians attack the Kurds was much the same as having the Turkish attacking the Kurds on the northern border between the countries. It saved Iraq the trouble of attacking the Kurds and Saddam could concentrate his efforts elsewhere!

I put a kilo of chilli peppers out in the afternoon sun to dry. When I returned to collect them the wind had blown the peppers all over the floor. I cursed and as I did so I felt my persecution complex tightening my chest but thankfully the sensation passed in minutes so I gathered up the peppers, threw them away, and went to the Hanoot to buy some more!

We dried the chillies as their availability and price as a fresh item compared with their scarcity and price as a dry product in the winter was vast. DIY was the way around this and for weeks 'wreaths' of assorted vegetables were strung all round the prison yard. Peppers, aubergines, okra, chillies and many more veg were left to dry in the vicious Iraqi sun. Many vegetables were unavailable for months at a time and this was the only way to have a supply of some items all year around.

Later that afternoon Adel was informed that he wouldn't be leaving yet due to a 'glitch' with his paperwork. I hoped he'd go soon. I was fed up with the prisoners fawning around him and his continuation as head grass.

After the final Muster of the day, a group of prisoners came to my cell collecting for Mimi. Adel Mansoor was walking out of prison abandoning his co-defendant and I thought this was a nice touch. Honour among thieves and all that!

Individually, a prisoner may be selfish and unwilling to help with the simplest request but gather a group of men around an issue and many would show their support for 'worthy' causes. I gave a couple of hundred Dinars as did the Swedish lads and the rest of the Western hostages. Then we got back to the serious matter in hand, a game of 'Trivial Pursuit' we'd been engrossed in which had been getting very competitive.

I had excess rice not finished with our evening meal and decided to try and make a 'rice pudding' with it. When he tasted it Kai donated a tin of Pineapple chunks and we sat there, Simon, Kai, and myself, eating rice pudding and pineapple as a midnight snack! Initially a tasty one-off, this developed into a regular event as I deliberately cooked too much rice in order that we would have enough to enjoy a midnight rice pudding!

Monday, 9th August.

Abu Athier called me to his office. Khalid Jerjes was sat there and with an 'Ealing-Comedy-style-Arab' grin on his face he told me that Julie and William would be in Baghdad from the 19th until the 23rd. As he spoke, he handed me a telex which told of Mike Dunn's arrival which was of no use to me and my heart sank at the thought he'd made a mistake. After a lot of paper shuffling and more inane grinning Jerjes finally found the scrap of paper referring to Julie and William's visit and relief rippled through me. Gone were the doubts, here it was in black and white!

Jerjes asked about my stance on the Britain/Iraq situation and also quizzed me about my financial status. Would my time in prison earn me a lot of money? I told him that due to my detention my salary had been halved and that my wife and son were reliant on charity to survive. I also made a point of saying that while the British and Iraqi Governments were not losing a penny over my being in jail, my life was in ruins.

He expressed surprise that the British Government were not giving vast sums of money to Julie to financially cover my detention. He said that it was realised in Iraq that I was a pawn in a game of chess and my detention or release was reliant solely on the British Government's attitude and compliance with Iraqi demands. I told him that the British Government didn't give a toss if I stayed in prison and that the rhetoric being used by the United Nations in Brussels and in London was just lip service for the media, a smokescreen to give the appearance of activity and commitment. I assured him that Julie, William, and myself were the only people 'paying' any price for this entire charade.

Once again I felt myself beginning to rage at the injustice of it all. The Iraqis, having made their demands, either couldn't or didn't want to understand that London would not treat me as a political hostage. I was the filling in a political sandwich they had made but no one wanted! I asked Abu Athier if I could leave saying I had some food to prepare. I had to get out of the room before I exploded and got myself into serious trouble. Abu Athier nodded and I thundered back to my cell in a furious mood.

In the evening, Ken Beaty called me into his cell and told me of the conversation he'd had with Abu Athier and Khalid Jerjes when he'd met them after I had said my piece in the afternoon. He told me that they had asked if what I said was true. Ken said he had assured them that it was true and not only in my case but in his as well. He said that he had informed them that he would be forced to sell his house to finance his stay in prison as the United States Government were not helping him financially either.

I couldn't understand why the two sides in this dispute misunderstood each other so completely and comprehensively. Baghdad was convinced that as hostages our governments would foot the bill, while our governments refused to acknowledge that we were hostages. Were we just 20th Century cannon-fodder? It seemed that way.

I hoped that this information would be passed through the Iraqi grapevine and that someone would understand that to hold us was not hurting the British Government and that their promise to hold us was no threat to our parliament. As had become the norm, I saw no positives and my diary entry read, "This has given them (the Iraqis) something to think about, but no one cares so what difference will it make!"

Tuesday, 10th August.

Daily routine was disrupted by the impromptu visit on an 'Amnesty Committee'. Disruptions destroyed my fragile state of wellbeing and security. Muster was five minutes late and even though this was a short period of time it was a major issue for me as I stood impatiently on 'my spot' awaiting the call. I felt vindicated when Muster was called and with a superior air I gazed at the somnambulists who dared believe that it would be overlooked and had remained in bed.

As my section hadn't congregated quickly enough for the guards we were forced to crouch in the blazing afternoon sun for 20 minutes. As we reentered the building I felt dizzy, my clothes sticking to my sweat-soaked and shaking body. I fell on my bed exhausted and sucked in cooler air from the air conditioning unit. Since I'd first been imprisoned I knew my physical condition had deteriorated and events like this made me aware of by just how much. I didn't want to die here as this would be a victory for these bastards!

In the afternoon I went to Section Two to visit Abet. I thought I could give him some much-needed moral support. He was very dejected. His new 'bedroom' was awful, he had been thrown into an 18-man cell that was a dirty, dingy, depressing hole. His cellmates were a mixture of Egyptians, Turks, Palestinians and Asians.

A couple of the Asians spoke excellent English and they fawned all over me asking for information. One of them was from Kuwait. We'd been in the same prison for months and not known it! He'd been taken over the border by the Iraqis. Working for the KOC (Kuwait Oil Company), he'd been sent to the area to conduct a survey to build a new petrol station! We chatted a while, I told him how things were for the other Kuwait hostages and about the possibilities for our release. I didn't know if they would apply to him, I hoped that they would but we were in Iraq so who knew?

Abet's cell was more crowded than most 18-man cells I'd seen and the condition of the belongings in it told me that the inhabitants were not receiving many visits or outside aid. Threadbare clothes, tatty remnants of luggage, and a smell of age and decay filled the cramped environment. The windows were blocked and the air was stagnant, moist, and fetid. As I looked around this dungeon of despair I likened it to a laboratory petri dish in which bacteria that might spawn an epidemic were being cultured!

Things never ceased to amaze me and as I checked out the cell I noticed a set of boots which struck a pre-prison-life chord with me. They were the same style of safety footwear Taylors supplied our Asian employees in Kuwait. I laughed and told the KOC-worker about this. He'd purchased them from one of the Taylors lads in Jahra who preferred to wear lighter flip-flops. I was speechless! A man in prison in Baghdad was wearing boots I'd delivered to Jahra nearly 1000 klicks away. I'd been begged to get these safety shoes for the Taylors staff there and felt a proper mug!

I left Section Two with a promise to return to see Abet and my newly-discovered fellow hostage. The relief he displayed when he realised he wasn't alone in Abu Ghraib was astonishing. I hoped the new-found optimism this 'news' gave him wouldn't be misguided.

When I returned to Section Three I had my hair cut. I didn't get the same hairstyle each time it was cut, but at a price equivalent to 10 pence I could hardly complain.

The Swedes and I went to get a cooling shower at midnight. Stefan had just 'soaped-up' when the water stopped running. He wasn't happy about this and started cursing repeatedly in Scandinavian. Covered in soap and with no water coming out of the taps he ended up using some water that was in a nearby dustbin to rinse the soap off meaning he was dirtier than when he started! The rest of us waited for the water to come back on, but in the end I lost patience waiting and went to bed.

I couldn't get off to sleep. The heat was oppressive and my head was full of negative mental boulders which were rolling around distracting me. I tossed and turned until about 2.00am when I thought I heard running water. I rushed to the shower area and found all the taps were still full on and gallons of water had flooded out all over the floor. I shut off the taps, fetched a bucket and enjoyed a refreshing shower which cleared my head and I was able to fall asleep straight away when I returned to bed.

Wednesday, 11th August.

I tried a new exercise regime out on the sports field. I walked a couple of laps to rid my body of the stale atmosphere of the section then I ran at pace for a while before walking some more to get my breathing back to normal.

At the sports field I also had the opportunity to meet up with friends from other sections and catch up on all the latest gossip. I heard that Mohammed the Tunisian had been bitten by a rat! Later I wrote in my diary, "Heard this morning that a rat had bitten M'hmd al Tunsi last night. I said there was no need to clear out the room and kill the rat as it will die anyway! What a horrible bastard M'hmd al Tunsi is!"

Simon, Kai and I had an agreement concerning meal preparation. We'd agreed they'd prepare a 'lighter' lunchtime meal while I'd prepare a more substantial evening meal. Simon and Kai were sleeping all morning and making a packet soup after the 1.00pm Muster. This was not in the spirit of the agreement, I was getting 'hung-angry'!

Sleeping was a coping mechanism for Simon and Kai and it frustrated me. In certain scenarios I have encountered since my release I have found that stressful situations leave me feeling exhausted and needing to sleep and it reminded me that I hadn't coped well with other people's methods of dealing with our captivity!

A perverse character trait of mine compels me to 'lead by example' and the efforts Simon and Kai put into food preparation spawned greater culinary effort on my part. It was an attempt to inspire them to bigger things – I hoped. That evening I prepared barbecued chicken, Arabic rice, and a full barbecue sauce. It was very well received and I hoped Simon and Kai would 'follow my lead'.

Thursday, 12th August.

A couple of prisoners in a nearby cell were removing all their possessions to give it a thorough cleaning when they disturbed a rat which scurried into the corridor. A hue and cry ensued as an increasing number of inmates gathered brandishing heavy objects with which to dispatch the rat. Mohammed the Tunisian was conspicuous by his absence, he realised he'd met his match!

Up and down the corridor the rat scurried attempting to find a bolthole with no success and the prisoners finally cornered it, kicking and beating it to death! The rat's shattered body, about 15 centimetres in length, was paraded as the spoils of the hunt.

Friday, 13th August.

Ong gave me a Thai meal for lunch. This had as its main dish a plate of raw mince! Now under normal circumstances I would have said, "fine", and not even thought of the health concerns, but being in Abu Ghraib I held back – just a little! I puzzled over it for a while then thought that the longer it remained uneaten and raw the more likely it was to upset me – so I wolfed it down and it was lovely!

Saturday, 14th August.

Adel finally left the prison. I wondered if he would be able to get home straight away or would he, like many others, spend weeks and months in Tasfirat, the Iraqi equivalent of purgatory, until transport was found to return him to the point of arrest which was standard practice in Iraq.

Tasfirat was a mixture of 'coming' and 'going' bodies. Some were awaiting the trip to Abu Ghraib to commence their sentences, I had endured this hellish experience, while others, some with many years of existence in Abu Ghraib behind them, were awaiting the final move in the dance of freedom. From Tasfirat they'd be returned to the police station where their experiences first began. At this point, the local police would make checks to confirm there were no further charges against them on file and then after many weeks and in most cases months prisoners were released or transported to Iraq's borders for a hand-over to the police or army of one of its neighbours. The act of being handed over to another authority could mean death! Many people I knew in Abu Ghraib were in fear of this day as they were considered criminals in their own countries and were facing the death penalty!

The Swedish families and Robin, the wife of Ken Beaty, arrived at the prison for visits. Once again I got very little information out of the Swedes but Ken was in good form that evening gushing how proud he was of what his wife had uncovered. Using the US' Freedom of Information Act she had been able to discover that both the US and UK had comprehensive daily information about the situation within Abu Ghraib! I couldn't imagine who was providing these 'reports' and hoped it wasn't the moron Khalid Jerjes. I imagined the rubbish he'd include to elevate his own importance and make the prison appear bijou!

Our governments were passing the buck and trying to avoid responsibility for our situation. They blamed the UN for the imposition of 'punitive sanctions' on Iraq, saying that nothing could change until the security council altered its attitude towards the country.

I said to Ken that the fools in government must think 'us' stupid. The UN was not despatching its edicts from outer space, it is an organisation over which the US and UK has vast influence. If the UN sanctions were the only thing holding us here, then their continued imposition should be examined. They were not hurting Saddam but killing the Iraqi people through illness and malnutrition.

As I walked around trying to file and quantify what I'd heard from Ken I saw a sight that told me how tough things had got in Abu Ghraib. A prisoner was taking a nylon rice sack apart very carefully and with the resultant pile of threads he was weaving sandal straps onto an old pair of soles which he had reclaimed from the rubbish! The prison was full of items created by the inventive use of cast-offs, but it appeared that things were now getting to rock bottom!

As I went to sleep, I laughed at something Ken told me Abu Athier had said to him. He couldn't go to the hotel where his wife was staying, but if he wanted to spend the night with her, they could be together in Abu Athier's rear office where there was a bed. I imagined what Julie would say if she were offered something like that!

Sunday, 15th August.

Robin Beaty went to the Ministry of Foreign Affairs in Baghdad and pushed the humanitarian angle trying to use Ken's health problems to get him released. He came back into the section full of hope for her visit, and on a high about the way things were going.

I spoke to 'Clown Prince' Khalid Jerjes to arrange for Julie, William, and myself to spend the night in a hotel as we now had the dates of their next visit. This was something that had been promised, but now Jerjes was saying the same as Abu Athier had said to Ken – that we may have to spend the night in the prison. I told him under no circumstances was William going to spend a night in a prison locked in a 'cell'. He was two-years-of-age not an old lag! Jerjes told me that he would sort something out for us, but my diary entry said in two words exactly what I thought about this. "Lying Bastard!"

The three Swedish lads came back to the section earlier than usual and Stefan said it was because their families also had an appointment at the Ministry of Foreign Affairs to discuss their continued detention, or more accurately their chances of release.

In the evening, Adel Mansoor returned to the prison in a foul mood. He had been refused entry into Tasfirat because his passport, which had expired while he was in Abu Ghraib, was no longer valid. Despite my negative feelings toward Adel this wound me up and I lay awake feeling angry until 3.00am.

Monday, 16th August.

The 9.00am Muster was called at 8.45am, this tiny change in routine angered me, and the rantings of one of the guards increased my unrest.

He yelled at me to squat and I gave him a 'hand signal' to slow down but actually I meant 'Fuck Off!' The guard then walked away to harangue the occupants of Section Five but was soon back hassling me and ordering me to sit down. I was seriously pissed off and shouted back, "Ana Inglisi, mo kalb!" (I am English, not a dog!)

A gasp and silence rang around the yard but nothing was said and the tiresome prick walked away to hassle Section Five again. I am not a brave man, and I am not trying to paint the picture of a hero in any sense of the word, but I'm proud. If I believe something to be true I will defend it to the hilt and I deem the adage 'do as you would be done by' to be good and proper. I will not be 'put upon'. Now, years later, I'd walk away, but as you will understand I was not able to do that in Abu Ghraib.

Later that morning I was told that their were rumours circulating saying I had been called a dog by the guard. This was typical of Abu Ghraib, if it was possible to get something back to front or completely wrong then these idiots would manage it. I was disappointed to be included in another rumour and annoyed it had been so wrong.

Ghassan came to my cell late in the evening and tearfully informed me that his brother in Syria had died. He wailed deep, heart-rending sobs saying his sentence was destroying his family. His parents now had no one to keep them in their dotage as he and his younger brother were in Abu Ghraib. His distress seemed genuine, but I wondered if it was a charade designed to gain something for himself and so I held back on any sympathy.

Tuesday, 17th August.

In the morning I took some plates into the Swedish lads and their families who were having a buffet. While I was in the visiting room, Christer's wife Liisa asked me, "Has Julie made her trip to the USA?"

This was a new one on me and I simply shrugged. It hurt my feelings that apparently everyone apart from me was aware of what Julie was getting up to. I left and returned to my cell still smarting from embarrassment at my ignorance.

Abu Athier came to my cell during the afternoon and asked if I wanted to see Julie and William on Friday as they were due to arrive on Thursday. I replied, "I'd love to, if it's possible."

"Friday is my day off," he countered.

"Oh! Okay, then I'll wait," I said, shrugging my shoulders. As I was still speaking, Abu Athier added, "But I will come in anyway."

I really don't know if he did these sorts of things to bait me or to generate feelings of gratitude. I understood the way he worked and tried to ignore him but it was difficult.

Later that evening, a crowd of us were playing 'Trivial Pursuit' when the 'case of the stolen pork' came up in conversation. Simon and I declared that the son of a bitch responsible should be made an example of to the other Islamic inmates and as we spoke the Swedes fell into an embarrassed silence. After a pause of a minute or so they exchanged words in Swedish and then Leif and Stefan tried to apologise for the mistake which had led to them eating the pork! Thinking that they were the only people in the section likely to have pork they had taken the meat and used it in late July. They were ashamed of their actions and a replacement was promised.

I felt a twinge of guilt at the curses which I had bandied about in accusation of the other inmates being responsible for the 'theft', but these lasted seconds as I was more interested in continuing our game of 'Trivial Pursuit'.

Adel Mansoor left the prison again, this time making his bid for freedom armed with a 'laissez-passer' (temporary international travel document) which was valid for one month. I wondered if the wheels of Iraqi justice would grind fast enough to get him out of Iraq before it expired. This time his departure celebrations were muted. The attitude among everyone now seemed to be, *If you're going – for Christ's sale go!*

Two new prisoners entered the section today who'd been charged with illegal entry from Turkey. These poor bastards weren't even given a translator in court and were staggered by their sentence. By now I had an impervious shell which prevented the plight of others from affecting me so I shrugged off their situation as 'just another case'. At that moment this was exactly how I felt; pitiless.

The rest of the day was normal and boring right up until lock-up Muster was interrupted. A commotion started in Section Four and when I looked across I saw the deputy governor screaming at a prisoner kneeling in front of him. He then started slapping him repeatedly across the face before kicking him in the genitals. I couldn't see if the prisoner had said anything to warrant the last part of the assault but after he'd fallen screaming to the floor the deputy governor, ('Psycho', as I would now refer to him), laid into him with his boots, kicking him until he passed out. At this point, Psycho lost interest, the body was removed, and Muster completed. Such assaults, although not always as vicious, were a daily occurrence. There was always some unfortunate who would be kicked, slapped, or hung on a fence at the whim of a guard.

Wednesday, 18th August.

As Julie and William were arriving soon, I had my facial stubble 'trimmed' by a 'professional' barber. This is a form of 'torture' I had never experienced before entering Iraq and something I reluctantly exposed myself to on too many occasions for my liking while in Abu Ghraib.

Abu Athier said that each time I had it done I resembled a Palestinian terrorist. *This is a bit rich coming from a state-sponsored terrorist!* I thought to myself.

The process hurt like hell. A length of cotton thread was taken by the barber and secured on his left hand, then the threads hanging from his thumb were twisted in such a way that a spiral of thread, which was held against the face of the 'victim', was tightened and locked onto the facial hairs against the thread. The barber then pulled on the other end of the threads, which were held in his mouth, and this action tore the hairs from the face!

Obviously the barber had been performing this act for many years and he 'operated' at great speed. He even removed the fluffy hair from earlobes, foreheads and the bridges of noses. Most of the Arabs had apparently experienced this since their manhood and facial hair first arrived, I on the other hand nearly died when I first allowed this to be done to my face. My facial hairs were possibly made of tougher stuff than some of my fellow prisoners, that or my skin was not as tough! Maybe the fact that I had not been through this ordeal before added to the discomfort. All I know is that the pain was excruciating and the fact that my face glowed like a beacon for two days after convinced me that the Arabs I was held with were masochists.

A fresh rumour circulated the prison after lunch. An unusual story that all the Sudanese were going to be released in a special amnesty negotiated by their government. This was as believable as anything else in this 'asylum' and with 15 days being the mentioned timescale, we were all going to be watching and waiting.

With their families still here, the Swedish lads were, as usual, playing their cards close to their chests. I noted in my diary, "The Swedes have been quiet all week, as is usual on their visits. This is now the fifth visit. Christmas, February, April, June and August – they go sort of funny as if talking to us will spoil any chance they have of freedom. It is all secretive, our sources-our-information-syndrome, with the attitude that 'we' know what is going on and 'you' don't. I felt personally that it was all hopes, rumours and conjecture as they were told in a letter that they would be out by the 15th of December last year!"

I promise you this was not sour grapes, but rather a wish that my fellow hostages would accept that whatever we did, the Iraqis would let us go on a political timetable and not due to 'our' behaviour.

We were good friends to each other while held in Abu Ghraib, but on occasions the pressure for each of us wanting freedom led to some distance opening up between us.

Thursday, 19th August.

Whenever I had been expecting a visit from anybody, but especially Julie, I became hyper and had to find things to do in order to occupy my time lest I did something 'silly'. By 'silly', I mean something spontaneous or rash; an argument, taunting someone, falling out and fighting, writing a stroppy letter, etc. I realised I was a nuisance and my own worst enemy.

Did this realisation keep me in check? Not often! As happened today!

Following 1.00pm Muster we had returned to our cells when another Muster was called and back we went to the hot concrete yard where confusion reigned. 350 prisoners were behaving like bovine specimens, brushing against one another as if walking unaided was more than they could manage. They swayed about the yard as if Muster were a new experience rather than something they'd done four times daily for years. I began shoving the other inmates physically to give myself the space I wanted and then my temper exploded and in my rage I grabbed a couple of 'sleepwalkers' and threw them away from me. "FUCK THESE PEOPLE! FUCK THIS PLACE! FUCK MUSTER!" I screamed.

Being a lifelong football supporter, my shouting voice is loud and once I had taken my place in line and my head had cleared I gazed up and saw the savage face of Psycho. I could see that he was enraged by my outburst, and later I wrote in my diary, "I know he wants to do me, but if he hits me I'll hit him back!"

The man frightened me and I knew that if he struck me and I fought back it wouldn't help me, however this was the only way I felt able to deal with such a threat. When we got back inside our section, the other prisoners were laughing about my outburst saying that it had been funny to see Psycho's face because he couldn't do anything.

Evening Muster was called at 7.20pm. Normally, at this time of the year, the call to Muster came at 8.15pm and so not expecting it I had just put our kettles on to boil the water for our tea and coffee. Annoyed, I went out and joined a line and within minutes Psycho appeared informing the guard that we should sit on our haunches and he'd be back to count us soon. Everyone did so, apart from me. My kettle was the whistling type, and as the water inside it was now boiling I heard the whistle start and so I went and filled our flasks before returning to sit on the floor. The guard who always gave me grief shouted at me to crouch and as he did so feelings of anger, contempt, and hatred began to pulse through my head. Slowly, I stood up and looked around at everyone else crouching and then glowering at the guard I shouted, "ONE DAY I WILL BE A FREE MAN IN ENGLAND! – WHILE YOU WILL ALWAYS BE AN IRAQI IN IRAQ!"

The guard went around to a lot of the prisoners who spoke English asking them what I had said but none of them would give him an answer, each saying that they had not understood. He persisted in trying to find out what I had said until Psycho returned to count us, at which point I crouched down. *There's no point pushing my luck!* I thought.

Maybe I had overstepped the mark and had been lucky that the other prisoners had not revealed what I had said, but rather than be disturbed and then relieved when I had not been punished I felt bored, irritated, and that the whole thing was stupid. Not that I had acted stupidly. Oh no, I was maintaining my dignity and independence or so I convinced myself!

This was not an opinion shared by Kai and Simon who were worried that my outbursts would cause problems for all Western hostages. To be honest they may have been correct but I would rather have had problems then the void I had been forced to exist in for over a year now. The vacuum was a total abomination to me. I had always led a full and interesting life, one in which I believed I had control.

I spent time with the Swedes that evening and was entertained by Leif and his revelations about what I refered to as the 'Swedish Situation'. I noted in my diary, "Leif told me the Iraqis were saying that they were concerned about the condition of the three Swedes as they wanted to maintain the good relationship between Iraq and Sweden. I laughed as if it was all some sort of sick joke. Why don't they just let them/us go and have good relationships with all countries instead of fucking about and antagonising everyone!"

I then go on to say, "Everyone has come to the same conclusion that I have, and that is while we are in prison and the (allied) bombings go on then the sanctions won't be lifted."

I felt that this was the heart of the issue. Saddam's regime had demanded 'conditions' for our release and as the UK were refusing to talk about any subject apart from our unconditional release I sensed we were due a long stay in Abu Ghraib!

Friday, 20th August.

Trying to prepare for Julie and William's arrival was not as easy as you might think. It was a general visiting day and the showers were in demand from other prisoners. Patience was not my strong point and the eons they took to shower had me tearing my hair out. The more I tried to hurry them up the slower they went. I should have remembered this from my time in Arabic countries, Inshallah! But under stress it's the details you forget; the important little details!

Later, I saw Ken Beaty walking from the clinic to Abu Athier's office with his wife Robin. I'd heard she was leaving Iraq today and didn't expect to see her. I thought this was probably a drop-in visit on her way out of Iraq as Abu Ghraib was to the west of Baghdad en route to Jordan. Given this, I thought no more of it until a very agitated Ghassan came to my cell asking me to 'comfort' Ken.

Robin had left and Ken had believed he'd be leaving with her but this obviously hadn't happened and he'd fallen apart. His distress could be heard throughout the section. Ghassan felt that I was the person to comfort him but I refused as did the Swedish lads. We told Ghassan that in his own time Ken would calm down and until that point he would want to be alone. Ghassan left with confusion and disgust written all over his face.

As we had said, Ken eventually 'got a grip' and normality returned. None of the us had the bad manners to mention his distress to him or to each other, it never happened. What 'emotional cripples' we'd produced in the 'stiff upper lip' regime we had developed in the West.

This incident saw Ken's attitude change from having a polite adoration of the "long-suffering Iraqis" to total disregard for the "lying, deceitful, Iraqis". In my opinion he was adopting a very acceptable attitude towards the entire situation.

Julie and William didn't arrive which was a source of concern and consternation for me. To distract myself from morose thoughts I spent the evening in competition with Kai and Simon playing board games. Kai had taught me how to play Backgammon. He was very good and took great pride in showing me the rudimentary tactics and then trouncing me.

I was really agitated as I tried to sleep. Visions of my family stranded in the desert or sat in a barren hotel room haunted me. I cursed Khalid Jerjes, the bloody idiot couldn't even arrange a visit. How the hell was he ever going to get us released? Everyone should have been aware that coming to an Arabic country on a Friday was not a good idea. I cursed everyone who had made me miss one precious day of a visit.

Saturday, 21st August.

Gleb Desyatnikov informed me that my family hadn't been granted a visa and had postponed their visit for a week and would now be arriving on the 26th. Addressing our Western hostage group he also said that politically nothing had changed and our ongoing detention seemed likely. Simon was not elated by this information and became extremely aggressive and moody for the duration of the visit which included learning the riveting news that the Iraqis were going to put on a third TV channel, as if we didn't have enough to suffer with the existing two!

I learned that the prisoner from Section Four whom we had witnessed receiving a horrible kicking on the 17th had been beaten intermittently all night long as well. His crime apparently had been to stick a piece of wood up the rectum of another prisoner. Whether this was a sexual or aggressive act I never found out, but the punishment received for this 'poking' was well over the top.

Sunday, 22nd August.

I went out for exercise and met Abdul Baki who said his family were in Baghdad. The Iraqis had not granted them permission for special visits, and they had been sat in a hotel for nearly a week. Abdul said Khalid Jerjes had promised assistance. I thought, *God help them!*

I asked Abdul to loan me the cash to pay Jerjes off, saying I didn't want to get out of prison and be so deep in debt to that bastard that I spent the rest of my life paying him back. He said he'd be happy to loan me the money. During my life, men with huge problems of their own have shown me the most generous side of human nature and Abdul Baki was always such a man.

We walked on and then stood open-mouthed as a sanitation truck drove onto the sports field and proceeded to disgorge a full tanker-load of raw sewage directly onto the exercise area! The smell was appalling. I shuddered to think what the health implications were and with this in mind Abdul and I cut short our walk-and-talk and returned to our respective sections.

The ICRC visited, which was all very nice but as there was no change in our situation the meeting only lasted five minutes. After lunch I went to see them on my own and explained that the stories being written in the British media about Michael and I were a fabrication and could they put a halt to this. Did they believe me? I don't know. The stories in the media didn't stop so I guess they didn't.

That evening, Ghassan told me that the deputy governor, Psycho as I now knew him, was on medication for mental problems! This came as no surprise given what I'd seen. The man really was a psychopath!

I went to Section One in the afternoon to visit Abdul Baki and continue our conversation. As usual the entire section made me feel very welcome and comfortable and I spent an enjoyable couple of hours away from the boredom of my own cell.

During my chat with Abdul, I decided I would write to the British Embassy in Amman and request that Khalid Jerjes be taken off my case. I noted in my diary, "Due to his constant talk of good relations, and bribes etc, I don't want to get involved, I don't want to bribe my way out of here, I want my human rights, a release, and reparations for my time in this shithouse."

Thursday, 26th August.

The 26th was the revised date I'd been given for my family visting me but I'd heard nothing more for a week and had lost hope it was going to happen. I was exercising on the sports field when I was told to make my way urgently to the office as 'someone' wanted to see me. Excited at the possibility it might be Julie and William, I dashed to my cell, put clothes on my sweaty body, and ran to the office only to find it was Khalid Jerjes who wanted to see me basically to cover his arse about my family visit being held up!

My diary entry reads, "Jerjes comes out with so much bullshit that I just see red. I told him to arrange to have my brains blown out. That way I would at least be out of prison. Julie is being messed about by the British Government, I'm being messed about here! I ran six laps of the sports field to get Jerjes out of my system. God, I hate that man!"

Omar was moved from the punishment cell to the prison hospital and reported as being sick. This was a move clearly designed to prevent him from complaining to the ICRC about his treatment. The Iraqis were well-versed in dealing with international inspections. No one ever saw anything other than what the Iraqis wanted them to see.

At the end of the ICRC visit, each prisoner was given a biro and a cigarette! The foreign section was given six new basketballs, six new volleyballs and six new footballs. Of the 18 balls, only one new football was actually given to the prisoners. The rest of the balls mysteriously disappeared – they always did! Huge amounts of stationary that had been given for the prison school was 'confiscated' by the guards who used the materials for personal use or to profit from their sale.

The only piece of good news I learned today was that the previous evening Chelsea had beaten Queens Park Rangers 2-0 to record their first win of the new Premier League season which had started ignominiously with two defeats and a draw.

Friday, 27th August.

Abu Athier came into my cell and asked, "Is Madam Julie coming to see you today?"

I was in a prison and had been in the damned place for over a year and I replied, almost mockingly, "I haven't got a clue!"

I think my frustration was showing. Abu Athier gave me a hateful gaze and, without another word, turned and walked away.

Saturday, 28th August.

I awoke needing to pay a visit to 'hell'. I got up and made my way through the silent echoing passage from my cell to the toilet block. As normal I had taken a couple of pieces of toilet paper with me, just in case they were required. I never dropped them into the small hole in the ground, but instead rolled them up into a small ball which I threw into the rubbish can.

Some months earlier, one of the Egyptian lads, Reziq, was trying to clear a blockage with his hands and had his entire arm down the hole in the floor. He berated me about my use of toilet tissue exclaiming I had blocked the toilets. He ranted and swung his filth-covered hands about while clasping the toilet paper he'd retrieved. The sight of Reziq covered in urine and excreta berating me for using toilet paper as he resembled a demon from the bowels of the Earth and smelt like a slurry tank will never leave me and this is why I now used the rubbish can!

I was attempting to wash my backside in the Arabic fashion and as I reached for a water jug used for this job I felt something and acidic bile rose in my throat. The toilets were dark, the only light being in the sink area. Blankets which doubled as a toilet door kept all but the faintest slither of light out. I raised my hand to my face and inhaled – yes, some bastard had managed to get excreta on the handle of the jug. My hand was now covered in someone else's shit!

I struggled on, cleaning myself up as best I could, grateful that I had the toilet paper in my pocket. When I reached a stage where I could get out and wash my hands, I scrubbed them in a relentless manner like I'd never done since my first use of an Arabic toilet over a year before which now felt like a lifetime away.

After Muster, I exercised and had a talk with Noufal. He told me that my situation was not unusual in the prison. The Iraqis liked to use psychological stress as a tool to distract and control people. I didn't feel better but I realised that Khalid Jerjes was part of the system feeding my anxiety.

Noufal also said that I should learn to be more hypercritical and not to wear my heart on my sleeve and that I should get any ideas I had of 'revenge' against Abu Athier, Jerjes and Ghassan out of my head as they were not feasible and causing me further distress. International politics is all too vague and nebulous a concept and I couldn't 'attack' it, so I gave my torment a physical shape; Abu Athier, Jerjes, and Ghassan.

Abu Athier came to my cell and informed me that Julie would be arriving in Baghdad on Monday or Tuesday. I didn't feel joy, the news gave me an acidic taste in my mouth and a feeling that I was about to evacuate my bowels. I almost feared the next arrival date being announced, as I knew it would start the entire anticipation process again, very likely with no outcome!

Sunday, 29th August.

I went to Section One and had a chat with Abdul Baki and Noufal. Abdul was ill and looked dreadful so he didn't say much and Noufal and I continued our conversation from Saturday. Noufal said that Abu Athier was a good man, but his position within the Iraqi system meant that to stay alive he had to be seen to act in a certain manner. To be fair Abu Athier never caused me any harm, more mental anguish, but my hatred was driving me mad and rational thought was not my top priority.

We chatted about food and wine and I mentioned to Noufal that I was good at making home-brewed wine. He asked me if I could brew him some wine here. I said it would be very dangerous and that during the fermentation stage the brew would give off a strong aroma. He told me that among the filth and crap of his cell it would be a pleasure to wake up to a "new and fresh smell" adding that he would be held totally responsible if anything should go wrong and the wine discovered. I said I'd think about it, but the devil in me fancied the challenge the minute Noufal uttered the question!

At the 1.00pm Muster I had a word with Psycho and asked why was a new inmate called Haji Ali continually staggering out five to ten minutes later than everyone else causing us to be held in the crouch position until last for counting. I told him that unless something was done, I would take the matter up with the office as I was fed up of block punishments due to one idiot. I was told to sit down and shut up and I did shout "BULLSHIT!"

loudly as I crouched down to be counted.

When Muster was over, I dashed across to 'Donkey Ali' as most of the prisoners knew Haji and berated him about his continual tardiness. Psycho then ran into our section and told us to go back out to the yard where gave us a lecture about our attitude. Having heard about the commotion, Abu Athier arrived and told me to go back into the section. As I was turning and walking away Psycho shouted, "IMSHI!" An impolite way in Arabic of telling someone to go away. In other words, "Piss Off!" In hindsight, I realised that the probable reason for his lack of action over Donkey Ali's tardiness was the fact that it gave him something to punish us for!

The Western hostages agreed with my attitude and actions. Some of the Arabic prisoners were also in accord with what I'd done. I realised that most of these poor sods were not able to express their feelings at all. To act as I had would mean for them a trip to the solitary cells and some serious beatings until they forgot what they were complaining about in the first place!

In the evening, Ranko came to my cell and told me not to aggravate the guards as they would beat me. He was a good man and in many ways he saw me as a son, but he didn't understand me or my situation. When it came down to why we were in Abu Ghraib, he had killed three men in a motor accident while I had driven up the wrong road! I wasn't for giving in or lying down. When Ranko left, I lay awake for hours replaying many different events from the past 13 months. Scenarios flashed through my head as I contemplated what the near-term future might have in store for me and if anything might change that would bring an end to my living hell.

FAMILY COME AND THE SWEDES GO

August had been traumatic. I seemed to be attracting more attention, and trouble, from the guards, and my intransigence was worrying the other hostages and prisoners. I was scared; scared of being forgotten, scared of being ignored, scared of being beaten, scared of impulses that I felt I scarcely controlled. As September began, mentally I grew weaker and I was taking more and more chances with my life.

Wednesday, 1st September.

Gleb Desyatnikov arrived and brought with him three boxes of food. I wondered if he travelled to Abu Ghraib on a white horse, because at times he certainly saved me from unspeakable degradation. Gleb was taken for granted, but did a marvellous job with the minimum of fuss and great dignity, often in the face of immense provocation from Iraqi officials and prisoners alike. He informed me that Julie still hadn't been permitted a visa, however it was possible that she'd arrive at very short notice as and when this was arranged.

I said Khalid Jerjes had been speaking about attempting to get us out using bribes and that I thought this stupid, irresponsible and doomed to failure and would probably result in further charges. Jerjes was a complete buffoon and I wished more than ever that I could get him off my case. Thinking about him decades later, the greater I understand his frivolity; the trouble was, in 1993, I was cast as Stan Laurel to his Oliver Hardy! An odd couple, joined at the hip but separated at the heart. A dark reality that has haunted many a double act.

The foodstuffs were inspected by the Iraqis and, as per usual, large amounts stolen. This really made me angry because I'd been told that Julie, despite her horrendous financial situation, was paying for all my food now and the bloody Foreign Office couldn't protect the items they sent to me. This was more inflammable material thrown upon my already combustible, tinder-dry, psyche.

Later in the morning, when Gleb was gone, and Abu Athier was not in the prison, I was called to the office and questioned by the section manager about the 'incident' between Haji Ali and myself. I said he was a liability and was angry that the section kept receiving block punishments because of him. Haji Ali arrived towards the end of my explanation and added, like a cringing school kid, that I was calling him names. The section manager said that I was wrong for insulting him and sent me to the punishment block which after the insanity of the main prison I found to be quiet, peaceful and actually quite glorious as there were no lunatics milling about! On the negative side of things, my cell had no fan, cooler, or mosquito net, but I could put up with that and so I lay on the concrete floor and relaxed!

Thursday, 2nd September.

I was asleep when a noise woke me. I sat up disorientated as it appeared to be coming from every part of my concrete bunker. As my eyes grew accustomed to the light, I saw a pair of eyes peering through a hatch in the gate and recognised them as Abu Athier's. He was here to 'let me out'. I don't know whether my spell in solitary, a put-up job, was designed to 'scare' me, if it was, it failed miserably as I enjoyed the peace and quiet!

Were these tactics used by the senior officers to extort items of food and cigarettes? One played the 'bad cop' who threw me into solitary, and then along came Abu Athier, the 'good cop', getting me 'released' and then hitting on me for various things that we had delivered in our parcels from Amman? I could be wrong, but paranoid delusions were gaining the upper hand and faintly ridiculous notions became entirely plausible in my head.

The Swedes 'paid back' their share of the pork that had been eaten by mistake the previous month and Simon cooked bacon, sausage and beans which for him was a culinary dish of some magnitude! I felt that the 'honeymoon' was over for Simon and Kai as they were now sleeping even longer each day and producing only the most fundamental food. By now I'd begun to feel as if I was being made a fool of as I was preparing food for them and putting real effort into it, and I didn't like the increasing feelings of resentment that kept fogging my head.

Sunday, 5th September.

I weighed myself on the scales in the 'clinic'. 59 kilos! I was genuinely shocked. Not used to metric weight at this time, I calculated this was 130 pounds or nine-stones-four-pounds. I was well on the way to weighing 14 stones (89 kilos) when I'd been abducted!

I heard on the news that Mohammed Hamza al-Zubaidi, Iraq's Prime Minister, later to become Queen of Spades in the deck of most-wanted Iraqis playing cards issued to US soldiers by the US Defence Intelligence Agency at the start of 'Operation Iraqi Freedom' in 2003, had been 'redeployed' by Saddam and many more elected officials also 'dispensed' with. Iraqi democracy in action!

In the afternoon, Khalid Jerjes came into the section with the Swedish Embassy staff and told me 'Madam Julie' would probably be here on Tuesday, and then he made a priceless comment that placed everything he ever said to me into perspective. "We are doing everything. Believe me. I am suffering more than you."

Sorry Khalid old son, but I really don't think so. I didn't then. and I still don't now!

Tuesday, 7th September.

No sign of Julie! I spent an entire exercise session being harangued by Arabs and Eastern Europeans about my relationship with the guards, especially Psycho, the management, and Abu Athier. The consensus was that I should be more like Ian Richter who had good relations with them and was given whisky and beer! I said that I didn't want good relations with any of them, all I wanted was for items delivered to the prison for me to be given to me!

I cooked a lasagne which under the circumstances was bloody marvelous. Gordon Ramsey wouldn't have thought much of it, but how would he have got on in this environment? Positive experiences such as a meal that worked or being able to explain my position on things in the prison lifted my spirits but it didn't take much, the sanitary conditions for example, to bring me back to reality with a crash.

I wrote in my diary, "Today the water ran out (again) but more importantly the toilets on the other side are all blocked, so now with over 250 inmates in the section we are all using just two toilets! There are queues all day long and the damned toilets are filthy. God this is an awful place!"

Wednesday, 8th September.

My diary records the distress caused by Abu Athier's hints that Julie will be here; today, tomorrow, next week. Please, try to imagine how I felt, stuck in a foreign jail with my wife and son traipsing across the globe to a place mostly filled with danger, to visit me. I wrote about my anxieties for them both, mixed with a deep desire to see them again. "One of my fears is that William won't recognise me. He is only young, two-and-a-half and I have changed a lot in the past 14-and-a-half months – how long will this last?"

That afternoon Simon was called to the office and on his return I asked him if he'd heard anything about Julie's arrival and he said it would probably be Saturday or Sunday now which added to my misery and frustration.

I tried to switch off to reports of Julie's 'imminent' arrival and was about to go to bed when I heard that a World Cup qualifier between England and Poland was going to be shown on TV between midnight and 2.00am. England won 3-0. It wasn't a classic, but it was a bit of home which was a comfort to me.

The days dragged as I waited for news of my family. On the upside, the toilets were repaired – on the downside, for a couple of nights, Psycho started coming into the section conducting midnight cell inspections! When he came to our cell I didn't stand up as I was meant to because I had no respect for him. I didn't sleep at all well after his visits – the sick bastard worried me.

Saturday, 11th September.

My daughter Rhian's birthday. Another family occasion missed through being in this shithole. In the evening I listened to radio commentary of Chelsea's game with Manchester United at Stamford Bridge. The Blues won 1-0 with a goal from Gavin Peacock, and World Service broadcaster Paddy Feeny announced, "Paul Ride in Baghdad will be going barmy about the Chelsea result!"

How bloody right he was. Simon was chuffed that we'd been remembered. It was a special day for us all. Later that night we listened to the 'Last Night of the Proms' and I had a lump in my throat for most of the performances especially 'Jerusalem', a favourite of mine for years. It's strange how things from everyday life take on extraordinary meaning when you are unable to be part of the everyday. Thank you; Paddy, 'Sportsworld', the 'Proms', and the World Service.

Sunday, 12th September.

I was exercising and heard an announcement in Arabic that Abdul Baki translated as, "Immediate release for all Jordanian and Palestinian prisoners". As I walked back to my section the Jordanians and Palestinians were stood outside the library being processed! Would they go? Who knew? But hope is better than despair.

Michael discovered that he'd had 20,000 Greek Drachmas stolen. 5,000 had been 'found' on an Egyptian and he was put in 'The Sheraton', my whimsical new name, after my stay, for the punishment block. There was little doubt that he would get a beating, probably not for stealing the money, but for getting caught!

This Egyptian was a nasty little bit of work who claimed to have stolen the money over five months ago! I struggled at this stage of my captivity to find any compassion for anyone or anything; prison sucks the humanity out of your bones until all that's left is the bitter dust of resentment. *Fuck him! He deserved it!* Were my feelings about his punishment. It's awful to relive that emptiness now, three decades on, but to ignore it is to deny the truth.

Monday, 13th September.

Jean-Luc Barriere, the French inmate, was taken to see the prison psychiatrist. He'd taken to wearing a dishdasha (a long white robe traditionally worn by men in Middle East) which we ribbed him mercilessly about. This was his third visit to see the shrink and it made me think about what was going on inside his head, as I often thought about what was going on in mine – which wasn't good!

Kai had a diplomatic visit and was told nothing would be changing for six months. He was having problems with his supplies and so Abu Athier sent Ghassan to ask if he had a list of items he was meant to have received, Kai said yes but he refused to let Ghassan or Abu Athier see it!

Stefan told me later in the day that he'd just bought a property in Taiwan for $70,000! Nice! Even in jail he was still flush, while I was slipping inexorably down the rubbish chute of life with no visible means of escape. "Still these are the breaks," I wrote in my diary with a mix of sadness and jealousy.

The water had been off for most of the day and when it came back on at 4.00pm I was able to prepare an evening meal and have a hot drink. When I went out to the preparation area, Ismail, one of the Egyptian mafia, was cooking on Kai's stove with my gas. I challenged him, and he said indignantly that he was cooking for Mohammed the Tunisian and his sidekick Hadi. If he thought that this would make me back off, it had the opposite effect. I told him they were both useless pieces of shit, worthless spies who if they needed anything could go to the office and get it off of their 'friends'. I told him that if I saw him cooking their food using my gas again then I would take it up with Abu Athier. I ranted and raved and was well over the top, but just the mention of those two sent me into paroxysms of rage.

Wednesday, 15th September.

Michael and I stripped our cell, cleaning and scrubbing it to prevent infestations. The entire process took over two hours as we had to wait for floors and walls to dry before we could replace our personal possessions.

Khalid Jerjes told me that Julie would be here on Friday. While I wanted to see my family, this was ridiculous and I struggled with the stress that went hand-in-hand with the anticipation of their arrival. Jerjes questioned me again about the 'financing of my case'. He was doing a job for some other nationals but as far as we Brits were concerned he was as much use as a chocolate teapot. Once more he said, "Surely the British Government would be paying my costs after all this was over?"

I told him, in no uncertain terms, that this was not the case. He said, "But they must pay your expenses! After all this is a political case!" And then with typical Jerjes idiocy he said, "I will push them and so will other international groups!"

Jerjes asked why there was such a discrepancy in the coverage between the Swedish and British Media and I told him that London's population alone was the same as Sweden's in total, and that the British populous had plenty of other things to worry about! He also commented on my appearance saying that I looked thin and drawn. *Well what a bloody surprise!* I thought. My diary entry reflects my uncaring self-perception. "He hoped to see me put weight on. I don't think I will. I've either got worms, or the worry of this is keeping my weight down, or I've contracted Aids!"

In the evening I deliberately stayed out of Kai and Simon's cell as Simon was in the middle of a serious depression which I couldn't deal with.

Thursday, 16th September.

We had to wait an eternity for midday Muster in the hot sun. I wrapped a wet towel around my head and when the officer eventually arrived he asked why I had my head wrapped up? I explained that it was hot and I was trying to keep cool! "God! What am I seeing?" exclaimed the officer, laughing as he spoke. All the guards were entertained by my appearance, pointing and making jokes and then Abu Athier appeared and added to the party atmosphere by telling me Julie would be here on Friday – though he didn't say which Friday!

Friday, 17th September.

A general visiting day. "Oh joy!" I wrote sarcastically in my diary. Visiting day's still wound me up and I was feeling flustered right up to the minute Abu Athier came to my cell and told me to smarten myself up as Julie and William were here at the prison! The rest of the day was a blur of love, hugs, cuddles, and games.

At 6.30pm Ghassan, whom William described as a "stupid man", came and told us that I had to go back to my section for the night. He had been in and out of the room for much of the day and had crossed swords with William about 'whose daddy I was' hence the 'stupid man' tag. I'd not seen William's development, and his next comment choked me up as he said, "I love you very, very much daddy". So much for being forgotten!

Saturday, 18th September.

I'd spent Friday evening unpacking and storing the supplies that Julie brought with her and then on Saturday morning I started to read the letters and newspapers that were also in my packages. Among the newspapers was the 'Mail On Sunday', the edition containing the article George Galloway had written in which he alleged I had told the Iraqis that Michael had assaulted me. When I read it in full I was stunned. I sat on my bed with my eyes stinging with tears of rage. I'd been told most of the content in letters I'd received, however, seeing the actual article made my blood boil. I wrote in my diary a note to pass on for future reference. "George, I gather that you like boxing. Want to go three rounds with me mate?" (Curiously, 15 years later, I encountered

Galloway purely by chance as I was riding my motorcycle down St Paul's Road in Highbury. He was aboard a campaign bus canvassing for the now defunct Respect Party. To cut a short story even shorter, after a brief, "Remember me, I'm Paul Ride", exchange, I 'offered him out' and as the bus predictably drove swiftly off I shouted after him, "CUNT!" and he shouted back, "THANK YOU VERY MUCH!"

Today, William was a little calmer and had a sleep in the afternoon which allowed Julie and I to have an in-depth conversation about how she was doing, what she was doing, and how things looked on the international political front. She also told me that Khalid Jerjes had visited our house and stolen from her! The rest of the visit was a blur; the British Government were allowing a man like Jerjes the freedom to travel to and around London and abuse the trust placed in him.

When the visit ended and I returned to Section Three my head was spinning. As I began to unpack the latest things Julie had brought in I realised that large amounts of the delivery had been appropriated. I decided to 'threaten' Jerjes with exposure to the Foreign Office and the British media if the items were not returned. I would say he was responsible for 'aiding and abetting' the theft of my property from deliveries to Abu Ghraib and from my house in London.

I hated the person I'd morphed into, but prison squeezed the last of the humanity from the drying husk of a man close to the edge. I had become as insidious as the people I despised and most of my waking moments were full of desire for revenge.

Sunday, 19th September.

The last day of Julie and William's visit and my son discovered a great new game – running around and around in small circles, well at about a metre they were six of seven steps for him. I was virtually spinning like a top, nauseous, and dizzy as I played with him. I'm glad he hadn't discovered this game when they'd first arrived!

Today's visit was wonderful and everything I'd asked Julie for was delivered. Food, toiletries, household items, hardware, disposables and clothing all arrived. She even brought 'extras' such as a cool box and other items she'd had to negotiate hard for. She expected me to bring these 'luxury items' home when I was released. I tried to explain that I was at the mercy of the Iraqis and knew that they wouldn't allow me to take things she'd bought out of Abu Ghraib. She said, "Fine, then smash them! Just don't leave these bastards anything!"

I knew her anger was aimed at the Iraqis and not the other prisoners in Abu Ghraib who I hoped might benefit from my departure – a long shot but I lived in hope! Julie had also brought with her $1000 for Ong from his sister in America. It was the money he'd requested at the start of the year. When she passed it to me we had a brief chat about the scenario and then spoke of it no more as we had our goodbyes to say and my family was more important.

Wednesday, 22nd September.

I retreated into my shell for a couple of days after my family departed and didn't bother delivering my ultimatum to Khalid Jerjes, because I thought I'd be an easy target and, more importantly, so would Julie. Instead I wrote a strongly worded letter to Colin Cooper, the British Embassy official in Amman.

The visit of my family was already a memory and I had to get on with life in Abu Ghraib. I went to see Ong and gave him the $1000. I'd delayed doing this because I wanted Julie and William to be safely out of the country so they could not fall foul of Iraqi currency laws if anything went wrong. The biggest problem with doing anything for other inmates in Abu Ghraib was the fact they felt 'compelled' to declare that 'a Westerner' had helped them out. It was almost like a 'badge of honour' and I knew Ong would not keep his new-found wealth hidden for long.

During the afternoon, Simon dashed into our cell yelling that the Swedes were being released. It was true! I went into their cell to say goodbye and became involved in a 'feeding frenzy' as multiple inmates struggled to benefit from their release; begging, pleading, and stealing, anything and everything they could lay their hands on!

I hugged the guys and wished them all the best and then Abu Athier arrived in the section shouting that everyone should leave the area immediately and return all the goods they had already taken! Christer gave me the last of their Iraqi money and following this last kind gesture the Swedes were gone!

Abu Athier told me that he hoped this would be the beginning of the end for all of us Western hostages. Carl XVI Gustaf, the King of Sweden, was allowing his private jet to be used to fly them home direct from Baghdad. I wondered, *"Does Elizabeth II, the Queen of the United Kingdom and many other Commonwealth realms, even know who I am and where I am?*

The release sparked a wave of speculation about our 'impending' release; Kai, Simon, Jean-Luc, and Ali all had their own theories. I knew that before we could even be considered, Ken Beaty had to be released. We sat up until the early hours of the morning trying to work out all the permutations, but none of it made much sense. *Why should the end be logical?* I thought to myself.

Thursday, 23rd September.

Psycho visited me three times during the course of the day and night asking if I was okay and did I want anything! The first couple of visits were so bizarre that when I saw him approaching again at 11.30pm I felt uncomfortable and went to have a shower hoping to avoid him! Younis, a

Sudanese Maraheb, followed me into the toilet block and asked where I was going because Psycho wanted to talk to me! I told him I needed a shower and leapt into the slimy cubicle!

I don't know if the Iraqis thought I was ill, but the following day during Muster another officer asked me if I was all right, in good health, not too hot, and numerous other questions, to which I replied with a solitary Arabic word, "Mumtaz!" (Excellent!)

That evening Hamo asked if I wanted to transfer into the Swedes old cell alone! I said I didn't mind and left it at that. *What are these bastards up to?* Suddenly everyone wanted to make sure I was fine and would do anything for me! It felt as if I had won the Football Pools!

Saturday, 25th September.

The Swedes made a press statement saying that while we were in good health the British Government was doing nothing to help us. I was grateful that they'd spoken out but understood that the government were past masters in deception. Listening to a news bulletin on my radio that mentioned the press statement, I also heard that the government were sending two diplomats to see us. I'd known they were due for a month and I also knew they were coming to check on British property in Iraq which for me watered down the prospect of anything positive being achieved in respect of our cases.

Rumours abounded that Ken was going to be released on Tuesday and that it would be my turn next Saturday. I would gladly be a part of this if it were reality, but I wasn't hanging out any flags or holding my breath. There were two reasons to be cheerful though. Chelsea beat Liverpool 1-0 at Stamford Bridge, a result which buoyed my mood as did Paddy Feeny giving Julie a mention. This was a novel idea I'd come up with so I knew she and William were safely back in the UK!

Monday, 27th September.

A peaceful start to the week was fractured by Abu Athier telling me that Colin Cooper and Marc Le Goy had arrived for a visit. I spent a long time asking question after question of the two diplomats, and to my surprise I came away feeling that I'd been heard and, more importantly, received some honest answers. They brought with them supplies and everything I'd asked for arrived, nothing was taken. This was the first and last time this ever happened.

Julie sent a nice fax message saying she was sorry it wasn't me who'd been released the previous week to which I thought, *You're not alone there girl!*

When I'd returned to my cell, Ghassan came by and said, "The officers are having a meeting in the office and they need a packet of cigarettes. You did get a carton of Marlboro today?"

I told him that I'd lost an entire carton on Julie's recent visit and that because of this the carton I received today might have to last me over a month. The short translation of this? *FUCK OFF!*

Khalid Jerjes came into the section at 5.30pm and professed his innocence about the thefts from our supplies, telling Simon and myself that he owned ten houses in the best part of Baghdad and that as he was a millionaire he didn't need to pilfer from prisoners' provisions. I'd grown accustomed to his patter and ignored the stupid sod, but Simon lost his rag and abused him about his attitude and effort. The pressure was starting to tell on the remaining hostages now.

Tuesday, 28th September.

I received a bumper pile of mail. Some letters were complete, however numerous envelopes and packets were in a dreadful state; ripped, parts missing, inserts stolen – but it meant that people still cared and this gave me a terrific boost just when I needed to feel supported.

I was pulled into the office by Abu Athier and forced to write a letter exonerating him for the thefts which had occurred since my arrival at Abu Ghraib. From what he said I think the problem had now been raised at ministerial level and people were running for cover so as not to get covered in the metaphorical shit that had hit the fan!

In the afternoon I was in Section One having coffee and a chat when Abu Athier arrived advising that Jean-Luc's pal Ali Autout was being released in the evening. Ali was terrified that as a Moroccan he would end up being left here as the rest of us were released and yet here he was heading home before us.

Wednesday, 29th September.

Khalid Jerjes came in with the letter I'd written for Abu Athier which left him high and dry. He berated me that I needed him and said he'd placed the bag in the office in good faith as he'd been busy with the Swedes. *The story of my life*, I thought. He said the things had been taken when the bag was "temporarily unattended". It was a crock of shit, but it was bloody heart-warming to see the obsequious little prick squirm!

While Jerjes was burbling, Muster was called and so I walked straight past him and out into the yard. He followed me saying, "Why don't you say 'excuse me' are you insulting me?"

I had to bite my tongue at what he said next!

"The only way you are getting out of Abu Ghraib is with Khalid Jerjes and with nice words from Britain!"

I told him that there would be no nice words coming from Britain and that I would therefore be in Abu Ghraib a long time. I held this idiot in such contempt that memories of him still colour my perceptions of the legal profession.

The fact he had the letter I'd written for Abu Athier the day after I'd penned it confirmed for me, not that I really needed any validation, that Jerjes and Abu Athier were in collusion about all events that went on in the foreign section. I fumed as this officious buffoon, full of his own self-importance, railed against me in the public arena of the yard. I viewed it as another demonstration of his blind panic.

Colin Cooper and Mark Le Goy told me later in the day that I'd have to learn to put up with Jerjes! *I've been shot in the foot by my own Foreign Office!* I thought. They also showed our British hostage group a letter, so that we didn't have to speak and be heard by the secret microphones, that informed us to be very careful if we were 'paraded' in front of TV cameras by the Iraqis, and to be discreet until we were in a safe location! Cooper also told me not to write any more letters! It was all a bit cryptic and I didn't understand what it all meant. This would only become obvious as hours passed in the wake of their departure.

Once they'd gone, Abu Athier told me to have a shave. I enquired if he meant on a daily basis to which he replied, "No! Just today, because you might be going to do something – but I don't know what!"

My first thought was, *My God! The bastards are going to let us go!*

The next couple of hours were a blur as Simon and I got ready for what we thought was now the inevitable. I tried to remember where I'd hidden all sorts of things, and generally prepared to be released.

Khalid Jerjes then called us into an office and told us that we were going on TV to answer a few questions. He tried to coach us about answering carefully and I remember thinking, *This is all just a dramatic prelude to our release!*

Jerjes drove Abu Athier, Simon and me to the centre of Baghdad and the Al Rasheed Hotel. As we got out of the car, cameramen began filming and in a surreal vignette we walked into the hotel and across a mosaic of George Bush Senior that Saddam Hussein had ordered be laid across the entrance! Once we were in the hotel Abu Athier told the film crews to stop filming until we were ready to answer questions.

I asked to use the toilets and saw my first stand-up urinals in over 15 months! We then walked down a long hallway that led to the back of the building. Suddenly, a bank of lifts appeared on our right and we were escorted past them and up a staircase into a mezzanine area that was filled with seats and had a table at its centre which we were asked to sit at.

Microphones were placed on the table and almost immediately after we sat down the questions started. The first couple concerned Michael Wainwright and his whereabouts which Khalid Jerjes dealt with unsuccessfully in my opinion – but then I knew the truth! Jerjes said he felt too tired and did not want to come. The reality was the Iraqis knew Michael would say what was in his head, and that even though he could sound like the most brilliant philosopher of the 20th Century, unfortunately, he could also come across as monosyllabic and irrational.

The questions were predictable but 'suggested' that Kuwait was the guilty party, at least as far as our arrival near the border, and subsequent detention was concerned. Surely Iraq was just confirming the integrity of its frontiers!

I said that I saw myself as an object in a diplomatic gambit, a totally innocent party in a 15-month game of international politics and I would be seeking compensation when released.

The interview was mercifully brief and then Simon, who answered his questions with admirable grace, and myself were taken down into a restaurant and bought a couple of Iraqi beers that looked and tasted like pale ale but had a mighty kick.

I was still savouring the taste of the beer when an Iraqi arrived whom I recognised as the 'Major' from the 'Ministry of Justice' who had interviewed us at the beginning of August about our written statements related to our 'capture'. He told us that the Iraqis were willing to let us go! All that was required was a "British Statesman" and a humanitarian to visit Baghdad to secure our release.

There were a lot of little asides and this entire charade I felt sure had been an exercise in futility. It was simply the Iraqis 'getting their money's worth out of us', and using us to have a go at the Kuwaitis. They had by now realised that even if they held us for the entire term of our sentences, the only losers would be us as individuals. The British Government was intransigent and the Iraqis simply wanted to find a nice easy way of getting rid of us with the maximum positive media exposure they could obtain from the event. *Lovely jubbly! Everyone's a winner!*

Khalid Jerjes then drove us back to Abu Ghraib. In my diary a Freudian slip of enormous magnitude is revealed as I wrote, "And then Jerjes drove us home."

My soirée into the free world, and alcohol, left me feeling terrible. Later that night, after trying valiantly, with Simon, to write a letter outlining what was required to secure our release, I fell into bed shivering with a fever. My second September in captivity was coming to a shuddering end.

HURRY UP AND GET US OUT!

Friday, 1st October.

Simon and I had finally managed to get a letter together to send to his father and Julie respectively.

> "Urgent message:
> For the attention of: Julie Ride and Michael Dunn
> From: Paul Ride and Simon Dunn
>
> Today we appeared in an interview, which was of our own choice, and the statements made were a true account, as you know, of our detention and situation.
> Subsequent to the interview on the afternoon of the 30th of September, 1993, we were more or less told that our detention is over and that it is only polite diplomacy that is required to ensure our release. The Swedish delegation came and presented a letter from their King, and they were representatives of the Swedish parliament, and we think that if a recognised statesman, i.e. Mr Edward Heath, a person from a humanitarian agency, i.e. Michael Whitlam, director of the British Red Cross, and also a recognised person from the governing party in Britain, were to come with a letter requesting our release from the Government, this would be a guaranteed way of allowing the situation to be resolved, to everyone's satisfaction.
> When trying to arrange this delegation please ensure that it is known that we feel this is a 'rubber stamp' to legitimise our release. The decision is made; however, it is extremely urgent, and vital to our subsequent release, that the delegation is able to come to Iraq as quickly as can be arranged. We feel that this will create the necessary climate that will facilitate our release. We usually don't beg, but in this case, we beg that you ensure that every body concerned understands the urgency of this whole situation. As you know, we are innocent and this has now been recognised by the Iraqi authorities who now wish to resolve this situation as quickly as possible.
> We don't feel this is asking too much, it is just an official request for our release.
>
> Signed
> Simon Dunn and Paul Ride"

In the wake of the interview, I tottered around the section like a man on drugs. I failed to settle, instead I fidgeted and jumped between tasks. I hoped official contact would occur independently of anything we did and that my imprisonment would end soon.

Saturday, 2nd October.

Michael, Simon, and I were taken to the office to meet with Gleb Desyatnikov. We tried to explain to him just how finely balanced things had become. We had done all we could, now the responsibility for getting us out of Iraq was with the British Government! We let him know that we'd be upset, a mild understatement, if they refused to send anyone to negotiate our release.

I spent the afternoon in a state of frustration which wasn't eased in the evening when I listened to 'Sportsworld' on the radio and among the football results was a 1-0 defeat for Chelsea away at West Ham United!

Sunday, 3rd October.

Khalid Jerjes came to collect the letter for the British Government and demonstrated what a greedy, grasping clown he was. He 'interrogated' us about the wealth of Ali Autout's family. Ali was gone; what did the wealth of his family matter? Ah no, Jerjes revealed, Ali was still in Baghdad, his departure home was delayed. Still these vile bastards were trying to milk this situation for everything they could. I never knew if the interest in Ali's family was Jerjes' alone. He took a bag that had been delivered for Ali and said he'd pass it to him. Did he? I don't know, but I doubt it!

In early October, the spy network was working overtime constantly telling all the hostages they would be free in days. I tried to ignore it all, but I'll admit I thought that they might just be right – this time!

I was still making bread but, as the temperature was falling with winter approaching, 'proving' took longer and longer. What had been a two or three hour job in summer took an entire day now. We were locked up earlier during the winter and irregular Muster times made the entire bread making process more and more stressful. I know this might sound ridiculous, but I'd become obsessed with getting things correct and believed I was expected to maintain standards as I was a professional chef! This was a self-imposed sanction but I'm hard on myself, which is why I find it so difficult to be forgiving with others.

I had several people who wrote regularly to me. It was very kind of everyone who did so to take the trouble to write these letters and it always gave me real pleasure to read and reply to them. Some were very revealing about family matters and daily events in people's lives and in their own way they were like regional soap operas. Each had to be imagined being delivered in a Scottish, Welsh, Irish, Dutch or English regional accent, but as I love accents that was part of the fun! I was so grateful to have this correspondence, and I still am.

Some people who wrote to me had to suffer replies that were written during some terrible depressions when I may well have come across as rude, dismissive, and petulant. Not only was this unnecessary, I realise that it was damaging to all concerned. If you received one of my 'distressed' letters and felt offended, I am truly sorry. I can only blame my situation for the negativity.

Saturday, 9th October.

Back in the doldrums regarding any news about a possible release, I complained in my diary notes about the price of food in Abu Ghraib! "I paid my shopping bill today, another 450 Dinars. Simon gave me 125 Dinars towards yesterday's chicken but I've heard nothing about the 400 and 150 Dinar bills I paid last month – I want to prepare food alone – I want to be nice – but not get screwed – which is how I feel at the moment."

This was a perennial problem. Food, and the money to pay for it! I worried Julie was going short supplying me with provisions and not getting best value for money was bothering me. This was another example of the 'need to get it perfect' syndrome that shrouded me.

Saturday, 10th October.

Kai got a visit from an Iraqi representing German interests in Iraq who told him that as far as the Iraqi people were concerned we were guilty but as far as the government was concerned we were out and only a delegation was holding us here! I cannot imagine that most Iraqi people had any idea we were being held and doubted whether they cared.

Ken Beaty was having a tough time with his health and the VOA (Voice Of America), the American version of the BBC World Service, commented that Rolf Ekeus, director of the UN Special Commission on Iraq, who led the inspection team looking for nuclear and chemical weapons in the country, was being given the run around. Ken, like us, believed that the Iraqis wouldn't let us go if the political situation was negative, and he was not happy.

Thursday, 14th October.

I'd stayed up late the previous night to watch football on TV. Holland beat England in a World Cup qualifier and I wasn't in the best of moods when I was shown an article in an Iraqi newspaper which when translated claimed a British delegation was coming to Baghdad the following day! I pooh-poohed the report and got some stick from Simon. Anything at a political level is slow moving, and two weeks was not long enough to get a 'delegation' together.

Friday, 15th October.

World Cup qualifiers were a welcome distraction again. Having progressed from the first group stage, Iraq now faced sterner opposition (Saudi Arabia, South Korea, North Korea, Japan, Iran) to qualify for USA 1994. I watched on TV as they had a man sent off in their first game, a 3-2 defeat to North Korea. There were plenty of cheers from Section Three during this match!

I spoke to Abu Karim and Simon at different times during the evening and they both got really upset when I told them I was keeping a diary. I couldn't see the problem. I had written the bloody thing and if it caused a problem it would be my arse that got burnt. I noted in it, "Christ! Everyone in here is paranoid!" Prison, incarceration, detention, a custodial sentence – whatever – does strange things to a person's head as by now I knew only too well myself.

I also lost my patience with the food situation that evening. When meals were prepared by the others they were always smothered with garlic, and while I can eat it, I am not a lover of the residual smell so I decided to quit the collective food preparation and eat alone. I made the break with enough good grace to enable the three of us, Kai, Simon, and myself to remain on good terms, but I couldn't go on eating food that tasted of nothing but garlic!

Monday, 18th October.

As the weather had cooled with the changing of the seasons, I was exercising frequently again. I adopted the tactic of getting out quickly after Muster, running quite fast laps and then diving back into Section Three so that I didn't have to talk, deal with, or engage the inmates from other sections in the exercise area. Previously I'd enjoyed this, but now I found the ritual information swapping pointless and annoying because invariably it was little more than conjecture – and most of that was very uninspired!

Reports filtered through from the Iraqi section of the prison about an inmate who was beaten so badly that his eye came out! My diary entry simply read, "God help us!" Violence in Abu Ghraib was the norm. I'd heard stories about bottles jammed into rectums, electrical generators connected to various bits of anatomy, beatings, and numerous other assaults, but on this occasion the report really struck home and I remember physically shaking at the thought of what had taken place.

Ken Beaty had a diplomatic visit and he told us that Khalid Jerjes was telling lies all over Baghdad about him, his wife Robin, and Ali Autout. Jerjes, was now recognised for the idiot that he was by the other hostages. One-by-one he had alienated them with his stupid behaviour.

Tuesday, 19th October.

I heard on the radio that Iraqi Deputy Prime Minister, Tariq Aziz, was in Paris undergoing medical treatment in hospital and my immediate thought was Jean-Luc would be on his way home soon!

Wednesday, 20th October.

Gleb Desyatnikov came to visit and asked where Khalid Jerjes was! Why did people insist on asking me, a man in prison, where anyone was? Nobody had a clue where he was and there were rumours that he'd lost the plot and disappeared. Maybe he'd upset, or crossed, one of his Iraqi leaders and was being sent to Coventry – Iraqi-style – in the desert!

Gleb said that London was 'considering' whether to send a delegation and asked the Russians to confirm the 'release' stories. He said another pair of diplomats were coming in December and implied that we might not be here to receive the visit. It wasn't confirmation we were being released but, from the usually reticent Russian diplomat, it was very positive!

After the visit, Hamo asked if Michael had been given any money. I said I didn't know, but thought not. Simon told me that Michael had run up a bill of over 2000 Dinars at the Hanoot! I wrote in my diary, "What a case!"

Friday, 22nd October.

Recently, the 7.00am and 9.00am Musters had been combined into one at 9.00am. This morning, the authorities reinstigated the two original Musters. I'm an early-riser, so this was not a problem. Kai, Simon and the other Rip Van Winkles of the section hated the double requirement to get out of bed just to be counted!

Sunday, 24th October.

Iraq played Saudi Arabia in their latest World Cup qualifier. The game ended in a 1-1 draw. Matches featuring Saudi Arabia on Iraqi TV were censored! If a Saudi prince or member of the royal family was shown, the screen would blank for a second and a replay of an Iraqi goal would be shown! This action typified the childish and puerile attitude of the Iraqis to numerous other nations. Iraq was the most xenophobic country I'd ever 'visited'. It appeared to hate the rest of the world or at least its leaders did!

The day had been surreal. Three separate inmates approached me and said they had dreamt about me, and that I would soon be free! This came in the wake of another two inmates saying the same thing a couple of days previously. I wrote in my diary, "I'd better get out before everyone in the bloody prison is dreaming about me!"

Ong brought me a carton of cigarettes which on top of the regular and superb Thai meals he still cooked for me was a very generous gesture. He really appreciated the fact I'd been able to help him out.

Monday, 25th October.

Jean-Luc had an Embassy visit and brought me yet another batch of mail; more letters I was now struggling to reply to. The routine of prison life was a drag and even though I am writing now about the events that happened, they were in reality few and far between. The simple fact is, nothing much changes in prison. What happened yesterday will happen again today and it's probable that the same will be repeated tomorrow. Unless someone or something was inspiring, it was getting difficult to put anything original, fresh or witty in my mail, as I'm sure my dedicated correspondents will confirm!

Ken Beaty informed us that a 28-year-old prisoner had died of a heart attack. I thought, *At least he's out of here now!* Then I thought, *Was it a heart attack?* And then, *Is his body in the vegetable delivery van?* And finally, the thought that always played on my mind. *Will I die in prison?*

Wednesday, 27th October.

Simon asked me how much I expected to get as compensation for my time in Abu Ghraib? We hostages all hoped that reason, fairness, and some sort of justice would mean that we would be compensated for our time in Saddam's hellish prisons. To this day that aspect of the affair is unfulfilled. When I last contacted the Iraqi Embassy in London, I was advised that I need to take my case through the Iraqi legal system. I thought, *What and trust another fucking idiot like Khalid Jerjes and pay him for the 'privilege'? No thanks!* In any case, I was tried in a military court, or so I was told, so would probably be exempt from any recourse to the 'legal' system.

In the afternoon, Nicanor my Filipino friend was released. I was delighted for him as he was petrified that the Western hostages abducted from Kuwait would be released and he would remain a forgotten prisoner in this hell hole. As it turned out he was among the privileged early departees.

To my eyes at least, it did appear that the Iraqis were playing it straight down the line at the moment. A delegation from the Philippines had travelled to Baghdad with a letter requesting Nicanor's release and as a Kuwaiti detainee he walked! I wrote in my diary, "I hope the UK doesn't take too much longer!"

I lost my temper with Obet, one of the original group of Filipinos I'd befriended, who tried to give me some crumbs of comfort about the release of Nicanor and the general situation with the Western hostages. He was being supportive but I heard mocking and bit back unnecessarily, informing him that I was the first of the hostages to be abducted from Kuwait and certainly didn't want to be the last man out!

In the evening, the final round of Asian qualification matches for the 1994 World Cup were played. The conclusion was exciting. Japan drew 2-2 with Iraq in Doha, Qatar. I thought Japan were robbed of the result when Iraq scored a stoppage-time equaliser. Had Japan won they would have qualified for the finals, defeat saw Saudi Arabia and South Korea go through instead meaning Iraq also failed in their endeavours. Just as well considering where the finals were being played!

Saturday, 30th October.

After the last Muster of the day I went in and had a chat with Jean-Luc who told me that he'd seen Abu Athier wearing one of his sweaters which had been stolen from a clothing delivery that Colin Cooper and Marc Le Goy had brought with them from Amman. The bastard had more front than a row of shops, not only was he stealing from each of us, but now he didn't even have the decency to hide the fact that we were supplementing his lifestyle!

To add to my annoyance, Chelsea lost 1-0 at home to Oldham Athletic – enough said really!

Sunday, 31st October.

Halloween! Apart from a nonstop deluge that went on all day, the only thing of note that occurred was Simon going 'Trick-Or-Treating' with a sheet on his head and a cucumber sticking out of his crotch! My diary entry reads, "I am worried about that boy!!"

Due to the ceaseless rain, a rainbow had formed over Baghdad during the afternoon and I wrote, "At 4.30ish we had a rainbow over Baghdad – the only rainbow with a crock of shite at the end!"

SOUR GRAPES!

Monday, 1st November.

November started with a disappointing visit. Gleb Desyatnikov arrived with no supplies, no mail, and no news. He told us that, "The British and the Iraqi governments have no common ground!"

He regularly made statements that clashed with my take on reality and I could hear a voice in my head screaming, *WHAT ABOUT ME?*

The visit left me with the fear that the British Government were not going to go 'cap in hand' to the Iraqis with a letter requesting our release delivered by a statesman of international standing.

Abu Athier then informed us that my Mum, Julie, and Simon's father would be coming to Iraq for Christmas! I had only just recovered from the two-month anticipation of my family's last visit. The almost daily, will-they-won't-they expectancy had exhausted me mentally and physically, and I couldn't broach getting into that state again so I ignored Abu Athier and, after briefly talking it over with Simon, left him alone because he could not leave it alone! I didn't blame him for his constant updates and understood why he thought it might benefit me to have the information, but in truth the joy of receiving visits was wrung from me because of it.

Tuesday, 2nd November.

Gleb showed up with parcels for Simon, Michael and myself. Most of the stuff that arrived for me was a delivery for Ong from his sister sent through the British Embassy in Amman.

I was struggling to stay sane and healthy. The prison was a leech draining life from a body unable to escape the deprived surroundings that had become home. Food a delay, Muster an inconvenience, sleep fleeting, reading pulp fiction, talking gobbledegook; my life was wasting away like a kebab on a spit. Hot-warm-cool, it all depended on the prison thermostat which I had no control over. Bringing the day's tedium to an end, a power cut and darkness. At 11.00pm I went to bed. Why fight the inevitable? I slept immediately only to be rudely awakened at 1.00am when power was restored and the lights came back on!

Re-reading my diary now I realise how bitter and twisted I'd become. Many of my sentences are the distorted ranting of a man approaching his breaking point. "An Iraqi policeman was shot in Umm Qasr – and in an open UN observed convoy! Good shit!"

A man, probably with a family or someone's child, had been murdered and all I could think of was my own personal desire for revenge and my need for my captors to feel pain. I couldn't see beyond my experience and realise now that I was genuinely lucky that in a place filled with torture and hurt I experienced none. I'd lost my freedom, that's true. Yet even while I witnessed people lose their sight, their ability to walk, and their bodies abused by numerous vile means – some even losing their lives – my pain was still greater. I struggle now to see the logic behind my reasoning, but I understand that there was little genuine thought; every impulse was driven by one instinct – survival!

As I lay in bed that night struggling with my demons, Hamo came into the cell and informed me that he was going home the next day because people with short sentences had been given an amnesty. *So they do happen,* I thought! I wrote in my diary that this would mean drug smugglers would be released while people with driving offences would remain! My attempts to sleep after Hamo left were futile due to the noise the young Egyptian made as he celebrated his impending release with friends in his cell.

Wednesday, 3rd November.

At the first Muster of the day, Ghassan came out late and complained that he was tired and returned to his cell muttering about exhaustion! I shouted after his retreating diminutive form that we were all tired. In my case it was thanks to the fact that he'd been in Hamo's cell bullshitting all night!

I just couldn't leave things alone! I had become absorbed by drivel and tiny inconsequential asides had taken on great importance. With little else to do in prison, each sad bastard inmate starts to over-analyse every minute of every day, and with everyone doing the same thing, you end up confirming other prisoners distorted images of the truth as reality. It all makes perfect sense, in the scheme of things, to those convicted and incarcerated. Why struggle against the tide? Be washed along in the flood. Don't be a sore thumb, be a lemming! Regularly now, I slept for hours at a time. I cannot remember any disturbing dreams, why waste your time on dreams when the reality of every day was a fucking nightmare!

I soiled myself mid-morning. I don't know what happened, I suddenly had a warm sticky feeling between my legs. I don't feel uncomfortable writing this because stomach disorders were common. When a fever hit, it was actually better if it were so severe that delirium ensued rendering you unaware of what was happening to your body. Since I'd been to the vile and filthy asylum that the Iraqis dared to call a hospital, I had a morbid fear of becoming ill enough to warrant a stay there so I had to cope, pull myself together, and get cleaned up!

In the evening I went to Jean-Luc Barriere's cell for coffee and a chat. Jean-Luc had formed a great friendship with Abu Karim, a fiercely intelligent prisoner who had been transferred in from Section Two who I grew to like immensely. We had a wonderful conversation in which we attempted to put the world to rights and I felt uplifted. Thank God for people like Jean-Luc, Abu Karim, Abdul Baki and Noufal. Without their good spirits, help, and support I would not have survived the rigours of the Iraqi penal system – light in darkness, hope in despair, friends when the need was great.

Saturday, 6th November.

Chelsea lost 4-1 away at Leeds United. A shocking result for every Blues supporter to stomach especially one being held hostage 5000+ klicks from home.

Kai had a visit from his sister and father. Barbie, Kai's sister, brought me a fax from Julie which told me about a trip she'd made to Stamford Bridge. A collection had been made and she'd been presented with a cheque for over £2500. It was great to know that the club I'd followed my entire life had been so generous. I knew that collections were also being made for me around the British Isles and the generosity of the public allowed Julie and William to survive for 18 months, a period when my reduced salary was not covering the bills.

I wrote letters expressing my thanks to Ken Bates the Chelsea Chairman and to 'Onside', the club's magazine. It was a strange experience having to write letters that would have meaning for hundreds of people. Trying to sound grateful while being honest was difficult. I felt humble, but my feelings were tempered by my belief that I was being used and treated like a commodity. Paranoia and my surroundings had converted my emotions into the written equivalent of distorted soundbites. I struggled to find a way to say thank you for what my twisted 'working-class' understanding was 'charity'. The Iraqis had turned me into a bloody charity case. I felt cheap.

Wednesday, 10th November.

Kai was told by his family that they had met the Bishop of Baghdad. The opinion of the Christian clergy in Iraq was that we were political prisoners and should be released. Kai reported that there had been a 'positive' attitude from all the agencies that his family had contacted. Cynically, I wrote in my diary, "Positive response all around from the outside – we're political – we should go – yawn – old stories!"

I realise now how bloody ignorant this comment appears when Kai's family were trying to give him, and us, some hope. I'd taken the position of devil's advocate in any discussion about release, politics, sentences, developments, etc. What a miserable bastard I'd become! Most of the time, there was little joy in anything for me. Humour was sarcasm and bellicosity, and my outlook on life stank. Basically I'd decided that if I fell into a bath full of pot pourri, I'd emerge smelling of dung!

Jean-Luc adopted a similar stance to me and became very morose,

Gallic and withdrawn! He did it so well with his chiseled good looks and accent. He was very 'bon chic, bon genre', a term the French use for the posh Parisian in-crowd whose London equivalent we call Sloane Rangers. All I had was a glare and a vile temper. It just wasn't the same!

In my diary I offer the reason for Jean-Luc's change of demeanour as the approach of Christmas and that perhaps he was starting to realise we were going to spend it inside Abu Ghraib.

Thursday, 11th November.

Ken Beaty was taken to the hospital in Baghdad. I questioned if this was the way he was going to be released? Whisked to an infirmary and then his arse thrown onto a jet and spirited out of Iraq and away from the whole bloody mess.

I went to the Hanoot for some bits and pieces; vegetables, potatoes, eggs, and that sort of thing. I noticed the meat they were selling was from Waterford in Ireland. I'd also seen meat and produce that had been packaged in Australia, New Zealand, the USA, Belgium, France, Jordan, Saudi, and several South American countries! *Some embargo,* I thought to myself as I bought two kilos of the Irish meat and some very rare butter of the same origin!

Saturday, 13th November.

The cell that had once housed the Swedes was robbed of its air conditioning unit! God knows where it went. No doubt to one of the Iraqi prison authority's houses or to the highest bidder.

I wore mittens inside for the first time this winter. At times I really felt the cold and this made me tired, especially during the evening. I noted in my diary, "I came and lay down on my bed and slept for two hours – full of dumplings – lovely."

Let me explain. The Irish meat was the best beef that I'd seen since I'd been in Iraq and it had a good layer of creamy white fat on it. Many people might see this as a negative but I made some gorgeous dumplings with it and cooked a delicious stew that was a joy. Comfort food eh – the rattle of a simple man!

Sunday, 14th November.

The temperature outside and inside the prison plummeted and my hands got so cold that I was unable to write letters after the first Muster. After lunch, I listened to World Service coverage of the Annual Service of Remembrance on my radio. I found it very distressing as I have many similar events in subsequent years. I've tried to analyse why certain things make me feel the way that they do now and concluded that part of my problem is the fact that veterans of previous conflicts have comrades that they can discuss their shared experience with, while I can only tell and re-tell stories of what happened and there is no one whom I've ever met that knows how I feel or really understands the experiences that I've had. 30 years on, this is still the way it feels to me.

There was some entertainment to be had in the afternoon when the Iraqi section football team played our team of jolly foreigners. The game, which in truth the Iraqis should have won, ended in a 1-1 draw.

In the evening, I was reheating some leftover chicken and was halfway there when my gas ran out, meaning my dinner was lukewarm and I'd just finished eating it when I heard the section erupt with the screams and shouts of guards, Marahebs, and prisoners. Eventually I discovered that Jean-Luc's training shoes had been stolen! The section was torn apart as the guards searched for them. I knew that they wanted to find them, not for Jean-Luc – their desire was to find them and beat the crap out of the person that had stolen them! They weren't found and so Jean-Luc was taken to the Iraqi section as their football team were suspected of transporting the footwear out of our section. He returned empty handed!

Later, Simon told me that Ghassan had said to him earlier that he'd overheard prison officials saying Ken was about to be released on humanitarian grounds. My diary entry reads, "We'll see – I hope so!"

Time has done some strange things to my memories of Abu Ghraib. I now realise that I was quite probably in the 'primary stages' of a nervous breakdown or at the very least physically coping with a situation that my mind could not deal with.

Monday, 15th November.

My first task after Muster was to get a replacement gas bottle as I didn't want to eat cold food. I reheated the remainder of the stew that I had left from a couple of days earlier. Oh My God! It was just as good!

I'd washed up and was trying to have a snooze when I heard Ken Beaty's voice. I shouted to Simon, who was in the corridor, outside my cell, "Close but no cigar!" Mocking the fact that he'd believed the stories about Ken being released.

Seconds later, Simon pushed his face against the netting on my cell door and said, "I'll have that cigar. Ken's going!"

I didn't rush to see Ken thinking I'd give the man time to get organised without a circus going on around him and then I heard he'd left. Just like that! I was outraged! How could he walk away without even saying goodbye? My diary entry read, "I was really pissed off and offended that he hadn't had the decency to come (next door) and say goodbye. Ignorant bastard!"

With time, hindsight, and in retrospect, I realised that the way the Iraqis 'organised' the release of hostages was specifically designed to disorientate their captives and in all probability Ken had been informed that speed was important. Who would want a second longer than they had to endure in the shithole that was Abu Ghraib?

Part of my anger and distress was down to the fact that I was the first of the hostages and therefore deserved 'special' recognition. I was deluding myself. A state of mind that encompasses many mental health issues – the perception that you, as an individual, hold some extraordinary importance in the general scheme of things.

The BBC reported the news about Ken and it fragmented in my mind. The oil man – missing in Kuwait – six months in jail – he was sick – an American Senator requested his release. The entire bloody episode made me angry. I questioned how a man could work in several Middle Eastern countries but be too sick to put in a Middle Eastern jail! It was sour grapes on my part, combined with jealousy, pride, anger, frustration, and fear. Every fibre of my body ached for freedom and now someone else had been awarded 'my' prize.

My dark mood wasn't assuaged by the constant stream of inmates who came by to inform me that Ken was on TV! I deserved to be released as much as any bastard in the entire bloody prison. Why had they let others go when I was as deserving, no, more deserving? After all, I'd been here a long time! The unfairness of every development swum around and around my head for the rest of the evening. None of this was fair!

Tuesday, 16th November

'The Donkeys', as I now referred to the inmates who couldn't or wouldn't get their sad arses outside at 7.00am in the morning for Muster, were locked into the section. Eventually they were let out and the officer doing the counting threatened them with a trip to the punishment block and a good kicking if they didn't get out of bed for morning Muster.

The poor showing at 7.00am resulted in another Muster being called at 8.00am. After we'd lined up we were left waiting for an age. I'd been cooking porridge between the Musters so I went to collect it. I stood on the Muster yard and waited, eating my breakfast. After I'd finished, I said to Ghassan and Haji Salim, "If they wanted me in the office, I could be found inside in my cell. I didn't mind going to the punishment block, but would not stand there like an arse!"

Later that morning Simon, Kai and myself ate some bacon that Ken Beaty had left. I didn't enjoy it. The meat was fine, but it filled my mind with memories about his release and his treatment compared to my treatment. *Fuck! Fuck! Fuck!*

In the evening I sat with Jean-Luc and Abu Karim and had a chat about the world and its worries. Really, it was all about our situation. It makes me quite sad to realise how insular and introspective I'd become. As we spoke, Ghassan entered the cell – he still went where he liked without asking! As he had a direct line to Abu Athier, I began mouthing off about the hostage situation and Ken's release. I was rude and abusive about the Iraqis, the jail, and my situation. I'd stopped thinking logically by this point and instead I'd started being more outspoken, which at best was very dangerous. In retrospect I can see that I lived right on the edge and I often saw the burning fire of hate in the eyes of the Iraqi guards.

Wednesday, 17th November.

The cells vacated by the Swedes and Ken Beaty were reallocated to four Arabs. The noise and hullabaloo this created was staggering.

An Iraqi official came in and began to speak about the "Ameriki". I pointed out that there was no "Ameriki" in the prison, just the "Inglisi", to which he made a dismissive gesture with his hands and said, "Mafi mushkila! (No problem!)"

"No problem?" I replied, "It is a fucking mushkila actually!"

He gazed at me and smiled as if he was dealing with a child who just didn't understand.

Later in the day I had a chat with Kai who was full of 'piss and vinegar' following the visit of his family and charged with the belief that being German he was not part of the sanctions and that Germany would come and release him, and it wasn't his concern if Britain was dwelling on its Empire!

So much for being an EEC brother, I thought! The truth of the matter was that anyone of us would have taken any route out of prison; no matter what it involved – doing, saying, pretending or being. Kai was simply attempting to use another line of argument to justify his release and in a manner of speaking he had a perfectly good argument – but things weren't that cut and dried in Iraq.

I was listening to FM Baghdad on the radio in the afternoon when Jean-Luc crashed into my cell shouting that Abdul Baki and Abu Karim were being released. At first I thought he'd said they were 'asleep' and for a second I couldn't grasp the importance of the situation. I came out of the cell and went to see Abu Karim and he confirmed the news. (I think a huge bribe had been paid.) His surprise and joy was evident.

We had a hug and he left the section only to return an hour later. He had to spend another night in prison as his paperwork wasn't complete! He left mid-morning the following day but returned yet again as his paperwork still wasn't in order! Perhaps he hadn't paid a big enough bribe I scoffed!

Thursday, 18th November.

In the evening Psycho came into our cells and asked if we were all right. These 'regular' visits were disconcerting. It was better, in my opinion, to have as little to do with this crazy bastard as possible. We told him we were okay, and he went away. What was it all about? I couldn't work out why he was coming into the section at night. Was it just to check on us or was there an ulterior motive?

Saturday, 20th November.

Our diplomatic visit was a real let down with no news or information in respect of our release. To my mind, the official angle on the entire situation was getting more sinister with every passing day. We were being checked at night by the officers and told by other inmates that they were sure we would be out soon – but actual information from British Government agencies in London and Amman had all but dried up.

On a personal note, I received letters from some old friends and a parcel from my Mum containing training shoes – which was nice.

Later in the day I listened to commentary of Chelsea's home game with Arsenal which didn't help my mood one bit as The Blues lost 2-0.

We heard on the radio that the UN was sending more troops to the Iraq/Kuwait border, to use force to stop Iraqi incursions into Kuwait. Simon said that if that had been arranged earlier then we wouldn't be here! Possibly, but it was much too late to think like that.

There was news also that the French Constituitional Council had sent a Judge to Baghdad. My immediate assumption was that it must mean the imminent departure of Jean-Luc, what other reason was there for them to be here?

Sunday, 21st November.

After several farewells and swift returns during the preceding days, first Abdul Baki, and then a couple of hours later, Abu Karim, left Abu Ghraib for the final time. On this occasion, Abu Karim didn't say goodbye, but we'd had so many false dawns that I suppose he feared that he'd be back anyway! I wrote in my diary, "He flew, didn't say bye, but was probably rushed. I hope he's well. We were told that he wouldn't have to go to Tasfirat – lucky for him!"

The rest of the day, and long into the night, was a battle to try and prevent everyone, guards included, from attempting to steal every possession that Abdul Baki had left behind. It was chaos as people literally crawled into the cell, as if that made their sad arses invisible, and grabbed anything that they could lay their hands on. It didn't matter if the items had belonged to Abdul Baki, past tense, or still belonged, present tense, to Jean-Luc!

Jean-Luc gave everything Abdul Baki owned (that wasn't stolen) to Tariq, a forger who'd previously (unsuccessfully) asked me for a loan, and Hamo, but this still didn't stop the constant flow of pitiful wrecks from turning up at his cell door and begging for anything.

Jean-Luc was angry that the French Judge hadn't made an iota of difference to him or his situation. He'd packed his bags during the day but said that it was bullshit and he wouldn't be going anywhere. I still had a feeling that he could be on his way. Don't ask me why I felt so positive about Jean-Luc when I thought the rest of the situation was 'crap' – it was just a feeling.

Tuesday, 23rd November.

The radio was busy with stories about Iraq. Tariq Aziz had departed Paris for New York. The UN had a team of soil experts looking for weapons in southern Iraq. A Royal Air Force fighter plane went down in northern Iraq, the pilot was safe. There was nothing major happening that might put a block on our release, but would it happen? Would Jean-Luc get out? Would any of us?

Michael injured his foot which he said Ghassan had caused, but Ghassan was more concerned with Michael's finger which had something wrong with it. Ghassan said he might lose the finger if it wasn't operated on. Another 'piggy in the middle' scenario for me to contend with, but what could I do? Anything I said to Michael he perceived as some sort of trick, a sleight of hand to be ignored. Ghassan persisted, insisting that I speak to Michael.

Friday, 26th November.

The tedium and repetition of prison 'life' was impacting me. I was stuck in a cycle and realised it. I didn't want to write a diary with a 'recipe of the day', an account of the weather, what I was wearing, the events that occurred 24-hours-a-day, seven-days-a-week – and my entry for today reflected this. "I am running out of ideas and getting fed up!"

I wanted a series of notes written in one of the most notorious prisons in the world to inform the rest of humanity how an ordinary, totally innocent man could be eaten up and used, moulded, manipulated, and played by a foreign government while his own, a so-called world super-power, wrung its hands in impotent horror and appeared to be doing little else.

In the afternoon I visited Noufal in Section One. I was still carrying a bit of depression about Abu Karim's release and was hoping to share my loss with one of the only other people in this crazy place whom I felt close to. Noufal cheered me up with a jocular story about Khalid Jerjes returning to Abu Ghraib.

Later in the day I was sat talking to Jean-Luc in his cell when the entire section went crazy. The Arabic prisoners always did excited with great gusto and now they were beating their chests, leaping into the air and screaming and shouting; united in a wall of sound that drowned everything else out.

We left his cell and ventured out into the 'Arabic Quarter' of the section. *Christ almighty!* It was a scene akin to New Year's Eve in Trafalgar Square with a touch of punk rock concert and a dash of religious revival meeting melded in. Men were kissing, hugging, dancing, laughing and running about like fools. Eventually the noise level dropped enough for us to hear that a TV report said the UN sanctions were going to be lifted!

I learned subseqently that the only development was an Iraqi acceptance of UN monitoring. Nothing more. No suspension or lifting of the sanctions, no general amnesty, no presidential declaration, nothing. All this mayhem was based upon was the Iraqi announcement that it was willing to let UN weapons inspectors into Iraq, with no lifting of the sanctions for six months. That was it; and from this The Donkeys had decided that the sanctions were to be lifted and their release would surely follow! It really annoyed me.

Saturday, 27th November.

Morning Muster was delayed because some people were unable to get up! The Maraheb was trying to work out who wasn't there and so I thought that I'd save him some time saying, "The German and the 'Little English' (as Simon was affectionately known) are still asleep!"

The Maraheb went to wake The Donkeys and they arrived as the guard began the count. His blustering didn't scare Kai and Simon who slept through this Muster and the one that followed at 9.00am as well!

Later in the day I listened to 'Sportsworld' and heard that Chelsea had lost again! 1-0 away to Sheffield United! The reporter said they had "looked good" which was no consolation really. I'd rather look like a dog and pick up three points every weekend!

Sunday, 28th November.

Simon was locked in the section along with The Donkeys who were unable to get up for Muster. I feared he would get into trouble as Psycho was taking the session and then just at the last moment they were all let out to take their places.

We were called to Muster at 12.00pm and informed that prisoners were being inoculated against meningitis! Thanks, but no thanks. The Western hostages refused, all feeling like me that having a disposable hypodermic syringe stuffed into the arm was a shocking idea. The unsanitary conditions and the worry that the needles might be contaminated and/or shared brought with it fears of contracting Aids or other diseases.

A very unpleasant event happened in the afternoon when an inmate in Section Four was crucified on the chainlink fencing that surrounded his block. I have no idea what his infringement had been, but with a great deal of screaming and shouting the poor bastard had been tied to the fencing by guards and left to hang there for hours. In one respect he was quite fortunate; the ferocious heat of summer had passed so he was gently barbequed by the much milder late November sun. I dare say he didn't see this as a particularly valid point as he dangled there until dusk.

There were news reports in the Iraqi press that filled me with despair; among them an article claiming that a speech made by Prince Charles had destroyed any progress that had been made regarding our release. Mirroring this misery, Kai had a visit from German diplomats and was shattered by the news that the Germans were not requesting or sending a delegation to secure his freedom.

Simon loaned me a copy of 'Tornado Down', a book written by British pilots after the first Gulf War. I found the whole thing a bit 'Tally-ho', but I had a jaded perspective of men in warplanes carrying multiple weapons being held for weeks, while I, in a Land Cruiser, with three pairs of sunglasses, a solar-powered calculator, and some paperwork, got seven years!

We decided to draft a letter to John Major, informing him once again of our situation and requesting that he did everything he could to secure our release as soon as possible. Simon showed the letter to Michael, for his signature, and he said that he agreed with the sentiment, and we should tell him, John Major, that the government were not doing enough!

SIR EDWARD TO THE RESCUE!

Wednesday, 1st December.

'Martyrs Day'. A Muster with a minute's silence to show respect for the Iraqi dead of the Iran/Iraq war. Despite the fact that my mind had been bitterly twisted by my abduction and imprisonment I did, and do, feel great sympathy for the Iraqi people who were compelled to endure the tyrannical dictatorship of a madman.

Jean-Luc had a visit from a Catholic Priest later in the morning and among the snippets of information passed his way he was told that a delegation from France would be here in January and he would be allowed to have wine for Christmas! He probably wouldn't need it as Abu Athier said he would be out before then! This mixed message of a French delegation coming in January and release before Christmas didn't make sense as any release was supposed to hinge upon a delegation!

Full of supposition, questions, and ever-changing possibilities, we Brits waited impatiently for Gleb Desyatnikov to arrive. Given there might only be one more visit before Christmas I wondered if he would he bring anything 'festive'. My diary says I doubted it, perhaps to insulate myself against disappointment! I hoped for a spectacular gesture, but I had become so used to let downs that I didn't want to get hurt again!

The atmosphere was very tense and then Gleb arrived and broke the spell and told us that Colin Cooper and Marc LeGoy were going to be visiting again. We were close to the horror of another Christmas in prison and I said I didn't want to spend Yuletide in Abu Ghraib again. All things considered, it was a positive meeting especially for Simon who got a new heater and mattress!

I was ordered to see the visiting optician. I went along but never saw him as the queues were too intense and I realised that the need of those scrimmaging to be seen exceeded anything I felt. I'd also recently received a fully serviceable pair of glasses, sent, without charge by Dr Amin, my optician back at home in Walthamstow. Thank you Dr Amin.

I returned to my section and had a look at the newspapers that Gleb had brought with him and then I opened my mail. What a bunch of clowns! Instead of going to the British Embassy in Amman to be passed on to the Foreign Office in London, the mail I'd sent out last month had been returned to me in Abu Ghraib!

Thursday, 2nd December.

I struggled in the cold to get myself together for 7.00am Muster and then

I strip-washed in freezing water! I could feel the last vestiges of what little heat was in my flesh and bones draining from my body as we were told to wait in the glacial winter shadows for 9.00am Muster! I gestured towards the administration block and used colourful language to explain to the assembled prisoners that if the officers wanted me I would be in my cell because I was not interested in standing outside like a bloody fool.

After a while I calmed down and remembered I was in prison. This wasn't fun, nor reasonable, but what the 'guilty' had to expect! But then I'd get angry again! My problem? I wasn't guilty as I had committed no crime. The more I thought about it, and the more I was challenged by the authorities, the angrier I got. This anger became my problem. It was the weapon I used to defend myself. Delusion as I now understand it. But when a person is faced with situations on a daily basis that they fear, self-deception is always likely.

Lunchtime Muster was a repeat of the morning's events. We stood, we waited, I exploded. I'd then march inside informing anyone who was interested, and listening, that I was not going to stand about outside like a fucking idiot! To cap things off, evening Muster was also delayed because Psycho was playing ping-pong with an Egyptian prisoner!

The rest of the day was uneventful, and thankfully the distress that these delays caused slipped into my unconscious. I realised I had become obsessed with detailed routine and that if events, for example Musters, didn't occur in a 'regimented' fashion I really struggled to retain equilibrium and self-control. The more this went on, the more my coping mechanisms were being stretched to their limits. An analogy I use to explain the situation is to say that it was like an expatriate mentality. An expat travels with a bucket in each hand; one for gold and the other for shit. When one is full up it is time to quit and come home. My problem was that my shit bucket was overflowing but I was denied the opportunity to quit as this was a seven-year contract!

Friday, 3rd December.

I got out of bed at 6.55am and went berserk when I discovered that there was no hot water to have a shower. The Muslims had used it all for washing in preparation for prayers! Some people would say that this was a good use of hot water, and in one respect I'd have to agree, but what really annoyed me was that for the rest of the week the same odious idiots wouldn't go near water! If the Prophet hadn't told them to wash before prayers, I doubt whether some of the foul examples of humanity I was interred with would ever have washed their fetid bodies!

I had a cold shower and refused to Munster. I blamed the freezing water but my growing belligerence was the greatest factor. I'd long felt as if the entire situation was an affront designed to humiliate me personally which made me seethe. Not a good way to start the day.

I'd been getting headaches of an increasing severity for a week or so and I now felt as if I were getting a cold as my body was aching and I kept shivering. I went to bed relatively early and fell asleep immediately. Prison had made a virtual insomniac of me, and usually I didn't sleep until 2.00am, but tonight I was asleep before 11.00pm.

Saturday, 4th December.

A general visiting day that I made no comment about in my diary. Was this out of mundane acceptance of the bi-monthly debacle or more a case of 'it is what it is' resignation?

Afternoon Muster was a farce as we were called to the yard for counting and stood there like fools for an eternity. The reason this time? Psycho was playing football and we had to wait for him to count us! In my diary I noted, "He is like a fucking demigod!"

I listened to the football results on the World Service with Simon. Chelsea didn't have a game today so I described the whole affair in my diary as 'boring' but had the good grace to reflect that some of the results were 'good'. What a well-rounded supporter I was! I was struggling to cope and wrote, "I hope to start running again soon. My nerves are like Shredded Wheat (brittle and easily broken)."

Later that evening I was having coffee with Jean-Luc when Ghassan came in and told him that it was 75 percent certain he would be released in the next few days. Jean-Luc said he'd seen the psychologist that morning and he'd said the same thing. To my shame I couldn't feel as happy as I should have for him. The first thought that filled my head was, *How long do I have to put up with this shit in the name of the British Government?*

Resentment was so close to the surface that even good news for a fellow inmate could, and did, inspire a tirade of vile, and jealous, thoughts. Day after day, I felt traumatised. I was convinced that my life had been destroyed. I would never be able to get another job overseas again which meant a life sentence as a chef in the UK. My imprisonment was unfair, unjust, and unnecessary. The only person losing anything at all was me. The Iraqis were not gaining from holding me and, having realised this, wanted to get rid of me. The British Government were not losing anything either but didn't want to show any sign of weakness in asking for my release, so here I sat with my entire world under my bed in cardboard boxes. My grasp on reality was slipping into a paranoid abyss. I went for a walk to clear my head and mused that I would need to walk to Jordan to do so!

Section Three was expecting to receive a visit from an important Iraqi minister and this caused the usual panic and 'pre-visit sanitation' of the block. I never did see this important visitor, but I can't honestly say that I really looked too hard! I was sick of these ignorant bastards turning up at the prison expecting prisoners to leap about in feigned respect and honour of their position within a corrupt and abusive regime. I hated the fucking lot of them anyway and my biggest problem had become not being able to show it at every opportunity!

Tuesday, 7th December.

I noted in my diary that I'd finished reading 'Fever Pitch', Nick Hornby's book about his life and a season following Arsenal. Like all football supporters, I enjoy the bit where he writes about my team. Locked in after a game at Chelsea he, and the rest of the Arsenal fans, were 'abused' by a groundsman who gave them the traditional English insult, a V sign. Football violence is wrong, but banter and contention are what make the game the world's greatest sport. Years later, I bumped into Hornby in a shop at Highbury Corner (close to the old Arsenal Stadium in North London) and recognising him I asked, "Are you the Arsenal supporter that can write?" He looked at me with a pained expression and nodded!

Wednesday, 8th December.

I had a serious row with the guards at first Muster. At 7.15am I went out and joined a line of four, we Mustered in rows of five. The Donkeys were late as usual and Psycho told us to sit on the floor and wait until he came back to count us. I'd been in this situation before. The floor was damp and very cold and so I refused and stood my ground. Once he'd gone to another section I went inside yelling that they could put me in the punishment block again if they wanted and I went to my cell to wait for the shit to hit the fan.

When Psycho returned and came into my cell to tell me that he was going to report me to the section manager I countered that I would be speaking to Abu Athier about the crap we had to put up with due to The Donkeys. As he stood looking at me with a tick in the corner of his insane jet-black eyes I shouted "GOOD!" at him for his threat, and at that moment I felt hatred for every Iraqi, I despised the lot of them. I truly feared this psychotic bastard. I'd seen him beat other inmates to bloody lumps of humanity, and then kick the hell out of what was left – but something drove me on. Call it stupidity, lack of self-regard, I have no idea why I wouldn't or couldn't back down in the face of such obvious danger.

After 9.00am Muster, Abu Athier and the Justice Minister, who I hadn't seen since our TV appearance weeks earlier, came into the section and walked into my cell. I told him about the performance at the 7.00am Muster and he asked which officer had been on duty and told me not to worry as he would speak to the manager and sort it out.

Shortly after Abu Athier left, Simon came in shouting that Heath was in Baghdad on our behalves. "SHUT THE FUCK UP!" I shouted, and threw a ladle at him! I know I did it in a semi-joking fashion, but it caught him, and he screamed at me that it hurt, which I don't for a second doubt. I apologised and tried to explain that I couldn't go through another stage-managed wind-up as I was in a place where I felt unable to cope with any more disappointment – I really couldn't.

After evening Muster, and lock-up for the day, we had a couple of visitors advising us that they had heard reports about our situation on their radios. I still 'denied' the news by 'rubbishing' each visit we had, and then suddenly there was a dramatic turn of events. Other prisoners filled the corridor outside our cell. Dozens of Arabs were shouting that they had heard reports on the radio from Dubai, Jordan, Egypt and the Emirates all with news of our imminent release which was due to the arrival of a British ex-Prime Minister – Sir Edward Heath! Maybe Simon was right!

I capitulated and agreed to listen to the BBC World Service who would surely be reporting on the story if it were true. We heard nothing at 8.30pm, but with each subsequent news bulletin that commenced on the hour there were some details, sketchy at first, but coloured with more information from media sources as the night dragged on. It didn't make me feel that I'd be out soon, but rather it awoke the memory of all the previous occasions when my mind had been assaulted by hours, days, and weeks of agony as a promised release, visit, or amnesty, failed to materialise.

I wrote in my diary, "I stayed up until 1.45am, but still couldn't sleep as I was full of ideas! Dear God! I hope that this is true and it's the end!"

Thursday, 9th December.

"The British Government has agreed to allow Sir Edward Heath to visit Iraq and request the release of three British hostages, Paul Ride, Michael Wainwright and Simon Dunn."

The newsreader speaking in perfectly enunciated English was easy enough to understand. I was almost sick thinking about release, but the fear that it would all come to nothing still haunted me. I began to mentally and physically prepare for freedom by trying to adopt a positive attitude and I began to tell people that they were welcome to certain of my belongings if, and when, I was released.

Radio bulletins reported that Sir Edward had seen Tariq Aziz the previous day and I hoped that this was a prelude to further developments today, as I wrote in my diary, "With the radio saying that Edward Heath had seen Tariq Aziz yesterday – hopefully he will see Saddam Hussein today, but today has been 24 hours long already and it is only 12.15pm!"

I went into Kai and Simon's cell after lunch, having already noted in my diary that, "Simon is a little tense. Who isn't? Time is slow today." These were the last words I ever wrote in Abu Ghraib.

As I sat talking to the lads, Abu Athier came into the cell and told me to get a shave – we were being freed!

I was stunned. I'd waited 18 months for this. In retrospect I'd like the opportunity to repeat the entire release again and be more aware of every emotion and feeling. The reality is, I felt as if I'd been robbed, and the pleasurable feelings and joy I think I should have had were nicked. My memories of my release are a jumbled ragbag of detail, some of which are so bittersweet that I'd rather have forgotten them.

As Abu Athier spoke, I jumped to my feet and asked him to repeat what he'd just said. In his slightly melodic Arabic voice he said, "Please get yourself shaved. You're going to be released today."

THREE MONKEYS!

I spun around silently as Simon stood up asking if he was also being released. For a split second the cell grew small. It was shrinking around me, I thought, *Is the cell shrinking or am I expanding?* Maybe the cell was too small to hold me. My head filled with sound, a mix of roaring waves and rushing winds, which made it difficult to hear anything said to me. I felt as if I'd been plunged into cold water. My breath caught, I felt weightless and a surge of energy prickled my body. I turned into the cell and a yelling Kai leapt into my arms and hugged me. He was trying to say something which I neither heard nor understood. As the two of us hugged, jumped, span, and screamed in delight, I planted a kiss on his cheek!

People grabbed my hand; pumped it, smiled, laughed, asked questions. I couldn't hear, and they weren't speaking they were screaming. I could see their faces passing me contorted in paroxysms of expression and yet the tempest in my head masked every word they bellowed at me. I staggered to my cell and ripped at my boxes searching for my shaving kit I'd not used for months. I knew where everything was and yet the razor and shaving soap had gone!

When longing is so close to fulfilment, our lives seem cursed by problems determined to frustrate good fortune. In my paranoid and slightly bemused mind this lack of shaving apparatus would cause the entire release to be cancelled. I would be left in Abu Ghraib and it would serve me right, after all I repeatedly refused to shave and now I was hoisted by my own petard!

I became Basil Fawlty in 'Fawlty Towers' as he searches in vain for a roasted duck which has been switched and replaced by a dessert trifle, the more I scrambled in the boxes the less I could see. I ripped open packets of pasta and fumbled with tins of processed meat. I found things I'd forgotten I had and as bile burnt my throat and the roar in my head became almost unbearable, the errant shaving equipment revealed itself. *Oh! Sweet God! Thank you!*

I stumbled toward the toilets. My senses were in hyperdrive and an acrid smell of ammonia and faeces slapped me in the face as I stepped into 'hell'. I stood still trying to regain my equilibrium, shaking, not only with emotion, but with a chill I felt on every inch of my flesh. Ideas and thoughts – very fast. Movement and progress – very slow. *Is this what a heart attack feels like?*

I began gasping in deep draughts of fetid air, I had to control myself. I shivered and started to shave, I don't think I was scared, well no more than normal, but I couldn't stop myself shaking. *I hate shaving. I always cut myself. I hate it.* Finishing with very few self-inflicted wounds, I congratulated myself and took one last breath of disgusting air in the vile and unforgettable toilets.

The hallway back to my cell was a mass of prisoners. The sudden popularity of the "Thalatha Inglisi" (Three English) was, now we were being released, unrivalled. Our possessions could be given, taken, or stolen and distributed amongst the 'salvage team'! Prison mafia chased prisoners away from our cell. Why would thieves, extorters, liars, and cheats want to share the bounty, our belongings, with anyone who would eventually be forced to buy it? The threats did not stop dozens of penurious, desperate, and determined individuals from begging or grabbing whatever they could from our cells. We attempted to stop the craziness while struggling to get the hell out of this hole forever.

Order, of sorts, descended on the section when Abu Athier returned. Standing a little over five feet tall this tiny man had the presence of a giant. His impact is difficult to put into words. Arabic prisoners understood something we, the Western hostages, never did. We were fortunate to remain ignorant of the capacity for evil that inspired such unquestioning respect.

He came into our cell and said to Michael, "The store tell me that you owe them more than 2000 Dinars. Is this correct?"

Michael, in his Yorkshire brogue, responded, "Ay, tha's reet." He pulled at his money belt and scowled at the meagre contents. This show of willing raised expectations with the gathered collective who ran the Hanoot, but it was as far Michael got. He'd run out of money some time ago and the bill at the Hanoot was not forgetfulness but penury. Questions rang out from the crowd and eventually Hamo wailed to his 'audience', which included Abu Athier, that he had to have his money.

My blood ran cold. Was this another reason to stop us leaving? I had developed a captive paranoia, and for every glimmer of hope my slightly fucked up head arrived at several, very serious, reasons why the glimmer would mutate into a shit-storm of problems. By the time of my release I had developed some mental health issues but I never realised this during that period, and would not have agreed with anyone who suggested it. All I understood was, *I'm going. I don't have any debts!*

I don't remember if I was asked, but with Michael's debt preventing us from leaving the crap-hole I leapt to my feet and pulled out some Iraqi Dinars I had in my pocket and offered them to him. He waved the money away. *Oh come on!* For a moment I thought he might be willing to stay in Abu Ghraib rather than accept my help!

Abu Athier gestured to Hamo that he should take my money which amounted to about 3000 Dinars. Hamo snatched at my hand and took most of it. Hours before the money had kept me from destitution but at this moment in time it was little more than tissue paper.

Money gone, bill paid, we moved on! An occasional hand still slipped into the cell; behind backs, over shoulders, between ankles, behind bottoms, in a display that resembled a naked puppet show.

Trying to concentrate on getting ready to leave, I thought, *Well, this is one hurdle over!*

Julie wanted me to bring as many of items she'd brought, as I could manage, out of Abu Ghraib. Many of the things left behind would have been nothing but sad reminders of 18 months of fear, deprivation, and worry. The unwritten rule of leaving is what you've acquired in Abu Ghraib is 'bounty' gifted to the poor bastards you leave behind. Prisoners in Iraq survived on second-hand goods and hand-me-downs; to take any items would have been to impoverish men surviving on the razor's edge of existence or expiration.

I understood why Julie wanted me to remove all I could from Iraq; the thefts, and loss of so many things, had left her feeling like a victim. As it happened, I returned home with nothing – and Julie didn't complain once. I left everything in my cell and walked out of the section in my 'Going Home' clothes. I knew what I wanted to wear, and they were stowed in a special, talismanic, release box, under my bed.

We came together, the 'Thalatha Inglisi', and, with Abu Athier leading, were walked almost ceremoniously from the section. Crowded up against the entire length of chainlink fencing skirting the foreign block were prisoners of myriad nationalities all desperate for a glimpse of the 'Inglisi' walking to freedom. I stumbled along, not sure I knew where I was going, but wanting Abu Ghraib to be in my past. Every step we took was accompanied by hushed whispers from the men we were leaving. "Ma'aasalaama" (goodbye), "Alhamdulillah" (praise be to God), "Bil tawfiq" (good luck), and a collection of other invocations. The event went some way to explaining Abu Athier's mystique. He took people with long prison sentences and walked them out of the gates to freedom!

We were led into the relative gloom of the administration area, a place I'd not seen in nearly 16 months. I stood still at an office counter, terrified that this would be revealed as a sick joke! Michael and Simon were given back their passports and they checked them as if looking for visas and travel stamps! Of course I didn't have a passport as I'd never intended to leave Kuwait and if an overweight, overzealous, overbearing, over-armed, arrogant bastard, and his team of gunslingers at the border, hadn't overreacted, then perhaps I wouldn't have been incarcerated for the last year-and-a-half!

Slowly but surely, it was starting to feel as if we would actually get out of this bloody awful place. Feelings in the pit of my stomach were struggling for supremacy as fear and worry challenged the joy I knew I should have been experiencing.

ID passes, a few coins, pieces of paper and some other small bits of detritus that had been in my pockets at the start of a journey that began a lifetime ago in a place far away tumbled out of an envelope that was placed in front of me. Each item was touched and checked off an inventory by a pair of Iraqi guards who then pushed them across the counter towards me. I half-smiled as I recognised the items I'd possessed on the day I was abducted. Some articles were missing – my valuables, the keys to the Land Cruiser and the contents of the vehicle. I didn't mention these items. I wasn't about to create a reason to slow, delay or derail our release. I never expected the Land Cruiser to be returned but I did wonder who had it? Was it a senior Iraqi official? Was it a Mukhabarat officer? Was it Abu Athier? If it was, he would need a 'booster seat' to see over the steering wheel! A few thoughts, a few fears, leaving with a tiny bag of possessions when I been detained with a car full of 'equipment' and personal effects. I expected nothing – the Iraqis never disappointed me!

The ritualistic return of our possessions seemed to take forever and I could feel sweat trickling down my back. It was more than I could deal with at that moment and the stress was killing me. Finally, we were 'signed out' of Section Three by a couple of the guards whom we had dealt with for many months and Psycho. Even at this point he was someone I was 'fearful' of. The evil, deranged bastard was just so unpredictable.

Escorted out of the section by three armed guards and led by Abu Athier we made our way to a vehicle and were ushered into the back seat. Crammed together with our meagre belongings on our laps we set off. The journey to central Baghdad was cramped, painful, bumpy, hot, and uncomfortable. We passed through streets filled with market stalls and row after row of vehicle repair shops. Then we bumped and jolted through an area of office buildings and on further until we came to a residential area in suburban Baghdad and we stopped outside a high-walled house.

We were ordered out of the car and stood huddled on the pavement in the late afternoon heat with gusts of wind blowing sand and rubbish across the ground in small spiralling dust devils. One of the guards unlocked the metal doors which provided access to the premises and pulled them apart. The shrieking sound this made filled the silent afternoon air with a tortured metallic noise. It was obvious they hadn't been opened for a long time and I didn't know what to expect next. Were we going to be staying here? I thought our release meant leaving Iraq!

The guards were silent, surly, and belligerent. They all had weapons which made me nervous and the looks they gave us suggested they'd happily open fire to end this charade. As I looked at them and then up at the house I noticed there were metal bars on all its windows. It looked as much a prison as Abu Ghraib! If this was freedom, suddenly I wasn't enjoying it!

With grunts and gesticulations we were ordered into the house. Inside, the air smelled stale and dust danced on rays of sunlight piercing the gloom through cracks in door frames and closed window shutters. I grew accustomed to the murk and followed the others into a lounge area which looked liked it had last been furnished in the 1960s. We were told to sit down on a large sofa and as we did so clouds of dust rose from its long-unused cushions and joined the detritus twirling in the chinks of light.

I didn't feel good about these developments. I was confused and my head was struggling with a series of fears and questions. *Where is Edward Heath? Where are Marc Le Goy and Colin Cooper?* I had run out of faith in developments orchestrated by the Iraqis a very long time ago. What was going on?

Abu Athier entered the room and sat down, generating another dust cloud, and said, "You will stay here tonight to keep you safe!"

I'd felt a damn sight safer in Abu Ghraib. Here we were in an unknown location with a man feared for his violence accompanied by three armed men all of whom seemed less than pleased to be in our company, and this little bastard was speaking about safety!

"Tomorrow you will be taken to the British delegation," proclaimed Abu Athier.

"Why tomorrow, why not now?" I countered. "What is this charade all about?"

"Mr Paul, we will take you and get you a picture to put on your laissez-passer then you will be able to travel," replied Abu Athier in an officious manner. "I will return and then these things will be arranged."

So I was the only one not able to travel! These bastards had dragged me into Iraq without paperwork, but now they were suggesting that I may not be able to leave because I had no paperwork! Abu Athier departed the room leaving us in the company of the guards and for a while we struggled to find our voices. One of the guards left and returned with cups of tea which had a tainted taste like the dust enveloping us.

I'd begun to worry that it was getting too late to have a photograph taken when Abu Athier returned with a couple of Mukhabarat officers. I couldn't understand why the Iraqis needed such a heavy presence to guard us. I was a shade under 60 kilos, Simon was built like a very long pipe cleaner, and then there was Michael. Surely a couple of guards, minus guns, would have sufficed.

Escorted by the Mukhabarat officers, I was led out of the house by Abu Athier and we got into the car and drove to a market which was alive with activity. By now it was the middle of the evening and we walked around the area trying to find a photographer who could produce an image of me that the authorities could use to create my travel documentation.

As I walked along the road encircled by Abu Athier and his henchmen, a woman dressed in traditional Muslim clothes approached me and began to move her hands in an imploring, begging motion. Abu Athier thought that this was really amusing. A foreigner imprisoned for the last year-and-a-half should become the target for a woman so desperate that she was forced to beg. I had little to give her because Hamo had grabbed most of my Dinars. After the initial shock, I saw the pathos in the situation – however at that moment, all I wanted to do was get my damn picture taken and get the hell out of Iraq.

We walked the streets entering barren shop after barren shop, and Abu Athier became defensive, if not a little embarrassed, repeating, almost like a mantra, that, "The reason for the shortages was the unjustified Gulf War and the evil sanctions now imposed upon Iraq by the West."

His reasoning didn't make me feel responsible, guilty, or able to do anything about it. I didn't reply but thought to myself, *Oh yes! I've spent 18 months in this shithole as you have a problem with Bill Clinton and John Major and I'm a 'Western doppelganger'. How could I forget?*

By now I was getting close to having a panic attack and then finally we found a shop to take the bloody photo! As I walked in I was struck by the perversity of my situation. I'd been imprisoned for 'illegal entry' into Iraq and now here I was in a camera shop in Baghdad having photos taken to get out of the country!

Instead of waiting in the shop for the photos to be developed, Abu Athier suggested we have a stroll around the nearby stalls and shops! I felt as comfortable as a waiter serving sushi to a Scouser! Eventually we returned to the shop, collected the photos (I don't remember paying) and returned to the 'safe house'. I was mightily relieved the event was over and my laissez-passer could be completed.

Some food was delivered to us. Lukewarm, tasteless fodder; kebabs, rice, chips, salad. I ate not for pleasure, but in case it was the last offering for a while. There was no conversation. This wasn't a social event and as I ate I couldn't decide if I felt full, sick, or in need of more food! The guards decided they knew what I needed and 'suggested' it was bedtime and we were shown to a communal sleeping area upstairs where I slept fitfully with one ear trying to hear what the Mukhabarat thugs were up to. I hoped it would be the last night that such things would occupy my mind.

Friday, 10th December.

Awake, I found the courage I thought I needed to ask if I could shower and, when I did so, I found the experience completely bizarre. Try to imagine, if you can, standing under a shower and feeling water falling onto your body and soaping it. Normal, well yes it is – but for the previous 18 months I'd had to pour buckets, jugs, jars, beakers, and cups of water over me. Now, here I was, in the 'lap of opulence', stood in a filthy bath enjoying the miraculous sensation of water flowing from a shower head! The house was without heating and being December was freezing cold, this meant that I shivered as I dried myself with a cloth-come-towel that felt like a scouring pad. You can't have everything!

With morning ablutions completed, we gathered downstairs like the three wise monkeys, *See No Evil, Hear No Evil, Speak No Evil*, and nervously awaited the next stage of our 'Magical Mystery Tour'. I didn't get to look round most of the house, but I did glimpse the kitchen. What a mess. As I was in catering, I had a sudden and somewhat perverse desire to clean the place up!

At 9.00am, a car arrived and we were instructed to get in the back. It felt like we were children on a family trip; we had to be there, but were just a bloody nuisance to our parents!

We travelled through Baghdad along a series of empty, potholed back streets. If this was freedom, it didn't feel like it yet. The sun hurt my eyes, the smell of the river seared my nose, and fear gripped my bowels.

20 minutes later we arrived at a walled, gated villa that was surrounded by dozens of vehicles. We were told it was a presidential guest house and once inside we were shepherded into a room set out for breakfast and invited to help ourselves. Melon, sweetmeats, and many other delicacies were piled onto plates. We were shown, by decorous waiters, to a huge dining area and banquet table. I sat nervously at one corner and ate the food. Again, this was energy for my body not a pleasure for my senses. My sense of taste was flawed, even the sweet melon syrup that clung to the fruit had no flavour on my tongue.

A person I recognised, entered the room – Sir Edward Heath! My first thought was, *Are we really going home?* I felt the food I'd just swallowed rise to my throat. I didn't know what to do. *How should I address him? When are we going?* Questions, some sensible, others bordering on insanity flooded my mind.

Well into his 70s, Sir Edward was a vast man with a girth that was inverse to anything I'd been used to in Abu Ghraib! He looked well-fed – I'd grown used to emaciation! Polite handshakes followed together with a bit of sycophantic drivel from me. Give me a break though, this man was releasing me from a hell I had never imagined in my entire life prior to the 28th of June, 1992. He was entitled to everything I offered – and a bloody sight more!

When feeding time was over, we had to pose for the media. Sir Edward made me remove my top, emblazoned with legendary slogan 'Chelsea – The Pride of London', because he didn't want to be regarded as partisan! If he'd said I had to leave naked, I'd have done it – anything to get out of this damn country!

Sir Edward, Simon, Michael and myself then stepped through some doors onto a patio where the gathered media surged towards us. We stood to my mind like three naughty schoolboys and allowed the media a good look at the British Hostages! I cannot recall if we were asked any questions during the Q&A session with Sir Edward – I think we were there to illustrate his diplomatic skills and demonstrate the mercy and benevolence of Saddam's regime.

When the media had finished with us we were stuffed, almost literally, into the back of a car and driven away as part of a convoy of vehicles which soon began to hurtle at breakneck speed across Baghdad. Like the parting of the Red Sea, traffic and pedestrians were halted and directed aside to allow us through.

I was feeling nervous and uneasy as I sat with Simon squeezed between Michael and myself. In front, next to the driver, was an Iraqi with an automatic weapon. Leading the cavalcade was a Mukhabarat vehicle, its wailing siren fracturing the morning peace. Directly in front of us was a limousine carrying Sir Edward and behind us more cars, more motorcycles, more sirens, more Iraqis and more guns! The cacophony tortured my ears.

I looked at Simon, we spoke, but it was the chatter of monkeys. Banalities, gallows humour; it all flooded out in an incontinent stream. Verbal diarrhoea; words pouring out, keep talking, don't stop talking. Don't stop the car, don't stop the chatter, don't stop the feeling, don't fucking stop! Don't think, with thinking comes negatives – with negatives comes disappointment, don't slow down – faster, faster!

It all felt like a scene from a Hollywood blockbuster movie. Any second now the director would lift up his megaphone and yell, "CUT!" I'd been there before with this 'movie scene' thought process and was hoping once again that the madness would stop. Every time the Iraqis put me in a car I'd ended up in more trouble. The bile of breakfast, a tasteless dream, now burned the back of my throat.

I scanned blurred images; scared people staring at a passing procession. They see but don't want involvement, being involved is trouble, the faces have enough trouble. Cars stood on their noses, as petrified drivers slammed on brakes to avoid our speeding cortege. Siren wail, thump, rattle, monkey chatter, siren wail, thump, rattle monkey chatter. I thought my ears were going to bleed and my head was going to split open. Stress brought on by the terror of confinement and the incessant chatter of nervous monkeys.

We'll be there soon. We'll be there soon. My inner-monkey-self repeated. *Little monkeys, cheeky little monkeys, all excited about going on a journey.*

The chattering monkeys had just been promised another ride and I was sure I'd heard the word 'helicopter' mentioned. A voice in my head hissed, *When will you grow up?* Another voice replied, *Tomorrow, if I live that long, I promise!*

In the shimmering heat, the world turned to jelly and wobbled in front of me. My mind was seared with images of hades. My eyes, filled with sand, dry, not a tear in sight.

The cavalcade approached some gates and the three monkeys lurched about as the motion of the vehicle threw them against each other. A barrier was held open by saluting soldiers, the sirens still wailed, the monkeys still chattered. As the line of cars swept forward, I saw freedom and was relieved as the vehicles including ours, slowed and stopped. No more spine-shattering thumps, the siren wailing faded and only the nervous chatter of the monkeys remained – momentarily. And then there was silence as they gazed at freedom, a means of escape, a 'magic carpet' – a helicopter – to carry them out of Baghdad.

We were ordered out of the car. Would the monkeys get onto the 'magic carpet', or was this the cruellest trick yet? I watched Sir Edward Heath shake hands with Mohammed Hamza al-Zubaidi, the former Prime Minister of Iraq who'd played a key role in suppressing the 1991 uprisings and had been seen on TV kicking and beating rebels. Were we also to be brought all this way just to wave him goodbye? No! Brusquely we were directed towards the helicopter, but first a parting shot from the Iraqis. Zubaidi, in the guise of an Iraqi Bernard Manning, was cracking 'jokes' to the last – his delivery at our expense! Funny? No! But we were still in Iraq, so the monkeys laughed.

I smiled at Zubaidi and my head screamed, *GET OUT OF MY WAY!* And then another voice asked rhetorically, *Why are you stood there mouthing banalities? Why are you stood between us and the helicopter?* My head knew he was bullshitting because he could. I desperately wanted to say, *For Christ's sake stop!* But Zubaidi or Bernard Manning, or Tommy Cooper, or Peter Sellers, or whichever comedian he thought he was, ploughed on with his final gag, "Next time make sure that you come with a passport and visa when you cross a border, or you will need rescuing again, yes?"

Waves of warmth and love for this oaf, and all he represented, flooded out of the three monkeys. They recognised that the 'magic carpet' behind him was their means of escape and to hasten their departure they smiled, laughed and agreed with him. The three monkeys were wise because they kept their council and didn't tell Zubaidi, the crap comedian, murderer and torturer to fuck off!

MAGIC CARPET RIDE!

Saddam's henchman stood aside and gestures suggested that we should approach the helicopter. I'd never been in a chopper before. I'd seen them taking off, flying and landing for as long as I could remember as I'd lived across the River Thames from Battersea Heliport when I was a kid growing up in London.

Perhaps I should have been nervous, and maybe I was, but such was my desperation to get out of Iraq I think had they said there was no room in the helicopter for one of us I would have volunteered to be strapped to the outside of the bloody thing! We clambered in and I remember thinking that perhaps this was how American servicemen in Vietnam felt, the Iraqi military helicopter we had just boarded was a Huey, the model made famous by the antics of the United States Cavalry in 'Apocalypse Now!' and numerous other films about the conflict in Southeast Asia.

The noise the Huey made was staggering and we were all handed a pair of headphones fitted with a jack-plug and a microphone that we could use to communicate with each other over the noise of the engine. We were airborne almost immediately after the doors shut and we had all fastened the buckles on our safety harnesses.

The rotors appeared to make the sand around the aircraft 'boil' and the desert rose and engulfed the weightless 'magic carpet' on which we sat. I felt like a 'volunteer from the audience' involved in a magic trick, suspended in the air, not really understanding how it was all happening. In the blink of an eye, the Huey emerged in the clear air above the mechanically inspired maelstrom and figures on the ground fell into the distance and then disappeared as the transition from vertical to horizontal flight occurred.

The now airborne monkeys were still chattering! I tried to talk to Simon and Dr Jeffrey Easton, Sir Edward Heath's doctor, who had accompanied him on the arduous journey, and we valiantly fought the deafening noise of the rotors for some time. The view was boring, mile after mile of burning sand. We flew over several areas that were obviously military installations with tanks parked inside defensive positions, and perimeters delineated by the movement of soldiers and other military vehicles along well-scarred routes. An occasional lorry, perhaps delivering desperately needed supplies to the markets of Iraq, passed along distant highways. As the flight continued, the noise of the rotors became more and more like the beat of a savage drum; regular yet unnerving and strangely overpowering. I can't say I enjoyed my first trip in a helicopter, but then the circumstances were quite trying!

Without notification, the Huey started to descend and almost immediately buildings and scurried human movements were visible on the ground far below. As we descended, I grew increasingly apprehensive as the distance to terra firma diminished. I realise how stupid this sounds but I was still anxious that my release could be threatened, or revoked, by a radioed message from the Iraqi regime to the pilot of the helicopter. I was fearful, and no amount of smiling by the other monkeys raised my spirits or erased my fears.

How many people had I witnessed leaving Abu Ghraib euphoric, only to return hours, days, and in a few cases, weeks later? I was travelling with a former Prime Minister of the United Kingdom and still my nerves were taut and my head screamed that this didn't matter as he may go, and I might stay! After all we were still in Iraqi airspace, weren't we? I felt that no one understood the mad bastards as well as I did and my fear grew as we descended, but I wore a sardonic grin – when in Rome and all that!

My pulse raced as a chainlink fence disappeared in a dust storm as the helicopter sank ever closer to the ground and we landed. *Oh God! Let me off of this damn thing!* I thought, and then the door opened and I slid out of the shuddering machine. Keeping my head low and clutching my bag of belongings, I followed the others towards a building in the distance. Rotor wash whipped at my clothes and the sand danced in pulses around me as I walked along the ground but this soon faded and died as I neared the sanctuary of bricks and mortar. Once inside the building my fear subsided a little. At least now 'it' couldn't see me. In a short space of time, the helicopter had taken on the persona of a living entity and I felt the same way about it as my captors, loathing!

I became aware of people around me. I was offered a drink, I think, and the room span. I remember asking, "Am I still in Iraq?"

The reply was like opium to an addict. "No! We are in Jordan."

"How? Why? Surely, we we're in an Iraqi helicopter? How did we get into Jordan?" I asked, with stammered questions. Right to the bitter end, none of it made any sense to me. I thought that Iraq had been locked into its own borders. I suspected a trick!

Calm voices soothed an irrational madman with advice that special arrangements had been made to allow the Iraqi helicopter to fly over the border and land in Jordan. It was further explained, as the 'madman' continued to pull an incredulous face, that this was done to make the trip less arduous for Sir Edward Heath. What wasn't added, and not necessary, was that the chattering monkeys were not a consideration!

Minutes, several minutes, an hour, more – I have no idea how long we spent at the border. I was told to get my belongings and prepare to leave. I had no idea about anything. *Where was I? How far had I come? How far had I still to go?* I'd had a feeling that someone had said Amman, but I didn't have a clue how far away that was!

We went outside, and were directed to another helicopter, a huge Puma belonging to King Hussein of Jordan's Royal Flight! When our release had been negotiated, the King had offered Sir Edward one of his aircraft to assist with logistics. I realised that the arrangements were made with Sir Edward in mind, I'd feared my release may entail my return to Tasfirat, Al Alwiyah, and God only knows where else so I got a result as well!

We climbed aboard, strapped ourselves in and were rapidly airborne. We were separated from Sir Edward in the Puma. He sat in dignified silence with Doctor Easton, while the three chattering monkeys sat in the darker recesses of the cabin which although more spartan than the Huey was more spacious.

The noise inside the Puma seemed more deafening than Huey and it curbed my urge to talk. I realise I keep going on about the racket of these helicopter engines, but for 18 months I'd heard very little mechanical noise and so the din I was now experiencing felt so incredibly loud it was almost painful at times.

I felt like Jonah inside the belly of the whale, moving without seeing what was going on outside. The windows of the Puma were tiny in comparison with the huge glass doors of the Huey. Thundering through the air I suddenly realised I was free! It was a strange sensation that didn't fully register due to every thought being whipped into a froth by the throbbing of the rotors.

After a far shorter flight we descended towards an airport and made a calm landing, it was just after 1.30pm. After what felt like a very long time, a vehicle approached the still and silent Puma. As it drew up alongside the huge sliding doors on the helicopter were drawn back and in the wake of Sir Edward Heath we were allowed to disembark. Waiting on the tarmac to greet us were our parents, my wife Julie and son William. Hugs were exchanged all round and then I experienced confusion. Suddenly, I didn't feel anything and I wasn't elated. I was probably a bit taken back by the emotion on display. We don't do emotion very well in my family, to such an extent that I told my Dad to look after himself – as if he was about to get on a train, and not a person I hadn't seen for over two years!

After the reunions we were put in a car and driven to the airport terminal. As we climbed out of the vehicle and made our way into the building, I began to understand what Julie and William had endured for the past year and half. Climbing the steps, the waiting journalists and television reporters formed an impenetrable wall, a seething mass of people, cameras, and microphones.

I realised that this was a very determined group who knew what they wanted and were determined to get their equipment to the front of the melee. The physical crush was preventing us from getting into the building and the environment was not calm and orderly enough for an interview; it was a huge scrum of bodies each attempting to gain an advantage. In the middle of this circus, Julie's voice suddenly rang out and she shouted that her son was getting crushed and that the crowd needed to back off.

Arrangements were then hastily made for a press conference and the media reluctantly moved away from their objective. This still didn't prevent a few dedicated hacks, determined to get an 'exclusive' or 'the first words', from thrusting microphones and cameras in front of us and calling out questions in the hope of a word or two they could use!

Once we actually managed to get inside the building there was an air of frantic activity as civil servants, the Ambassador, his staff and seemingly dozens of other people dashed around. What they were doing I haven't the foggiest idea, but obviously it was very important given how many of them were scurrying all over the place.

I sat on a huge sofa with William who had an 'Action Man' toy he was fascinated with, so we played a little and I became aware of how calm he was, or appeared to be, in the middle of all this lunacy. We were given drinks and there was some food laid on as I remember, but I have little recollection of what it was; not surprisingly I had other things on my mind.

A short while later we were told that we were to be put in front of the world media, apparently this deal had been struck before or during the scrum as we'd entered the terminal building. We were led into a huge room filled with what appeared to be hundreds of people facing the table which we were directed to sit behind. I edged my way along between the seats and the table and sat myself down with William in my arms.

My memory of my release was a bit blurred, I was told to go, and I went. Sir Edward Heath told us that we should refrain from 'attacking' the Iraqi regime because, as he rightly pointed out, Kai and the other hostages were still being held and we might compromise their release if we spoke out.

As we sat in front of the media, some cameras clicking, others filming, questions were asked and polite replies made and this little monkey started to feel overwhelmed. The only question I remember being asked was how I coped, and somewhere in my reply I said that keeping an eye on Chelsea Football Club, and their results, had been an important factor; to which my Dad cried out about their league standing. When I'd been abducted, The Blues were considered to be a top-six Premier League side and at the time of my release they were languishing in the relegation zone!

When the interview was over we were herded into a waiting area, and then came the moment that I'd dreamt of for a year-and-a-half – we were told to get ready because we were about to board the Virgin Atlantic Airlines jet that Richard Branson, the Sir would come later, had provided to get us home.

Carrying William in my arms, as I walked out of the terminal building and headed towards the huge aeroplane which was only about 200 metres away, I felt afraid; afraid of what I'd lost, afraid of what I'd become, afraid about the future, afraid of what I'd seen, heard and experienced. I climbed the aircraft boarding stairs and when I reached the top step I turned towards the building and asked William to wave at the gathered crowds of cameramen, reporters, and diplomatic staff. William waved and some of the group waved back while others filmed the scene and then after a minute or so I turned again and we boarded the aircraft. In this moment of freedom I thought my nightmare was finally over; I didn't have the faintest idea that it was only just beginning.

FLIGHT TO FREEDOM

I stood still for a few seconds just inside the aircraft door, my breath caught in my throat. The interior of the plane felt unexpectedly dim and cramped. The confines of the aircraft made me shudder and, having just stepped in from the brilliant sunshine of a Jordanian afternoon, I blinked repeatedly trying to accustom my eyes to the subdued lighting.

As I walked along the empty aircraft's aisle I struggled to understand that this huge plane had been made available to us by Richard Branson at no cost at all. I felt very humbled by the entire situation, but glad that I could be, almost, 'alone'. I had been in dozens of aircraft flying to and from work in various countries, but the space and size of this flight for the few of us on board was making me feel very strange.

The plane took off and I remember feeling incredibly uncomfortable. I couldn't relax and felt that I should be 'somewhere else'. Where that was, I didn't know, but this whole experience felt other-worldly to me. I knew this was real as opposed to a fitful dream, but I couldn't comprehend why it was making me feel so overwhelmed, tense and nauseous. I could tell that Julie was edgy, but I put it down to the stress of the past 18 months and a realisation that things were not getting back to normal any time soon. I realised that one part of this circus had come to an end but knew that I still had to get my life back to normal and my first thought about that was, *No problem!*

As I sat in my seat, struggling with my emotions, the cabin crew were kind and solicitous taking great care to offer everything they thought we might want but withdrawing if the timing wasn't right, allowing us the privacy I craved. As we cruised at high altitude Sir Edward's doctor, Jeffrey Easton, came and sat alongside Julie, William and me. He asked me about my state of health, both mental and physical. I tried to explain to him that I felt fine physically and further clarified that everything was as well as could be expected and that what I really wanted, and needed, was to get on with my life as quickly as I could. What worried me at that point was getting back to normality and carrying on with the basic day-to-day events that routine lives are comprised of. I don't think I ever thought about the status of my mental health beyond headaches and feeling, as I was right now, exhausted and brittle.

I recall telling Doctor Easton about the euphoria I felt over my release and that I had plenty to tell people when the time was right. I said that because of the hostages still being held in Iraq I would not be able to tell my story straight away. Easton told me that my ordeal was now over – and I believed him!

A couple of journalists were on the flight, there I assumed at the behest of Sir Edward Heath. I say this because they 'spoke his language' and, I'm sure, had given promises of providing 'tasteful' and 'politically aligned' reportage. I had no experience of the media at this stage, and in all honesty, I wish this had stayed that way. The best way to express how I feel about the media now is that I rarely watch the TV news and I have not purchased a newspaper in what is now nearly 28 years!

As the journalists approached, I noticed a change in Julie's attitude and she became uncharacteristically aggressive. Beyond that, I cannot remember now the questions that were asked or the replies that were given. All I recall was feeling incredibly nervous during the whole 'interview' process.

As we flew on, the cabin crew were available on request to provide food, soft drinks and champagne. I enjoyed the hospitality and had plenty of glasses of champers, but something was missing. I didn't get the warm, glowing buzz I'd always associated with having a 'proper' drink.

The plane's intercom crackled into life and the pilot announced that we were going to land in Bari, Italy, to refuel, and a short while later we were on the ground and I noticed how dark the nighttime outside looked.

Every minute that we spent on the ground was an eternity for me. Glancing out of the small window adjacent to my seat, at any moment I expected to see uniformed Iraqi soldiers marching towards the plane as it sat immobile and connected to a tanker pumping it full of fuel. With the gift of hindsight, I realise that my state of mind was totally irrational. I'd spent a couple of wonderful holidays in Italy and found it a beautiful, serene and safe country and yet here I was now sitting fidgeting and watching everything and everyone with mounting anxiety fearing that at any second I would be dragged off the plane and thrown into a cell. Something was not right, yet I had no idea that it was me. I was not right. I was already deep in the grips of a psychosis but had no idea that was the case!

I was deeply afraid that something, anything, could, would or should happen. I heard not what someone said but my own deranged interpretation of their words. My mind had imploded. After months of relying on half-truths and lies, I'd lost the ability to accept a statement at face value. Every word, I was sure, disguised a hidden meaning. My body had been released from prison, my mind had not.

The flight back to London became part of my release; a release that has flown from my memory and returns now only in small vignettes. Did it happen to me? My recollection of some of it is so disjointed that it almost feels as if I was at a cinema with a limited view – so-much-so that to me my opinion seems barely valid!

Having continued safely on its journey from Bari, a couple of hours later, circa 9.00pm GMT, the plane landed at Gatwick and as I climbed off the flight with William in my arms and staggered into the dark, cold night of a British December I shivered as a unique and biting chill I'd not felt in nearly two years enveloped my senses. I clutched William close to me and my teeth chattered as I realised that I was ill-dressed for this moment and the winter wind was finding it easy to permeate my flimsy clothing and pinch at my skin.

At the foot of the steps I became confused by the phalanx of lights, gathered people and vehicles that all appeared to be coming towards me. I have since seen video footage of the event and as I reach the bottom of the plane's steps I thank the flight crew and then turn and attempt to get into Sir Edward Heath's vehicle! I snap back from the car and stand shaking, confused and disorientated and am then directed towards a minibus.

The minibus drove around in what seemed like circles before it eventually arrived at a terminal building which we were quickly ushered inside. I was grateful to be out of the cold and didn't pay much attention as we were being shepherded into a room but after a few seconds I realised that it was a VIP suite full of people celebrating our arrival or was it our release? I couldn't decide which at the time. Among them, my aunts, uncles, cousins and various other members of my family. Michael's family were there along with Stephen Howarth and Heather Taggart from the Foreign Office and many other faces, most of whom I had never seen in my life.

I was taken aback by this reception, but never once did I feel close to shedding a tear. What was the point of crying anymore? At once I was being hugged, my name was being called and pandemonium erupted as the waiting group surged forward. I was hugged, kissed, and a procession of well-wishers shook my hand – but I felt done-to, rather than a person actively taking part in the greetings and congratulations. It all seemed unreal and very strange.

As soon as the tumultuous welcome subsided an official took Sir Edward Heath out of the room by a side door and we were beckoned to follow. Once outside the hubbub of the reception room we were told that Sir Edward wanted us to attend a press conference with him. Dressed in a Virgin Atlantic sweat-vest and holding William, I followed Sir Edward into another room with Julie and the rest of the 'interview group' following us closely.

Before I knew it, I was sat alongside the ex-Prime Minister in front of dozens of microphones and cameras. I felt like an imposter, I'd done nothing, but here I was with my fellow released hostages facing a wall of Fleet Street's finest. I thought we'd get a fair-shake, but I now understand that only the distorted and salacious utterings of the press sell newspapers. I can barely remember speaking. Most of the questions were dealt with by Sir Edward, whom, when I did speak, I thanked along with Richard Branson, the Foreign Office, Julie, and all who had written and assisted in any way at all.

The events of the past 24 hours or so felt like an 'out-of-body' experience. Imagine you spend a year-and-a-half in an Iraqi prison so different from anything you could have ever imagined and then you are flown out of the nightmare in a helicopter supplied by Saddam Hussein.

Then you are then put on another helicopter belonging to King Hussein of Jordan and eventually flown home from the Middle East by Richard Branson and at the end of each leg of the journey comes a fusillade of questions asked by the world's media. I couldn't take it all in. Did these events happen the way I was expecting? Not by any stretch of the imagination. Was it what I wanted? Not in the least. Was it more than I could handle? Most definitely, yes! Was my release a good event? Yes, of that there is no question. Is my memory of the day something I cherish? No, it was like a drunken ride on the last bus home! I didn't realise then, but this was the first day of the rest of my life – and I'd forgotten how to live.

We walked back into the reception room and were met by a crush of happy smiling people. Suddenly, my cousin Peter thrust a replica Chelsea shirt into my hands and I pulled it over my head instantly. I loved it, and it felt like a life raft of normality in a vast sea of crashing waves that were drowning me.

Everything felt new and strange. Toilets had 'furniture' in them and were not just the holes in the ground surrounded by slimy concrete walls I'd grown used to over the previous 18 months. People were smiling, I hadn't seen a lot of genuine happiness in a long time. Alcohol was in every hand. Everyone was relaxed – except me. I wanted to disappear and desperately craved being alone and still for a second.

I scanned the room looking for a way out and saw my ex-wife Delyth and daughter Rhian who I hadn't seen for eight years. Many more faces from my past came at me. This was crazy, I felt like I'd stumbled onto the set of the TV show 'This Is Your Life'. All it needed now was for then host Michael Aspel to walk out from behind a sight screen carrying his famous 'Big Red Book'.

I was aware that Julie had difficulty being 'involved' with issues connected to my past and so I decided to take Delyth and Rhian into an adjoining room to speak to them in order, I thought, to save any distress for all concerned. My tactics failed and the first problem of my homecoming was finding myself the 'piggy in the middle' – caught between two women, one I'd formerly been married to and the other who I was currently married to, both attempting to do the best they could for their/my/our children. I never considered myself to be a good husband, father, or homemaker for any of them, but this felt immaterial; I was a victim of my own history. Swinging in the wind, I tried to please everyone and less than an hour after arriving back in the UK I'd come unstuck. Happy days!

Time passed and people began to leave and head back to their homes, some many hours from Gatwick. As the room emptied and I settled a little, Heather Taggart came over to see me. Smiling politely, she thrust a bundle of letters that I vaguely recognised into my hands. Now you might think that this would be perfectly normal as she was the woman who sent the mail out to me via the British Embassy in Jordan, however this was a batch of mail that I'd written weeks previously that she was just about to pass to Julie for posting!

I know that this seems almost petty when all things, my release, transport home, and all the logistical work that had gone on, are considered, but at the time I was very bitter about this aspect of my detention. The Iraqis always saw me as a political hostage, the Russians always regarded me as a 'pawn', yet the British Government, or at least their mandarins in Whitehall, seemed to treat me as nothing more than a prisoner. I admit I was charged by an Iraqi military court with illegal entry, but the charge was fictitious and my conviction a sham. Given the truth of the matter, I felt like I'd been hung out to dry for 18 months.

I discovered later that Julie, who received very little in the way of financial help from the government, paid for most things that were delivered to me and also picked up the cost of posting the huge bundles of mail I sent out. Fortunately, charitable donations by members of the public proved to be a Godsend to my family during my incarceration and I am eternally grateful to everyone who helped them.

As the last of the well-wishers departed, I left the suite with Delyth and Rhian to say goodnight and thank them for coming up from South Wales. Unfortunately, as soon as we got outside, I fell into a media trap. BBC Wales were there to film 'the Welsh angle' of my release! To keep everyone happy, I went along with this and recall saying I hadn't been involved much in Rhian's life, but I hoped that this was going to change. Rhian said that it was nice to have me free and I think that when I spoke I used bits and pieces of Welsh language I'd been taught by Delyth. Once the news crew were sated, they all climbed into a minibus and left – I was tired of being the performing seal already.

This 'innocuous' bit of TV fluff sent Julie into a foul mood which I understood but could do nothing about. We left Gatwick in a taxi to take us home to Walthamstow and with Willian soon asleep the entire trip passed in virtual silence. The only conversation between Julie and I concerned the motives of the occupants of a car that appeared to be tailing us.

Saturday, 11th December.

We arrived home in the early hours of the morning and had only just got inside when a reporter and photographer from a 'popular' tabloid knocked on the door and asked for an interview and some photos! Julie went ballistic and there I was, stupefied, exhausted, confused, and desperate for some sleep caught between Julie and her nemesis – the British media! They were told to leave and did so without even trying to put a foot in the door. We went to bed immediately and when I woke up a few hours later I didn't know where I was.

AFTERMATH

The sun streams through the patio doors of our new house. We'd had to move as the media would not give us any peace. A wonderful day is a joy to experience after the hell of 18 months in an Iraqi prison. Waves of contentment wash over me as I observe ordinary everyday things a free man takes for granted; birds gathering in flocks in the branches of a tree, buses passing by in the street, the sound of children playing in a park, a normality I feared I'd never experience again.

I am reclining on my back on a settee and lying on my chest is my son William. My wife Julie asks a question as she enters the room, I answer her in an off-hand, matter of fact way, and continue to 'play wrestle' with William.

Everything is calm, and a loving feeling permeates the room. Relaxation for me after the terror of being held hostage and forced, hooded, interrogations by the Iraqi secret police. My mind drifts and I realise that time has been a great healer, just as everyone said it would be, and now I am starting to get back on my feet again. God knows it's taken long enough.

Suddenly, shattering the moment, the room is cast into shadow. Time takes on a slow-motion quality and images change into a stuttering, frame-by-frame montage. Micro-seconds take hours to pass. My body springs into self-preservation mode, somewhere in my mind I know I've been here, or in a similar situation before. My muscles tense, my heart races, a pulse throbs in my head, my limbs snap as adrenalin courses through my veins and my vision becomes tunnelled. I attempt to locate the imminent, impending danger. My body is ready for whatever is coming next as my sensory stimulation increases. I become aware of every centimetre of the room, as I attempt to identify the threat. The weight on my chest fails to comprehend the danger, thinking my fear is part of our game. My son fights playfully and as I attempt to push him to relative safety my worst fears become reality. Glass shatters with a deafening roar as the love recently filling the room is replaced with hate and the accompanying roar of hell.

I turn towards the patio doors as they implode turning into a haze of shattered fragments. In their place are silhouetted assassins, dark figures wearing identical masks and sunglasses. They enter the room veiled in smoke and debris. Their automatic weapons, held at waist height, barking and spitting white hot death.

I try to sit up. Around me, elements of the room and the furniture within it implode in a froth of innumerable particles. Swirling in the air, the shattered fragments reflect the sunlight and form rainbows in the moving light. Sickening thuds accompany the rending of wood and mark the strike of a thousand bullets. Ceramic, mahogany, glass, fabric, and plaster fall victim to the deadly assault.

I scream Julie's name and as if I've signed her death warrant with my lips her body explodes in a spray of crimson flesh. Her torn and dismembered corpse is tossed across the room on a wave of lead, crashing into a wall. The violence continues at dual-speed but my mind takes hours to watch each hissing bullet contribute to the obliteration of my world.

I am about to die. All I can think of is how to save my William who screams as the roar of machine guns combine into a cacophony of sound which tears at my heart and soul. William is shaking and clinging to my shoulder. I touch him and he vaporises in a mist of hot, sticky, death. His blood splashes my face, pieces of his young body are smeared all over me. The fear and shock that my family are dead and I am about to be executed paralyses me. I turn to face my assassins, but rather than a volley of bullets my fate is a fusillade of laughter. With this final twist of the knife, they turn as a unit and walk away from the smoke-filled abattoir that my home has become. There is only one thing left in the room physically unscathed by this monstrous violence, me!

The horror of the event takes only seconds but it feels to me as if it lasted for hours. Freed from the frozen grasp of death and destruction I draw some fetid air into my gasping lungs and let forth a piteous scream.

In a panic I wake up, the scream has broken the spell of the nightmare that enveloped me. I leap into a sitting position and realise that the moisture dribbling off my flesh is not my son's blood, but rivulets of sweat coursing from every pore of my body. Confused, but slowly realising this is all part of the trauma-filled existence my life has disintegrated into, I shudder as another desolate day begins.

Following my return to the UK, this was a frequent nightmare I struggled with, and the experience left me shattered before my day had even started.

Saturday, 11th December.

At first, being released from incarceration is a wonderful and, if you'll excuse the pun, liberating experience. Each daily event, from making a cup of tea to using a toilet or buying an article from a shop, is given a special meaning when measured against the reality of a prison sentence.

With this in mind, you can imagine the significance of going to see Chelsea for the first time since I returned home. It didn't take long. A few hours in fact. At 7.00am, I was awake. No Muster, thank fuck! I dressed and was out of the house double-quick and on my way to Stamford Bridge to watch the Blues take on Ipswich Town as a special guest of Ken Bates! The day was a whirl but among my memories was a visit to the dressing room to meet the manager and the players and afterwards Mr Bates giving me a lift in his Rolls Royce to a relative's house which was nearby. In between, Chelsea didn't do anything to improve their league position (third from bottom) by drawing 1-1 with Ipswich Town in front of a sparse crowd of 12,508 which would have been 12,507 if I hadn't been there.

Monday, 13th December.

The weekend melted away in a blur of family fun in Chelsea and handling calls from the media when I returned to Walthamstow. Their pursuit seemed relentless. Monday came and I'd arranged to go and see various people in London to ascertain just where I stood regarding employment, finances, and the rest of my life.

One of my first ports of call was Taylors office in Pimlico. Here I met with directors of the company and administrative staff. It was all very sociable and relaxed, but the bottom line was that I was out of work! Contracts had come and gone while I was in Iraq and I was surplus to requirements. I knew that I'd done little to ingratiate myself with either my fellow workers or my employers, but it hurt deeply that my services were no longer required. I was told that Taylors were willing to pay me the 50 percent of my salary that they had been giving Julie for the past 18 months, for the next three months. This would take me to the end of February 1994, and after that I was unemployed!

In the wake of this discovery, I went to the Embassy of Kuwait with Steve and Josie Brooks, founders of the Gulf Support Group, an organisation battling for compensation for UK citizens who had been taken hostage and used as human shields during and after Iraq's invasion of Kuwait. We arrived and were allowed in after our identities had been checked by the security staff; then we were shown into a huge room on the ground floor and a short while later a senior Kuwaiti diplomat arrived and began to discuss the Iraq/Kuwait situation, as he saw it. I've got to be honest here and say I wanted some money. Because of the inability of the Kuwaitis and the United Nations observers to do a better job of watching the de-militarised zone between Iraq and Kuwait I'd spent the previous year and a half in a bloody prison!

I had no idea then, but I was a minnow in waters filled with international political sharks. Every person that I approached had an agenda or programme that they were duty-bound to fulfil. The Kuwaitis wanted me to use my unjust, and frankly irrational, imprisonment to attack and vilify the regime of Saddam Hussein. To be honest, I had no problem with doing this as I felt it was, and still is, the truth. I was told that I could be put in touch with an Arabic writer from a major newspaper and that he would help me to write a book. We spent quite some time manoeuvring around this topic and finally, I think, I agreed to send in some notes on my experiences that could be worked upon in the near future.

I hated the entire experience. I felt like a specimen that the Kuwaitis were manipulating to display in its best aspect. Their comments, words, and demeanour told me that they really had little consideration for what I had been through. They simply wanted to use my experiences to reiterate their opinions about the Iraqis and the political situation at that moment.

Finally, we got down to the financial side of the meeting. The Kuwaitis said they would give me some money, which they were at pains to point out was not an admission of guilt, to help me through Christmas! I thanked them and said that help, no matter where it came from, was gratefully received at that stage. One of the diplomats in the meeting left the room and returned a short while later with a bundle of notes which he handed to me saying, "This is a gift from the Kuwaiti government. Enjoy the holidays."

I'd seen piles of Iraqi Dinars very recently, but not a wad of sterling like that. I had no idea how much was there, but I felt much better for having it in my hand. The diplomat then said, "It's £1000. We want to give you and your family some money for presents at Christmas time."

I felt so grateful and thought that this was the start of the different lifestyle that people I'd seen over the weekend had spoken about. I recall that shortly after the Kuwaiti official had given me the cash I'd wanted to get as far away from the embassy as possible. Why? I can't say. It's possible I feared they would take the cash away. It's possible that I feared I was surrounded by people who looked very similar to the evil bastards that had locked me up. It's possible I had the desire to count the money and gloat over it. I can't really say much apart from the fact that the urge to run was never far from my mind.

As the week progressed, every TV station and newspaper was either on the phone or knocking at the door asking for an interview, but we refused them all. The logical question that needs to be asked and answered is why did we not take the thousands that were offered at the time? The answer is quite simple. Kai Sondermann and Jean-Luc Barriere were still in Abu Ghraib, and I'd been warned that any revelations about my imprisonment might result in them having to spend a lot longer in jail as a consequence. I kept quiet. I spoke only to the local 'Guardian' in Walthamstow, and that was a very low-key interview. Suddenly, the same story was on the front page of the 'Daily Telegraph', purporting to be written by a man who I'd never heard of, never met, and certainly never given an interview to! I was furious for two reasons! Firstly, Kai and Jean-Luc were still in bloody Iraq! Secondly, why should they get a story for nothing that I had refused to sell to other newspapers!

Wednesday, 15th December.

Kai Sondermann and Jean-Luc Barriere, the last Westerners known to be jailed in Iraq on charges of illegally entering the country flew to freedom after politicians from their countries met with Saddam Hussein in Baghdad and appealed for their release.

*****

In the wake of the news of about Kai and Jean-Luc I subsequently agreed to go on to the 'Big Breakfast' early morning TV show with Gaby Roslin who came across as a nice person. She interviewed me about my experiences in Iraq, and I revealed that the previous Christmas I'd been so depressed I'd asked an Iraqi soldier to blow my brains out. By midday, London's daily newspaper the 'Evening Standard' hit the streets with my revelations in there, reported in such a way that it appeared they had direct access to the story!

I made an appointment to see the editor of the 'Mail on Sunday', the newspaper that had published George Galloway's story about Michael Wainwright and me and his visit to Abu Ghraib. I told him that the story Galloway had written was at best a terrible distortion of the truth or alternatively, and in many respects, a pack of bloody lies. His reply astounded me. He said that it was the newspaper's opinion that, "As an elected Member of Parliament, George Galloway's account of events carried more weight than my denials, or any allegations I made that such a man had lied."

Nothing was going the way I thought it would in respect of gaining recompense for my troubles, and a further hammer blow came from the office of Prime Minister John Major who advised me to take up my grievance case with Saddam Hussein and his government, via the courts in Iraq! I remember thinking, *Mr Major, we all had a good laugh about the Citizens Charter and the Cones Hotline, but you really are taking the piss this time!!*

The fragile veneer of calm sugar-coating my mind was being chipped away. I started reacting to things rather than living a normal life. I know I drove Julie to distraction when I spent over £400 of the money the Kuwaiti Embassy had given me to buy presents for my family on a new carpet for the living room of our house. The only reason I could give her, myself, or anyone else, was that the old carpet appeared similar to me to one that had been 'laid' on the floor of a prison cell I'd occupied, and this was causing me genuine distress. What I failed to realise was that this was the tip of the iceberg. As time passed, the memories of Iraq and Abu Ghraib should have faded from my mind but a total inverse of this was happening and the consequences would be both terrifying and horrific.

I experienced the nightmare I described at the start of this chapter, and it started recurring. When I was up and about and out of the house, I'd regularly get stopped in the street by people I didn't know who recognised me from the TV or newspapers. I found it disconcerting that they knew my story and although they meant well, I'd frequently hear the line, "It's over now Paul. You're back home and everything's all right." The truth was that flashbacks and disturbing memories were making it impossible for me to reconcile my existence with my Iraqi experiences. I'd maybe agree that it was over and I was back home however my head was screaming, *BUT I'M NOT ALL FUCKING RIGHT!*

Small events like this started to feed the paranoia that had developed during my time in custody. I realised that Iraq had fundamentally changed me, but I couldn't get the rest of the world to accept it and the self-imposed pressure of having to find a job wasn't helping my frame of mind. With 1994 underway and the Taylors wages soon to cease I started to trawl deeper into my contacts file than I had in a long time to see if I could find a route back to work and eventually got in contact with a company based in France called Sodexho. I'd been interviewed by them before about a contract in the Congo, but it had fallen through. Feeling like a leper, I wrote to them again about prospective employment and they got in touch and following an interview in Paris it was arranged that I would go to Kazakhstan and work as a camp-boss on a gas field development project. I was told that it was minus 40°, and that I should prepare for the weather! I had a medical in London, physical only – if there had been a psychiatric element to it I'm not sure if I'd been hired.

Saturday, 19th February, 1994.

Since my return I'd been going to watch Chelsea regularly. Manager Glenn Hoddle had marginally improved the team's league form and progress had been made in the early rounds of the FA Cup. Today I found myself at the Manor Ground, home of Oxford United, for a Fifth Round tie. For many years The Blues had a bad habit of getting knocked out by lower-league opposition and when Oxford took the lead I thought, *Here we go again!* Fortune was to favour Hoddle's men who fought back to win 2-1 with goals from John Spencer and Craig Burley. It was a great day out and I made the most of it, as my new job in Kazakhstan was due to start and I'd soon be back to listening to football on the World Service.

Wednesday, 23rd February.

I flew from London Heathrow to Paris and there I boarded an Aeroflot flight to Moscow. The plane must have seen service during the Second World War! It was dirty, smelly and a part of the floor was ruptured! I sat huddled in my seat. I was frightened by the foreign voices. Words spoken in a language I did not understand now left me with worrying feelings of self-doubt. We took off and almost instantly the plane became a whirlwind of activity. It seemed as if most of the people on the flight knew each other, or if they didn't then they were trying their very best to get to know each other. Bottles appeared from every seat in the plane and toasts were drunk repeatedly by a group of huge bear-like men who spoke some English and were in the company of several gorgeous women one of whom invited me to have a drink. I was soon chatting about my immediate past and my struggles because of it which gained me a wider audience of passengers who all had bottles of alcohol in their hands and kept refilling my glass to keep me talking and on it went across a continent.

By the time we touched down in Moscow I was absolutely hammered which made clearing customs an ordeal and if that wasn't testing enough I then had the challenge of finding my way to the gate to board a flight to Almaty, the capital of Kazakhstan at this time, and from there I had to get to Tengiz, the place where I would be working for the next three months.

The challenge soon developed into a major problem. I was far too drunk to be able to make any sense to anyone, or, and here is the important point, understand anything that any of the hundreds of workers at the airport who I asked for assistance actually said to me. I spent several hours traipsing around the airport building trying to get directions without any success until eventually I did what all English people of my generation were instructed to do at an early age if they ever got lost, I asked a policeman. Big mistake; the next thing I knew I was in a police cell and I soon felt it's walls closing in on me. Déjà vu?

Fortunately, freedom from my detention for being drunk was obtained by handing the desk sergeant the contents of my wallet, namely a 50 Franc note (about £5) and I was allowed on my way. The first thing I did was to find a phone and try and place a call to my employer's office. Having failed, and in an increasing state of panic, I contacted the emergency number for the French Consulate in Moscow and eventually I managed to speak to someone I could explain my situation to and told them I was working for Sodexho in France and said I'd got lost in Moscow airport and requested that the British Embassy be made aware of these facts.

Now you might be thinking, why did I make such a ridiculous phone call? The answer is very simple. I was overseas, and the last time I was 'detained' in a foreign country I lost the next 18 months of my life. I wasn't well and, in all honesty, I shouldn't have been allowed out alone never mind being taken on by an international catering company and sent to a place of work in a situation the idea of which had increasingly terrified me. Eventually I got some sleep in the airport, and a few hours later a Sodexho employee arrived to take care of me. He began by asking where I'd gone to the night before. I told him the truth. Nowhere! Apparently I was in trouble because flights to Almaty were every three days, and so now I was stuck in Moscow!

I stayed at a company flat in the city centre for a couple of nights and was eventually 'hand-delivered' onto a flight to Almaty and from there the final leg of the journey to Tengiz was made in a battered, stinking, noisy helicopter that redefined for me my concepts of feeling unsafe. The chopper ride was a pre-cursor to a hellish experience in Tengiz, a location I dubbed the 'Bolshoi Tyurma' or big prison! I doubt very much if the place would have existed without gas and oil. There was a cracking plant, where crude oil was separated into its component parts, gas, and oil etc, and this had a 20-mile 'dead zone' around it, an area that contained no inhabitants – just in case a mistake was made that could lead to fatalities! Beyond this were the camps where I was to work. It was a cold, depressing place and an environment which inspired a set of questions in my head that had me wondering if I would ever be fully functional again.

I struggled with the job, the location, and my head from the moment I arrived. I woke up most mornings not having a clue where I was, almost expecting to have to go out for Muster! Bizarrely, most of the chefs that I'd worked with in Kuwait were here in a neighbouring camp. I found out that they were contracted to work six weeks on and two weeks off, while I was doing three months on and two weeks off for less money! This wound me up as did the people I had to work with and cater for. Looking back, none of these annoyances were any worse than those I'd encountered previously when working abroad – my current problems in Tengiz were all in my head.

Why was I putting myself through this hell? I'd been an expatriate worker since 1985 and, to be frank, it was the easiest way I knew to earn good money. When I write about good money in 1994, I am talking about earning circa £1300 per month. After my experiences with food in Iraq I found the concept of working in catering repellent, but it was all that I'd ever done with any level of success. It was the way in which I could best earn my living and pay the mounting bills!

My mind went to pieces in the Bolshoi Tyurma as I was overwhelmed once more by the gamut of emotions and situations that I'd experienced in Iraq in which food had played a major and powerful role. In the Mukhabarat complex with its rice soup. In Al Alwiyah with its food in dustbins. In Abu Ghraib's reception with food being passed through iron bars. In Section Three where food was begged, borrowed, and stolen. With so many foul memories of food, its preparation and the entire concept that was now a fixed understanding in my mind, I concluded that I couldn't do the catering thing anymore. I couldn't be that person who handled the animals, dealt with the grease, the grunge and detritus anymore. I knew I was done. I had to get out of this place and get home.

Salvation and an excuse to quit came courtesy of Chelsea Football Club whose progress in the FA Cup I'd been following with mounting excitement. Wolverhampton Wanderers were beaten 1-0 in the quarterfinals and Luton Town 2-0 in the semi-finals. The Blues opponents in the final would be Manchester United who were leading the Premier League on goal difference from Blackburn Rovers. The Red

Devils were clear favourites to win the cup, but the fact that Chelsea had beaten them home and away in the league had me thinking they had a punchers chance, and I fully intended to be at Wembley to see if they would take it.

Tuesday, 12th April.

I flew home to London. When I'd resigned my position, I'd given a garbled story to my employers about missing my family and wanting to watch Chelsea in the FA Cup Final – the truth of the matter was I simply couldn't cope in Kazakhstan.
    Trying to put a lid on my negative thoughts, I slipped straight back into going to watch the Blues and at every match I found myself getting more and more involved in the activities of the Chelsea Independent Supporters Association. I was able to get a ticket for the Cup Final and I also landed myself a new job working in the kitchens of the BP offices at Finsbury Circus in the City of London. I still couldn't escape catering, however the kitchen staff here were lovely. Many of them, including Ricky Groves who would later train to be an actor and appear in 'Eastenders', came from the Walthamstow area and so knew about my past.
    A strange but true story that occurred one day while I was at BP is worth telling because I feel it demonstrates how a vast majority of the population might think and react in similar circumstances. During a break, a few of us were sat around a table eating lunch when one of the permanent chefs made a comment to a young relief chef who was covering a holiday absence that assumed he knew about my experiences in Iraq. He didn't have a clue what she was talking about, so she explained that I'd been a hostage for 18 months. His first reaction was a bemused, "You're joking!"
    Then after other chefs at the table had thrown their contributions in, I confirmed that everything they said was true. The young relief chef sat in silent contemplation for a few moments and then as he was raising a forkful of food to his lips he asked, "Did they fuck you up the arse?"
    As the entire table exploded with laughter I replied, "No, I wasn't fucked up the arse!"
    The rest of our break was full of the usual questions. As I answered them in a parrot-fashion manner I could cope with, I realised the reason for the young lad's question was not a desire to embarrass or upset me, it was simply that being male-raped was the worst outcome he could imagine happening during an overseas prison sentence.
    This is one of the reasons why I decided to write this account of my experiences. I want people to understand that the horrors of a situation are sometimes not what actually happens, but traumatic events that the imagination fears might occur. The contraction of diseases and illnesses that are deadly under the wrong conditions. Feet beaten until they

resemble the size, shape and colour of an elephant's. Electrodes being placed on naked flesh, or genitalia being connected to a mains power supply. Being forced to torture another human being. Being forced to self-abuse with a bottle or another sharp and deadly instrument. These are fears based on reality. Salacious fears are hardly ever accurate, they exist in comfortable fantasies not the real world.

Wednesday, 4th May.

I went to see Sir Edward Heath at his house in London. I was nervous about the meeting. It played on my mind that I was a scruff from Chelsea and he'd been the Prime Minister, and was, at that point, Father of the House (House of Commons). I'd also been struggling with flashbacks again which fuelled my apprehension.

Sir Edward put me at ease and listened to what I had to say which I imagine probably came across as the rant of a madman. He asked me how things were regarding my employment, finances, and health. When he asked me about my health, I think I became ultra-defensive and delivered a story that hinted at my real state of mind but stopped short of revealing that I felt as if I was about to fall apart. In truth however, I think that a man of his experience would have been well capable of seeing that I was in distress and in need of psychiatric help, though he did suggest that I make an appointment to go and see Dr Jeffrey Easton, his personal physician whom I'd chatted to on the flight back to London following my release.

Saturday, 14th May.

Cup Final day! What a disappointment! I was a Wembley to see referee David Elleray make a catalogue of shocking decisions that helped Manchester United win the match. The record books do not state this, they show that Chelsea lost 4-0, however every Blues supporter present knows that despite this thumping margin of defeat, but for the width of a crossbar and the complete ineptitude of the match officials, the game could have gone the other way.

Wednesday, 1st June.

I went see Dr Easton in Salisbury and with the best of intentions he gave me advice that he thought would be the helpful to me. What he failed to realise, and what I didn't discover for many months was that I was suffering from Post-Traumatic Stress Disorder (PTSD). By now I had already created some extensive coping devices, strategies, and defences against externally received messages which challenged my distorted understanding of any situation.

I spoke to Dr Easton about the press and the media in a venomous tone and he said that my exposure and dealings with them were in the past now, and so I should stop worrying about them and their activities. I was astonished by this, so much so that my memory of our conversation has never faded. I came away from Salisbury feeling, if not angry, then at the very best genuinely confused. I'd made the trip to get help for the problems that were starting to control and direct my life and felt that I'd been given an 'arm-around-the-shoulder' chat loaded with well-meaning support, but containing no devices or tools I could use in any practical way to deal with, or resolve, the issues that were steadily forcing me into a vortex that was about to take control of my mind and encourage, dare I say 'make', me do things that would change my life forever.

When I got back to London, I went through all that had been said, and realised that I simply had to 'man up' and 'pull myself together' or at least that was the way I interpreted the advice. So what does a working-class boy do in order to 'get on with it'? I threw myself into the task of working and trying to climb out of the hole I'd been shoved into through honest endeavour.

During the summer of 1994 I experienced an increasing number of behavioural aberrations which impacted my relationship with Julie and William. As an example of this I can remember a journey we tried to make on the London Underground. We walked to Blackhorse Road, our nearest station, and went down on to the platform to wait for the train. When we arrived, I checked the information display panel and saw that the first train going to Brixton was due in five minutes. I paced up and down the platform feeling uncomfortable, trapped, and aroused. When I say 'aroused' I mean hyper-vigilant and ready for something to happen. I scanned the display panel and watched the arrival time reduce, agonisingly slowly. From four minutes to three minutes. From three minutes to two minutes and, finally, from two minutes to one minute. Suddenly the screen went blank. I couldn't breathe. I sensed the temperature on the platform slowly beginning to rise as I stood staring at the screen willing it to display the information I wanted to read that the next train was approaching!

Nothing happened – the screen remained blank.

"Display you bastard!"

I felt my blood beginning to boil – the screen remained blank.

"DISPLAY YOU FUCKING BASTARD!"

Suddenly, the display obeyed and told me that the next train to Brixton was in seven minutes! The previous train had been cancelled without notification. I exploded! A human bomb waiting for a trigger. The cancellation of a tube train was that trigger. I swore, I cursed, I threw punches around and then I waved my clenched fists at the display and beseeched God to deal with this slight, this very personal slight, against me.

To other passengers waiting on the platform I must have seemed like a madman and the reality wasn't too far removed from this.

Explosive events similar to this became my normal state of mind and I lived on the edge every minute of the day, capable of detonating into a towering fury at the least provocation. Julie and William were both, justifiably, terrified of me. I wasn't aware of this fact however for many months and maybe even years. In my mind they were as guilty as anyone else of marginalizing me, ridiculing me, ignoring me, and generally doing all that they could, as was the rest of the human race, to make my life intolerable.

My illness progressed unchecked and undiagnosed and as an unannounced consequence of this Julie left me taking Willian with her. They spent time at her sisters in Devon where I tracked them down and asked them to come home. Julie returned, but our relationship was never the same. She was scared, I was mad, and William was caught somewhere in the middle.

I took a permanent job as a night chef/manager for a company based on the Isle of Dogs. It was hell. I couldn't handle the demands of the job, or the hours, and I certainly couldn't deal with the people that I worked with. It wasn't the people themselves but rather it was them as human beings. I just couldn't deal with people on any level. I resented them, I distrusted them, I despised them, I hated them – much as I did the rest of humanity.

Monday, 31st October.

I returned home from work early in the morning, and Julie told me that she wanted a divorce. I'd been to see my Doctor, and his locum had given me some Diazepam, anti-depressants, to help me cope. I'd never been a pill-popper and so 28 of the 30 tablets I'd been prescribed remained in the container they'd been dispensed in.

Julie and William were the 'thing' that got me through the ordeal of imprisonment and my time as a hostage. I felt as if I'd lost the power of thought when I heard the request for a divorce. I struggled to reconcile myself to the reality that it presented but I was tired, emotional, and in the middle of a nervous breakdown. I wasn't thinking straight and reacted to the situation rather than responding to it.

Reaction was, by this stage of my illness, my normal course of action. The path of least resistance. I hardly ever made plans, I simply staggered from one, usually cataclysmic, event to the next. I was blinded with self-obsession. An obsession that was coupled with a belief that my own feelings were an accurate reflection of the events unfolding around me. I decided, at that moment, that life was not going to be worth living if I didn't have my family. I took the remaining 28 Diazepam and climbed into bed.

I woke up that evening feeling slow and stupid. I could hear Julie moving around the house, but I couldn't make sense of anything. I wanted everything to stop. I wanted the confusion to cease. Then I remembered she wanted a divorce. Julie told me that she was going to stay with friends and that she was taking William with her. Having failed earlier, at this point I decided to do the job of ending my awful life properly. It was the only way I could make all this shit stop.

Julie left with William and the house was empty and still. I dragged myself out of the house to a local Off Licence and bought a bottle of brandy and a bottle of Southern Comfort and once I was back home I rifled through drawers looking for anything that resembled a pill. I tried to set up the video to record an explanation as to why I committed suicide, and then I started drinking and necking the various pills I'd found which in the main were painkillers. I drank as fast as I could, glass after glass that brought tears to my eyes as it burned my throat.

Numb, but very much alive I realised I must be a hard bastard to kill and so I kept searching for things that might speed my demise. I ate packets of rat poison that I found under the kitchen sink and drank more of the booze. I felt sick but I was in no way dying. "CHRIST! I'M INDESTRUCTABLE!" I screamed. My mind whirred. I had a new idea. The final act of my futile life would be to light fire in my bedroom. The resultant smoke would asphyxiate me and my vile body would die once and for all.

I went to the bedroom and prepared the scene. I didn't want to die in a pile of crap, I wanted to be found like a mummified corpse; smoked by the product of the small bonfires I was about to light. I stripped down to my underwear, glugged down the last of the alcohol, struck a match, started a fire and laid down on my bed and waited for my life to end. As I listened to the crackle of flames which were starting to consume furniture my head screamed, *No! No! No! This is wrong!* I didn't want to burn. I didn't want to feel pain. I wanted to slip away heroically and painlessly, I wanted smoke and unconsciousness.

Suddenly I realised that things had gone badly wrong. My intention to create smoke had disappeared as my fire lighting skills, honed as a Boy Scout, had created not a pyre of smoke but a pillar of flames which were about to barbeque me! Thoughts, some even logical, crashed around my stupefied brain. *Don't let it burn. Everything that Julie and William have is here, they are not part of this. I don't want to feel pain. I don't want to burn. I don't want to burn my house. What the fuck am I going to do?*

I lived 500 metres from Walthamstow Fire Station, I would go there for help! Ignoring the fact that I was dressed only in my underpants I ran out of the house and went to summon help!

The fire-fighters were magnificent. I had stumbled back to the house and looked on as the flames were doused. They reacted so quickly they even preserved most of the furniture, however my funeral pyre, the bed, was a write off! A policeman who was in attendance approached me and ushered me into his car. I was still dressed in my underpants only, so he handed me a blanket. I covered myself and cursed my luck. I couldn't even kill myself properly!

Eventually a plain clothes policeman arrived. He introduced himself as Detective Constable Franks and had a chat with me. He said that the fire crew had spotted three separate seats of fire which indicated that the fire might not be an accident. I told him it wasn't, and he asked me to explain what had been going on. I told him things had gone from bad, being a hostage, to worse, my wife telling me that she wanted a divorce. Due to this and my inability to cope I'd decided to stop the bus and get off, I didn't want any more of this shit!

He asked what I had consumed and then conferred with a colleague at which point I was taken to Whipps Cross hospital where the contents of my stomach were pumped out. I'd completely lost track of time, but it wasn't long before I was back at my house where DC Franks informed me I was going to be arrested. He told me that this was being done for two reasons. Firstly, the police considered that I was a danger to myself. Secondly, they couldn't do anything about it unless they arrested me as they had no right to detain me unless they did so. I was arrested for my own protection and taken to Chingford Police Station where I was put in a cell.

Tuesday, 1st November.

I was interviewed by DC Franks who told me that the entire incident would come to nothing as I had been arrested for my own protection and as soon as something could be fixed up I would be going home. Later the same day he returned and explained that I would have to appear in court; "A formality," he said, and then things would progress. He asked me if I wanted anything from home, as I'd have to stay in the cells. I asked him for some toiletries and he said he'd see what he could do. In the evening, a police constable came into the cell and handed me a plastic shopping bag with some personal items brought from my house.

Slowly, as my brain fought its way out of the fog of a drink-and-drug-induced psychosis, I began to detect an alarmingly familiar pattern to this detention scenario. Initially, in London, I'd been arrested for my own protection and then I'd been told that I'd have to appear in court. In a flashback, in Iraq, when I'd been taken over the border, I had been told that it was a common occurrence and easily dealt with, then days later I'd been told that there would be charges.

The entire scenario left me feeling used, depressed, and just as suicidal as I had been the previous day. I put the plastic shopping bag over my head and attempted to asphyxiate myself! Exhausted, I passed out. My latest plan to kill myself was however flawed because there were some small holes in the bottom of the bag that allowed enough air in to keep me alive. I came round the following morning with nothing more than a sweat-soaked head and a terrible hangover to show for my efforts. Another dismal failure!

RIDE TO HELL

Wednesday, 2nd November.

I was transported to Walthamstow Magistrates' Court where before my hearing I met Elliot Stern, my court appointed, legal aid, solicitor. At Chingford nick he'd listened to my version of the events that had shaped my recent misfortunes and said that the charge of arson being brought against me was such that when my mental health was taken into consideration I was likely to be remanded in custody. As I sat in a transport wagon on the way to court, thoughts of a similar journey in Baghdad came to mind. It brought back memories of paying for the pleasure of the awful journey from Tasfirat to Abu Ghraib and everything that entailed. This made me shudder with apprehension about what the future might hold for me now.

At court I met Elliot again in a small room, and he stated that the locations for my remand would either be Claybury, a secure psychiatric hospital in nearby Woodford Bridge, or HM Prison Pentonville in London. I told him that neither worried me, and that they might as well throw me into Pentonville as I felt I'd be able to cope there; after all I understood prison! He replied that he thought I'd struggle in Pentonville and that in any event I would be far easier to contact in Claybury. He was the solicitor, and I bowed to his professional knowledge and agreed that I'd be willing to go to Claybury. He then called the police officer who was stood outside the room and I was escorted to the court area and sat in a glass dock.

I realise, looking back, that to the magistrate I must have resembled a zombie from the gates of hell. I sat there with my face still covered in streaks of soot from the fire and my hair tousled like that of a scarecrow. After various conversations and deliberations, the magistrate asked if I had made the suicide attempt as a "cry for help", to which I replied with great sincerity, "No! It was a cry for death!"

The magistrate looked at me with a mixture of sadness, pity, revulsion, and a million other expressions, and then remanded me to the custody of Dr Harish Ghadvi at Claybury Hospital. This part of my case was at an end, but I understood that the déjà vu which surrounded the entire event was not.

In Iraq – Oh, no prison for you Mr Bol. (Paul)

In London – This court appearance is a formality.

The result of my Iraqi court appearance was a seven-year sentence for illegal entry with a serious allegation of spying. The result of my London court appearance was the dubious pleasure of being remanded to a hospital which when it first opened its doors in 1893 was known as the Claybury Lunatic Asylum. Just when I thought it couldn't get any more trauma-inducing, my living nightmare had a new twist to it and the more I tried to elude the grasp of the tormentors besieging my mind, the more their number increased. Where was this all going to end?

The first couple of days of my stay at Claybury were benign. I spent them sitting around as I was still feeling anaesthetised from the drug, poison, and alcohol cocktail I'd tried to kill myself with. Even though I'd had my stomach pumped, all that muck had got into my system and my body was taking a while to cleanse itself. I was examined by doctors, 'observed' by nurses, and undertook various tests.

I learned that the local media present at the magistrates' court had sold the story to the nationals. I was told all hell had broken loose with the hospital switchboard being under siege from the press. All calls attempting to contact me were screened, and I was asked to say if I knew who callers were and if I wished to speak to them or not.

I had visits from Elliot Stern and his colleague Donal O'Riordan who came to interview me and take further statements. Deborah Clark, my MPs personal assistant, brought me fresh clothes and toiletries. I liked her and she tried to explain how Julie felt about me. She stayed with me for about 40 minutes. As she was leaving, she did the most wonderful thing. She put her arms around me and gave me a hug. I was touchable.

Time passed slowly. The day-to-day monotony was familiar and crushed my spirits but this time around I had welcome visits from family members to break up the hours and improve my mood. One day, my cousins John and Andy came to see me and we went for a walk around the hospital grounds. It was pouring with rain, but this didn't matter I was glad to be out of the ward and breathing fresh air. On another day, Julie, William, my brother Phil, his wife Helen, and their son Thomas arrived. This was amazing even if though I became increasingly agitated by the behaviour of some of the other patients on my ward.

Monday, 7th November.

The morning was filled with what I referred to in my diary as "just the normal lunacy". You become very self-centred when suffering from PTSD, and my entire time in Claybury was spent attempting to distance myself from everyone and everything and being totally unsympathetic towards most of the other patients. In the afternoon, My Dad arrived. He'd made the trip up from Devon on the back of a night shift and looked shattered, but he brightened up as the afternoon went on and I was really grateful he'd made the effort to travel all this way to see me.

Wednesday, 9th November.

I noted in my diary that, "I've been sleeping badly for two or three nights now." It was getting worse as I became more aware of the nocturnal activities of the other patients. I had trouble relaxing as a constant stream of people came and went all night; talking, laughing, and arguing with themselves, and winding each other, themselves, and me up. My patience frayed swiftly. At tea-time I threw a fit. A visitor who'd just popped in to see a friend, ate my meal! I couldn't believe the way I felt.

Homicidal would be putting it mildly! I frightened myself. This bloke would probably have killed me, but suffering with PTSD, I felt totally indestructible. This might sound corny but I would come to learn it was one of the symptoms of the illness.

Thursday, 10th November.

This was my worst day in Claybury, my lowest ebb if you like. I woke up 'aware of something' and sprang aggressively out of bed, instantly pumped up and ready to defend myself. A patient called Colin was stood at the end of my bed drinking a beaker of water gazing down at me. I always pulled the curtains around the sides of my bed, so I knew he'd actually had to come around the screens to look at me. To my mind he was invading my space. I delivered a series of expletives, making it totally clear that if he didn't move immediately I would get extremely violent. Colin recoiled as if he'd come into contact with a toxic substance, crying, "No! No! No!"

I dropped back onto my mattress and pulled the blankets over my head and put cotton wool in my ears to keep the noise out. I was absolutely fuming. As I dived under my bedclothes I looked at my watch, it was still only 4.45am. The tension was hurting my stomach and I thought, *This place will make me ill.*

At breakfast time, I complained to the nurses about Colin. In a mental hospital, for whatever reason, it seems to me that patients are not thought of as people who could possibly have rational complaints, and rather than dealing with problems nurses tend to ask patronising questions such as, "Are you dealing with this rationally?" To be fair to the staff though, Colin was spoken to, but it didn't work and he kept talking incessantly at every opportunity.

As I could perceive little difference between my treatment at Claybury and Abu Ghraib, I adopted the position of a prisoner. I wrote in my diary, "I'm playing the bastards at their own game!" I refused to leave the ward. I said that if anything was required of me then it would have to come to me. I would not be going anywhere. I thought that if I could survive the Iraqi prison system then I could cope with the rest of my 'detention' in Claybury. I had coffee, books, and a head full of hate. I would get through this!

In the evening, Julie, William and Deborah Clark came up to see me. Everything went well until I saw Colin approaching Julie while I was playing with William. My immediate rage was uncontrollable. "THAT BASTARD HAS BEEN WARNED," I screamed. "IF HE DOESN'T FUCK OFF, I WILL KILL HIM!"

I am ashamed when I remember that day. I find it so unbelievable to realise how low a point I'd reached. Fear was the overriding factor. I'd been violated, both in Iraq, and here in Claybury. Irrational, yes I know, but self-preservation is the strongest human instinct and I was frightened.

The realisation that I belonged in Claybury hit me. The other patients were all staring at me. I felt exposed, vilified, fated, and hated. Deborah Clark was giggling, embarrassed by my outburst. She, Julie, and William left shortly afterwards. I felt alone that night. It was at the moment when I'd seen the terrified look on my little boy's face and the horrified, frightened, look Julie was giving me that I finally understood that I was mad!

The days that followed had set patterns to them. I wasn't being offered enough medical treatment and the flashbacks that I'd had when I first arrived at Claybury started again. These weren't dreams, and the term nightmare really doesn't encompass the full horror that I experienced night after night. It became so frightening that I became scared of going to bed. Abu Ghraib felt as if it were 'right in my face'. Set routines, classic 'institutionalisation' flashbacks were occurring all the time now and it was beginning to grind me down, just as it had done prior to the fire. Life was a roller coaster of emotions during this period. My nightmares had recurring themes, as did my daytime flashbacks, but these were taking place without warning and being inspired by different catalysts, so it wasn't possible to avoid a certain activity, as at one time or another, everything, and anything, could trigger them off.

I would be walking along and see a person who would, in my mind's eye, be the spitting image of a person I was in prison with. This would stop me dead in my tracks. It was as if a bowl of liquid nitrogen had been poured down my throat. My whole body would stiffen and turn ice cold as a monumental shudder of fear coursed through me.

Eating a meal, the food on my plate would trigger a memory. Reading a newspaper or magazine, I might come across an article or photo that would leave me trembling at the memories it brought to my mind. Throwing away a piece of rubbish, I would stop myself and think so-and-so could use this. Lying in bed at night I would wake drenched in my own sweat, with my sheets soaking wet as if they had just been washed. I felt constantly tired, restless, and angry. Relaxation and a peaceful night's sleep were beyond me.

Monday, 28th November.

I was up at the crack of dawn to get ready for my next court appearance. Elliot Stern drove me to Waltham Forest Magistrates' courthouse where I was met by my Dad. I had one thought running through my mind as I went in front of the magistrates, *Dear God! Please don't let them send me back to Claybury!*

For once, fortune smiled on me and in his summing up, the Chief Magistrate said to me, "Mr Ride, it is the decision of the court that your bail order be altered and you no longer need to reside at Claybury to fulfil its conditions. You are allowed to go with unconditional bail as the order the Court has decided upon, but, should you break your bail, this will end in a custodial sentence! Do you understand?

I replied that I did and thanked the court, at the same time thinking, *I've been to prisons that these simpering people couldn't even begin to understand! Did they honestly believe, and think, that if push came to shove that a UK prison would be unbearable!*

This is an example of how deranged my thinking was. I was so constantly pumped up that nothing was impossible and no situation too tough to cope with. Today, the thought of prison fills me with horror, and possibly in my sub-conscious mind it did even then – but I would have never admitted it!

Christmas 1994 came and went. I still had my troubles, but at least I was at home. Steve and Josie Brooks from the Gulf Support Group asked if I, along with Julie, would assist with an article a 'Sunday Times' journalist was writing about the situation post-Gulf War. They asked us to do it because the developments in my life mirrored the troubles other expatriates affected by the Gulf War were experiencing. I had serious misgivings about dealing with the media, but after giving it some thought, and taking into consideration the lofty reputation of 'The Sunday Times', and the assurances I was given that the focus would be on the trauma caused by events in Iraq and not my private life, I agreed to the interview.

I should have known better. When I read the article, my immediate reaction was a sense of boiling rage mixed with déjà vu. There was little mention of the human shield hostage scenario I had elaborated on during the interview, the story mainly concerned itself with exaggerations and fabrications about my mental health and the breakup of my marriage. Seething, I phoned Steve Brooks who shared my outrage and took up the situation with the newspaper's editor who insisted I had willingly taken part in an interview about the matters included in the article, and that it was unfortunate that I had failed to realise the implications of the entire process. I'd been duped by the press once again!

I contacted the Press Complaints Commission and eventually received a letter clearing 'The Sunday Times' which stated that the request for an interview to compile an article about one issue, and then publishing an article with an entirely different slant to it was in fact 'editorial licence', which they informed me was beyond their remit. At the time I was incensed, the only reason I'd let the media back into my house was to try and get the entire problem of compensation from Iraq, for all its victims, back on the agenda. All that had been delivered was another horribly distorted assortment of lies and half-truths that served no one apart from the journalist and the paper.

At the time these abusive assaults by the media caused me terrible pain and anxiety. The experience affected me so much that I can remember being perfectly willing to serve time in a British prison if only I could get redress, and I would go as far as saying by way of physical violence! I had difficulty in dealing with a mind full of detritus left as a 'scar' of my experiences in Iraq but the media cared not a jot, and they exposed me to the most distressing episodes of worry at a time when I was at my lowest ebb, both physically and psychologically. I received not a penny in payment for my time and felt horribly abused. The struggle inside my mind was overpowering and, to cap it all, I still had the case to answer at Walthamstow Magistrates' Court!

By now the media had stopped calling at the house, opting instead to lie in wait and ambush me as I arrived at the courthouse. At the time my feelings of disgust for any representative of the media were at their height and the matters were worsened by my case repeatedly being adjourned during January and February 1995. On each occasion a new date for my hearing was announced, this gave the media the opportunity to plan their ambushes, which led to further harassment and humiliation for me. I'm not sure how many times this took place, maybe two or three, all I know is that internally, in my brutalised mind, it felt as if these events had taken place six or seven times. I felt sick and my head was screaming, *SEND ME TO JAIL!*

Outside the courthouse I'd face a barrage of questions from shouting voices. The entire freak show was more than I could deal with, and on one occasion I made an obscene gesture at one of the cameras. That evening, as footage of me gesturing like a man out of control flashed across TV screens in households across London that had tuned in for the local news, I recall the 'deeply-offended' reporter asked, "Should ex-hostage Paul Ride be shown mercy?" The implication being that mercy was for people who acted reasonably but my actions were, quite obviously, entirely 'unreasonable'. It was in the public interest to know that I'd attempted to asphyxiate myself, but there was never any mention made that I was in the middle of a nervous breakdown and that no one in authority appeared to give a damn. I was unable to work and nobody was willing to broach the subject of compensation and, even worse, no one was able to stop the thoughts in my head which were driving me out of my mind. Without this basic knowledge why would viewers think I should be shown mercy?

My final appearance at Walthamstow Magistrates' Court had a sting in the tail that I couldn't have imagined in my worst stages of paranoia. I was told my case was being passed to the Central Criminal Court of England and Wales, commonly referred to as the Old Bailey! This was the place for serious offenders and, just as before, just like Iraq, the realisation of the awful truth crushed me. As I staggered out of the courtroom, I could hear the platitudes being mouthed by my solicitor. "Most unfortunate." "Unexpected." "Inexplicable." They left me cold. I was about to be tried as a major criminal, like one of the Great Train Robbers, when in fact I was just an empty shell of a man, being blown from one catastrophe to another.

RIDE TO HELL

Friday, 28th April, 1995.

Eventually the date set for my appearance at the Old Bailey arrived and my Dad came up to London to stay with me and offer moral support and Deborah Clark came to try and assist me in holding myself together.

In the morning, I turned on the TV to watch the news. It was a morbid curiosity that made me listen to opinions the media offered about me and sure enough there was coverage on the local London bulletin which went along the lines of, "Paul Ride, the former detainee freed over a year ago following 18 months as a prisoner of Saddam Hussein's regime appears at the Old Bailey today charged with Arson."

On this occasion it was not the words that left me gasping for breath, instead it was the footage used to illustrate the piece. The images that flashed the screen were of a house gutted by fire. Its exterior was blackened and flame-damaged, and all the windows were smashed. It was a scene of total devastation. Here I was, stood in the house that they were purporting to be showing on the screen and it didn't damn-well look like that. I exploded into a towering rage and screamed at the TV, "YOU LYING, STUPID, FUCKING IDIOTS! THAT'S NOT MY HOUSE!'

I ranted, and stormed around the house. Now even the media were openly lying about what I had done. My head rang with the questions of a man on the edge.

Is this a plot?
Are you out to imprison me?
Why are you lying?
Why are you doing this to me?

On and on the stream of paranoid questions flooded. Looking back now it all seems so unreal, but at the time I was sure, no, I knew, that this was a major conspiracy. I had no answers to any of my questions and was left thinking that If the Iraqis could jail me for seven years for driving up the wrong street, then British justice could put me away for life based on the 'evidence' I'd just seen.

Expecting the worst, there was however to be one final twist in the plot. When we arrived at my barrister's chambers in the Temple my barrister (£200 per hour) unexpectedly said, "If I told you that the CPS (Crown Prosecution Service) were going to drop the case against you, what would you do?"

I struggled to hear him properly as the pulse in my head meant that I could hear the blood rushing through my brain, and the gushing, pumping sound almost drowned out his voice. I asked him to repeat the question, which he did, and when the penny slowly dropped I replied, "I'll do a lap around the Old Bailey with no clothes on."

"Go on then," came the jaunty riposte. "The CPS is not offering any evidence against you!"

I didn't do the naked lap because suddenly everyone was congratulating and hugging me. To what purpose I really didn't understand, after all I'd actually done nothing; as with the rest of my life during this awful, awful period, I felt like a victim of the entire process. I couldn't have effected any change even if I'd known how to do so, that feat was accomplished by Deborah and her persistence on my behalf. She'd written letters, had meetings, and lobbied on my behalf for weeks prior to the date of the trial. At the eleventh hour her persistence had carried the day, and it appeared that this nightmare was really at an end. Well almost, it soon transpired that I would still have to go in front of the Judge and the drama eventually concluded in the afternoon following a drawn-out exchange of legal deliberations.

I recall at one point the Judge saying, "I hope Mr Ride is not suggesting that the British legal system is, in anyway, like that of Iraq?" He spoke with humour and incredulity in his voice, and then the case moved on and the moment was gone. He was right though. I felt that the British legal system had been as negative towards me as the Iraqi one had. It's difficult to explain, but so many of the negatives in Iraq were mirrored by developments and events in London.

Suddenly, it all felt as if it were happening to another person, the court case was over. There were more details, things said, comments passed, but as I now realise it was all specialist language designed perhaps to disorientate the subject of the event. I know that's how many of the people whom I have met that have any experiences of courtrooms regard the events and the theatrics. In court, just about the only thing most of them admitted to understanding was the term of their sentence. It's a funny old world!

There is little doubt in my mind that the outcome would have been vastly different if Deborah Clark had not fought for the case to be dropped. This is not because my solicitor didn't want to win the case, but simply because he was my court-appointed legal representative and as such he was drowning under the workload of the other cases that he was being given on a regular daily basis. Deborah quite possibly, saved me from a custodial sentence and I am so very grateful for all her efforts and never-ending patience with a man designed to wind people up. Me!

EPILOGUE

It's now 27 years since I was cleared of arson at the Old Bailey and many changes have taken place in my life. In June 1995 I commenced a two-week Post-Traumatic Stress Disorder course at Ticehurst House (now part of the Priory Hospital Group) in East Sussex. Deborah Clark had written to former hostage Terry Waite to see if he had any ideas about how I could be helped. Waite put her in touch with Dr Gordon Turnbull, creator of a PTSD therapy unit at Ticehurst, whose team had treated him on his return from Beirut where he'd been kidnapped and held captive for almost five years by the Islamic Jihad Organisation.

I experienced many difficult emotions while at Ticehurst and want to say a big 'thank you' to Dr Gordon Turnbull and his team for their work and research in the treatment for sufferers of PTSD, and on a personal note, for their support, patience, and help.

Ticehurst was a key turning point for me and when I got home, armed with a clearer train of thought and much encouragement from friends, I made the decision to quit catering and further my education. A couple of years studying and taking exams culminated in the offer of a place to read history at Queen Mary and Westfield College (now Queen Mary University of London). In 2000, at the age of 40, and having had a fabulous three years, I graduated with a two-one. I followed my degree up by completing a PGCE (Postgraduate Certificate in Education) course at Greenwich University and an MA in Local and Regional History from Goldsmiths, University of London.

Having qualified as a teacher, I took a part-time role at Newham Sixth Form College teaching AS/A Level History, GCSE English Literature resits, and Citizenship, and while there I also applied to work as a lecturer within the prison system. I wrote a generic letter and sent it to the education departments of several prisons and got a reply from HM Prison Pentonville. Following three failed attempts I eventually got to see the Deputy Education Manager, a top man called Peter Jackson, who offered me a position as an adult educator. I had an enjoyable six years there especially working on the prisoner resettlement programme. I now work on offender behaviour programmes and interventions which aim to change the thinking, attitudes and behaviours which may lead people to reoffend.

I was divorced, quite rightly, by Julie in 1995 however I'm happy to report that we have been in a long-distance relationship for about 11 years now. She lives in Devon and we see each other as often as possible, which is like working overseas!

I returned to my roots and have lived in the area of Chelsea I grew up in for some years now. I've just renewed my season ticket to watch the Mighty Blues and am optimistic for what the future might hold under the new owners.

The diary I used to write this account enabled me to tell a story of prison life. The regimes, the squalor, the horror, the filth, the stress, the stupidity, and, most of all, the horrendous boredom. I am not an erudite person and feel that whatever I write can never recreate images that properly explain where I've been, what I've seen, or the things I've had to do. The more I discuss it, the more I understand my experience was like a bad 'B' movie.

I was raised in a stressful environment and only later in life did I come to terms with the fact that the issues of my childhood haunted and defined my adult persona. I was a working-class bloke from Chelsea, badly equipped to deal with the web of international politics I was drawn into and the sheer hell of prison 'life' in Iraq.

Requirements in a prison are self-reliance, and the ability to cope with the suspension of normality. I managed some things better than others, but the fear that was born in prison troubled me for years. The experience made me cold and withdrawn. Like many inmates I closed down many humanistic areas of myself. Why? Because to leave them open would just invite hurt and pain. Why feel suffering when you can go numb! The sort of experience I had isn't full of drama, sex, and excitement, but rather it is a vacuum of fear, folly, celibacy, and tedium. I'm sorry I cannot write pages about torrid, illicit liaisons, daring do, and excitement, but then I'm not Andy McNab. I was never trained to kill, and I certainly wasn't prepared for 18 months as a hostage!

I have received lots of support, help and encouragement getting my expansive notes, made over the last 28 years, into a coherent form and I would like to thank Mark Worrall for his diligence and hard work getting this book into print.

Paul Ride
London
July, 2022.

Printed in Great Britain
by Amazon